The Historic
District Action Guide

lectual, scholarly, and educational texts. To submit a proposal or manuscript to the series, please request proposal guidelines from AASLH headquarters: AASLH Editorial Board, 2021 21st Ave. South, Suite 320, Nashville, Tennessee 37212. Telephone: (615) 320-3203. Website: www.aaslh.org.

ABOUT THE ORGANIZATION

The American Association for State and Local History (AASLH) is a national history membership association headquartered in Nashville, Tennessee. AASLH provides leadership and support for its members who preserve and interpret state and local history in order to make the past more meaningful to all Americans. AASLH members are leaders in preserving, researching, and interpreting traces of the American past to connect the people, thoughts, and events of yesterday with the creative memories and abiding concerns of people, communities, and our nation today. In addition to sponsorship of this book series, AASLH publishes *History News* magazine, a newsletter, technical leaflets and reports, and other materials; confers prizes and awards in recognition of outstanding achievement in the field; supports a broad education program and other activities designed to help members work more effectively; and advocates on behalf of the discipline of history. To join AASLH, go to www.aaslh.org or contact Membership Services, AASLH, 2021 21st Ave. South, Suite 320, Nashville, TN 37212.

The Historic District Action Guide

From Designation Campaigns to Keeping Districts Vital

William E. Schmickle

ROWMAN & LITTLEFIELD
Lanham • Boulder • New York • London

Published by Rowman & Littlefield
A wholly owned subsidiary of The Rowman & Littlefield Publishing Group, Inc.
4501 Forbes Boulevard, Suite 200, Lanham, Maryland 20706
www.rowman.com

Unit A, Whitacre Mews, 26-34 Stannary Street, London SE11 4AB

British Library Cataloguing in Publication Information Available

Library of Congress Cataloging-in-Publication Data

Names: Schmickle, William Edgar, 1946- author.
Title: The historic district action guide : from designation campaigns to
  keeping districts vital / William E. Schmickle.
Description: Lanham, MD : Rowman & Littlefield, [2018] | Series: American
  Association for State and Local History | Includes bibliographical
  references and index.
Identifiers: LCCN 2017060860 (print) | LCCN 2018017891 (ebook) | ISBN
  9781538103555 (Electronic) | ISBN 9781538103531 (cloth : alk. paper) |
  ISBN 9781538103548 (pbk. : alk. paper)
Subjects: LCSH: Historic preservation—United States—Handbooks, manuals,
  etc. | Historic districts—United States—Handbooks, manuals, etc. |
  Historic preservation—Government policy—United States. | City
  planning—United States—Citizen participation—Handbooks, manuals, etc.
Classification: LCC E159 (ebook) | LCC E159 .S (print) | DDC 973—dc23 LC record
available at https://lccn.loc.gov/2017060860

∞™ The paper used in this publication meets the minimum requirements of
American National Standard for Information Sciences—Permanence of Paper
for Printed Library Materials, ANSI/NISO Z39.48-1992.

Printed in the United States of America

For Charlotte.

Contents

Preface

It is the power of the stars.

—Taylor Wilson, Nuclear Physicist

The "it" in Taylor Wilson's observation is the fusion of two atomic nuclei, producing heat and light. In historic preservation, metaphorically, it occurs when politics fuses with preservation in a historic district. The heat produced is the passion to do good things for a community, and the light is intelligent insight into how to accomplish them.

Are you a preservation star? You are in my book if you have proposed creating a historic district, are running a successful campaign for district designation, or are engaged in running an established district in your community.

THE CENTRALITY OF POLITICS

Why politics? Jon Dewey has written me from Utah saying he wishes he had known about a first edition of this work when campaigning for historic district designation in Salt Lake City's Yalecrest neighborhood. "Honestly I didn't know this was going to be a political challenge, and really that's ALL it was. It does comfort me to know we are not alone and that the same struggles are felt universally."[1]

The book he referred to was *The Politics of Historic Districts: A Primer for Grassroots Preservation* (2007). The *Guide* you're reading now is an updated and expanded edition of that work that combines it with a second book, *Preservation Politics: Keeping Historic Districts Vital* (2012). The National Trust for Historic Preservation has named them to its list of "essential" books in historic preservation.[2]

The Historic District Action Guide takes you from the dawn of the idea of establishing a historic district through a successful designation campaign to the problems and prospects of older districts as we strive to keep them vital. I have used examples from all around the country, and you will have the benefit of transcribed conversations I've had with political actors, planners, consultants, opinion shapers, and preservation leaders. My goal is to show you how to think politically for successful action.

That will be my story: how to recognize and use politics from your district's conception to old age. Hurtling through brief chapters, we will end up light years from the start. So hold onto your seat and let's get started!

NOTES

1. Email on file.
2. Emily Potter, "Fourteen Essential Preservation Books," National Trust for Historic Preservation, www.savingplaces.org/stories/10-tuesday-10-preservation-books#.WdkxODApDIU, January 14, 2014.

Acknowledgments

"Feeling gratitude and not expressing it," William Arthur Ward wrote in *Fountains of Faith*, "is like wrapping a present and not giving it." How could I do that when so many people gave me the gift of their interest in my work?

I wish to thank Mitch Allen of AltaMira Press, Bob Beatty of the Association for State and Local History, and Charles Harmon of Rowman & Littlefield for encouraging my writing.

I am indebted to those who sat for interviews: Bob Agee, Ross Arnett, Dan Becker, Peter Benton, Cathy Purple Cherry, Don Deline, Kaye Graybeal, Eric Holcomb, Jeff Horseman, Tom Marquardt, Eric Nelson, Maggie O'Conner, James Reap, Joe Riley Jr., Greg Stiverson, and Elizabeth Watson. The richness of their observations is matched only by their helpful candor.

If you are not a member of the National Alliance of Preservation Commissions, then join! I have benefitted immensely from their efforts on behalf of historic districts everywhere.

Jim and Kathy Cully in New York; Dan and Michelle Brown in Vermont; Allan Pitcher in Washington, D.C.; and Sharon Kennedy in Annapolis have borne up under my endless discussions of the politics of historic preservation. I fear that my sons Andy and Greg, and their spouses Zuleyha and Shannon, have grown too accustomed to them also. I appreciate everyone's good natured tolerance.

Most of all, my wife Charlotte has given me intellectual and emotional support as well as the time to read, develop my thoughts, and write. She has always lovingly supported my enthusiasms, among which she has been the greatest of my life.

Annapolis, October 2017

Introduction

What D'ya Know?
Not much, you?

    —Michael Feldman's radio program, *What D'ya Know?*

Isn't that the way it goes? You start a project and when it's finished you say, "If I'd only known then what I know now. . . ."

MY START

Some years ago I stood in front of a North Carolina Department of Transportation survey map hanging in the gym of the Oak Ridge Elementary School. Sketched on it was a highway improvement plan that would devastate our old crossroads community.

The proposal surprised my neighbors, too. Several spoke in the whispers of the already defeated. One said it was a "done deal." Another said you can't fight DOT.

INTRODUCTION

But there was another fellow there, a Guilford County planner. He quietly told me that Oak Ridge could gain clout if we became the county's first rural historic district. I took his business card like a drowning man grabs a straw.

I spread the word. Soon a few of us were driving down to the county offices. It was the last moment of real peace we'd enjoy for two years. If we'd only known then. . . .

LEARNING THE BASICS

What do you know about local historic districts? I knew next to nothing then, not even the difference between federally designated and locally designated districts. So I also didn't know that local districts are the ones with teeth in them—the ability to enforce compliance as part of the local zoning code.

I still had to learn that the most typical form of local designation is the overlay district. That's where the district is superimposed over existing zoning without affecting underlying permitted property uses.

A rough working definition of a local district is a defined area of historically, visually, or culturally related properties that are designated and administered by a city or county government to preserve the community's identifying character. But a definition can take us only so far. We need to add that:

- District ordinances derive their authority from state and federal enabling legislation.
- All district properties are designated as contributing or noncontributing, though work done on all of them is subject to regulation.
- Historic districts are typically administered by an officially appointed Historic Preservation Commission (HPC).[1]
- HPCs issue Certificates of Appropriateness (COAs) as part of the local permitting process.

Not knowing that, I knew nothing about getting a district designated. I just assumed we'd ask the County Commission to approve ours. You see, I didn't know that:

- A district has to meet criteria for certifying its historic significance and integrity.
- Designation typically involves due process hearings before the HPC, Planning Commission, and the City Council or County Commission.
- The process can take many months, even a year or more, to complete.

And I didn't know all hell would break loose when we took the plan to our neighbors.

I found that attitudes toward districting cut across all lines—political, economic, gender, ethnic, educational, or what have you. Any national statistics on preferences simply dissolve into individual personalities at the local level. Some folks you know will be just great. Some will break your heart if you let them.

On the up-side, I had no idea how many fine people I'd meet in the preservation community. Local preservation groups pitched in, as did the statewide nonprofit group, Preservation North Carolina, and our State Historic Preservation Office (SHPO). The National Trust for Historic Preservation and the National Alliance of Preservation Commissions (NAPC) were invaluable resources.

WHY AN ACTION GUIDE?

They all helped us learn what we didn't know about preservation. They taught us what to say.

But how to win, there was the problem. We got bits and pieces of political advice, all of it good, yet nothing systematic. I was intrigued by how little other folks actually thought about politics when politics was what they were doing every day. That holds true for running established districts, too.

So, tell me now, as you step out to win your district's designation: What do you know about preservation politics? If your answer is "not much," then turn the page.

NOTE

1. Or some similar name, such as Historic District Commission, Landmarks Commission, Board of Architectural Review. I will use "HPC" throughout for generic discussions.

Part I

PRESERVATION & THE POLITICS OF HISTORIC DISTRICT DESIGNATION

Chapter One

Before You Take Another Step

History may not always repeat itself, but it sure tends to rhyme.

—Thomas Boswell, sportswriter, *The Washington Post*

Initiating a districting campaign is a great idea, but not an easy plan to carry out. Are you hesitant about stepping forward, wondering how to begin without getting off on the wrong foot?

If you are, I have a simple answer. Do nothing until you get comfortable with the idea that preservation is only what you do get *out* of your campaign. *In it*, you'll be doing politics for the foreseeable future.

That's obvious, isn't it? You yourself can't create the historic district. All you can really do is start the designation process rolling, unsure of where you're going next and what you have to do.

Well, you're not alone and you no longer have to rediscover the wheel. Others have gone before you, and Tom Boswell sums up my discovery: that although each historic district is unique, there are still enough similarities in those experiences to permit some general observations to help you think more clearly.

Your basic story line has played out again and again across America. Local activists propose a historic district. An opposition arises. A rancorous community debate ensues. A divided city council or county board of commissioners[1] looks for a way out. Usually an up or down vote settles the question. Sometimes, like in Newnan, Georgia, a compromise is struck that strings out hope beyond reason.

LOST CHANCES

"We could have been the best of the small towns," Newnan's Georgia Shapiro said in 2003.[2] You might know her town. It's where *Fried Green Tomatoes* and *I'll Fly Away* were filmed. But to hear her tell it, what was happening to Newnan's first historic district brings to mind another Southern movie, *Dead Man Walking*.

"Every day is a danger," Shapiro said. She was referring to the City Council's last-minute decision to set up voluntary design guidelines instead of the proposed historic district with mandatory review and compliance. The city's planning staff suggested the change as a compromise. Realists on both sides of the issue knew it was largely an empty gesture. The ordinance afforded no dependable protection, even from a property owner bent on mischief. Newnan's historic properties were living on borrowed time, trusting in luck for a daily reprieve from the inevitable.

Now I'll bet that's not what you wish for your own community. Yet it's not an isolated event. From Palo Alto to Staten Island, elected officials often react coolly to the notion that communities with historic resources need the shelter of enforceable law.

Why? At a very basic level, your average local legacy just doesn't look like important history to many of them.

Let's call it the George Washington syndrome. I'll lay you odds that once you start your districting campaign some opponent at a public hearing will complain, "Why is my property historic? George Washington didn't sleep there!" It's amazing how many people think such a lame line is brilliant analysis.

My guess is that every place George slept is either gone or somehow already protected. He never even napped in most of the 2,500 districts across the nation. Some cities are chockablock with districts. Baltimore with thirty-three has more than twice as many as all of Arkansas. New opportunities abound.

In fact, we'll never run out of new places to nominate. What is new sooner or later becomes old and may acquire historic significance. A presidential bedroom is no longer needed to justify interest, nor is a Frank Lloyd Wright design. A Michigan preservationist has argued that while Hartland Township hasn't a single important structure, taken as a whole it's historic.

But what does that signify? Opponents charge that we've sacrificed any meaningful definition of historic to a sacred cult of the merely old. As Mayor Bill Welch of State College, Pennsylvania, said when he vetoed the city's preservation ordinance in 2002, "When everything is historic, nothing is historic."[3]

So, unless you discover George slept around in your neighborhood, you've got your work cut out for you.

ALTERNATIVE FUTURES

So what's a preservationist to do? Quite a bit, actually, as you'll see. But while we're here, let me try to get you to look at this from another angle.

As the case for outright *historic* preservation has become increasingly difficult to make stick, we've actually shifted much of our talk over to the kinds of *futures* we prefer. Since its Charleston inception in 1931, the historic district movement has become strikingly forward-looking.

This is something politicians can understand. Their eyes may glaze over when you mention ambience, character, sense of place, an intangible heritage, or cultural landscapes. But you speak their language when you bring up property values, economic vitality, tax bases, mixed-use development, managing sprawl, and securing a wide array of other measurable benefits.

Councilwoman Wendy Scatterday in Wheeling, West Virginia, is convinced. She has said that "the purpose of historic districting is an economic development program, as well as a means to protect historic assets."[4]

If you worry that she's putting preservation in the backseat, change your thinking. Those other interests can power up preservation for where we want to drive it.

PLAYING THE GAME

There is a downside, of course. Historic districts that are designated for any number of economic and social advantages may in fact have little to do with genuine preservation. Sometimes it's just preservation as decoration. Other times, it's not even that.

My wife, Charlotte, and I once drove 8,000 miles coast to coast looking at historic districts. Some, like Santa Fe, were truly remarkable. Some unfortunately looked like they had never seen a design guideline, voluntary or not. If the local town council is trying to entice travelers to the bric-a-brac shops and alternative café at Broad and Elm, why worry about front porches on Third Street? Sometimes you just keep on driving.

Even in our least successful communities, you can be sure that someone like you meant to do better. But historic district initiatives get shuffled together with all sorts of conflicting ideas, principles, and interests. Preservation gets you a seat at the table, but you don't get to deal the cards.

Which reminds me of something I learned on a Las Vegas stopover: If you want to preserve your resources, you'd better know how to play the game.

Our game is the politics of historic districts. As in any other game, politics has its own rules. They are largely impervious to our preferences, and you ignore them at your peril. If you think that's overly dramatic, I suggest you think again before you take another step.

NOTES

1. A note on terms: As a rule, I will specify "city council" to denote any local legislative body, be it city council or county board. Capital letters will refer to a specific "City Council" or the generic one I'll use for instructive purposes. The same will go for mayors as well as other local bodies or positions of authority. To avoid tedium, "the Council" will usually mean "the Mayor and City Council," except where a distinction is made concerning powers, as in chapter 31.

2. Kevin Duffy, "History a Matter of Heart in Newnan," www.ajc.com, June 9, 2003.

3. William Welch, "Why I Vetoed the Historic District Ordinance," www.centre-daily.com, September 9, 2002.

4. As reported by Alec Berry, "Review Process Sought for Wheeling Historic Property Demolition," www.theintell.com, October 5, 2016.

Chapter Two

Thinking Politically about Historic District Designation

You can't reorder the world by talking to it.

—Buckminster Fuller

Like Tip O'Neill's view of politics, all preservation is local—and nowhere more so than in the creation of a local historic district. From initiative to designation, the process is local. When the issue is in doubt, the process is also almost exclusively about local politics.

ON WINNING

Getting local designation under these conditions typically means winning a hard-fought political contest. For every successful campaign, other deserving proposals fall short. It is only by winning that we are able to translate what we want into public policy.

Evidently that's not as obvious as it seems. Some preservationists deplore the imperative to win and the competitive strategy it implies. They prefer a path of educating for consensus, trusting in reasoned discourse and the final persuasiveness of their vision. This approach has its advantages, but it's hardly ever enough.

John Herzan of the New Haven Preservation Trust in Connecticut reportedly was "shocked by the 'level of discontent' in response to the proposal to expand" even one of those minimally burdensome National Register districts. "We really thought we were doing a service to the people who lived in the area."[1]

The worst thing in politics is to be right and to lose. And still, as Peter Branson says, "You learn by doing, and by falling over." Or, thankfully, from observing others.

ON PRESERVATION ADVOCACY AND POLITICS

We don't win historic districts because we're right. The political landscape is littered with the bones of just causes. We win by outmaneuvering our opponents.

When we fail, it's often because we've confused issues with politics, overemphasizing *policy* relative to *politics* in the policy-making process. We anticipate an issue-driven designation process, only to find that policy considerations are but one—and not clearly the most important—factor in the political calculations that determine the outcome.

Politicians are happy to use our arguments for preservation, or those of our opponents against it, as cover for the positions they end up taking for such political reasons as public opinion, ideology, party discipline, and political ambition. Their own personalities and subjective biases may also deflect an issues-focused agenda.

At best, policy issues are the *input*, and politics the *process* in public decision making. To mistake the one for the other is like confusing grain with the gristmill.

National, state, and local preservation organizations have done an outstanding job of supporting citizen activists who typically spearhead the toughest historic districting campaigns. District proponents are time and again the best-informed party in the local *policy debate*. So how is it we can get outpointed in the *political contest*?

Isn't it because we like to think "politics" is what other people do? Other people, you know, like developers, who challenge us with change—as if preservation were the norm! When preservationists are forced into politics they like to dress up their politics as "advocacy."

Consider the session titled "Advocacy: An Advanced Guide" offered at the National Trust's 2003 National Preservation Conference in Denver. Its program blurb stated, "Successful advocacy for historic preservation is as diverse as the resources it strives to protect."

Not quite. If every preservation fight were that unique, what could we possibly learn from studying them? Battles won by heroic effort would simply pass into Homeric tales told around conference tables—or maybe just abbreviated into the "inspiring three-minute success stories" previewed for a Denver luncheon.

I see it differently. Preservation campaigns are indeed very different when we're looking at *what* things are to be preserved—a public space, a working-class housing tract, a waterfront commercial district—and *why* our communities should protect each one. That's what I think of as *advocacy*.

But when we look at *how* we actually win decisions to save historic resources, we find that the dynamics of what we do are essentially the same from case to case. Now that's *politics*.

When advocacy and politics are made to travel together, politics may get put in the trunk like shameful luggage. The moderator of a roundtable at the 2004 meeting of the NAPC in Indianapolis recognized a questioner who asked about politics. He froze, looked around the room, said "Ohhh . . . *pol-i-tics!*" and quickly changed the subject. And so it goes, more often than I can tell you.

NO FAULT ZONE

So who's to blame? No one, really.

Politics is a natural activity, but hardly pleasant. It speaks a harsh language of power. Wanting to avoid it is a healthy impulse.

Most of us prefer to orient our lives toward other pursuits—and our communities are better off for it. The proper study of preservationists is preservation, just as it is the law for lawyers, wealth for economists, and faith for ministers. If they all thought first in terms of politics, what a dreary and luckless world this would be! So, it's right and proper for preservationists to hew to what they know best: our historical, architectural, and cultural legacy.

But avoiding politics is one thing. Responding to it in ways that suit us rather than politics' own requirements is something else altogether.

I think we'd all be far better off if we simply broke politics out from under the cover of advocacy and gave it the attention it's due on its own.

ON POLITICAL THINKING

The best way to start is at the beginning with Politics 101.

Politics—any politics, not just preservation politics—arises where interests come into conflict. Basically, two things can happen:

1. The parties share enough common ground to resolve their differences and reach agreement, or

2. Where agreement isn't possible, politics decides the issue by a vote that favors one party over the other.

Advocacy, by which I will now mean *persuasive education*, plays a different kind of role in each scenario, as represented in figure 2.1.

In the first, where conflict is low and agreement is possible, politics is mild background noise. Here the preservation specialist—maybe with the aid of an experienced mediator—may nudge differing interests toward final consensus by educating the parties to the merits of preservation on a case-by-case basis. In this high consensus/low politics setting, much hangs on the advocate's technical excellence in framing the argument and getting the message out, saying the right thing the right way with the right attitude to the right people at the right time.

But as conflict among competing interests escalates, the prospect for mediated consensus fades and advocacy is downgraded to a supporting role. In the high-intensity world of many preservation battles, the activist must take dead aim at winning the vote for designation, whether or not this involves changing people's opinions by reasoned argument. Politics at this level values strategic thinking and tactical agility over technical expertise, and excellence is known by winning.

The difference becomes obvious in a hotly contested campaign to designate a historic district:

- Going in, you'd better be superbly briefed as an advocate on all your preservation talking points: what designation does, what the law is, why the district deserves protection, and so forth.

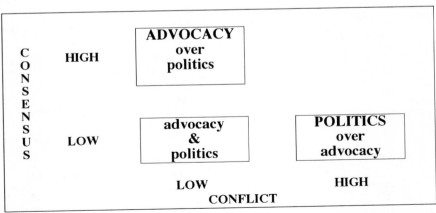

Figure 2.1. Where the degree of consensus among interests in a district is high (vertical axis), advocacy will be more important than politics in securing designation. Where conflict is high among interests (horizontal axis), politics will play the critical role.
Created by the author.

- Yet it is possible to know all this and still enter the fray as the *best informed* but *least prepared* participant—unless you yourself are politically astute enough to grasp the flow of the political contest on your own.

This is why learning to think politically about preservation *now* will be critical to your success *later*.

Preservation politics is about assuring we have an advantage over our opponents when we need it. Advocacy always plays the leading role in defining and nurturing worthy preservation ends for the community. But it can't substitute its own standards and methods, which aim at specific outcomes, for the fluid expectations of competitive politics.

Where conflict over districting remains unbridgeable, the political process—at its best—aims at balancing our interests against those of our adversaries. Exactly where this balance is struck when the votes are cast is settled by the relative influence each party brings to bear on the moment of decision. Our job is to see to it that our interests are heard by decision makers and that our influence prevails.

FUSING POLITICS AND PRESERVATION

From a strictly preservationist point of view, politics is rarely satisfying. Yet the principles you advocate as a preservationist will be judged politically in the long run by your ability to apply them to practical effect in advancing your community's welfare.

Even then, *the politics of district designation are more than just technique.* As preservation goals inform designation politics, so do political considerations reshape preservation goals.

Aristotle summed it up for us: "In framing an ideal you may assume what you wish, but you must avoid impossibilities."

Only by engaging in politics are you able realistically to explore the limits of the possible. Those limits are defined by the scope of the historic district ordinance you can win and what overreaching goals you can't. As you move through the designation process to your City Council's final vote, you will be striving to put forward a plan that maximally satisfies your preservation interests while meeting the political requirements of success.

ON LEARNING FROM EXPERIENCE

Such challenges are reborn with each new local campaign. Every new effort repeats the experiences of the others, within a fairly limited range of variations in the roles played by elected officials, property owners, consultants, public administrators, the media, and private sector associations.

Each designation campaign will have its own peculiar features. But time and again, experience shows that the main dimensions of the process are both regular and predictable. The political dynamics that can be distilled and taught include:

- Mastering the political process.
- Planning and strategy.
- Campaign organizing and the qualities of leadership.
- Framing a practical vision.
- Anticipating and handling the opposition.
- Conducting community meetings.
- Managing issues, petitions, and public opinion.
- Dealing with public officials.
- Strategizing for public hearings.
- Winning the vote for district designation.

The way most of us first get involved in preservation just about assures our coming late to political sensibility. So now I want us to cast our thoughts back to beginnings so that we may find our way forward, as Plutarch said, "like watermen who look astern while they row ahead."

NOTE

1. Aliyya Swaby, "Opposition Kills Historic District Expansion," www.newhavanindependent.org, July 11, 2016.

Chapter Three

How It Starts

I guess it's time you heard our story.

—Humphrey Bogart, *Passage to Marseille*

Thousands of local preservationists just like you have been baptized by fire. They haven't become preservationists because they're architects, historians, city planners, lawyers, professors of fine arts. They've joined our ranks because they have found value in the legacy of some local property that they have fought very hard to preserve.

In this fight, they have experienced politics in the trenches. They have done battle all along a learning curve from reasoned arguments to adversarial gamesmanship to backdoor politicking. Some have won. Too many have lost. Others are fighting still.

Of course, not everyone's challenge has been so daunting. Some districting has begun under fairly auspicious circumstances. Sometimes the local government has sponsored the plan. Other times the social situation is settled and the district becomes a public celebration of civic pride.

But often preservationists-in-the-making don't get interested in politics until they find themselves in the middle of a high-stakes contest among conflicting interests. They're behind in the game and pressed for time. So like the ever-late White Rabbit they hasten to make up the deficit. Upset by the course of events that has brought them to this pass, they often fail to understand their place in the process.

How about you? Wherever you are, and whatever the peculiarities of your situation, I think you'll find something instructive in the generic tale I have to offer.

JUMPING INTO POLITICS . . .

We preservationists have an unusual ability to make a personal connection with property we don't own. "The second my husband and I started driving up and down these streets," Paula Soest says in Orange, California, "I just fell in love with the whole thing."[1] We tend to infuse places—from open farm-land to old town centers—with significance because those places have taken on meaning and value in our own lives. Thus New Orleans's French Quarter is described as "the physical essence of who we are."[2]

Some of us come to believe that the time-softened places we hold close are special and somehow safely apart from areas that have been touched and spoiled by others. So when the hand of change falls upon us, it seems to come out of the blue. The more sensitive we are, the more we express outrage at what for others is a commonplace occurrence. We seek a political solution. Sometimes it begins to take the form of getting a historic district designated.

I suspect you're like most Americans who are fortunate enough not to have to think about politics on a daily basis. So you probably think that because the political process is receptive to your claims, the process somehow begins when you get involved.

The truth is that politics is a continuously flowing river. When you step into it for the first time the experience is new only to you. Usually by the time you and I get involved, the political process of change has been going on for a long, long time.

Developers—to pick one group whose actions trigger historic districting campaigns—are different. As Baltimore preservationist Brad Rogers observes, they think in terms of markets and ordinances, not meaning and value. By the time their project comes to light, they have typically invested much time—perhaps years—and borrowed money to negotiate sales with property owners, to conduct market studies, and to get zoning ordinances changed at those boring commission meetings no one else much attended. ("I'd rather watch grass grow," confides a friend.) With these land usees and other major matters well behind them, they are locked into the project personally, emotionally, and financially.

It's just then, when the developers are eager to finalize such details as deed transfer and construction permits, that you want to be heard. More than that, you actually want to start the whole discussion over again. Of course, you don't want to talk about just the project at hand. You want to get back to basics. Basics like, what is truly good for the community and how does it relate to the built environment?

Out of this comes your proposal for district designation. This is the moment when you're most vulnerable. Smart opponents will jump on your plan as a desperate reaction—an afterthought devoid of real, compelling, intrinsic merit. And unfair. "We all play by the rules," said attorney Andrew W. Miller in Philadelphia, adding his client had relied "on existing laws" in obtaining a demolition permit several months before local activists took action.[3]

. . . AND SKIPPING OUT AGAIN

Can you blame developers for being exasperated? As one critic reasonably charges, preservationists who come late to the game "shirk responsibility. [They] do not plan ahead, but wait until new construction nears and then cry for government to intervene."[4]

This reflects a contemporary belief that elected officials ought to do whatever we tell them. "Our councilman is not a developer. He is supposed to be *our* voice," claimed activist Deborah Tempera of Fells Point in Baltimore, angered over James B. Kraft's decision to back away from height restrictions to allow for development.[5] When officials don't reflect our interests, we're likely to blame them and the "rigged system" as accomplices in unwelcome change.

But do you see what's really happened?

Coming late, we've hardly wet our feet in the river of politics-as-it-actually-is before skipping out again. From their place in the real, continuing flow of political events our opponents can't help but feel a bit like the hit-and-run victim who reported, "An invisible car came out of nowhere, hit me, and disappeared."

So be careful. We can become so intoxicated with our vision of a well-preserved community that we can't see straight when politics intrudes on our reverie.

If that's the case, then we're going to make the cardinal mistake of thinking that preservation is one thing and politics something else—an incompatible and inferior interloper. "Mere politics," a Philadelphia preservationist says, hoping his city's heritage won't be dragged down by it. A Boise activist sees her situation similarly. "It's a very emotional issue for us," she says. "We need to get the politics under control and do what's best for our future."[6]

How do you see politics? Here's a quick self-test: What's your first reaction to the West Coast preservationist who writes of his cause, "Let's see if politics can be removed from the issue and let it become a black and white issue of 'is there enough evidence to nominate the district by itself.'"[7] If you said "uh-oh" when you read that, then you're on the right track.

A REALITY CHECK

Isn't it obvious that politics doesn't interfere with preservation so much as we force preservation onto local politics? When we go to politics to enact our districting legislation, it is politics that sets the rules, not preservation.

We have some nerve, then, when we confront politics as it actually is with an abstract ideal of how we think it ought to be. That's why finding out how the political process actually works can be a sobering—and liberating—experience.

NOTES

1. Michelle Gringeri-Brown, "Inside Preservation: A Grassroots Effort Pays Off," www.americanbungalowmagazine.com, 2002. Also see, F. Andrew Taylor, East Valley Neighborhood Designated by Las Vegas City Council as Historic," www.reviewjournal.com, November 18, 2016.

2. Christopher Tidmore, "New Orleans and the Charleston Experiment," www.itsonlypolitics.com, August 20, 2003.

3. Valerie Russ, "Despite Landlord's Objections, Rowhouses Get Historic Status," www.philly.com, July 10, 2016.

4. Rex Curry, rexy.net, n.d.

5. "Kraft Explains Why He Withdrew Height Restrictions from Fells Point," www.baltimorebrew.com, November 18, 2016.

6. Emily Simnitt, "Boise OKs Historic District," www.idahostatesman.com, June 1, 2004.

7. www.mkhelp.com, July, 1998.

Chapter Four

A Walk through the Designation Process: A Guided Tour with Planner Kaye Graybeal

"Why," said the Dodo, "the best way to explain it is to do it."

—Lewis Carroll, *Alice in Wonderland*

When you were in school, did you enjoy the lesson on how a legislative bill becomes a law? Yeah, me neither.

Few things can kill an enthusiasm for politics as quickly as an organizational chart of local governmental operations. So instead of going through "the-head-bone-is-connected-to-the-neck-bone" exercise until our sit-down bone gets numb, let me walk you through a simulated, quite typical real-life experience.

The facts in our simulation won't match up precisely with yours. Not to worry. Being good at politics isn't mainly about facts. Facts change over time and they differ from place to place. You'll need to find out the specific process in your own community. But good questions about how political processes work and how to win are everywhere the same, and they're always in fashion.

An exercise like ours, which is driven by questions and leading statements, can serve as an imaginative bridge between where you are at the start and where you need to go with the designation. At the very least it should help to demystify City Hall where zoning rewrites can be "like walking into a fog."[1]

A SOUTHERN DIALOGUE

Come along with me now as we travel to the lovely port city of Wilmington, North Carolina. We're going to walk into City Hall just as if the only thing we know about historic districts is that we want one. I've picked Wilmington because of Kaye Graybeal. In the early 1990s, Kaye was our consultant in Oak Ridge, North Carolina. She soon became Wilmington's Historic Preservation Planner, the position Maggie O'Conner now holds after Kaye moved into a position as planning manager.[2]

I've arranged for us to meet with Kaye in her top-floor office. Maggie has come along to offer insights. The room with its conference table to one side looks as I had expected, knowing Kaye. It's bright, well-organized, and efficient. Preservation and community service awards fill one wall. The large window looks out to the Cape Fear River in the distance.

What follows is a slightly edited version of an unrehearsed and unscripted hour-long conversation among the three of us. Oh, yes . . . and my neighborhood community is fictional.

Me: It's a pleasure to meet you, Maggie. Thanks for joining us. How familiar are y'all with old Alopecia Shores out toward Bald Head Island? Our historic area is receding alarmingly and we think district designation could help. What can we do?

Kaye: The first thing we should do is check to see if your neighborhood has already been surveyed and qualified for the National Register under previous grant studies.

Me: But all we want is a local district. And anyway someone's told me that a National Register district doesn't have any teeth, but a local district does.

Kaye: That's right. But if it has already qualified for the National Register we can assume it qualifies as a local district. But if it hasn't, we'll have to start from scratch.

Me: What do you mean "qualify"? We're one of the oldest beach communities around.

Kaye: Yes, but you're asking for a new zoning overlay for the district that will basically regulate its design features but not the use of properties. The HPC will need documentation that it's worthy according to criteria set by state enabling legislation and our local preservation ordinance. National Register criteria track along the same lines. From the HPC to the Planning Commission to the City Council, everyone has to be able to point to documented evidence.

Me: Why so many steps? What's so difficult?

Kaye: Every city or county has its own procedures guided by state enabling legislation. Most of them, unless they're very small, have at least one advisory commission that handles technicalities and makes recommendations based on their expertise. They're made up of citizen volunteers who are charged with the responsibility for getting a well-prepared proposal to the final decision makers—the elected officials.

Me: I see. So what if we haven't been surveyed?

Kaye: Then we'll have to decide whether we can budget for a consultant to do the study next fiscal year. Or you as a neighborhood might want to raise the money to pay to have it done. That would be quicker.

Me: Would the City decide to fund this because they want us to have the district?

Kaye: I think we should first send you back to Alopecia to get a feel for the degree of support. We can't just take your word for it. [Smiles.]

Maggie: When we go to the City Council we need a lot of people saying "yes, yes, yes"—more than say "no, no, no." Even if you pay for the study, you'll still need support, because politics is involved. If you don't ask people to join early on, their feelings get hurt, and they're against it because they don't know why they're excluded and they don't understand the regulations.

Kaye: And that it's done behind their backs, or it's a plot. So you have to talk about the benefits, get people excited . . .

Maggie: But even one person can get things started. That's why we went ahead today and met with you. The main thing you need to know is what a district is and why you want it.

Me: OK. So who down here makes the decision to budget for the study?

Kaye: If we think the project looks feasible, we'd ask the City Council to approve a budget enhancement in our consultant line item. We could just ask for funding "for historic designation survey and report." Then we would use it for your neighborhood if there appears to be interest and support. That would avoid asking the Council specifically about your neighborhood before we're ready to go ahead with designation.

Me: So we wouldn't have to go down to the Council to get them to give you the money?

Kaye: You could, but that could be too much too soon.

Me: That's good because we worry that as soon as word gets out about our proposal, people will start fighting it without knowing what it's about. When you ask for a show of support, isn't this biasing the process by giving early warning to our opponents?

Kaye: You'll have to go to the community with a public meeting before the report comes out, to inform them about the possibility. You might show them a vague or broad boundary with a disclaimer that it could change.

Maggie: You might want many community meetings. The first one would be for information: what it means to be in a historic district, what's going to happen, the positive benefits of it. And the drawbacks.

Kaye: But don't label them drawbacks. We say, "Here are some things you need to consider to decide whether the process will benefit you."

Me: So we have a community meeting, you get the funding, and the study is favorable. Whose proposal is this now—yours or ours?

Kaye: It would be a staff proposal if the City paid for the study, with a recommendation of approval to the HPC, the Planning Commission, and the City Council.

Me: Who has control over the details of the proposal? For example, can we leave out property owned by die-hard opponents?

Kaye: Zoning laws don't promote "Swiss cheese" holes in the district. That could be considered illegal spot rezoning. What you'll have is an overlay district on top of underlying zoning, and the district has to be made up of contiguous properties. But you could leave out properties on the periphery. It would be a judgment call. That's where politics enters in, depending on how strong you think support will be for what you want.

Me: If we do that won't we be open to charges of gerrymandering?

Maggie: You don't want to leave properties out just because of present owners. Properties change hands. This is where you have a community meeting, to bring people around. You've got time to work on them.

Me: How long? We'd like to get it done yesterday!

Kaye: Maybe a year, more or less, after funding the survey. There's the study, and the time needed for it depends on scheduling and the district's complexity. We'll send the completed report for comments from SHPO. [She pronounces it "SHiPO," the State Historic Preservation Office. Every state has one, by one name or another, pursuant to the federal National Historic Preservation Act of 1966.] They have the opportunity to speak to the integrity of the proposed district. Then if you look at just the formal meetings, it'll take one month for the HPC, one for the Planning Commission, and one for the City Council to review it, if all goes smoothly. If it doesn't, any of them could continue their deliberations longer, send the proposal back for more study, or ask for more information.

Me: How much does the City Council pay attention to SHPO?

Kaye: They need something to hang their hat on if they are going to vote in favor of something that some citizens are going to oppose. They can at least say, "Well, the State says it's very worthy." I think sometimes decision makers don't necessarily trust the Preservation Commission, so if the HPC can add credibility to the proposal by saying that SHPO approves, they'll have a stronger case.

Me: Why wouldn't they trust the HPC?

Kaye: It depends on who's in office—maybe a property rights advocate—and who's on the HPC—a few zealous commissioners can make the entire HPC appear unreasonable.

Me: What if SHPO isn't fully supportive? Will we have to redo the report?

Kaye: Yes. Or we can go forward and make a case for doing something locally that SHPO doesn't agree with, if we feel we have the support for it.

Me: Who's the "we"? Who's going to make those kinds of decisions? We in Alopecia Shores or you downtown here?

Kaye: It's a partnership. If the City has paid for the survey report and the planning staff is bringing it forward to Council, the staff will work with the community even if some people are likely to stand up and object. It's a subjective call for us, though the technical merit of the proposal is objectively defensible. At some point staff has to make the decision: Can we lend this support? Is this a proposal that most people are behind? If we have broad consensus, we can take it forward while acknowledging there are people against it. Because we're making the recommendation, we have to be confident that the proposal meets our zoning regulations and is something that can be politically supported.

Me: When you write the proposal, are you going to run it by us for our opinions? What about our opponents?

Kaye: We'll make sure everybody, including opponents, can obtain a draft copy either here or online, or we'll pass it out at public meetings.

Me: Will you amend it just to suit the opponents?

Kaye: No, it's still a partnership with you, with the whole community. If we find out there are people extremely opposed to parts of it then we would need to assess whether we need to bring it back to the community to get consensus or whether we've done all we can and take it on to the commissions and the City Council.

Me: But once people state their positions, isn't it hard to change them?

Maggie: I think you're wrong. People listen and change. Some may become strong supporters. They need to understand what it means to be in a historic district—what you can do and what you can't do, and that's when you talk about the design guidelines.

Me: What guidelines?

Kaye: Once you are designated, the HPC will apply design guidelines in evaluating applications for certificates of appropriateness for work projects in the district.

Me: When do we write the guidelines—or do you do that?

Kaye: Unless there is something really special about some aspect in your district, the guidelines that the HPC already uses in other districts will apply to you. But we don't want a lot of conflicting norms out there among the districts—we have five already. That would complicate the HPC's work and maybe open us up to legal challenges.

Me: So we can't really negotiate much on the content of the guidelines.

Kaye: Maybe a little, but not really much. If you were the first district, you'd have a lot more flexibility. But here, you'll probably just want to explain the guidelines very clearly so people don't think they're more of a burden than they actually are.

Me: Is it right to say you'll be handling the official process with boards and commissions downtown and it's up to us to handle things in Alopecia Shores?

Kaye: Once staff gives the proposal to the HPC and the HPC supports it, the HPC will be the petitioner of record who asks for Planning Commission support and final Council approval. You will be able to testify at each stage and so will your opponents. How that goes depends on what you've accomplished in your neighborhood.

Me: What exactly is the Planning Commission's role compared to the HPC's?

Kaye: The HPC verifies that the proposal is justified in preservation terms. The Planning Commission—because the district will be a zoning overlay—considers how the proposal conforms to zoning code and whether it conflicts with other City interests and plans. The City Council looks at anything at all that it thinks is important.

Me: What if the Planning Commission says no?

Kaye: The HPC can decide to appeal the decision to the City Council.

Maggie: That's why you need community involvement. You don't want to just leave it up to a consultant or us or the HPC. You want to show it's about community pride.

Kaye: And you have to find all the intersecting interests in the community that will support you.

Me: So will you be on our side?

Kaye: What we do as staff is present the technical merits of the case. We act as advisers to the Council. We have to know what Council members like—what their interests are—but we are also trying to do what's right for the community. When I was in Maggie's job I once asked, "Can I be an advocate in presenting this proposal? I am the preservation planner." My supervisor, who had the job I have now, said I didn't have to be just neutral and technical. That's a judgment call, too. As staff, you have to realize that you're going to be criticized by the district's opponents, and Council members might see staff as trying to ram something through that people don't like. You have to be careful about the degree of advocacy and passion that you show. If you can present the case so that it's undeniably worthy of historic designation, then you don't have to espouse all the other benefits of preservation. Just show that it meets all legal requirements for merit. That's best. If you do that, you've done your job as staff.

Me: How about the City Manager's role in this?

Kaye: The City Manager is at the top of the City's administrative hierarchy. The City Manager is the Planning Director's boss and the Planning Director is the Preservation Planner's boss. The City Manager would be informed by subordinates about the plan and might oppose it for any number of reasons and stop it. It's up to staff to persuade everybody right on up the administrative line, including the City Attorney.

Me: Would we as citizens lobby the City Manager if there were resistance to the district?

Kaye: You can ask for an appointment with the Manager or you can go to the City Council. The Council is the voice for the citizens in City affairs and can tell the Manager that citizens should be allowed to pursue their initiative. But if we do our job as staff that shouldn't be a problem.

Me: What about the Mayor? Will you talk with the Mayor or should we?

Kaye: Historic Preservation staff may or may not talk with the Mayor, but that's typically the job of the City Manager. The Planning Director might suggest a meeting with the Mayor, department heads, and staff. It's a good idea to get the Mayor onboard before going to the City Council.

Me: Is there anything else that can be done to improve our prospects with the Council?

Kaye: We could request a work session with the Council to educate them—tell them, here's what people think the pros and cons are. We'd tell them how staff has addressed those concerns. Citizens can attend this type of session to listen, but not speak. Then we could summarize this presentation in the public hearing.

Me: How would you handle the benefits side?

Kaye: We could use case studies from other communities, with hard numbers to support economic arguments, for example. We could say we've seen it work in other places, so we think it could work here. So you try to back up an opinion or a recommendation about a particular benefit with evidence on here's why or here's how it has worked someplace else.

Me: I'm uneasy about the community meetings. We're not preservation experts. Should we coordinate with you and have you speak for us?

Kaye: From experience, that could be a problem for staff to meet with advocates ahead of time. We'll come and talk about what a historic district is and what it'll mean to your community. But it's your meeting and you'll be the ones to convince your neighbors.

Me: Maybe we need our own preservationist to advise us.

Kaye: You could hire your own consultant, even if the City does the survey study. Or you could contact SHPO. They keep a list of qualified consultants.

You can also invite SHPO to come to a meeting. Also think about inviting such private sector organizations as Preservation North Carolina or Historic Wilmington Foundation.

Me: Do we need an attorney?

Maggie: When you go to the HPC or the Planning Commission with an attorney it sets up this other world. Everybody suddenly gets very tense, very careful about what they say. People stop working together, and you need people to want the district.

Me: So what do you think we have to do next?

Maggie: You have to have a plan. But what you do depends on how you read who's sitting on the City Council, because some politicians may be leaning more heavily toward preservation while others aren't. So what kinds of risks you can take in the campaign depends on Council members. You might have a very favorable Council when you get there, and the opposition won't matter. But you could have a Council that doesn't want to approve it, and every single supporter will be important to you.

Kaye: That's when you talk about economic development, creating a protected investment environment, and other benefits. You need as many people from the community pushing their interests with you as you can get together. You need to know the people you'll be working with in the community and on the City Council.

Maggie: And you need patience . . .

On that calming note, I thanked them for their time and assistance. By the time I had crossed back over Cape Fear, I was already seeing implications for planning and strategy rising to the surface.

NOTES

1. In the words of Baltimore homeowner George Frazier, www.baltimorebrew, October 20, 2016.

2. Since this interview appeared in the first edition of this material, Kaye has taken a position in Knoxville, Tennessee.

Part II

CAMPAIGN STRATEGY

Chapter Five

On Planning and Strategy

You might not be interested in strategy, but strategy is interested in you.

—Leon Trotsky

We got a friendly reception in Wilmington, didn't we? If you're not that lucky in your first encounter with local government, well, it's good to be put on notice sooner rather than later.

So what did we learn? That when you take your districting idea to City Hall, what you see is what you get. It's not what you'd like to hear, that the way ahead is clear.

YOUR STATUTORY SETTING

So let's take care of first things first. Pick up the phone, call City Hall. Ask to speak to a planning official and make an appointment to meet face-to-face. While you're on the phone get yes or no answers to the following basic questions:

- Does the City have a *preservation ordinance* that provides for local historic districts and specifies the designation process?
- Has the City put in place a *historic preservation commission* charged with design review and designation responsibilities?
- Are there *design guidelines* in place that will apply to your historic district?
- Does your City Planning Department have a *preservation specialist* on staff or at least someone conversant with local historic districts?

Just as soon as you can, get copies of the ordinance and guidelines—if there are any—to read before you go in for a chat. This will save time and make you a more intelligent listener. We could've been better prepared for Kaye and Maggie, don't you think?

But what if there is no ordinance where you live and you have to start from scratch? That's just a complication—an obstacle, not a barrier.

In fact, demonstrating support for districting might just be what it takes to get an ordinance passed and a HPC set up. The Huntington Woods, Michigan, City Commission created its Historic District Commission in 2003 for the express purpose of studying a districting proposal.

In such cases, we—and I mean you and all the folks in and out of government who'll be working on the project—don't have to come up with an ordinance and HPC design entirely on our own.

Every state government has preservation statutes on the books to guide us. We, at the local level, will be able to decide a good many particulars. But anything the City does will have to conform to state legislation governing the establishment of districts and HPCs. To find out more about your state's statutory framework, contact your State Historic Preservation Office.

So keep that appointment downtown. Find out how your local designation process really works, what falls to you to instigate and what kind of people you'll have to work with.

Don't hesitate. "Questions," cinema sleuth Charlie Chan once said, "are keys to door of truth." Ferret out where your input can make a difference and where you shouldn't tread. Bear in mind that when "no" means "no" for a good reason, that's a good answer too.

The more you know the less likely you are to think, say, or do foolish things.

LOCAL PROCEDURAL DIFFERENCES

Did you notice that Kaye and Maggie didn't start by asking us what we wanted them to do? They just laid out the planning procedure mandated in Wilmington and told us what they could do in terms of:

1. Budgeting for a study.
2. Surveying district properties and preparing a map.
3. Getting the City administration onboard.
4. Developing the draft proposal.
5. Getting SHPO evaluation and comments.
6. Submitting the proposal for HPC review and recommendation.

7. Submitting the proposal for Planning Commission review and recommendation.
8. Submitting the proposal for City Council consideration and vote.

This is exactly what we needed to hear. We could plan on it—if we were pursuing a district in *their town.*

What about in yours? Municipalities seem to enjoy coming up with their own ways of doing things. So get with a planner and map out the way it's done in your town. I want to assure you, though, that no matter how different your flowchart might look from others, the politics that courses through it will be the same.

We'll be using Wilmington as our model town because its process is common, simple, and straightforward. Once you know what you're facing, you'll need to make mental adjustments to adapt what we say here for your own purposes as you plan your campaign.

ON PLANNING

But you know what? The more you think about it the more confusing the very idea of a *plan* becomes.

Follow me for a moment: Let's say we've gone ahead and developed a plan that's tailored to our own town's designation process. But what do we actually *do* with a plan? Well, we implement it, of course. But what does *that* mean and how does it work to get us what we want? How should we *conceptualize* the process to make sure we're in control of what happens?

Should we think that implementing a plan is like assembling a jigsaw puzzle? Do we line the pieces up then fit each into place, moving from success to success, until the puzzle is completed. Is that it?

If that's the plan, then we're in trouble because we haven't accounted for politics. A *plan* is just a plan until it comes up against competing interests. That's when we need a *strategy* for checking our opponents and winning over decision makers.

So what's holding us back? Well, I think maybe we just don't want to fight with our neighbors. It's not a pleasant experience.

So we delay, maybe with our fingers crossed that we'll be as lucky as resident Steve Davis in Norman, Oklahoma, where 78 percent of property owners supported local designation. Not only did no one file a formal protest, but he reported, "We just haven't heard anything negative from anyone, not even any phone calls."[1]

Still, given that one well-aimed protest can blow a plan apart like a Clint Eastwood's 45 Magnum in *Dirty Harry*, you have to ask yourself: "Do I feel lucky?"

THE DESCENT INTO POLITICS

Even if you realize you can't duck politics forever, the way the formal designation process works can lull you into procrastination. The first few stages in the Wilmington model deal almost exclusively with preservation matters right up through the HPC hearing, pushing politics to the sidelines. But just like with any protected enterprise, the longer we put off facing up to our competition the more perilous our position becomes as we descend into the much more politically complexioned worlds of the Planning Commission and elected officials.

The hard political truth is that those who sit on the City Council are free to ignore every staff and commission recommendation that crosses their desks. Planning staff are employees, and commissioners are no more than citizen advisers to the Council in the policy-making process. Their support is an advantage, no doubt about it. But it's in no way predictive or binding on the City Council. Their recommendations carry no more authority than individual Council members are inclined to give them.

What's your Council's record? Unless it has a proven track record of deferring to the HPC, I'd advise you to prepare for the worst.

If you walk into the Council chamber with nothing more than a solid proposal, staff support, and a couple of advisory commission recommendations, then all bets are off. You may have done everything by the book, hit all your procedural marks, satisfied every legal and technical prerequisite for designation, and still lose the final vote. In fact, your Council members may actually say they agree with every argument you make for districting *and still refuse to do what you ask.*

So *what* can we do about it? And *when* should we do it? These are strategic, not planning questions.

ON STRATEGY

Do you remember Kaye's offer of a partnership with us? It captures our strategic challenge brilliantly.

Look at the list of procedural steps again. They involve us, and yet there's *nothing there that you and I are personally required to do.* But if you pay close attention to what she and Maggie said we can do to help our cause, you'll see that there are actually *two* processes running on converging tracks toward designation.

- The first is the *formal* procedure that runs its decreed course from the resources study to designation.
- The other is much more *informal and political*, and it's our particular contribution to the effort.

This second, strategic line of action begins back in our community. That's where we lay the political groundwork for the proposal's favorable reception before the HPC, Planning Commission, and City Council.

Get it? On the one track, we do *what is required*. On the other, we do *what it takes* in terms of:

1. Initiating the process.
2. Influencing the study.
3. Holding community meetings.
4. Carrying out a petition drive.
5. Managing a media campaign.
6. Testifying before the HPC.
7. Testifying before the Planning Commission.
8. Lobbying and testifying before the City Council.

Flip back and forth between the lists. Do you see them twinned and pulling together like the two sides of a zipper as we close the gap to district designation?

No part of either track is ever complete in itself, and no single accomplishment is ever certain until the final vote is taken. Even momentum has no loyalty.

That's why politics is more like a game of chess than a jigsaw puzzle. With a jigsaw puzzle you know when you've made a good fit, you know that the piece will stay put, and you know you can build confidently upon it. But in chess, as in politics, the game changes with every move. You can never know for certain that any move is the right one because you can never be sure how the other player will react.

A political strategy is practical only if, like chess, it embraces fluidity, uncertainty, and only general predictability. We know just two things for certain: where we start and where we want to end up. After our first move, everything is tactical improvisation looking for advantage in swiftly moving events. But the long thread of our effort, what connects all from beginning to end, must be our sustained strategic effort to bend the course of events our way.

Chess grandmaster Savielly Tartakover once explained the difference between strategy and tactics. "The tactician," he said, "must know what to do whenever something needs doing; the strategist must know what to do when nothing needs doing."

So in the early going, while things are still moving our way in the formal process down at City Hall, that's the time for strategic preparation. The first thing we need to think about is what it means to build community support in what will likely be a most difficult political climate.

NOTE

1. Jane Glenn Cannon, "Norman Neighborhood Seeks Historic District Designation," www.newsok.com, October 10, 2016.

Chapter Six

Our Strategic Line:
A Community in/within Conflict

The most basic decision in politics is whether to be conciliatory or aggressive.

—Dick Morris

We have seen how the district designation process works at City Hall. So what do you think our chances are with your neighbors? How should we approach them?

Should we be conciliatory going into our campaign or is it better to be aggressive? Do you believe that we invite trouble by looking for it? Maybe you're wondering how we can know the limits of cooperation if we don't pour all our energies into working together. For that matter, how can we be confident of any strategy?

Hard to tell, isn't it? So what do we do, just pay our money and take our choice? In truth, I suspect that we don't want to commit one way or the other until we see how things play out. We expect that our opportunities will be a mixed bag anyway, don't we?

Let me suggest an approach that allows us to be as conciliatory or as aggressive as circumstances warrant. Let's take a strategic line that combines the underlying political reality of a *community in conflict* with the possibilities of nurturing a newly vital sense of *community in the midst of conflict*.

EDUCATED ILLUSIONS

First, though, I want to know whether you can handle conflict. The first time I made the case for winning through competitive politics a conference

33

attendee accosted me. "I hear what you're saying," she said, "but I still feel that preservation is too important not to bring everyone along by educating them."

Educating them? You mean all they have to do is know what we know and they'll agree with us? Some, sure. But *all* of them, even *most* of them?

What a quaint notion. She's a perfect example of how we can get so deeply invested in preservation values that it distorts the way we see and interpret the once familiar world around us.

There was a time, I'm sure, when we were easy with neighbors who had views and aspirations of their own. Diversity of interests was healthy, wasn't it? But maybe we think that's a luxury we can no longer afford. Now anything different from what we want is all too easily held to be rationally, aesthetically, even ethically suspect. We brand our adversaries with being unschooled, unsophisticated, antisocial, spiteful, selfish, greedy, or some other slur d'jour.

Such immoderation in our judgment can't help but inspire immodesty about our own place in politics and lead us to folly. We need to get a grip on ourselves. No one I know ever won over the majority we need by being a snob for the truth—especially when that truth isn't a gold-plated self-evident one.

INSTINCTIVE POLITICS

An editorial in the *Florida Quest* said it as well as anybody: "There's a natural instinct among many to resist being told what they can or can't do with their property."[1]

Private property rights are indeed a far more commanding instinct in American politics than preservation. And long ago, even Machiavelli—the master political manipulator—warned his powerful Renaissance prince that he could do just about anything he wished as long as he left other people's property alone.

Have no illusions. Our opponents enjoy advantages that have little to do with being smart, and they instinctively seem to know which buttons to push to get other folks in a lather and send us up the wall.

Talk about an educational deficit! You'd think we'd know by now that politics runs more on emotion than intelligence. Didn't Sam Adams advise us long ago that people "are governed more by their feelings than by reason?"

So we've embarked on a political enterprise that is a great deal less thoughtful than we'd probably like it to be. We should expect that our ideas will be roughly treated by at least some neighbors.

A COMMUNITY IN CONFLICT

Much of the direct political conflict we'll encounter is just superficial and passing. Hostility and resentment are here today before the vote, gone tomorrow afterwards. But all of it springs from far deeper tensions among interests and feelings that are shaping—as they will continue to shape—our community.

These tensions simmer below the surface most of the time. They may bubble up here and there as specific projects—a new condominium block, demolition of a church—raise concerns. Once in awhile they come to a boil. No doubt our proposal will turn up the heat.

But the conflict that boils over into a community fight over designation doesn't begin with our initiative nor will it end with districting. The historic district will just be a different, and to our mind a more successful, way of dealing with it.

This elemental conflict is an inescapable fact of everyday life. That's why, when we think politically, we think in terms of a *community in conflict*.

A COMMUNITY WITHIN CONFLICT

Our focus on conflict doesn't stop us from working to alter the way people view preservation, even if their interests don't match ours. So part of thinking politically has to be devoted to community building, to molding individual attitudes and linking up diverse interests in support of preservation.

As we look around our neighborhood we should be scoping out how much room we have for invigorating a *larger sense of community within conflict*. Still, we know we're not going to win over everyone. Some of our neighbors will remain unmoved. Some will stand against us.

OUR DUAL STRATEGY

Taken together, these two perspectives frame what will be our two-part political mantra: *There is enough mutuality of interests to make a historic district possible, and enough conflict among interests to make districting necessary.* It's up to us to make our case on both counts and win the decision.

Our strategy, then, is straightforward. We will do what it takes to forge a broad coalition for districting wherever we can, and we will use that coalition to outpoint those who remain unalterably opposed to us.

In the process we will discover how much consensus is possible and how much conflict is unavoidable. This flexible approach gives the fullest practical play to our yearning for positive advocacy and consensus building while being thoroughly realistic about the practical requirements of political success.

In today's slang, we got game. Now let's go look at the field of play.

NOTE

1. Editorial, "Lake Helen's Historic District Changes Are Good," *Florida Quest*, September 14, 1998.

Chapter Seven

Makers, Breakers, Takers, and Shapers: The Political Field of Play

Who's on first?

—Abbott and Costello

What's on second base, I Don't Know is on third, and that's about as far as I can keep things straight in Abbott and Costello's hilarious baseball routine. Keeping the who's who of political players straight in your own districting campaign can be even more confusing.

At least in baseball you know the shape of the diamond and can put players on bases. But how should we diagram who's playing where on districting issues?

Do we sketch out left field and right field, who is liberal or conservative, Democrat or Republican? From where I sit, I think that's looking too far out into the haze of general tendencies to be of any real use. Better we pull back to the infield where we can clearly see that everyone's primary interest—whether in baseball or in preservation—is in real estate.

Home plate is the most valuable piece of property in baseball. The whole game is organized and played around that central fact. And so it is with preservation. You have to focus on people's primary interest in real estate to keep your head in the game.

WHO'S WHO?

So let's start identifying who's who politically by making real estate our base organizing concept. Our most important question, then, isn't who's for or against preservation. Not even close. The most important thing we need to know is who owns the properties we're going to include in the district.

37

Note: who *owns*, not *occupies*. When you send out notifications and announcements, you don't want them tossed out by some renter or leaseholder you *think* is the owner.

Every overlooked property owner—whether they live in the district or out of state—is a political and public relations strike against you. We just can't afford to lose support from mistakes.

Ownership creates an exclusive group of interested individuals for the key, uncontestable reason than the burden of districting falls most heavily on property owners. Others who live or work in the district have a right to express their opinions. But when it comes to districting, the City Council will *first* weigh heads and *then* count them. You'll find that the heads that count the most are the ones that voice the weighty interests of property owners.

Property interests, of course, aren't monolithic. And because those interests are not all the same, politicians aren't going to treat them all equally, either. Perceptions in both quarters—those of property owners and policy makers—are nuanced by any number of considerations, such as:

- Whether properties are owner occupied, owned by local voters, or owned by absentee landlords with few ties to the community.
- Whether properties are used for residential, commercial, institutional, governmental, agricultural, or other purposes.
- Whether owners are private individuals, corporations, not-for-profit institutions, or public governmental authorities.

These differences can create tensions among *groups* of property owners. The College Hill district in Greensboro, North Carolina, has had running conflicts because of its mix of family residences, a YMCA, a commercial strip, fraternity and other student housing, churches, and bars. But *individual owners*, too, will keep a skeptical eye on neighbors like themselves, ever watchful of their own particular interests.

Each owner, then, will approach historic districting through a different, carefully guarded perspective that passes through the lens of his or her own self-interests. But no matter how different they are, their attitudes will always be fundamentally different from those folks who don't own property in the district.

This won't keep property owners from working with non-property owners, such as groups concerned with gentrification and social justice. Yet the difference still runs like a fault line between them.

So the first thing you want to do is get yourself down to City Hall, go to the tax and property records, get hold of the property maps covering the district, and start answering these questions for each parcel of land:

1. Who is the owner of record?
2. Who pays the property taxes?
3. Is the owner local?
4. Is the owner an individual, or is it a corporate, governmental, or other entity?
5. How is the property used: residential, commercial, institutional, governmental, agricultural, mixed use, and so forth?
6. Is the property itself owner-occupied, rented, leased, or vacant?

Record all information you gather, including out-of-town addresses. List each parcel's acreage, if it's available, in case you need it later.

Don't assume that the City can give you accurate lists. If you want it done right, do it yourself. You'll never have to say, "That's not what they told me." That just makes you sound careless.

Precision is your byword. Activists in the Bungalow Heaven Landmark District in Pasadena, California, could attest to 962 lots and the inaccuracies of some public records. Now create usable lists of information from what you've found:

- List owners who live in the district in their own residences.
- List owners who work in the district in their own premises.
- List those who own investment properties for rent or lease.
- Make separate lists of properties by type of ownership: private individual, corporate, governmental, private institutional, and so forth.
- Make separate lists of owners by how their properties are used.
- Group properties under the individual names of owners who hold title to more than one parcel.

Your goal is to be the unimpeachable master of facts and details so you won't get caught making unsubstantiated claims.

As you work, you'll detect emerging patterns of mutual interests among your neighbors that are almost certain to be clearer to you than to the owners themselves. That's because few folks ever lift their vision beyond the immediate setting of their own properties—meaning that an understanding of their interests in districting needs, quite literally, to be mapped out.

WHO'S WHERE?

So let's do some mapping. You should be able to get a copy of the official tax map showing all the built features of the district's physical landscape and how they're zoned. Make sure your copy is big enough—blueprint size is perfect—for marking up individual properties.

Start by boldly outlining the district. Then denote all structures and features that contribute to the historic significance of the district. If you don't yet have a historic resources survey, then estimate them now and make changes later.

Next, devise a consistent legend for other group identifications. I'd suggest using a mix of transparent color markers that you may overwrite, colored pens, colored adhesive dots, and written abbreviations. Look at all properties, *both contributing and noncontributing*, and do the following:

- With transparent markers, color code each property by use: residential, business, private institutional, governmental, or other, including mixed-use.
- Identify properties that are owner-occupied.
- Identify properties by type of ownership: private individual, corporate, governmental, private institutional, and so forth.
- Draw lines to connect or encircle multiple properties owned in common and identify the owner.
- Indicate all properties that you believe are currently vulnerable.

Check with your Planning Department for a rundown of rezoning, building, or demolition applications as well as any preliminary inquiries that might affect district properties. You have a right to anything that has entered the public domain. Highlight the more important concerns, but mark even innocuous things on the map.

Property owners will also be influenced by developments immediately adjacent to the district. And owners just outside may be motivated to support or oppose designation depending on its spillover effects on them.

Now go find out what's important to your neighbors in the district. Talk *with* them, not just *to* them. But don't let them in on the district idea just yet. You don't want folks talking until you've made your first community presentation, as we'll see in chapter 18.

Has anything happened recently to agitate them? Are there any new issues on the horizon, like a school or hospital expansion, a road widening or cell phone tower? Is the quality of residential life under pressure in one particular quarter? How about economic decline among retailers?

Are there any issues in the district that pit one set of property interests against others, such as tearing down residences for church expansion? They needn't be so specific, either. General problems often percolate along lines where different property uses run alongside one another, as where a commercial sector abuts residences. List key issues in the map's margin and connect them by arrows or lassos to specific locations on the map.

Now sit back and look at your map. Don't just focus on problem spots. Where are the less marked up, quiet areas in the district? Owners in a well-maintained, especially affluent, neighborhood will be a tough crowd to motivate. Still, as Alan Prendergast observes in Denver, "Even in stately, don't-mess-with-success Park Hill, increasing anxiety over scrape-offs, pop-ups and new construction has led to a hotly debated proposal to set up a historic district."[1]

WHO'S WHAT?

Whether people back us or not will have little to do with their personal political views. Liberal Democrats can be just as prickly about property as conservative Republicans. Yet both will readily back districting if they see it's in their interest.

The usual left–right political labels don't really explain much. I'd like you instead to think of property owners in the district in terms of Makers, Breakers, and Takers:[2]

- *Makers* (that's us) have the vision, resources, and leadership qualities needed for bringing a historic district into being. We are convinced that our valued property and related interests are best secured by district designation. This in turn, we'll affirm, promotes the common good of our community.
- *Breakers* are inclined against districting from the start, and they have the resources to mount an effective opposition against us. They tend to find disadvantage for their interests under designation and are unresponsive to appeals to civic virtue. Breakers must be persuaded, co-opted, neutralized, blunted, or defeated.
- *Takers* are unconvinced but persuadable property owners. More or less satisfied with the status quo, and often having limited resources and interests, they don't yet see where the district will make much of a difference to them. They can't get excited about the district, yet they're not especially motivated to oppose it either. In the end, they'll pretty much take whatever happens in stride.

HOW THE GAME IS PLAYED

Now you know the field. It's time to play the game.

Takers straddle the line between our most ardent opponents and us, and they outnumber both. They are our main political interest, not Breakers.

Our *key strategic challenge* is not to beat our opposition in a head-to-head contest. It is to isolate its most adamant elements—those who will not let themselves be persuaded, cajoled, or enticed—on the extreme edge of opinion and so to split them off from more moderate doubters as we move to win the middle ground.

Non-property owners aren't going to choose sides unless they're fairly invested one way or another. Because they don't own property, few of them will have any real influence outside of group associations unless they have personal political influence.

Any number of organizations, however, may have a broad membership including both property and non-property owners who share ideas and interests—but not property—in common. So we can add to our taxonomy of property owners:

- **Shapers**, who act as individuals or associations, *independently of property status*, to influence the outcome of our districting campaign.

Shapers may be local, state, or national preservation organizations; property rights groups; tenants' and merchants' associations; a regional development board; the tourism industry; cultural heritage and political action groups; behind-the-scenes operators at City Hall; your local board of realtors, developers, architects and contractors; newspapers; and anyone else able to exert influence on public opinion and the political process. These relationships may be diagrammed as in figure 7.1.

LEVEL GROUND

We have explored the political inequities of property ownership. We've walked the district and found differing interests. We have split up the players into separate and competing classifications, and we've begun to think about the strategic implications of what we've found.

And yet in one area all the active participants—Makers, Breakers, and Shapers—stand on common ground and share the same objective. *They all seek to maximize their relative influence in the political process.*

By thinking this way, we are able to treat all parties with equanimity. We know that they must act under the same political compulsions that govern us. This basic fact means that we, as they, should be unaffected in our political calculations of standing and clout—in a word, power—by sentiment, animosity, principles, ideology, or any other motives.

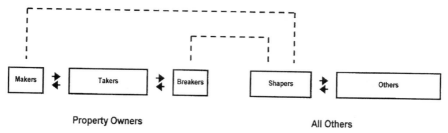

Figure 7.1. **Individuals are distinguished by their relationship to district real estate: some own property, the rest do not. All owners are divided into three groups, and Shapers are distinguished from other non-property owners who take no interest in districting. Arrows indicate individuals shifting between groups as they change their minds during the districting process. Dotted lines represent support or cooperation between Shapers and Makers or Breakers.**
Created by the author.

This necessarily level-eyed reading of the lay of the land gives us an advantage. *We see our opponents' true interests more quickly and even likely better than they see it themselves.* We can anticipate their best efforts and capitalize on less. Our own campaign, then, gains focus and economy of effort. And we ourselves gain clarity and confidence for the game ahead.

NOTES

1. Alan Prendergast, "Park Hill Neighborhood Divided by Battles over Historic District, Subdividing Lots," www.westword.com, September 28, 2016.
2. Stephen D. Krasner first suggested these shorthand labels to describe state actors in the construction of international economic systems. I have redefined them to suit our purposes. See "State Power and the Structure of International Trade," *World Politics*, Vol. 28, No. 3 (April 1976): 317–47.

Chapter Eight

Leadership and Organization

In politics, an organized minority is a political majority.

—Jesse Jackson

You will soon be the public face of your campaign. Next time you look in the mirror, think, "Who else ought to be in this picture?"

Effective leaders build effective leadership teams. Whether you're starting from scratch or within an established organization, the first thing you have to do is put together a campaign steering committee. "Politicians and non-elected citizen leaders agree," writes Danica Roem in Rockville, Maryland. "If you want to win on public policy and political issues, it helps to be well organized."[1]

THE STEERING COMMITTEE

Shaping public opinion is like working in wet cement: It sets more quickly than you want. Think like the audiences you want to influence at the start. The first time your neighbors come to a community meeting, who should they see? Who will inspire them? Who will give them the confidence they're doing the right thing by siding with you?

You can't do it alone. One person can make a difference, but not the whole difference. The history of many districts is written in the biographies of individuals with indomitable wills, such as that of St. Clair Wright, who saved Annapolis, or a special vision, like John Gaw Meem's for Santa Fe. But you can be sure that, to a person, they've known how to use the talents of others.

Reaching out to them doesn't mean pulling in everyone. The steering committee you want is a small, closely knit group of capable people who can work well together.

By small, I mean no more than can fit around a good-size kitchen table— and just that informal. You'll have a mountain of technical material to master, a multiphased process to attend to, and a neighborhood campaign to mount— all under the pressure of closing deadlines.

You will have to have each other's confidence that agreed-to tasks will be done right and on time. No excuses, no pettiness, and no hurt feelings, please. Check your egos at the door.

Take advice, share responsibility, and create an atmosphere of no-fault leadership within the circle. And since you're going to be scheming to win, what goes on in the group has to stay inside the group—*and off social media!*[2]

CHOOSING YOUR LEADERS

So who'll make up your team? Select them with these criteria in mind:

1. *Intelligence.* Everyone is going to have to be a quick study, with an ability to analyze problems and draw conclusions. You don't want the group dragging anchor in muddy thinking. Clarity is essential to crisp decision making.
2. *Personal Character.* Members must want to do the right thing, not just win arguments. Their public face should be one of integrity, dignity, and good humor.
3. *Discipline.* Tolerate no loose cannons. Everyone must agree to defend every group decision. Opponents will exploit dissent. Exclude anyone who can't keep confidences.
4. *Commitment.* A meeting missed is a meeting lost. Even one person's absence steals time and effort from everyone. At least two members will have to find time during the occasional workday for taking care of business at City Hall or special events.

That profile is ideal. But remember what Don Rumsfeld said: "You go to war with the army you have, not the army you want."[3]

What will make any team superior is *enthusiasm and generosity*. You'll want members eager for success, folks who look forward to meetings, who will forget the lateness of the hour, and who will cheer on each other with a forgiving spirit. That'll make the whole group greater than its parts.

THE CORE MEMBERS

Your *key decision makers* should be three to five members who own property and reside or work in the district. Anyone who doesn't own property has to be widely admired. You'll need:

- A torchbearer and lightning rod, a performer accustomed to public speaking and able to think in front of a not always friendly audience.
- A campaign manager for keeping the committee's work focused and on track.
- A member typical of the community's mainstream property owners.
- Members typical of other large constituent interests.

Because some property owners will likely see preservation as too "out there," make sure at least one member has a conservative occupational background. You want those people to think, "Hey, they're for it and they're okay, so it must be okay for me too."

Avoid flakes. Some self-styled preservationists provide the best possible targets for opponents. Simply shun fanatics, eye-rollers, and folks with obvious ties to other divisive issues. We don't need that kind of baggage.

All other members can be outside advisers. I recommend three types.

1. **A Preservation Specialist.** Ask your SHPO or a state-wide or local preservation organization for a list of qualified consultants, if you can afford one. If not, look for a young professional on the rise in a graduate program in preservation in your area. Your City's preservation planner will help with technical and procedural details, but public servants aren't actually "yours" and your opponents will say their tax money is being used against them. If things get hot, the Planning Department may back off and leave you hanging. Be aware, too, that whatever you say to staff is of legitimate interest to your opponents and may be in the public domain.
2. **A Political Insider.** Move heaven and earth to get someone who knows who's who at City Hall, who's interested in what, who's aligned with whom, and where the push-buttons and power levers are. A former official will do admirably, or what I call a political "gym rat." The first time I met one—a jack-of-all-trades in the land-development business—he was at a Council hearing, standing in the back, taking notes, whispering asides, chuckling, shaking his head. He would react to a quip, a ploy, a rejoinder, a close vote like a sports fan responds to a great play, a close call, a painful defeat. He could sense a shift in momentum, and he knew voting records like lifetime batting averages. He'd seen it all "a thousand times," he said, and everybody called him "Jim." Now that's the kind of guy you want to bring in for a briefing on how to win.

3. An Attorney. Districting adds to local zoning law, but you shouldn't need a lawyer unless the other side starts blowing legal smoke. There are several areas where knowledge of preservation law is indispensable:

• Credibly answering property owners' legal questions in community meetings.
• Explaining the constitutionality of historic districting.
• Correcting inaccuracies in references to the Fifth Amendment's "takings" clause.
• Riding herd on your City Attorney's legal counsel in hearings.

Be cautious about hiring a polished attorney to handle the burden of public speaking for you on other issues. You don't want to appear too uptown while presenting the case for districting back home. Get a lawyer who knows that a public hearing is not a courtroom.

Network to find one in the preservation community. In Oak Ridge we got invaluable assistance from attorney Myrick Howard, president of Preservation North Carolina.

YOUR LARGER ORGANIZATION

What do steering committees do? They plot the strategy and guide the campaign's course. They help a larger number of less involved but still important folks work together toward a common end.

Not every able seaman mans the bridge. There's more to running a successful campaign than making the key decisions. It's wonderful to be blessed with loads of volunteers who can work on publicity, serve as block captains, mobilize support for meetings, research public records, enter data, write supportive letters, lick envelopes, work their own contacts with policy makers and the media, help with documenting district resources, put together information packets, and do the many other things that need doing.

Effective leaders don't tell others what to do. They create conditions in which others are encouraged to do their best. Have your key leaders keep in touch with volunteers on a weekly basis. Once you're ready to take the campaign public, start holding meetings with them to reinforce their sense of value, to assure they're working together, and to improve ongoing planning.

There's a big difference between taking my advice on having a small steering committee, on the one hand, and turning away eager volunteers, on the other. Saying "no" to supporters who want to be part of the inner circle is simply impolitic. It's better to work out a kind of affiliate status. Give them significant responsibilities and bring them in for regular talks. Who knows? You might find talents you hadn't suspected before.

WEBSITE

As "information central," a website enables us to spread our basic message with maximum content control while reducing the time, effort, and costs. And Facebook, Twitter—

STOP! Social media is to be used sparingly in campaigning. Unless carefully considered, it can kill you. We'll explore social media in chapter 16.

Other website advantages include:

- Compressing our core message while providing click-throughs to more detailed pages and off-site resources.
- Keeping connected with supporters to share information only.
- Recruiting and coordinating volunteers.
- Advertising events.
- Facilitating carefully defined email messaging campaigns to influence officials.
- Improving coalition building with other groups and organizations.
- Providing easy media access to our campaign.

If you plan on using your site for fund-raising, be sure to incorporate your organization under 501(c)(3) IRS status.

A basic site may be managed by a high school student, though a professional operation is preferable. Your site should have the right look and feel for your community and be competitive with whatever your opponents put together.

Once you buy your domain name, put it on all your campaign literature. But remember that not everybody has Internet access. For many older or economically strapped folks, the Internet culture is still *terra incognita* and a political liability if you focus on it overmuch.

Keep the site simple and user friendly. But never think that a presence on the web can replace people working in the community. Even then, no combination of mere mortals is ever ideal. Go with what you've got and work your contacts. There's a political village of more or less ready supporters at the local, state, and national levels. So let's turn now to how we might approach them.

NOTES

1. Danica Roem, "WECA Activism Pays Off in Rockville," www.thesentinel.com, July 8, 2016.
2. See chapter 15.
3. "Troops Put Rumsfeld in the Hot Seat," www.can.com/2004/US/12/08/rumsfeld .kuwait/index

Chapter Nine

Working with a Local Historical Society: A Conversation with Historic Annapolis's Greg Stiverson

Our friends show us what we can do, our enemies teach us what we must do.

—Goethe

What other friends can we count on in this fight? Who are the Shapers—influential people or groups—who can help us win? What do you have to do to get them onboard?

Many folks have interests related to ours. Some want what we want. Others oppose what we oppose. But be cautious. It's often true that "the enemy of my enemy is my friend." Yet when you're both watching your adversary you're not always seeing eye-to-eye.

Once you identify potential partners with compatible records, how should you proceed? Do you just assume common cause and go in brimming with enthusiasm? Or will you find that you should have thought this through before you sat down at the table with them?

A SHAPER'S PERSPECTIVE

So let's go to an interview I did for the earlier edition of this work. What Greg Stiverson sketched out then is still deeply instructive. At the time, Greg was president and CEO of the Historic Annapolis Foundation (HA), one of the premier local preservation organizations in the country.

Me: Let me set this up for you. Assume I've caught on fire about getting a new historic designated. Next thing I'm in your office—or the office of someone like

49

you in another town. I just know you'll personally want to do everything you can to help us. Would I be right?

Greg: Well, a great deal depends on where my organization—the one you're going to—is in its own evolution. When you have a well-established, mature organization like Historic Annapolis, our response today would be different from what it would have been several decades ago when we were starting out.

Me: What sort of difference are we talking about?

Greg: Back then Mrs. Wright wouldn't share with anyone. She had one task and she stayed on it with great focus. She didn't want to have anything to do with any other organization in town. She wanted everyone to focus their energies entirely on Historic Annapolis and not on any other organization. And it worked.

Me: And now?

Greg: Today we want to share and expand the preservation world around us. We can and should assist groups like yours. But that takes time and resources away from other things.

Me: If that's the way you define your mission, what's the problem?

Greg: I don't know anyone sitting at a nonprofit organization thinking, "What can I do with my time? I don't have enough to do." So anytime you have an opportunity to work with others, you have to measure it very carefully against the fact that you'll be withdrawing resources from something else. It may be a very good idea to help get a historic district started elsewhere, because the two of us working together are going to strengthen preservation. But there is a cost to your own agenda.

Me: One of our concerns is that we won't see eye-to-eye and that'll weaken our community standing.

Greg: That's a real problem. When you're trying to build momentum you can't make room for all opinions and let people opt in and opt out. Mrs. Wright kept Historic Annapolis in crisis mode. If we don't do this now and this way, she'd say, then the community will have failed. She ended up with an effective organization that people loved or hated. No one was in the middle. You either approved of that kind of in-the-trenches, bare-knuckle, the-fight-must-be-won approach—or you said, "Oh, those Hysterical Annapolis people, they're just crazy." If you have to start with a take-no-prisoners attitude, you'll want everybody going in the same direction.

Me: Well, we're going all out to win. We assume there will be irreconcilable differences with some of our neighbors and other groups in the community.

Greg: And it's going to be hard for us to throw our hat into the arena that you must play in. Our priorities are different at this point. We're trying to work with all elements in the community rather than saying it's us against them.

Me: So what can you do for us?

Greg: We can counsel. We can pat you on the back and say "Atta' boy!" We have staff who can help you with preservation issues. One of the principal benefits of calling upon a mature organization is being able to point to it and say, "See, this is what we're trying to do, these people have done it, they think we're on the right track, they were at the same stage ten, fifteen, twenty years ago—and look at the good they've done. That's what we want to do." That helps you remove the issue from local personalities or a particular bone of contention. It's a role we certainly could play in community meetings or by testifying at critical hearings.

Me: How about personally? What can Greg do for us? I'll tell you straight out: We'd like you to join our steering committee and meet Tuesday evenings with us. What about it?

Greg: That's a serious issue, too. One would hope that a mature organization would be as generous as possible with its mentoring. It all comes down to a matter of resources and how much time we have.

Me: Sounds like you're saying, "No."

Greg: There are two problems here. The first is that everybody thinks they have to talk with the president and not with a staff person. Why? Because it just makes them feel better, even though staff may have just the hands-on experience they're looking for. It adds validity—if you have to report back to others you want to say, "I talked with the president." That's a fact of life for all organizations. People always want to talk with the person at the top.

Me: Sure. That's why I'm talking with you now.

Greg: But when it happens all the time, it puts a strain on the organization, especially if the higher up you go the more demands the organization itself is placing on its executive. It's a lot easier for me to delegate a staff member to go to another meeting, to spend two or three hours with you. But I couldn't do that myself all the time.

Me: We are trying to be respectful of your regular working schedule. That's why we're just talking about Tuesday evenings when you're off.

Greg: And that's the second issue: What's my commitment level? You've got a new group of all volunteers in your movement who are going to be passionate about your campaign. They're all charged up and won't think a thing about spending several hours at someone's home once a week. Sorry, that's not me.

Me: I appreciate your candor.

Greg: It's the difference between a new group and a well-established organization. Organizations have life cycles. At first volunteers do everything. The board is all volunteers. That's where you are. Then, if you succeed and stick with it, the organization begins to acquire staff. The board becomes more a board of directors. A mature organization has all the work done by a professional paid staff. The director becomes president and CEO with a board of trustees. And that's where we are.

Me: So it's not that we disagree on what's important; it's just that we see our work differently. Is that it?

Greg: Yes. It's one thing if you have passionate volunteers talking with passionate volunteers. But now you might be talking to someone who already works forty or fifty-plus hours a week as a paid employee. When you're all charged up it's easy to say, "Of course, that person will be glad to come out and help us because we're trying to do the same thing they did." In theory, that may be reasonable and true. But in reality, senior executives tend to have many commitments and might just not have the time or energy to give you. I also might have more academic or professional interests than a local activist who comes knocking on my door.

Me: Time, not interest, seems to be the constant issue here.

Greg: What you always hear people say who are in demand is that the most valuable thing for them is not money—it's time. And it really is true. As you get more senior what you really value more than anything is time to recharge your batteries by study and reflection. Sometimes you'd like to say, "I really can't come out to your meeting once a week on Tuesday evening because I'm just pooped." [Laughter.] But that's the way it is. You just can't say it.

Me: I've got an appointment to see you. What do you want to hear from me when I walk in the door?

Greg: Two things. One, I want to know what you really want. I don't want to hear you ask me, "What do I do?" I want you to come in and say, "Here's what we plan on doing and here's how we think you can fit into it." Two, I want you to tell me why you think I will fit in. Not, "You're head of Historic Annapolis and since we're doing something similar we know you'll want to be a part of it." I want to hear, "Here's what we'd like you to do: one, two, three. And here's why. Will you do that?" Be specific. You can always be turned down. But at least you'll know why.

Me: Do you already know what you'd like me to ask you to do?

Greg: Yes. Ask me to explain our success story to your group. Ask for staff help to share their experiences in very specific areas. And when you get to the point where you need to go to the Mayor or the City Council and you want someone to go along who has been through the process successfully, I'll be glad to go along with you. I know these folks. I can help you make the contact. Those are the kinds of things we can do, and I think you'll be happy with them.

Me: What are sorts of specific things you don't want us to ask you to do?

Greg: I don't want to draw up documents, or be the one to arrange meetings. Don't ask us to conduct the survey of historic properties for the district. Things like that—things that others can do just as well.

Me: How about making a financial contribution toward the survey, if we're trying to do it ourselves?

Greg: That's interesting. That's something a more mature organization like ours might do. It would further preservation without drawing down our people resources.

Me: How about helping us find other sources of money?

Greg: That's a little trickier. The people we'd send you to are the same ones we go to. If they write a check for $100, I want it to come to us. Then we might be able to help you, maybe not.

Me: But you could help us find a consultant, put us in touch with a preservation law specialist, and identify other people at the state and local level we could use?

Greg: You bet. We should have the phone numbers on our Rolodex of all the people you're going to need. We should be willing to share that with you and tell you to tell them I said to give them a ring. Making those kinds of connections for you is easy to do, and it's the collegial thing to do. It also helps the people you call to know you're not coming in from left field.

Me: May we ask for help from your board members, or is that overstepping the line?

Greg: The board is one of our really valuable resources. My experience is that the bigger an organization gets, with maturity, the more prominent the board members become and the more willing they are to do that sort of thing. They don't have a lot of but they can pick up the phone. They like to be considered decision shapers. If I were to call up and say, "We're working with a group, and we're going to see the Mayor, and it'd really help if you'd call and support them," they'd be delighted. They're happy to call their peers for you, because they're getting those kinds of calls all the time themselves. They like being able to say, "Now it's your turn."

Me: So in the final analysis, there are good reasons for coming to you—even if you're not going to be at the center of our effort.

Greg: Sure. You get our staff's help on my instructions. You get my help where I can give it. And you get the backing of our board. And I think that your readers should expect to get that kind of help from any organization like ours in their own locales.

I thanked him and said goodbye. Then it struck me that there had been no Historic Annapolis Foundation around to help out when HA started! The lesson? Experienced friends can help point the way, but we shape our victories ourselves.

Chapter Ten

A Practical Vision

The best way to predict the future is to invent it.

—Alan Kay

Legendary CEO Jack Welch has said that good leaders are known by their ability to define an inspiring vision, to identify themselves with that vision, and to single-mindedly propel the vision forward to completion. The last part is the hard part. Without it, a vision is just pie in the sky.

ON PRESERVATION VALUES

Visit your local bookstore and look over the racks of leadership books. Many are full of advice on finding meaning, clarifying values, and putting them at the heart of your mission statement. These are *not* the kinds of books preservationists need. We've got that stuff down pat.

National, state, and, where available, local preservationists are eager to help you put together a values-packed vision for your community. All you have to do is ask, and maybe send off for a few pamphlets. Work hard at getting the districting details right and professional preservationists will buoy your confidence and fire your enthusiasm at every turn. I've been on the receiving end of such support, and it can be exhilarating . . . until you run up against someone like my friend "Noel," who has owned a Victorian inn.

So here I am telling her about writing this book and she says, "Hel-*lo*! I care about old buildings, too, but why would anyone want to live in a historic district if they didn't have to?" Bummer. But instead of telling her to go pound salt, I realize, as Yogi Berra might say, you can hear a lot just by listening.

UP TO A POINT

First, her outburst puts us on notice. When we *think* preservation values and *say* historic district, she *hears* historic district and *thinks* government regulations. We don't have a *preservation* problem with her as much as we have a *districting* problem.

We need to stay alive to that difference. Just about everybody supports preservation values, but only *up to a point*. For you and me, districting is acceptable because it comes in under that point. For many others, like Noel, it just doesn't. They may see districting as carrying too high a price in terms of other perceived goods, even if those goods are just conveniences.

If you listen closely, you'll hear the same refrain time and again: "Many people support the historic district, but don't want more rules," says Tracy Bailey of St. Cloud, Florida. Sonia Schmerl, a former chair of Ann Arbor's HPC, was right in telling me that residents often are "more afraid of local government than they are of losing historic properties."

That's especially true if you've started with a single issue. Concern about "pop-ups" and "pop-backs" in blowing out row houses around Washington, D.C., has not overcome property-rights resistance in Capitol Hill neighborhoods.[1] Single-issue NIMBYism—"Not in my backyard!"—might kick-start your campaign, but you'll need more than that to win over unimpressed dissenters.

"PRESERVATION-PLUS"

Not all dissenters are dead set on breaking us. More effective advocacy may help some of them realize that protecting a larger historic legacy is important enough to bear districting. And the rest? How can we hook them?

Let me put it this way. When you go fishing, do you fish where you like to fish or where the fish are? Do you use the bait you like to use, or the bait the fish like? Campaign that way.

Get out and walk your dog. Talk with your neighbors. Appreciate the texture of their lives. Find out what they value, want, or worry about that districting can help them with. Start there.

Is it security of property values? Commercial vitality? Quality of life? Security for existing neighborhoods and local businesses? Tourism? Infrastructure development? Roads, parking, and traffic control? Utilities? Environmental protection? Beautification? Schools? Adaptive reuse of closed churches or public buildings? What else?

Be attentive, be imaginative—and be aware that nobody just wants old buildings standing around. Preservation has to *lead* to somewhere better, especially if the future is in doubt.

Think of it as "preservation-plus." A historic district can serve as a loom on which a whole tapestry of personal, corporate, and public interests may be interwoven, along with security of place. A district adds strength and identity to each individual thread—preservation included, but far from only preservation.

So whose interests can you pull together in your own community? The point is to be flexible, practical, broad, and welcoming.

Speak expansively of big-picture gains, yet give your vision a human scale. Make it relevant to each property owner. Pay them the respect they deserve by considering them as individuals. Make them part of your narrative and always be honest with them.

Don't denigrate the power of self-regarding interests. The folks you're trying to attract have to be confident that the district won't unreasonably impede their ability to use and enjoy their property as they wish while protecting their communities. The more you attend to the interests of others, the less you have to do to win them to yours. But win them you must.

Offer them very tangible benefits as the quid pro quo for backing you. Inspire their eagerness for things that they cannot have as assuredly without historic districting, without your support and your leadership.

Never use preservation *against* anyone if you can help it. Leave no doubt that you're absolutely pro-growth, pro-business, pro-prosperity, pro-real estate interests, pro-homeowners, pro-neighborhoods, pro-family values, pro-diverse community cultures—whatever the mix—and *pro-preservation through and through.*

Be the honey pot of possibilities. But don't mistake the tactical challenge at hand.

STRATEGY AND TACTICS

When we think politically, our primary objective isn't district designation. That's our strategic goal. Right now, our main tactical interest lies in gaining a competitive edge over our opponents.

So frame your vision to get it. You'll find your practical vision where your ambitions for preservation intersect political realities. It'll be made up of:

- What you want as framed by preservation principles.
- What your neighbors desire for themselves.
- What you should offer them concretely.
- What your neighbors will support.
- What you can accept.
- What you can get approved.

There's nothing formulaic here. Bear in mind that support and opposition will grow or shrink as your campaign evolves. Good folks, too, can back your district proposal for any number of reasons. Preservation may be your cause, but don't ask others to take a loyalty oath to it.

In your community-wide meetings, foster the belief that designation is the event through which all other aspirations must pass, so that it becomes a practical instrument of their fulfillment too. Speak expectantly and often of districting as a watershed for the community.

Lean into it. Politics exists, Aristotle said, for the sake of noble action. Think in terms of verbs, not nouns. Create a vision of achieving, not just achievement. Show them the contours of a journey that can capture their imagination and ignite enthusiasm. Call them to common purposes. Awaken them as civic beings sharing lives in a reimagined community that promises to give full play to their hopes and aspirations. Put your opponents on the wrong side of history.

Chief justice of the Indiana Supreme Court—and preservationist—Randall Shepard has championed preservation for its focus on "community building." Historic districts, he has argued, have become a form of community empowerment for influencing City Hall. They are the anvil on which new relationships, partnerships, and alliances are forged: perhaps, for example, with downtown commercial real estate interests, with various minority groups and their associations, and with leaders involved in public affairs.

Defenders of an existing community culture may not have recognized it as important until you propose the district. Make it their vessel, too, with safeguards for social justice as we'll see in chapters 11 and 61.

Being attentive to this isn't just clever tactics. Most communities have a form of comprehensive planning. Our historic district has to make sense within the context of broader policies. City governments can be just as anxious as private citizens about change and being hobbled by regulations.

The surest way to deflate your opponents' mischaracterization of districting as imposing a repressive bureaucracy is to inspire others—private citizens and public officials alike—to recognize that what they really want aligns with preservation. Be a visionary to stretch their perspective, but be practical to seal their support.

THE POTTER AT THE WHEEL

Are you up to it? Of course you are.

You are like the potter at the wheel. Your hands-on familiarity with the texture of community life gives you the feel of the practical craftsman for what you may reasonably expect to accomplish.

So, go ahead, roll up your sleeves. Plunge your hands into that pliable clay. Work around your opponents and bring forth from your community the best it has to give.

ON PRINCIPLE AND PRAGMATISM

My message—not to let pursuit of a preservation ideal get in the way of what's attainable—can be perplexing, especially for idealists, and we preservationists are a pretty idealistic lot. How about you?

If you're going to be any good at preservation politics, you're going to have to learn to think in two different ways simultaneously:

- *As an idealist*, you will always ask how your decision accords with preservation principles.
- But *as a political activist*, you must also question how a decision affects your chances of winning.

Unfortunately, the answer to one often doesn't square easily with the other.

Let me give you an example out of my own experience in starting our rural district in North Carolina. Suppose I told you that we announced during our campaign that vinyl-coated aluminum siding would not be prohibited by our design guidelines? Would your first response be a principled, "Oh, no!?" Or would it be a more politically perceptive "Why?"

We had bigger fish to fry. Unless we got the historic district, a super-highway would bisect the village and bring far greater pressures to bear on historic resources, property values, and local institutions like our antebellum military prep academy. Then, too, our County Commission was not at all well disposed toward our effort. Caught between its preference for 100 percent property owner support or exempting properties, we chose to force the issue with overwhelming community support. So, we had to keep our numbers in the upper ranges.

Aluminum siding was popular in Oak Ridge. Even more so was the young family man in our midst whose livelihood depended on it, as a critical few neighbors pointed out. We did what we figured we had to do.

Of course, at a very human level it's extremely hard for us to accept that the only way we can advance what we care about is by acting in ways that are likely to end up compromising it. So what will you do if a similar situation arises? Unfortunately for some of our well-meaning preservation friends, principle seizes them like rigor mortis, incapacitating intelligent movement, making them dead to political necessity.

ON COURAGE AND CONVICTION

Everywhere we turn today it seems some politician is taking pride in standing on principle against an alleged tide of compromise. But you and I know, unless we're gullible, that politics is not just about principle. If it were, all we'd have to do is declare the principle that settles the policy and then go home. No, politics is about the far more interesting problem of what you do with principle when real life demurs.

Having the courage of your convictions doesn't mean acting in divine disregard of present realities. Lead from conviction, by all means, but be pragmatic about the big picture.

What works is the right political choice. What's more, it's the right moral choice too, because winning is the only way you can move your markers forward to the benefit of your community. Conviction instills you with courage. And it is courage you need for doing those things, here and now, that you'd rather avoid.

To this day I don't really know if we had to exempt aluminum siding in Oak Ridge. I do know our ranks held. Minutes before the final vote, a key commissioner asked if I might agree to exclude acreage at the proposed highway's intersection in order to assure passage. With a high degree of popular support behind me, but unable to consult with the neighbors whose trust I held, I rolled the dice. I declined.

As it turned out, a one-vote majority approved our district after a two-year campaign. The highway plan bypassed us. The aluminum option was less than we might have hoped for, but more than we came close to getting. Today the little village has become a thriving incorporated town, saved and spurred on by district designation.

In my opinion, the so-called leader who listens only to the single steady voice of principle is just as inconsiderate of the public interest as one who heeds no principles at all. The former rarely wins. The latter is seldom right.

When you win, what you manage to achieve will always be judged in terms of preservation values. And believe me, someone who has stood on the sidelines will find you wanting. But take heart. No one stands on firmer ground for principle than the conscientious activist who finds a practical way to win.

NOTE

1. Martin Austermuhle, "On Capitol Hill, Tension between History and Growth Comes Down to a Single Street," www.wamu.org, September 13, 2016.

Chapter Eleven

Gentrification: An Exchange with the University of Georgia's James Reap

If that's movin' up then I'm movin' out.

—Billy Joel, "Movin' Out"

Billy Joel has a choice. Others sometimes don't. You might never encounter gentrification as a designation issue where you live. But if you do, you will want to respond with openness, sensitivity, and skill.

Here's the situation. As preservationists we find ourselves attacked for holding to the past. But that's not us, we say, in framing out our vision. Others then oppose us because they fear our future.

They worry that rising taxes, costs and real estate prices will force them out of homes they love and neighborhoods they care about while changing cultural landscapes. Stirring our souls in different places are issues of diversity and social justice.

With or without historic districts, gentrification happens. In the Boyles Heights section of Los Angeles, Jackson Defa and his partners opened Weird Wave Coffee Brewers on Cesar E Chavez Avenue and then found themselves ensnared in controversy.[1] The larger story was described as next-generation Mexican Americans returning to the impoverished Heights their families had abandoned in the 1980s, now spawning tensions with vulnerable working-class residents. "For those moving back," Jennifer Medina wrote in 2013, "the idea that they are pushing others out is the source of much consternation."

No one had proposed a historic district, but the concept of an arts district led to talks with community activists that ended up as debates about unwanted change. "We all can think of examples of neighborhoods we don't want to be," Evonne Gallardo told Medina. "But we don't know exactly what we do want."

That has been our challenge, too. Attorney Alfred Fraijo, who is described as a cheerleader for the Boyles Heights neighborhood, could be addressing us, though he's not: "It's really easy to say no to things, but . . . if we can figure out how to say yes to development and history at the same time, we can really be a model for this city that hasn't had one yet."[2]

I would like to think that the political skills we have been developing could be of service. But on the heels of this we have to ask, what is the effect of historic districting on gentrification?

We can approach the answer two ways: factually and politically. On the evidence, does districting itself initiate, delay, or accelerate gentrification? A recent study out of New York City is grounds for optimism about its impact on affordable housing.[3] But if you are outside of New York, the best you can expect is for those who feel at risk to say, "Okay, *there*. But what about *here*—what about *me*? Do you see my condition, do you understand and care?"

Gentrification means different things to different people.[4] Some of the most important and creative work being done in preservation focuses on underserved residents at risk from gentrification. As campaigners for new districts, we must acknowledge that the problem is compounded by the way the designation process operates. State and local enabling legislation values historic-resource surveys and property-owner opinion over, and usually to the exclusion of, impact studies and views on such matters as diversity, affordable rentals, and support services.

Do you see what this means? When we play according to the rules we are complicit in this institutionalized neglect. In the typical storyline I've chosen, where we've come late to the public policy process, we have little choice but to go along at City Hall. It's when we go to the community that we can make a difference.

Start where we began in chapter 10. As you go to home and business owners, look beyond them to the underserved. If the situation warrants, seek out official and private actors who represent their interests. The vision that you form for community empowerment should be shaped to resonate with them.

Ask what heritage they would like to shelter beyond the built environment. Don't downplay the risks of change or lead with talk of protections. The underserved would like to be better-served stakeholders, too, in vibrant communities moving forward. When the time arrives to broach district designation, tell them what you have to do to win. Your goal is to persuade them that they are better off supporting you than your opponents. That's the time to talk about ameliorating the downsides of gentrification.

I've asked James Reap to help us with an overview. He is Professor and Graduate Coordinator of the Master of Historic Preservation Program at the University of Georgia and a cofounder of the National Alliance of Preservation Commissions. As an attorney, James has trained many local HPCs through the NAPC's Commission Assistance and Mentoring Program (CAMP). That experience shaped his leadership in drawing up the NAPC's *Code of Ethics for Commissioners and Staff.* In 2016, he was appointed by President Obama to his Cultural Advisory Committee. James is also past-president of the International Council of Monuments and Sites (ICOMOS) and has served as a board member of Preservation Action and the Georgia Trust for Historic Preservation.

THE EXCHANGE WITH JAMES REAP

Me: As a practical matter, how have you encountered gentrification in CAMP?

James: Actually, it's seldom raised except when HPCs are considering the designation of new historic districts, particularly in low income or minority neighborhoods.

Me: What are the most salient concerns?

James: Everyone wants their property values to go up, but property owners on limited incomes worry about the higher taxes that can result from districting. Then there is the economic hardship issue related to higher historic district maintenance standards and commissions asking for more expensive solutions than owners prefer or can afford. The prospect is that districting will make it harder for low income residents to remain in the neighborhood. There's also opposition from those who claim preservation is the enemy of affordable housing, though we know this doesn't have to be the case at all.

Me: Still, there is the perception, a fear—

James: The *fear* of historic district designation in low income and minority communities is often encouraged by developers interested in promoting gentrification for their own economic interest. They want freedom to develop properties without having to deal with preservation standards and guidelines.

Me: But when we make that case, doesn't it sound like, you know, our regulations are better than you're your unfettered market? Shouldn't folks be cynical?

James: What property and free-market advocates can't give that we can is a greater measure of predictability and transparency in our ordinance and guidelines.

Me: That addresses risk. But what about the content of decisions? What speaks to the interests of diversity, cultural identity, and the underserved?

James: The NAPC's *Code of Ethics* calls on preservation commissions to respect the diversity of heritage resources that hold different meanings for various groups and communities. HPCs should proactively seek to make decisions in the best interest of the community. That means discussing gentrification in advance, to orient their work toward the rights of citizens—individually and collectively—to the beneficial use and enjoyment of their properties and other historic resources.

Me: And not just wait till issues arise and backfill to address them.

James: The NAPC suggests commissions face social justice head-on, even before gentrification is raised in the community. All Commission members should first become familiar with the real as well as the perceived issues—and the arguments, pro and con. But they also need to be aware that preservation *does not always* result in gentrification and that gentrification is not always bad, even for low income and minority communities.

Me: How so?

James: The case for districts can be made on matters like increased property values, better credit scores, lower crime, new businesses, more local jobs, public infrastructure improvements. Of course there *are* potential negatives: rising rents, higher taxes, cultural conflicts with new residents, and the loss of some established businesses that don't cater to the new residents.

Me: What can we do in particular to address those negatives?

James: Quite a lot, actually. Instead of just seeing them as *being* the problem, historic districts give us tools to help. Once commissioners inform themselves, they can advocate a variety of approaches. Practical programs should allow for the preservation-friendly redevelopment of historic low-income communities while helping vulnerable residents remain in place, if they choose to do so. On the other hand, some residents might happily accept the opportunity to capitalize on the increased values of their properties and locate to another area, something they may not have been able to do because of depressed values.

Me: So we ought to also think in terms of opportunities, though not unmixed with potential downsides.

James: When my students get fired up about the evils of gentrification, I point out to them that we live in a capitalist society largely shaped by market forces. Not discounting government policies and programs, those forces created the neighborhoods we see today and have largely shaped their evolution over time. I think it's unrealistic to believe we can stop and freeze neighborhoods in place. All communities need to evolve and change over time. We *can* ameliorate a number of the negative effects of those market forces—and celebrate the positive ones.

Me: That sounds like a tall order.

James: We need to work it into an overall response. We can urge that any municipal comprehensive plan—especially any preservation plan—address redevelopment and cultural resource protection in such a way that its negative impacts are addressed. Communities have used a variety of approaches to do this, including passing affordable housing or inclusive zoning ordinances. Senior home repair programs—to counter age discrimination by result—are an option. Then there are "hands-on" programs for low-income residents that utilize public and nonprofit resources to renovate homes in a preservation-sensitive way. Localities have also put in place property tax freezes and tax incentives.

Me: Like in Chicago, where I've heard from planner Peter Donalek that his condominium qualified for Illinois's real estate assessed valuation freeze. What else?

James: Other successful approaches include creating community development corporations that focus on serving struggling neighborhoods using such tools as home-ownership programs. There are also ordinances that give tenants "first right of refusal" for purchasing their units in condo conversions. Land trusts, lease purchase agreements, and vacant-lot urban infill regulations can be structured to provide opportunities for affordable housing without demolishing historic structures.

Me: All of this is good to know, but it has a great deal of policy wonkiness about it that won't play well in the trenches of campaigning. What should we carry forward?

James: At bottom, the *Code of Ethics* stipulates that commissioners should compromise or search for alternatives where necessary to provide substantial justice for all citizens.

Me: Individually, as they come before the HPC?

James: We made a point in the *Code* to stress that commissioners should be sensitive to the interrelatedness of *all of their decisions* and their long-term implications for both historic resources *and* the community. We need to be developing approaches that allow for redevelopment and community vitality while preserving heritage and enabling residents to be a part of revitalized neighborhoods without fear of involuntary displacement. Historic districts aren't necessarily a cause of social-justice problems. But they can play a central role in addressing them, better than can be done without them.

Me: That's a heartening observation. Thank you, James. It's time I hit the road.

What James just said about "displacement" we'll be looking at again as a policy issue in chapter 61 *after* we have won designation. If gentrification looms large in your campaign, you might read it now before taking up the next chapter on the politics of developing design guidelines for administering the district.

NOTES

1. Jonah Engel Bromwich, "Coffee Shop Tales," www.nytimes.com, August 14, 2017.

2. Jennifer Medina, "Los Angeles Neighborhood Tries to Change, but Avoid the Pitfalls," www.nytimes.com, August 17, 2013.

3. Historic Districts Council, White Paper, "The Intersection of Affordable Housing and Historic Districts," http://hdc.org/wp-content/uploads/2016/05/Intersection-of-Affordable-Housing-Historic-Districts.pdf, March 2016.

4. A good brief introduction to this complex issue and the many meanings associated with gentrification, see Kea Wilson, "What Does 'Gentrification' Really Mean?" www.moderncities.com/article/2017-aug-what-does-gentrification-really-mean.

Chapter Twelve

Thinking Politically
about Design Guidelines

Many people have accused me of being devious. They may be right.

—Archy McNally in Lawrence Sanders, *McNally's Puzzle*

Before we move on from the politics of vision, you need to anticipate that sooner or later you'll have to talk with your neighbors about how strictly the historic district will oversee what they do to their properties. When the time comes, you'll want to practice a little creative ambiguity.

Does that sound devious to you? Try to see it my way. A studied—yet honest—vagueness is an essential political skill.

The problem couldn't be plainer. We have to sell our neighbors on our vision of what the historic district can do for them. That means that our proposal has to be strict enough to preserve the legacy that is the key to everything else. But the more restrictive we make it, the more likely it is to encounter opposition.

Our political task, then, is to warm our neighbors to the historic district's benefits without overheating their anxieties about its costs. That isn't just a political necessity. It's also being responsible to them. The truth is that most property owners will rarely engage the district's review procedures after designation. And when they do, only a few will feel a regulatory pinch. If we don't discourage wild imagining now about how bad it could be, then we run the risk of losing the district—and that would be unforgivable.

So if you're to be a successful leader, you're going to have to help folks choose what is good in spite of themselves. If that's being devious, then let's be all for it.

YOUR CHOICE

The basic issue facing us here is whether—or how and to what extent—we'll make design guidelines part of our districting campaign. If you live in Wilmington, North Carolina, or a town like it, you have no choice. Kaye and Maggie told us in chapter 4 that our new district would be brought in under an already existing ordinance and a full set of guidelines, with maybe a tweak or two. The advantage there is that folks can see how the district has actually worked on behalf of property owners in practice.

Elsewhere, you may be obliged by statute or instruction to submit your guidelines along with the designation proposal. In most locales, however, guidelines just have to be adopted before the HPC starts issuing certificates of appropriateness.

There is, you understand, no such thing as a generic historic district. Property owners are bound to ask specific questions about specific work activities. They'll want to know:

- Which work activities will require full HPC design review and approval.
- Which activities may require simple on-the-spot staff approval.
- Which ones may be done without any oversight at all.

Still, other issues impinge. Will the HPC, for example, be given say-so over changes not visible from the street? Will noncontributing properties be treated differently? Questions like these may be anticipated in the district ordinance itself, but one way or another they'll influence public interest in knowing more about design guidelines.

So the question remains: How much are you going to say and how will you say it? In the end, your ability to win over supporters depends on whether they trust you.

TO DRAFT OR NOT TO DRAFT?

What do we have to do to earn their trust? Should we be drafting guidelines to show them? My answer is a firm "perhaps, perhaps not." You're simply going to have to decide what to do without any certainty that it's the right choice.

Informed opinion is divided. Some think it helps a campaign to have guidelines in hand. Others see it as an ill-advised complication.

What are folks—professional preservationists and city planners, your friends and allies—telling you? Keep in mind that making them at ease with your decision is a part of your political challenge, too.

So let's parse the problem. If we—let's say you and I, our steering committee, and a professional consultant or staffer—write up guidelines now that we'll propose to the HPC later, Breakers will say we're being dictatorial. But if we're seen as refusing to submit what we have in mind to public scrutiny, they'll portray us as trying to sell the community a pig in a poke before designation.

On the other hand, if we open up the process now to all interested parties—friends and foes and undecideds—then the guidelines will become yet another costly battleground in the districting fight. Even if we win the battle and the war, the guidelines will bear the marks of those who opposed them in the first place.

A MIDDLE COURSE GAMBIT

The best way to be trusted is to be candid with your neighbors. Tell them that the main question before us right now is simply whether we want the benefits of having a historic district. Once we decide that—once everyone's onboard who's coming aboard—then we'll get together and decide on agreeable guidelines. But ask them to hold off until then.

But why would they agree? Well, put yourself in their place. You see what districting can do for you and you're beginning to see that it's worth a price—that, as my friend Frank Whitaker has said, "The juice is worth the squeeze." That being the case, wouldn't you want to make sure that the hands that'll do the squeezing are friendly?

So when you talk with them, commit to making the drafting process open—but not just yet. They should see that if we were to open it up now, Breakers would do their best to make every aspect of the guidelines as onerous as possible to defeat us. It'd be plain dumb to let them in on what the rest of us will have to live with after designation.

Those who are considering their options have to know they can't just stand aside, either, waiting to see what happens. Sure, when the time comes everyone will have a chance to voice their opinions. But leave no doubt in their minds—though do it diplomatically—that what they do today with us to win the district will decide how their voices will be heard tomorrow.

There's nothing devious in this. We're offering Takers some bankable benefits for making the right choice.

A SECOND OPINION

Such was my thinking during our campaign in Oak Ridge, and so it still remained for the first edition of this work. This time around I've asked for expert advice. Why not before? If Oscar Wilde never said it, I'm sure he would agree: So much is unaccomplished when one invites opinions first.

So now I'm asking Peter Benton for his views.[1]

Me: Peter, you're a professional guidelines writer with Heritage Strategies in Pennsylvania. Is it advisable to develop design guidelines during a districting campaign?

Peter: Save them until later—first things first. The simpler the designation process, the better. Don't make it more complicated than it needs to be. It all depends upon the inclinations of the property owners. As for now, let's all agree that the neighborhood is special and should have a district.

Me: Even if owners would like to see them first, I imagine a draft set of guidelines could end up being—like a British critic once said about a Labour Party program—"the longest suicide note in history."

Peter: That's why it's better to achieve the historic district designation first. Save the complicated conversations and the details for later. Keep it simple. Emphasize community character. Almost everyone wants to strengthen the character of their neighborhood. You don't even need to use the words "historic preservation." Certainly *you* don't want to emphasize regulations.

Me: What about using the Secretary of the Interior's basic list of standards as a stopgap, if we need one?

Peter: If you decide to refer to the Secretary's Standards, emphasize their flexibility. Then anticipate the time when the degree of flexibility will be worked out based upon the nature of the historic resources and the inclinations of the property owners to accept design review.

Me: Which we shape in our campaign. Thank you, Peter, for your views.

NOTE

1. See chapter 42 for a dialogue with Peter Benton on developing design guidelines after designation.

Chapter Thirteen

It's Personal

All this criticism—it's like ducks off my back.

—Samuel Goldwyn

Where all politics are local, all preservation is personal. Every historic district is a slam-dunk great idea for fifteen minutes. That's about as long as it takes for people to start taking it to heart.

"I'm surprised by the intensity of the opposition," Mary McWilliams says in Evanston, Illinois.[1] Really? If *you* can get excited about property you don't own, you have to expect passion from those who do.

Historic districts hit home, literally. They touch us where we live and often how we earn our living.

But it's never just about the money. Anyone who says, "It's only business, nothing personal," is nuts. Folks may talk money, but it's like their own pictures were on every dollar bill. Touch one and you've laid hands on them and their families.

No, districting economics, like its politics, is intensely personal, too.

THE ATTACK

You're the messenger. Expect personal attacks.

Acquaintances may stop speaking to you. But it beats hearing them say, as others have in other places, that you're "arrogant," "sniveling," "frightening," "false," "obnoxious," "effete," and even—this from Seattle—fired by "yuppie-paradise, coffee-fiend pretensions."

71

They're mad, for sure. But what we want to know is whether they're politically smart as well. To get a handle on that, we have to look past what they say to see how they're shaking your tree.

It's all too easy to be rattled by the variety of opponents you can encounter, from the serious to the frivolous, rational to emotional, honest to dishonest, vocal and active to silent and passive, in-your-face hostile to behind-your-back-sneaky. You may, of course, run after every one of these detractors, trying to set the record straight. Play their game and you'll wear yourself out.

Dealing with the opposition is like courting the memory challenged girl in the movie *50 First Dates*. Each time there's a meeting you have to start all over again with the same people. It's like they remember nothing! They raise the same old questions, level the same charges, tell the same lies, commit the same slanders . . . and pile on more of the same. Nothing we say will change them. As it is, we're the ones who have to adjust our expectations.

THE TACTIC

So don't think that your adversaries will ask you questions to have them answered, or raise issues to have them resolved, or make factual errors to have them corrected. They're only interested in subverting your case for districting. If they can do it through misdirection and disinformation, so much the better.

They want to frustrate you, anger you, make you lash out, lead you into paths of condescension. They'll challenge your skills more than your intellect, and do all in their power to make you look the fool, the hack, the petty tyrant. The last thing they want is for others to take you seriously.

And you know what? No one has to take them seriously, either, for them to beat the socks off of you:

- They don't have to make a case, just prevent you from making yours.
- They don't have to have a vision of their own, just sow doubt about the one you're pushing.
- They don't have to do anything, just prevent anything else from being done.

So you go to meetings stoked to advocate preservation and they give you Greta Garbo: "The major thing we want is to be left alone," says a New England dairy farmer who has land for development.

Ironic, isn't it? We have to change the law to preserve the community. But if they can keep the law as it is, then they can pretty much change whatever they like.

DEFENSE OF THE FAMILIAR

Unfortunately for us, there are a lot of Takers out there in the middle ground of public opinion who'd be happy if the issue just disappeared. Whether he means to or not (and I can't decide which), ninety-three-year-old Dearborn resident Ed Klein gives comfort to our opponents when he simply says, "I'd like to see things stay the way they are."[2]

It's a common refrain. To our ears it harbors inconsistency. What "things" does he have in mind? Can he mean both the zoning law and the community which may be harmed by zoning law? Well, I think yes, he does.

Don't go looking for logic in politics. Many people don't parse these problems in terms of ends and means. Even if they do, they may ignore the conclusions. When it comes to where they live, they just don't want to lose the familiar.

You can talk till you're blue in the face that disorienting change is coming. And they look at you as if to say, "Yeah, tell me about it." You see yourself as a preservationist, the one who assures them of continuity. They see you as the present face of change, what with your new historic district and all. "And," they think to themselves, "*you're* asking *us* for *our* help to keep things as they *are*?!"

That other change you've been warning them about—the loss of this or that distinctive characteristic of the community—is, for a lot of good folks, just too abstract, too "iffy," too distant a prospect to get worked up over right now. *The Keene Sentinel* in New Hampshire editorializes that a proposed district would not be "as onerous as some critics portrayed it." Nonetheless, it says "neither is the threat it [is] supposed to ward off even remotely likely."[3]

Even if some current project is kicking up a ruckus, that kind of change is familiar. "Happens all the time," some folks will say. But the district? That's a different story. They know if it happens they can't duck it, and that scares a good many of them.

We wouldn't have to work nearly so hard at advocacy if the philosophy, law, institutions, and procedures of historic preservation weren't so unfamiliar and unsettling to the average property owner. People just don't want to wait to hear you out before they get all cranked up over it, either.

EXCOMMUNICATION

They start with the silly snicker about "hysterical" preservation. Then third-hand "horror" stories from other historic districts get passed around. Next, half-baked ideas are swapped on Twitter, over backyard fences, and in the checkout line. Opinions are quickly formed on the thinnest of pretexts. Disagreements follow.

Soon someone's accusing you of —do you see it coming?—"dividing the neighborhood" and "pitting neighbor against neighbor."[4] This is a pronouncement of excommunication in a community, so be prepared to deal with it.

Keep your composure. Politics happens. It's nobody's particular fault. Folks have interests and interests collide. That's all.

Blame is just a tactic, not a reality. Don't fall for their ploy.

It takes two to tango. The more you protest your innocence or make excuses, the more it'll smell like guilt on a sinner. Think about what the character Max said in the film *8MM*. "When you dance with the Devil, the Devil don't change. The Devil changes you."

A GRACIOUS DISPENSATION

Stick to the moral high ground. But be not self-righteous.

We all struggle *privately* with the conflict between what we desire for ourselves and what's good for the community. Districting brings that conflict out into the open. We get up in front of our neighbors and ask them to commit one way or the other, to stand with us for community or go their separate ways.

This call to a *public* decision is finally what makes districting so intensely personal. It publicly asks each of us as private citizens to make difficult choices that will affect the way we are viewed by others.

Carol W. DeGrasse of the Property Rights Foundation of America seems to admit as much. "This controversy," she wrote of the proposed, minimally restrictive Glimmerglass National Register District around Cooperstown, New York, "unfairly pits individuals who are concerned about regulation of their homes and businesses against people who would like to protect the historical beauty of the area."[5]

"*Unfairly?*" This is a personal complaint, not a policy difference. It's as if it were rude, uncalled for, or—in the words of one Santa Monican—"not proper" to hold each other accountable for how we choose between freedom and responsibility.

They say we're dividing the community. But it's this internal division between self and community that is at the root of their anger. You see what the real problem is, don't you? We're dealing with conflicted souls here. So the grace with which you handle the most obnoxious adversary will say more about your leadership than your most clearly reasoned argument or witty riposte.

NOTES

1. Jane Adler, "Preservation Haul," www.chicagotribune.com, December 28, 2003.

2. Craig Garrett, "Historic Designation Pits Neighbors in Dearborn," www.det-news.com, September 7, 2001.

3. "Sentinel Editorial: City Needs to Reflect on How It Goes about Protecting History," www.thesentinelsource.com/opinion, October 30, 2016.

4. See, for example, Catherine Van, "Plan for Historic Designation Splits Neighborhood," www.katu.com/news, October 23, 2016.

5. Carol W. DeGrasse, "Questions Historic District," www.prfamerica.org, May 7, 1999.

Chapter Fourteen

Sticks and Stones

Silence is the unbearable repartee.

—G. K. Chesterton

Some people are born ugly, but others are self-made. Here's a list of words they've used against us, taken from many actual designation fights (see figure 14.1). Tape them to your mirror and read them aloud. Get used to their sound because you're going to hear some of them in public. Learn to smile back. A friend of mine says that people never disappoint him; they always live down to his expectations. Just don't let them shake your soda.

hysterical
nosy
fanatical
arrogant
false
busybody
extremist
elitist
sinister
sniveling
obnoxious
self-appointed
priggish
obscurantist
paranoid
overreaching
frightening
outsider
mean
censorious
pseudo-intellectual
dishonest
history buff
overeducated
Volvo
volunteer petty
fetishist
whimsical
dictatorial
whining
careless
uncaring
idolatrous
arbitrary
controlling
zealous
romanticist
strange
dreary
sad
cavalier
comical

YOUR
PICTURE
HERE

laughable
sick
nasty
sorry
out-of-touch
statist
self-important
power hungry
grasping
insane
un-American
tyrannical
strident
pious
reactionary
liberal
fascist
left-wing
inquisitor
blood-sucking
cultist
brainwashed
ill-mannered
unhappy
desperate
frustrated
scared
pitiful

stupid
silly
ludicrous
fruitcake
slick
fuzzy minded
liar
yuppie
rat
rat bastard
troglodyte
jerk
new comer
old timer
senile
unpatriotic
enemy
idiotic
dreamer
house hugger
preachy
haughty
foolish
spoiler
storm trooper
Gestapo
spy
informer
underhanded
harebrained
crazy
gullible
masochistic
sadistic
highfalutin
grandee
over-educated
naive
snake-in-the-grass
spend thrift

Figure 14.1
Created by the author.

Part III

CAMPAIGNING IN THE COMMUNITY

Chapter Fifteen

The Campaign Kickoff

Gentlemen, it is better to have died as a small boy than to fumble this football.

—John Heisman

Every districting campaign should begin with a public kickoff. This is when you announce your intentions and state your case. Everybody should be there and attentive when you make contact and put the football in the air.

But bear in mind what also happens during a kickoff. Just like in football, we put the ball in our opponents' hands and try to keep them from running it back on us.

Influence is the yardage of politics. We're always in the process of gaining, holding, or losing it. It's not enough that we know our goal. Our opening play has to be designed to pin our opponents deep in their own territory and hold them there.

I want you to get ready now for that initial grassroots meeting in the district. It's your best chance to establish excellent field position.

Are you nervous? Of course you are. Joe Scarborough of MSNBC's *Morning Joe* speaks from long experience: "Most people who campaign don't love campaigning." And still they do campaign—and win.

THE COMMUNITY MEETING

Unofficial community meetings—and you should have two or more—are an opportunity and a challenge:

1. Early meetings can help head off charges that the district is a done deal with the city or that we're complicit in making an end run around the community.
2. They help us squelch rumors and correct misinformation.
3. They provide us opportunities to persuade others through advocacy.
4. They may settle at least some neighborhood differences over districting before we appear in front of official decision makers.
5. They offer us an opportunity to gauge and isolate our opposition as we head into the formal designation process.
6. They give us a chance to hone our message.
7. They provide a forum for building public confidence in our leadership.

They are also the best setting for talking to our neighbors about community itself before heading downtown to the polarizing public hearings that always seem to be filled with talk of "what I think," "what I want," and "what I need."

Of course, if we fumble our chances, these meetings can put us in an even more unfavorable light, harden differences, and give our opponents a chance to make significant gains at our expense.

FALSE STARTS

The hardest part of a districting campaign for political novices is knowing how to step out of the crowd and lead. And I mean *physically*, not virtually. Campaigning on your own two feet in front isn't easy even with experience. So I want you to imagine yourself getting up in front of your neighbors. Look them in the eye now and tell me what you see.

No, on second thought let me tell you. What you see are people who deserve your best effort. Don't worry about what they think of you personally for doing this. The main thing is they're here to listen to what you have to say.

Once you've crossed the floor to the front of the room, you've set yourself apart as a *leader*. Don't fall into the trap of acting like a *facilitator*:

- Don't start out by deferring to your neighbors.
- Don't act like the initiative has to come from them.
- Don't ask them how they feel about historic districts.
- Don't ask them what they want to do.
- Don't ask them how they want to proceed.

This may be a *community* meeting but it's not *their* meeting. They didn't call it. You did. It's *your* meeting. You're here for one reason only, and that is to sell them on your practical vision and get them to back the district.

Anything that keeps you from getting directly to your message is a false start from which it is tough to recover. Let me give you a few examples.

1. The Open-Ended Forum

I hear it again and again in tales of woe. It's like in the country song, how can anything that feels so right be so wrong?

You're excited by the idea of a historic district, so you get a few people together and call a community meeting to let everyone in on it. Once the basic facts are in evidence, you toss out the fatal open-ended question to the crowd—"Well, what do you think?"

This seems to be the right thing to do—to be seen bringing a good idea to your neighbors while showing yourself to be a good listener, not above others, and trusting of their judgment. Yet it is so wrong. It puts feelings—including how people feel about you—above policy. It's form at the expense of substance.

Don't ask people what they think until you've really given them something to think about. Otherwise you're just inviting trouble—a litany of criticism, dissent, silly comments, "what-ifs," and people talking about all sorts of other community issues.

2. The Public Study Committee

A variation on the theme is having a blue-ribbon committee conduct a public feasibility study that ends with a recommendation. It's supposed to be objective, of course. But anything that's intended to lead to legislation is always thoroughly political. Think about how a committee might be formed:

- Who will decide who's on the committee?
- Will they try to make it "fair and balanced" rather than focused and purposeful?
- Will preservationists be said to be too biased to be included?
- Will you be considered too political to be put on it?
- Who will draft the report, and who will present it?
- Who will define what "feasible" means?

And if the district's *political* feasibility is made part of the study, then what?

A study committee might well decide to conduct its own opinion survey *prior* to reporting out a developed district plan. If they (or we) go about polling neighbors on how they feel about districting before we take to the field, we'll have them deciding the game before seeing it played. And don't you think our opponents know that the best time to stop us is before we get started?

And if you can't avoid a separate study committee? In Massachusetts, for instance, the state Historical Commission specifies that, in the absence of an established HPC, a locally designated committee appointed by the City Council will conduct a property owner opinion survey, prepare educational materials, hold informational meetings, and prepare a preliminary study report.[1] If that's your lot, then say everything nice, and find an accommodation. But don't relinquish the political initiative in shaping public opinion in your community through your own campaign organization.

3. The Open Huddle

It's not a good idea, either, to advertise an early get-together for "anyone interested in a historic district." You can't have a meeting with some neighbors without causing problems with others in the long run.

What's to be gained anyway? You know the folks you're inviting will expect some kind of presentation from you, and anything you say will soon be common knowledge. If you're ready to talk to a few, then why not talk to everybody at once? There's a lot to be said for openness once we get to the kickoff. But if we let opponents into our huddle, we have to like their chances.

4. The Offside Call

Suppose we don't make any false starts. Say we get it right. We set the agenda, run the meeting, state our case . . . and soon someone's blowing a whistle on us. Our infraction? We jumped offside. We didn't ask them first. We get penalized for being arrogant, elitist, even conspiratorial.

So it's damned if we do, damned if we don't, isn't it? We go to the community either too soon or we go too late. Either way, we're going to lose ground.

The best we can do is to hold our first community meeting as quickly as possible. We can't wait to get it perfect. At some point we'll just have to stop the attrition by suspicion and take to the field.

And finally this, if a sense of urgency hasn't seeped in yet: There's always a danger that our opponents will jump the gun and call their own "stop the historic district" meeting first.

That's more likely to happen if you've been using social media. If you kick off your campaign online, it will be the biggest fumble you can make.

NOTE

1. For example, Christopher Gavin, "Hopedale Commission Looks to Form Historic District Panel," www.milforddailynews.com, August 21, 2016. See, too, Scott Merzbach, "Need for Local Historic Districts Debated in Amherst," www.gazettenet.com, April 6, 2015.

Chapter Sixteeen

Twitter Campaigning

"Birds do it . . ."

—Cole Porter

"Bees do it . . ." Just be careful, please, how you do it—don't fall in love.

The many varieties of social media have forever changed politics. And the glow of your iPhone is terribly seductive, like the bright side of the moon when you're sitting on a hill at night with that someone special—usually yourself.

But the change they've wrought, like the portion of the moon you see, is only half the story. New social media hasn't changed politics at all. Just the way we do it. But like the dark side of the moon, politics as it always is remains largely unseen by those who gaze atwitter at their screens.

The technology of connecting is changing far too fast for me to try to hit it like a speeding bullet. If you're smart enough to use it, you'll see its possibilities. I'll leave that to you. I will address some steady dangers pertinent to us.

TRANSPARENCY

Do you sing the praises of social media? It's time to change your tune. Think strategically. Follow Rule 1:

Put your hands in your pockets.

As you strategize, going dark is suiting up in armor for the fight. Transparency reveals weaknesses enemies will exploit.

Do not communicate even with your leadership committee online, except to arrange your meetings. Never reveal the topic. Leak nothing.

Behave as though you're going to work at the National Security Agency. Absolutely no one is allowed to take any kind of communications device inside. It will be confiscated if you try.

In your planning sessions and in between, follow Rule 2:

Keep them there.

PRE-KICKOFF BUZZ

Do you have a business background? Does social media work for you?

If yes, I understand. If you're rolling out a new product, you want heightened expectations. Whetted appetites. "Buzz." Social media is a great way to get it.

But those are wrong who say we should run government like a business when the business of government is legislating regulations. Folks won't salivate for more. No matter how you phrase it, if you float the idea of a district on the Internet then talk will be about controls on rights. You don't want your neighbors making up their minds in private, free of social pressure, before you publicly begin to *lead* them to acceptance of your plan.

DECISIVE LEADERSHIP

Nothing is more hostile to your leadership than social media. As Amy Jo Martin, author of *Renegades Write the Rules*, opines, "Social media is the ultimate equalizer."[1]

Don't believe Mark Zuckerberg: "When you give everyone a voice and give people power, the system usually ends up in a really good place."[2] That's an article of faith at best, a Facebook commercial, and to date counterfactual all across the nation.

Leadership—in contrast to running for office—finds a hostile environment on Facebook and other forms of social media.

COMMUNITY COMMUNICATIONS

Use a website *only* for FYI community-meeting and official-hearing announcements and anodyne policy information that gives away no strategy. Outside of that, follow Rule 3:

Repeat rules 1 and 2

A "Speed Bump" cartoon shows the three hear-see-speak-no-evil monkeys in a row with a fourth on a laptop saying, "No one said anything about blogging. . . ."[3] Okay, I will: Do no blogging. Do no tweeting, and so forth.

But *do read* everything everybody else puts online after you publicly launch your campaign. Mine it for intelligence. What issues, positions, and arguments are trending? Assume your opponents are doing the same to you.

Imagine what you'd love to learn about their counter-campaign. Then let them see none of yours from you. Not a single speck of insight into how you're thinking politically and what you plan to do. Someone will be trawling for it. As British actor David Tennant has observed: "Twitter! It's like being stalked by committee!" That right: their leadership committee.

In brief, don't do your opponents' research for them on your website. If you feel you have to state policy positions, then make them short, vague, and positive. If you craft them in response to attacks, that too will help your opponents prepare for public hearings.

DEBATING POLICY ONLINE

Resist the temptation to continue policy discussions online between public meetings. Even if your opponents do, don't let them bait you into saying things you'll later rue.

Columnist David Ignatius has summarized a growing body of research: "Arguing the facts often doesn't work; frequently, confrontation just makes people resist harder."[4] This is the "backfire effect" that David McRaney has advanced.[5] Breakers will not change their minds.

And stay away from extremists who try to draw attention to themselves with, in F. Scott Fitzgerald's useful phrase, the "foul dust floated in the wake" of their half-baked online rants and hothouse blogs. Responding to them makes you look small, desperate, and stupid.

Don't pick fights. Don't join fights. Do not try to end them. They're like flypaper: hard to disengage with all your body parts intact. Ignatius cites a study in the *American Political Science Review* that suggests "letting an argument die" for want of a response "usually works better."[6]

Never talk about Takers, Breakers, or Shapers online. Nothing substantive. Nothing personal. No rumors. Being talked about online has made people hypersensitive. Unless you are saying they are the best thing since sliced bagels, *anybody* is likely to feel violated, even your supporters.

An ill-advised statement can alienate everyone. I'd want to strangle any bird who tweeted: "Great plan! Let's see if the community is smart enough to back it." I've heard it expressed in private, but online? Zounds!

Those inclined against you will take a grain of what you say, bypass the molehill, and turn it into a mountain of trouble for you. They will twist even nice things you say and use it to their advantage. You say you welcome their views, or they make some interesting points, or they have a right to their opinions. They'll say you're a liar, you don't have all the answers, you admit you are dividing the community.

ONLINE GEOGRAPHY

Psychologist Daniel Goleman says, "Smart phones and social media expand our universe."[7] And that's another fine reason to stay offline.

Winning a districting campaign requires targeting a *select group* in a *geographically limited community*: property owners and some other key beneficiaries in your proposed district only.

You want to be the one who identifies them, not the Internet. You don't want others to self-identify, dilute your audience by showing up, or scatter your best efforts by tackling you online.

FAUX CAMPAIGNING

Don't be compulsively impulsive about putting yourself out there to be seen and heard online. Chris Pirillo, CEO of LockerGnome, has said, "Twitter is a great place to tell the world what you're thinking before you've had a chance to think about it."[8] Don't go texting down the sidewalk of Campaign Street and walk out into political traffic with your head down.

Most social media communicating is a colossal waste of time. "When you've got 5 minutes to fill," former Google engineer Matt Cutts says, "Twitter is a great way to fill 35 minutes."[9] That's enough time to knock on doors.

Don't kid yourself that online communicating has replaced the political advantages of face-to-face interactions in a small community like yours. If you don't want to have them, then you don't want to win. Don't hide behind social media as an excuse.

GROUPTHINK

Reflexive social media campaigning is suicide by groupthink. "Everybody's on social media" is a cultural observation, not campaign advice. Social media is not, as you might think, the way to build community. "Our technological interactions," E. J. Dionne writes, "create a connectedness among like minds that is also leading to ever sharper forms of separation from those who think differently."[10]

They also push discourse to its sharpest edges. Twitter feeds are especially dangerous. They have no room for the nurturing of judgment. They only telegraph conclusions across divides—the doubts of Takers—that must be bridged by understanding. Takers need to grasp why they *should side* with you instead of *picking sides* based on Twitter potshots.

LOSING BY ONLINE ABSENCE

All this said, today's online culture may punish your wise reticence to conform. Keep your antennae tuned to discover if and when you have to join the fray.

That can happen when your supporters don't keep *their* hands in their pockets and polarize opinion. Then go online to criticize no one but to change the conversation.

Chapter 21 will show you how to reframe issues to your advantage in community meetings. The technique is useful here, within limits. You don't want to substitute the distant firepower of Internet battles for the close-in, personally transforming engagements available in community forums.

For example, when angry and contending online parties split over regulations versus preservation, show up like the adult in the room. You might say you, welcome their involvement in the central issue on everybody's mind: how a historic district can employ the community's historic resources for everyone involved. Then say you are looking forward to their contributions at your next community meeting.

LOSING THROUGH WINNING ONLINE

"How dare you settle for less when the world has made it so easy for you to be remarkable?" writes best-selling author Seth Godin about the power of social media.[11]

Sorry, Seth, but this isn't about *me*. Hey, I'm as narcissistic as anybody out there. But at least I know enough to understand that collecting "likes" on Facebook and followers on Twitter is not campaigning.

Popularity that makes you feel "remarkable" is not the same as *influence*, the currency of politics. It won't win your district's designation. Signatures on hard petitions and votes at City Council do.

Only folks inclined your way will join your online choruses. You don't want to end up on the losing side like in Tom Lehrer's "The Folk Song Army" where the victors "won all the battles" while "we had all the good songs."

A CAUTIONARY TALE

I once attended a National Trust conference session on using social media in campaigning to save historic resources. The presenters were young and enthusiastic—and way more than just remarkable. Their excellent PowerPoint projections showed the outstanding building they had campaigned to save. They regaled the audience with their many online successes in advocating their cause and garnering like-minded support.

I kept waiting to hear how social media worked when they switched to politics from building their base through online advocacy. As time ticked toward the session's close, they put up a last picture of the ground where once the building stood. Standing in front of it they summarized the case for smartly using online technology for historic preservation.

"So what did you do wrong?" I asked when they took questions.

Blank stares. "Nothing. Why?"

"You lost."

NOTES

1. Blog, www.amyjomartin.com/?s=Social+media+is+the+ultimate+equalizer, January 19, 2017.

2. "The Best of Mark Zuckerberg," www.siliconangle.com.

3. Dave Coverly, "Speed Bump," *The Washington Post*, November 30, 2016.

4. David Ignatius, *The Washington Post*, July 19, 2017, A17.

5. David McRaney, "The Backfire Effect," www.youarenotsosmart.com, June 10, 2011.

6. See the full text at Gary King et al., "How the Chinese Government Fabricates Social Media Posts for Strategic Distraction, Not Engaged Argument," www.gking.harvard.edu/files/gking/files/50c.

7. Daniel Goleman, "Focus on How You Connect with Others," www.huffing-tonpost.com, January 23, 2014.

8. "Chris Pirillo's Top 140 Twitter Tips," www.lessonsfromsocialmedia.com/wp-content/uploads/2012/12.

9. "30+ Valuable Quotes and Advice from Matt Cutts," www.seoblog.com/2016/02/quotes-matt-cutts.

10. E. J. Dionne Jr., "Is America Getting Lonelier?" *The Washington Post*, August 7, 2017, p. A15.

11. "Lessons Learned from Seth Godin," www.sourcesofinsight.com.

Chapter Seventeen

Community Meeting Arrangements

Before everything else, getting ready is the secret of success.

—Henry Ford

A community meeting is no casual pickup game among friends. Historic districting is big-league politics to those involved no matter how small the community. Expect to be hit at every turn.

Of course, you might not end up bruised and battered. You know your own situation and might expect an easy go of it. But don't underestimate the value of being prepared for the worst.

Some folks will take exception to what you *say*. But has it occurred to you that meeting arrangements have political implications, too? Critics will jump on even minor errors to discredit the process.

THE MEETING PLACE

If your meeting venue is owned or managed by supporters, then opponents may say they felt unwelcome or intimidated. It's simply astounding how large the mere appearance of fairness looms in local politics.

Select a convenient neutral site if you can, such as a public school or community center. If you use a public facility, make sure you pay for it and get a receipt. If there is no charge, get it in writing. Watch the date and time, too. For instance, avoid a football Saturday afternoon if you're in a university community.

MAILINGS

Notify *all* property owners by snail mail even if you use email. Be a little paranoid. The first law of mailings is to assume that any announcement that can go astray will go astray if it's addressed to an eventual opponent. Double check your address labels against the list you developed earlier in chapter 7. Use certified mail if you've got the budget for it.

Don't wait till the last minute. Hell hath no fury like a retiree wintering in Arizona who gets forwarded mail after a meeting's come and gone. A notice that arrives late is the same as one not sent at all.

Remember: It's illegal to put unstamped circulars in mailboxes or through mail slots. Your opponents will have a field day with that fumble.

Why the concern? When the going gets ugly, the ugly complain about fairness and due process—even though due process doesn't apply to informal community meetings. An alleged failure to notify is just the kind of infraction that politicians find hard to ignore.

THE ANNOUNCEMENT

Say as little as possible in the meeting announcement so it will get read. Use the passive voice to keep focus on the meeting, not you.

Use a large font for folks with impaired vision. Put key information in boldface type. Sign it from your steering committee. Make sure the return address lies inside the proposed district. You've got a computer. Use it. Personalize every letter.

Sample Announcement

Interest has been expressed in designating our neighborhood a local historic district. You are cordially invited to a community meeting at (**location**) on (**date and time**).

If you cannot attend, please visit our website at **www.(name).org** or contact (**name, address, e-mail, and telephone**) to have materials and announcements of future meetings sent to you.

INVITING OTHER PARTICIPANTS

Assure that the **City Planning Department** is represented. Settle in advance what you expect of them. They're there to lend authority to what you say and to help with procedural questions. Some staff prefer to avoid confrontational meetings and others may take an unhelpful officious attitude toward the public. It's better to go it alone than go that route with them.

Your own **preservation specialist**—if you've managed to enlist one— should handle technical questions. Extend an invitation to your State Historic Preservation Office to help quell doubts about your objectivity while supporting you on matters of state law.

Be sure to invite private-sector **opinion Shapers** who support districting. Talk with them first, however. Make sure that they understand your agenda and how you'll conduct the meeting. Work out what they can contribute and how you'll use them.

Look at any **other constituencies**, a.k.a. stakeholders, besides property owners that you think will benefit from districting. If one of your goals is revitalizing retail business, then invite business owners. If it's keeping the old elementary school open, then invite the PTA. Invite any other groups whose absence would be a political faux pas.

How about the **local press**? It's never too early to start working the media. But as we'll see in chapter 29, reporters seek out controversy—because editors like it—and they will inflate your opponents' claims just for the sake of "balanced" reporting. It's better to invite a specific reporter you can prep ahead of time than to have to deal with one who just shows up cold.

Make a list of the most important people you want to see at the meeting. Have your steering committee call each one to remind them as the meeting approaches.

ROOM SETUP AND GREETING

Think carefully about seating. I'd advise you to ignore meeting consultants who want to diminish conflict by breaking into small groups around tables, each with its own moderator. We don't want to give our critics cause to say they were sidelined.

Do whatever helps you perform well. But I think that if you're going to lead, then you ought to get on your feet—never sit down— and lead from the front. Your opponents are sure to claim later that this made it *your* meeting, not a *community* meeting. But once you give up center stage you'll never get it back.

As folks arrive, greet them with a member of your committee, a sign-in sheet, the petition, and blank nametags to write their names on with markers *that work*. Give everyone a copy of your "Frequently Asked Questions" (FAQs) that we'll cover in chapter 19. Make sure printed material has your website on it, and post the site prominently at the front of the room.

It's best not to pass out cards for writing questions. A public session on a different matter—a proposed conference center in Frederick, Maryland, that had preservation issues—did it, to the organizer's regret. A reporter wrote that this style of taking questions—"more than the information presented itself"—was what "some people criticized" for leading to the conveners cherry-picking questions and avoiding confrontations. "If they were committed to dialogue," resident Mary Frances Mickevich said, "they would have let the people stand up and ask questions, the Frederick way."[1] Better make it your way, too.

Welcome everyone as warmly as possible—or at least cordially. If anybody jumps to an attack, just smile and ask them to keep an open mind. Don't let your colleagues stand around in cliques. They should be working the room, conveying friendliness, enthusiasm, and confidence.

And for heaven's sake, make sure the room is set up properly before anyone arrives. Nothing erodes public confidence like hearing you blame others for facility problems—a dead microphone, not enough chairs, a locked restroom. If you can't take care of getting the room right, how can you be entrusted with a district?

THE MAP TRAP

Hang a survey map of the proposed district at the front of the room, with the survey consultant standing by to answer questions. You'll soon understand that geography is political destiny.

How the map is derived can be political dynamite. It has to be defensible in preservation terms, with a density of contributing historic properties sufficient to justify districting. But no one benefits if the district is *technically* defensible yet *politically* unwinnable. Where the density of contributing properties thins out on the district's periphery, the question of including or excluding a street or block is a close call. If you give your City Council reasons to pare your map later on, they'll start cutting other things as well.

If the boundaries are still not firmed up by meeting time, make this abundantly clear by posting "DRAFT" across the map's top. No matter what you say, the opposition will probably complain later that the whole designation process was untrustworthy because "the map kept changing on us."

Make sure the map covers the maximum probable territory. You might get away with reducing the district later, but not expanding it. When the map is finally set, say so, and then leave it alone no matter what. That's the best you can do.

CIRCULATING YOUR PETITION

On your "top ten" list of things to get done at the meeting #1 is maximizing the number of folks you get to sign your petition. I'll be cold-blooded about this. Nothing you do to educate for preservation is worth much if it doesn't put signatures on your petition. Anybody can be for *preservation*. But only a signature registers support for *districting*. Politics has a built-in bias favoring numbers. And the only numbers that politicians will believe are those you have documented and verified.

Any name *not* on your petition will be presumed to be a property owner against you. Opponents always get the benefit of the doubt.

Work out a plan for canvassing the meeting. Make it easy for people to sign, but don't expect them to wait in line. Circulate clipboard copies before and after the meeting. Keep friendly hands on them. Tell your petition managers to steer clear of one-on-one arguments. If they get tied up in a knot of folks listening to attacks, then your opponents win.

Make sure your managers are eager and unapologetic about asking for support. Their attitude should be that signing is an opportunity not a favor.

Never, ever, let yourself get so caught up in the ebb and flow of the meeting that you lose sight of your goal. Nothing is more self-defeating than ending the meeting and then shouting out, "Oh yes—don't forget to sign the petition on your way out!" *No point that you'll make in the meeting will be as important tomorrow as the points you score on the petition today.*

Everybody exiting should have to pass by someone asking them to sign before they get out the door. Don't miss that chance. Be sure those who refuse are remembered.

COMMENT CARDS

I've suggested comment cards because you want to know what people are thinking. They also give folks a chance to blow off steam and then think better of it before expressing anger in public.

If you can print cards, include a place for name and address, plus a checkbox for requesting a personal follow-up at a specified phone number or email address. Be sure to collect comment cards at the end of the meeting and follow through on requests for information without delay.

RECORD THE PROCEEDINGS

Video, audio, or scribe. One way or another keep a record of what transpires. When you get to the Q&A, keep a record of what each questioner says. This is the raw data you'll need for refuting any later claim that opponents were shut out from participating in your meetings.

Keep the ball rolling by announcing the next community meeting before adjourning. Put that online, but keep your petition and comment cards close to your vest like proprietary intelligence.

THE DAY AFTER

Get together with your steering committee ASAP to discuss how things went and to agree on what to do next. Move quickly, preferably within a day or two, to contact folks who registered serious questions or who looked like they could be persuaded your way.

Whatever you do, don't leave the Monday morning quarterbacking to your opponents. Be seen out and about talking up the historic district.

NOTE

1. Nancy Lavin, "After Downtown Hotel Presentation a Chance for Questions," www.fredericknewspost.com, August 17, 2016.

Chapter Eighteen

Your Community Presentation

I only speak right on; I tell you that which you yourselves do know.

—William Shakespeare, *Julius Caesar*

"I am no orator," Mark Antony next told the crowd at Caesar's funeral. And you? Do you, too, say you "have neither wit, nor words . . . nor the power of speech, to stir men's blood?"

Don't sell yourself short. Like Antony you have conviction and a compelling subject. Like him, you know the time, the setting, the audience, and what motivates them to listen. The words will come.

But how little time there is to get your message across! Think. How long would *you* sit still for you? Let's be optimistic. You'll have some twenty minutes to introduce districting and to make your case. After that, it's all questions and answers.

We're going to make the Q&A session work for you. Handled right, it'll free you from numbing details in your opening presentation. Shakespeare gave Antony thirty-five lines to capture the crowd's attention, and then multiples of that in dialog to bend it to his purpose. So let's see what we can do for you.

THINKING AND WRITING

Twenty minutes to fill with words—a very few words, to be on the safe side. What will you say? Be brief, but beware: brief is hard. Charles Dickens once was asked why he wrote such long novels. "Madam," he replied, "I haven't the time to make them short." Let's take time now to get ours right.

98

Start with our practical vision for the community in chapter 10 and the suggestions there for what to do. Put it into words and write them down. Don't worry about brevity yet. Read what you've written out loud. How does it sound to your own ear? Does it say what you want it to say? Be honest with yourself. If it doesn't sound right, it probably isn't right.

Don't tell me that you're having problems with writing. There are no writing problems. There are only thinking problems. If you know what you think, you can write it down. Writing is the best self-test of clear thinking. The clearer your thinking, the clearer your writing will be and the better it'll sound to you. And the clearer your thinking, the fewer the words you'll need to express your thoughts.

SPEAKING AS THINKING FOR OTHERS

Thinking. Writing. Now speaking. You may think and write what sounds good to you. Political speech is for other ears.

Sometimes it just means telling folks what they want to hear. But if you want to *lead* them, then speak so that they recognize your expressed words as their own inarticulate thoughts made clear.

Leadership involves doing other people's thinking for them, winnowing out contradictory values and impulses, and getting them to act on the conclusions we promote. That's why our main targets are those Takers in the middle whose minds aren't made up yet.

What you'll say is framework for the longer dialog they'll be having with themselves once you get their attention. So give them the outline that takes them where you want them to go.

YOUR APPROACH

Surprise your listeners. They're expecting a history lesson and talk about regulations. Some are ready to pounce. Others just don't see what preservation has to do with them. "'Living in the Past' is a Jethro Tull album, not a strategy," as Richard Roeper says. So take a different tack.

Start with them and their interests. Talk about what *they* know first. This will get you beyond the blandishments—such as protecting our unique architectural history—and connect your purposes to their concerns—like property values. Then you can begin leading them into new ways of thinking about their investments in the community.

It's like the way preservation itself works to fit new construction into an older community. You can successfully introduce a new idea to your listeners as long as it's compatible with the existing architecture of their thought. This is how, as Samuel Johnson said of poets, "New things are made familiar, and familiar things made new." Make the familiar work for you.

Don't be the first one to raise objections to districting just because you believe you ought to address what *you* think will trouble your neighbors. There'll be time enough for that in the Q&A period.

Don't explain *yourself*, either. Explain the *district*. State your case as fact, not argument. That will underscore your confidence that they are up to this task. Make it a seamlessly positive presentation, and always talk up—never down—to your audience.

WATCH YOUR LANGUAGE

Respect for your listeners also means using plain, transparent, easy-to-grasp language. Don't muddy up your message with jargon. Preservationists can have difficulty with plain English. Don't speak of "historic fabric" when you mean old siding, windows, doors, and roofing materials. Normal folks will think you're talking about draperies.

Jargon is tempting shorthand. But I think the poet Horace gave us fair warning: "It is when I struggle to be brief that I become obscure."

1. Describing historic preservation. Plain old "historic preservation" is difficult enough. Christian Sottile at the Savannah College of Art and Design says that "*historic* is looking backwards, and *preservation* sounds like you're just kind of hanging on."[1]

Political difficulty attaches, too, to "building on the past," a phrase in common usage. But consider how our neighbors hear it. Its momentum ends on heritage, and so appeals to *us*. It leaves our neighbors wanting more, still uncertain where their interests fit.

In Anderson, South Carolina, Board of Architectural Review (BAR) member Dan Gregory turns preservation's face around: "We are bridging a gap between the past and preservation into the future."[2] There, like you, they're making *future* history.

That's the way you want to sound. Tom Liebel, an architect and the chair of Baltimore's HPC speaks of using "our great historic structures as a springboard into the future."[3]

A phrasing such as that will catch your neighbors' interests. You can use it to great effect to counter the image of historic districts than many bring in with them: as efforts to preserve communities in aspic.

2. Describing district regulations. Avoid all talk of "managed," "directed," "planned," or "regulated" change. Those politically fraught terms make us sound like we know better than our neighbors where it is they should be going.

We don't. Preservation works best where homes are enjoyable, businesses are profitable, and communities are livable. But you and I don't get to decide what enjoyable, profitable, and livable are. Homeowners, business owners, and other district beneficiaries do.

They will be the ones proposing change after district designation. What's more, we know that they'll be changing, too. Folks come and go. And everyone in time will find their interests changing also. We will have to adjust our expectations to do justice to them all *and* to preservation.

When you speak of preservation, of the future, and of the role of district institutions, stay on message. As often as you can, pledge:

- To *work for preservation*, and
- To *make preservation work* for all interests in the life of your community.

You won't be sounding like a preservationist who is focused on preserving the legacy of the past. You will be speaking as a campaigner who is out to win support for district designation.

A SAMPLE OUTLINE

Use this outline to jump-start your thinking on the details of your talk. Reshape it to your own liking and your own community's situation. Polish it till you can hit each point with very few sentences.

- Open with a **smile and welcoming comments**.
- **Introduce** those up front and others of importance.
- Explain that this is an **informal community meeting,** not a public hearing.
- Begin with your listeners' **invested interests in property**.
- Remind them what **they care about in the community** that supports those interests: For example, quality of life, security, family, and business values. If gentrification is an issue, address it here.
- Speak to **preservation values**. Say that you want the district to work for preservation while seeing to it that preservation works for every one of them.
- Establish the **preservation case** for districting, including the map's rationale.

- Make vivid the **situation** around them that has led you to bring this proposal forward—but make a villain of no one. If there is a crisis, this is the time to nail it down.
- Stress that you take no pleasure in putting difficult choices before the community, but that now is **the time for all of us to step up**. "Where is the man," Rousseau asked, "who owes nothing to the land in which he lives?"
- Create a sense of a community ready to embrace **change as opportunity**. Make it clear that a zoning overlay district doesn't stop change, but it can facilitate and shape growth.
- Stress good-naturedly that **2,500 historic districts** must be on to something.
- Make them **alive to the possibilities** awaiting them. As benefits are for all, responsibilities must be borne by all.
- Build **anticipation** through concrete examples taken from the experiences of similar communities.
- Drive home the idea that districting is **empowerment** (versus an oppressive layer of government), giving individuals and the community a greater say in City Hall over decisions that affect them.
- Stress that we, not the government, are doing this **ourselves**.
- Give a brief **synopsis of how the district will work**, pointing the audience to your FAQs handout (chapter 19).
- Recap districting as an **opportunity at an acceptable price** for doing great things together.
- Make it so that to miss this chance would be a **misfortune** for one and all. We will realistically have this one chance to create a district, but other forces will keep coming without letup or hindrance.
- Declare this moment a **celebration of our civic purpose**, of who we are as friends and neighbors coming together for the sake of one another.

Conclude with our mantra in chapter 6: That you know our neighbors, and know that happily there's enough abundant goodwill and good sense among us to make the district *possible* and enough of the opposite—here and there—to make it *necessary*. Pause. Let it sink in. Then say, "Questions?"

THE QUESTION AND ANSWER PERIOD

Now for the fun part.

The Q&A isn't something to be endured until you can head for the side door. It's where you're going to do your best work, out-point your opponents, and win over the undecided Takers. I want you to get clear on that before we turn to learning how to do it in chapters 20–24.

Knowing that the Q&A is coming enables us to discipline our opening presentation. We can focus on what we want to say, say it briefly, and stop. We know that if we get the broad brushstrokes right, there will be time enough in the Q&A to sketch in the details.

This makes us look good. We are masters of our material. We gain credibility by speaking directly to the audience and looking them in the eye. We are capable of delivering a lean and simple message—no complicating, hard to remember "ifs, ands, and buts"—so we won't have to read it.

Minimizing our presentation and maximizing the time we allow for Q&A will help assure Takers, who are willing to listen and be persuaded, that their opinions are heard and their questions are answered.

Breakers—our more resolute opponents—are different. We enter the Q&A inviting them to declare themselves. They will come hoping to use comment time to skewer our influence among the Takers. None of this surprises us. As we'll see in chapter 20 we know exactly what they're doing and where they're heading.

Being prepared for all challenges, we don't have to control the agenda and dominate the meeting. We can open the floor to our opponents and let them have their say. Because we do this confidently and welcomingly, we show ourselves to be tolerant, responsive, and settled. This will impress undecided fence-sitters and policy makers alike.

But the Q&A isn't just our questioners' time. We're going to use our responses to lay out all the other finer points of our case that we've held in reserve until then. Thus the Q&A becomes just an extension of our own presentation, part of our plan.

The more our critics accuse us from the floor, the higher the drama of the exchange will be and the more attentive our listeners. In this situation, the folks who are still undecided will naturally begin to pick sides and establish loyalties. We'll see to it that they come our way.

Rome wasn't built in a day. We can't expect to win all the support we need in this one meeting either. Others will be needed, and we'll be in this contest for the long haul. But then I'm sure you knew that already.

NOTES

1. Jenn Stanley, "Southern Rivals Struggle to Balance Historic Preservation and Modern Architecture," www.nextcity.org, June 1, 2015. Italics added.

2. Kirk Brown, "Preservation Poses Challenge for Anderson Residents," www.independentmail.com, September 24, 2016.

3. Natalie Sherman, "Historic Districts Proliferate as City Considers Changes," www.baltimoresun.com, March 14, 2015.

Chapter Nineteen

FAQs: Frequently Asked Questions

Good morning, Mr. Phelps. Your mission is . . .

—Mission Impossible

. . . to find a way to keep our community meetings from getting bogged down in details.

As we saw in our last chapter, many of our undecided neighbors—the Takers—will want straight answers to questions of fact. So what's the problem? If you know enough to answer them, you also know that almost every answer is loaded with technical details. But not everybody is interested in every question, and hardly anyone wants to hear everything that you might think they should know.

The solution? You and your committee should put together a handout of frequently asked questions—FAQs. Work up succinct answers to likely questions. Pass them out at your community meetings. You can then give short verbal responses while referring questioners to more complete answers in hand. This also works for those folks who've missed your answers at previous meetings.

THE QUESTIONS

Work with your preservation specialist, contact preservation organizations, and go online to develop your own answers to the following questions. Then decide which ones to put in your FAQs handout.

Keep the others in reserve for rapid response if you need them. Put all of them on your website, too, and update the list as needed. Just don't expect everyone to have handy access to it.

And, no, I haven't abandoned you here. Questions are always harder to identify than answers. If you haven't studied up enough to provide your own answers, then you're not ready for the Q&A. Divide the research among your committee members and share your answers. You'll appreciate the exercise when each of you has mastered what you'll all be responsible for in public.

One of the fine attributes of the preservation community is the general willingness of people to let you borrow text from their own materials. As always, be cautious about copyrights. But I think you'll find a lot of help out there when you go looking for it.

THE FAQS

So as Sgt. Joe Friday might have said on the old TV show *Dragnet*, here are "the FAQs, Ma'am, nothing but the FAQs."

1. What is a local historic district?
2. How is a district designated?
3. What are the benefits to me of designation?
4. What is historically significant about our community?
5. What is the legal basis for a local historic district?
6. Does district designation affect my property rights?
7. Why isn't zoning sufficient to protect historic properties?
8. What is a zoning overlay?
9. What is the difference between a contributing and a noncontributing property?
10. What are design guidelines? How are they applied?
11. What does "historic integrity" mean?
12. How does designation affect my property values and taxes?
13. What is the HPC?
14. Will designation prevent me from repairing, altering, renovating, or adding on to my property?
15. What projects need approval?
16. How does the Certificate of Appropriateness process work?
17. How are HPC decisions enforced?
18. What if the HPC denies my application? How do I appeal?
19. Are there extra costs and fees associated with district designation?
20. Does district designation require me to fix up my house?
21. Is there money available to help preserve old buildings?
22. Will the HPC tell me what color to paint my house?
23. Can I make my building more energy efficient?

24. Will designation mean that new construction has to be designed a certain way?
25. Will interiors be subject to review?
26. What about demolition?
27. Will the district be expanded to cover more properties?

As we'll see next, not everyone will ask questions so mildly. Our most aggressive opponents will phrase them as pointed challenges. So I think it's time for us to learn to think politically about questions and answers, don't you?

Chapter Twenty

Thinking Politically about Q&A: The Moving Pattern of Opponents' Challenges

Our foes will provide us with arms.

—Virgil, *Aeneid*

Districting campaigns are hard to win. But they are easily lost in the give-and-take of open community forums where we take to the floor to respond to questions.

There is a pattern in our opponents' questions where the ground shifts with every answer—a pattern that is logical and predictable. Learn this pattern now and you'll know your adversaries' plans before they do themselves. Master it and you'll perform to peak capacity in the Q&A.

POLITICAL THEATER

Imagine what it'll be like. You recognize your first questioner, hear the question, and then begin an answer. You owe the questioner a response, yet you can't ignore everybody else. So you look around the room and . . . do you know what hits you? You realize that they *might be listening* for your answer, but they *sure are watching to see how you do.*

This is public theater. Performance counts as much as the substance of what is said. Each speaker is judged by a critical and skeptical audience.

Of course you'd better know your lines. You must be prepared to answer any question about preservation, or know when to ask a specialist to step in for you.

But don't think your critics pose every question to get an explanation from you. You'll need to recognize when a question isn't just a question but a challenge thrown down by your adversaries—a challenge which you can learn to pick up and skillfully use to your advantage.

UNDERSTANDING QUESTIONS

Listen to questions two ways. Ask yourself:

1. *What does the questioner want to know?* This is how we usually hear questions because we're thinking about responding with facts and explanations.
2. *Why, and how, is the question being asked?* If we are politically alert listeners, each question adds to our understanding of how the political dynamic of the designation process is shaping up.

We often miss this second way of thinking.

TYPES OF QUESTIONERS

Two types of questioners provide us with political opportunities.

1. **Takers**, who are our unconvinced but convincible questioners. They typically pose questions for clarification as they decide for or against districting.
2. **Breakers**, who are our committed opponents. They ask questions or make challenging statements to sway opinion against us.

Unlike us, Breakers aren't responsible for a cogent plan, nor are they bound by fact or logic. They have an immediate advantage: the tendency of Takers toward inaction when confronted by a confusion of counterclaims and irreconcilable differences. What you and I might call an unhelpful, uninformed, or ignorant question is often for Breakers the smart political move.

DETECTING THE DIFFERENCE

You can usually distinguish between these two types of questioners by the way they pose their questions:

1. **Takers** typically ask *substantive* questions. For example, "What is involved in obtaining a Certificate of Appropriateness (COA)?" This is an

open invitation for us to tell them more. It's a chance for us to get our message across, and they'll let us know when they've heard enough.

2. **Breakers** pose *rhetorical* questions. "Why would anybody want an additional layer of government?" For them, the question is the message, their policy statement. They aren't seeking a convincing answer, and they are never satisfied with our response.

If you're not sure whether you're being led on by the first question a person asks, listen to the follow-up. Takers will typically ask for more detail: "Will I have to pay a fee for a COA?" Breakers, however, will become more combative: "Isn't this a burden on the elderly?"

THE LIMITED ROLE OF ISSUES

So the question-and-answer format is deceiving. It sure looks like an invitation to serious policy discussion—well, at least until you get into it.

1. Questions asked by unconvinced Takers are *opportunities* to advance our policies openly and fully. This is where advocacy as persuasive education plays its role and issues are important. Many conversations are ongoing. Your job is to establish a position and keep to it, reaffirming basic points and elaborating them as needed.
2. Our opponents' questions are *challenges* to be finessed and seized for the advantages they offer. Here political perspectives must rule and your responses should be politically calibrated.

One perspective stands above all others when it comes to dealing with Breakers: this is **not** a *contest of issues using reasoned arguments as weapons*, but a *contest for influence using issues as weapons*. The issues they choose are the weapons we will use to defeat them.

ANTICIPATING OPPOSITION STRATEGY

I'm not claiming that Breakers are actually conscious of the way they try to manipulate the Q&A to maximize their influence. It's enough that they *act* like they understand it.

Fortunately for us, their questions are driven by a political logic into a predictable pattern of arguments that offers us a ready-made strategy. When we learn to recognize this pattern, we are able to anticipate *what* they will argue, and generally *when*, before they know it themselves. Of course, if they're no good at this game, then so much the better for us.

HOW IT TYPICALLY BEGINS

The first move is to us. The historic district is our plan. We set the agenda. When we begin with advocacy, our emphasis is on historic preservation with the *historic* part—the valued legacy—emphasized. Our opponents see districting in terms of historic *preservation*—that is, protection—but protection *from whom*? They take offense presuming we mean from them, and they return the insult: "You don't trust us," responds Roger Weingarten in Montpelier, Vermont, "why should we trust you?"[1]

OUTLINE OF THE
MOVING PATTERN OF OPPONENTS' CHALLENGES

The pattern flows predictably between these two issues of trust. Between the one charge (that we don't trust them with their properties) and the other (that we shouldn't be trusted with power) lies an unfolding argument that appears in debate as a series of pointed questions or challenging statements.

There's a *pivotal shift* at the center of these questions around which everything turns. It occurs when opponents stop talking about historic preservation and start talking about property rights. If you listen closely, you'll hear that the arguments on either side of the shift evolve in a mirror image of each other.

Here's the basic outline of our opponents' moving line of attack using simple questions as examples.

Part One: Denying Historic Districting

1. **Arguments alleging our distrust of them.**
   Basic point: The district is personally demeaning.
   "Why don't you trust us with our property?"
2. **Arguments against the need for districting protection.**
   Basic point: Historic resources are already sufficiently protected.
   "Isn't this why we have zoning laws?"
3. **Arguments against the desirability of districting protection.**
   Basic point: The district will have undesirable consequences.
   "Why create a district that will lower property values?"

4. Arguments against historic merit.

Basic point: History isn't and can't be the reason for districting.

"Whaddya' mean historic? George Washington didn't sleep here!"

THE PIVOTAL SHIFT:
FROM HISTORIC PRESERVATION TO PROPERTY RIGHTS

Part Two: Affirming Property Rights

1. Arguments for property rights merit.

Basic point: Property rights are sufficient reason for opposing districting.

"You're violating my personal property rights!"

2. Arguments for the desirability of property rights protection.

Basic point: Property rights have consequences more desirable than preservation.

"I have a right to the highest and best use of my property."

3. Arguments for the need for property rights protection.

Basic point: Property rights are about to be lost to districting.

"The district's a done deal!"

4. Arguments affirming their distrust of us.

Basic point: The district is a power grab by preservationists.

"These people can't be trusted with this kind of power!"

Read over this outline until you get a sense of the flow of changing questions and challenges. We'll be looking at each of these parts in greater detail in the following chapters.

A SMORGASBORD

OK, I know what you're thinking: I must be delusional to claim I know exactly how the debate will unfold. And so I would be, *if* I were saying that. But I'm not.

Instead, I want you to think of a smorgasbord—an open buffet that has a rich variety of dinner items laid out on a long table and arranged in a natural and predictable order, from appetizers to desserts. Now substitute the categories of questions for the variety of foods and you'll begin to see how I say questioning is predictable.

At a smorgasbord diners are free to select items in whatever order they choose. If we watch them, and anticipate that sooner or later they will eat a complete and balanced meal, we will not be surprised if they pick here among desserts, there at salads, now at the meats, and later at the vegetables. Wherever they start, we see with increasing clarity where they will move next as opportunities for making new selections diminish. You can bet on it.

CATCHING THE PIVOTAL SHIFT

Our answers to their questions drive the changing selections. In part I we respond that district designation is about prudence not personalities, that it supplements zoning laws, and that government has a legitimate interest in protecting all kinds of historic resources and that preservation is indeed our central goal.

Because we have good preservation answers for every challenge, our opponents need to shift the focus of debate. The Q&A pivots when they declare, "This isn't about preservation. This is a property rights issue!" And so part II unfolds.

PROPERTY RIGHTS AS POWER

The predictive pattern that I've outlined draws upon experience for its particulars and upon the logic of power for its organization. Preservation is our primary goal, though it has other desirable results for us. But our adversaries see property rights mainly as an instrument—not an end—that enables them to do, or not to do, other things. Thus for them the property rights issue is about power or—in contemporary lingo—empowerment.

This political insight helps us stay focused. The contest isn't about the merits of *preservation* as much as it's joined where property interests collide with preservation over *districting*, for it's here that local law redefines the prerogatives of property ownership.

POLITICS NOT PRESERVATION

So we can't expect our adversaries to listen to us. They'll hear the points we advocate for preservation only to sidestep them. To do otherwise would be to arrest the momentum of their own necessary strategy.

They have no real choice but to ignore or misrepresent what we say about preservation in order to get to the pivotal shift to construct their own symmetrically opposite defense of property rights against districting.

That, in short, is the political logic of their situation.

Without this insight we're reduced to waiting to see what happens in the Q&A and improvising. With it we can seize their hostile questions and comments and make them part of our own strategic plan for defeating them while building a new sense of community with Takers.

NOTE

1. Gina Tron, "Design Review Meeting Long and Emotional," www.timesargus. com, June 10, 2016.

Chapter Twenty-One

Our Reframing Q&A Strategy

He must be very ignorant, for he answers every question he is asked.

—Voltaire

Let's look more closely now at how we'll respond to our opponents' questions in community meetings. Coming from our dyed-in-the-wool adversaries—the Breakers—these challenges are aimed at blocking our efforts to win over undecided Takers—those folks in the middle who are still making up their minds.

Breaker challenges may be posed as either questions or flat statements. I'll call all of them questions because each ends with the unspoken interrogative: "What do you say to *that*?"

OUR REFRAMING STRATEGY

We don't have to take the bait. We can decide how we want to "hear" the question and respond to it. We can answer it directly if it suits us. Often we'll reframe the question, taking a different angle that advances our message, not theirs, while still allowing us to be responsive. We don't want to get too deep into the weeds of their point of view.

Our Q&A strategy is simple and straightforward. We're not going to respond to our critics on their terms, much less argue with them. We'll answer them in ways designed to win over Takers in the middle ground and isolate our critics. This is a key part of our plan to build a vital sense of community in the midst of conflict and use it to defeat our opponents. Here's my format for the next two chapters:

- I'll state a typical question and follow it with a brief interpretative comment.
- I'll suggest either a direct answer or a way of reframing the question and responding.
- Final comments are meant to help you see the larger context out of which our initial response emerges and point you toward a fuller response if it's needed.

Your sense of the moment will tell you whether to reframe or directly rebut a challenge to stop it in its tracks.

THINKING FLEXIBLY

There's no one right answer to any question. Keep your antennae up to gauge the sense and direction of the meeting. A small, relatively friendly meeting invites one kind of response while a large, highly contentious one requires another.

I've composed my examples for the more difficult but not outlandishly hostile meeting. It's up to you to gear them up or tone them down as you think best.

Remember that the unfolding pattern of questions exists only in the abstract. Breakers will be asking the questions they want to ask whenever they want to ask them.

That's why you can prepare but you can't really plan for the Q&A. Think strategically, where discussion can turn on a different axis with each question posed and each response given.

Each meeting can have its own direction, too. One might be dominated by procedural issues and another by challenges to historic merit.

This is where our moving pattern gives you an advantage. When we've been through a difficult meeting, our natural tendency is to prepare to refight it with better answers at the next meeting. That's probably wise, but it's likely that you'll have to deal with a whole new set of questions next time. These chapters can help you focus in on them by a process of elimination.

SURPRISE QUESTIONS

We want to reduce your uncertainty, yet some of the best questions are surprises. "My neighbor's husband died and the house and Social Security are all she has now. She wouldn't come here today, she's so upset. What do you say to her?"

You look around the room and you realize this is it: the one you didn't anticipate. The one that can lose it for you. The widow-maker. It takes you to the heart of what you know and think and want others to understand. When you can answer it with confidence and compassion and get a nod from the questioner, then you know you've passed the public test.

The only way to prepare for the unexpected is to practice and practice again answering questions you think you might get asked. Somewhere in the seams of the responses you develop you'll find just what you need when the time comes.

KEEP CENTERED

The heat of Q&As can throw you off your game. Always remember you're not up there to fend off attacks like a batter fouls off pitches when the count is 3–2. You are driving home your points to Takers.

Batters step out of the box to compose themselves. You don't have time for that. Before you swing your bat, focus on this mental image:

A Better Community Future

▲

Your Interests ▶   Historic District   ◀ Others' Interests

▲

Historic Resources

It captures what we did in fusing together our practical vision in chapter 10 when we:

- Melded our preservation interests with other diverse interests on the horizontal axis in "preservation-plus," and
- Melted the divide between the past and future on the vertical axis in projecting our districting plan's role in mediating the place of preservation in our community's future.

The more you think about and see the axes clearly, the more the image will become second-nature to you as you shape your responses. Your task will always be to fuse your interests in sheltering historic resources with other interests while looking to the future, building on the past.

Chapter Twenty-Two

Answering Opposition Questions I: From "Distrust of Them" to the "Pivotal Shift"

Enemies are so stimulating.

—Katherine Hepburn

To recap: There are dozens of challenges that districting opponents across the country employ so regularly that we may treat them as inevitable. They can take the form of questions or challenging statements, but they are always argumentative.

Our opponents—the Breakers—will toss these arguments at us one at a time, jumping from one topic to another. But what appears to be random is actually rooted in an orderly progression of challenges.

The pattern has two main components linked by a pivotal shift of focus. The first attacks historic districting and the second affirms the sanctity of private property rights.

We'll begin here by considering Breakers' questions under the four headings of the first part that lead logically to the symmetrically unfolding second part in the next chapter:

- Arguments Alleging Our Distrust of Them.
- Arguments against the Need for Districting Protection.
- Arguments against the Desirability of Districting Protection.
- Arguments against Historic Merit.

What follow are the core, most often heard questions and challenges with examples culled from across the country. You're sure to hear their substance, if not the same phrasing angled the same way, in your own Q&A.

This selection is designed to get you thinking. Treat what I say as suggestions—examples—only.

PART ONE: DENYING HISTORIC DISTRICTING

A. Arguments Alleging Our Distrust of Them

1. *They say: Why don't you trust us with our property?*

Breakers like to portray themselves as victims. They're saying if we, personally, trusted our neighbors to be good citizens then we wouldn't be pressing this on them. They want Takers to feel the same way. "Houstonians are being told they lack any right—even the smarts—to determine the appearance of their property," an opponent writes.[1] Variations include *"they will tell us," "make us," or "won't let us"* do this, that or the other. As a Santa Monica homeowner puts it, "They just want to decide what's best for us."[2]

Variation: *We're caring folks, too, you know.* "We don't need a local historic district to do the right thing with our much loved buildings, history and heritage," protests Cinda Jones in Amherst, Massachusetts.[3]

Reframe: *Why did we call this meeting today?*

We respond: *Because we know that all of us care about our community. We believe that there is enough trust and confidence among us, neighbor to neighbor, to do this extraordinary thing for each other. Make no mistake: We're either going to have the community we earn by working together—or the one we deserve by failing to act. Right now we could use your support for the kind of community we need. So, what do you say?*

We're holding out a welcoming hand to Takers, asking for their help. And we're putting Breakers on the spot: put up or shut up. This offer of empowerment is our antidote to their claims of victimhood.

2. *They say: Why didn't you ask us first?*

Snubbed, that's how they feel. Bypassed, overlooked, taken for granted. Some mean it; for others it's just an incitement. "This has gone on for too long with too many people knowing too little," complains Jac Roth in Albany, Georgia.[4]

Direct answer: *Suppose we had called a meeting as soon as the idea popped into our heads. Would you have approved a vague notion then? Or would you have told us to go away until we had a real proposal? We thought the latter. So today is the real beginning. Nothing's been decided—except that we'd like you to join us.*

Because Breakers can't agree to join us, they insist the district isn't needed. The next section follows predictably.

B. Arguments against the Need for Districting Protection

1. *They say: If you trust us then why do we need more rules and regulations?*

This "if not . . . then" tactic tries to trap us in a contradiction, or an irrelevancy. "Where's the crisis?" we're asked in Camden, South Carolina. "It's called a racket: a solution to a problem that doesn't exist," comments a Baltimore opponent of the Federal Hill district proposal.[5]

Variation: *If it ain't broke, don't fix it!* In Evanston, Illinois: "We don't have people making stupid changes to their homes. A preservation district is unnecessary."[6] "Everything that's been done on Liberty Street has been done to improve the neighborhood," asserts Steve Murphy in Montpelier, Vermont. "Why go through these [expanded district] processes."[7]

Direct answer: *This isn't about you or me in particular. It's about how we can secure our community's future. Only by trusting each other today can we provide for tomorrow. And so we trust you'll join us in supporting the district.*

That's the way to avoid finger-pointing. It's different, of course, if you have a real crisis or gathering storm that's pushing your effort. Maybe there's no crisis now, but as a Floridian put it, "we don't know who will come in the future."[8]

2. *They say: Isn't this why we have zoning laws?*

As a Maine opponent asks, "Why do we need more ordinances when the old ordinances have been working?"[9] Zoning laws are said to provide ample and fair protection for all property owners, including preservationists. Breakers want Takers to feel we're asking a lot for no reason or little advantage, "like using a bazooka to kill a mosquito," wrote Matthew Turkstra in helping defeat a Washington, D.C., district proposal.[10]

Variation: *"We ought to fix zoning instead of adding new rules."* Denver activist Nancy Francis argues that "the underlying problem" turning "neighbor against neighbor" is the City's "refusal to do the right thing, which is to enforce the [existing zoning] code. It's like we're giving up on zoning as a tool to solve this."[11]

Reframe: *What will districting do for us that zoning laws can't?*

We respond: *It will protect us against identity theft.*

Each of us is invested, personally and financially, in our neighborhood, which has its own identity that we value and gives us value in return. Without the district overlay, zoning alone can't protect the community's historical integrity and distinctive character even *if* zoning is working, as claimed.

Zoning allows a wide variety of structures and landscaping without considering the unique character and needs of a particular area. As zoning changes, so do development standards. District designation still permits rezoning, but it establishes a constant set of development standards unique to the district that won't change with rezoning. The district will promote healthy change consistent with the visual character of our community.

Use this rule of thumb: The louder the defense of zoning the more the advocate (a) wants to introduce incompatible change and (b) believes that the district will in fact afford real protections to the community.

3. *They say: The free market can decide what's valuable and worth preserving.*

Districting isn't needed, critics argue, because the free market—which shows what people value by what they will pay for—is a more reliable indicator of what should be saved and how. Breakers may argue it, but they don't really care what the market says about preservation. They simply don't want anyone—not only preservationists—telling them what to do.

The market argument is a ready-made inducement for Takers to stop listening. Tim Shepard in South Windsor, Connecticut, brushes our perspectives aside: "You can sit down and have all the best answers in the world, but it's market driven."[12]

When folks are perplexed by choices, it's a relief to be told that the supposed automatic mechanism of the marketplace can take over. We need to shift their attention from theory to practice without, however, coming across as anti-free marketers. That would be politically stupid.

Reframe: *As a smart investor, don't you want to manage your risk?*

We respond: *Look, we're not indifferent property investors here. We don't care more for some abstract market theory than for how the market actually treats us. The historic district will give us greater security of investment, when the historic setting of each property is well maintained. There is a robust market for preservation nationally, and our purpose is to foster its ability to operate here to the advantage of all of us.*

There isn't just one market, and not all markets are equal. Diane Fox of the Greenwich Preservation Network observes that historic properties constitute "a limited market, but it works."[13] In New York

City, "the market itself shows that people like these [old] neighborhoods as they are." Roberta Brandes Gratz says, "Isn't it interesting that the [Donald] Trumps of the world fight to build these new monstrosities on the periphery of historic districts?"[14]

Without historic districting, property markets focus on short-term results at the expense of valuing the long-term benefits of historic preservation. Landlords in rental markets will damage buildings to maximize net operating income by avoiding maintenance or making harmful repairs and alterations. Long-term homeowners rarely have more than an abstract concern for the economic consequences of what they do to their properties. New building contractors in the redevelopment market will read the economic tea leaves in favor of teardowns. Realtor Bill Rothman in Carlisle, Pennsylvania, is a districting supporter who channels Joni Mitchell's "Big Yellow Taxi": "Someone can't just roll in, knock down a building and then use it as a parking lot."[15]

Built-in market correctives don't operate here, either. Once historic resources are lost through bad decisions, they can never be recouped. And the damage done to the rest of us can't be repaired by Adam Smith's "invisible hand" that shapes the general welfare out of selfish marketplace interests. As Indiana homeowner association volunteer John Tousley puts it, once historic resources vanish, "we become just another place on the map."[16] Regulation in these circumstances isn't anti-market. Districting keeps historic capital in play, ownership in private hands, and the market for historic properties fully operating.

As we move through defending the need for districting, our opponents will start focusing on its alleged limits and liabilities.

C. Arguments against the Desirability of Districting Protection
1. They say: You can't stop change.

This seems obvious to those who believe that preservation means shrink-wrapping communities or freezing them in time. One of my favorite examples is, "If Manitou Springs had a historic district when the town was created, we'd all be living in teepees." A more sophisticated version is that we will derail progress without achieving lasting preservation.

Variation: *You shouldn't even try!* "Using zoning as a weapon against legitimate progress is abhorrently wrong."[17] "Quit being afraid of change," says Albert Nixon in New Castle, Pennsylvania. "Change has to come in order for things to thrive."[18]

Reframe: *Change is certain, progress isn't and [expletive deleted] happens.*

We respond: *Let's go for solid growth built upon the past—real progress—not random, risky change.*

Remember to avoid any talk in any form of regulating or directing growth and change. That's a dog whistle to anti-government types.

2. *They say: But design is so subjective! Who can say what good taste is?*

We could talk all day about the problem of "good taste." Design review isn't at all about what we "like" or "dislike." That would be justifiable cause for complaint. Instead, the HPC looks for a project's compatibility with its setting in terms of recognized standards made locally more specific through design guidelines. Explaining this will get you only so far. There will be some listeners who are in thrall of a deep relativism that's skeptical about the very existence of dependable standards or anyone's ability or right to make decisions based on them. We hear this in, "Just because something is old does not mean it is good, just as because some improvement wasn't original, doesn't mean it is bad."[19] The best way to reach everyone else is by common-sense analogy.

Reframe: *Do you know the difference between an author and an editor?*

We respond: *Editors don't write the books; editors make them better. And what makes a good editor? The ability to help a writer choose what works best. For us, the question isn't how anyone can know what makes a good book. It's whether we want a good read. The role of the HPC in design review is very much like that. No doubt about it: the process helps owners make good choices. The real question is whether they want a good result.*

Once "disheartened and seething" over a HPC hearing on church signage, Ralph Faulkingham says that "with the passage of time, I look back on the process as worth every bit of what we put into it." Other members admitted to having "a result that they like, that is better than what they would have had."[20]

There's a big difference between being *subjective* and being *arbitrary*. Every day, democracies make decisions about what's subjective—such as what's ethically right and wrong—and then we make laws and establish procedures to see to it that our decisions aren't applied arbitrarily.

3. *They say: Preservation is just too expensive!*

Bear in mind that those who oppose districting always inflate preservation-related costs, and they'll find contractors who'll arm them with worse-than-worst case scenarios.

Variation #2: *Districting imposes unjust financial burdens.* In Durham, a planned rescue mission would encounter "astronomical added cost," and "it is not humane," says opponent Melvin Whitely.[21]

Reframe*: Do you remember the car service commercial, "You can pay me now—or you can pay me later?"*

We respond: *Valuable properties like ours become just old buildings when they lose the integrity of compatible materials and design details, and inappropriate new construction diminishes its setting and itself in turn. Substituting inexpensively is like taking part of the principal of your investment and throwing it away. Today the smart money is on preserving older properties intact. And the surprising thing is that over time, investing in preservation is cost-effective.*

Good design and construction will enhance the district, which, in turn, will lend its prestige to the security of our investments. There may be opportunity costs in building for prestige, but there are costs incurred if owners make inappropriate changes that detract from their own and their neighbors' properties. As Edmund Burke said, "Mere parsimony is not economy. . . . Expense, and great expense, may be an essential part of true economy."

Preservationist Jeremy Wells in Philadelphia gives Burke's point a modern phrasing: "The cheap quick fix is often the most costly fix in the long run."[22] Responsible repair and maintenance of older buildings can be an additional expense, as can appropriate renovations and new construction. But higher initial costs are generally compensated by stronger revenues and property values. HPCs should be open to proposals that are both appropriate and financially reasonable for property owners, with hardship provisions and guidelines suitable for financially strapped areas.

4. They say: The historic district will lead to lower property values when I go to sell!

"Historic district zoning," a North Carolinian claims, "reduces the number of potential buyers by eliminating those who do not want their property subject to the historic district bureaucracy; fewer buyers means lower prices."[23]

This argument is appealing in theory, but baseless in fact. Many realtors emphasize historic district locations. Urban districts may also be marketed for their scale and compactness, walkability and convenience to shopping, churches, and schools—all aspects of contemporary lifestyle preferences.

Reframe: *Why are realtors so eager to list historic district properties?*

We respond: *Properties in historic districts frequently—even sub-stantially—outperform sales of similar properties elsewhere. Where values are declining, preservation stabilizes them. Preservation sells, and not just because some buyers appreciate historic settings. Buyers are aware that a historic district signifies the presence of a whole mix of positive factors—social, economic, political, and cultural—that make living or working there desirable. They recognize the stability and strength of property values, too. The free market has demonstrated that people will pay a premium to buy property in sheltered communi-ties, whether in historic districts or in gated suburban developments.*

Don't be cowed by studies purporting to prove us wrong. Stick to your guns—and to documentation available through your State His-toric Preservation Office and the National Trust. Tony Felice, preser-vation officer for Mesa, Arizona, says that creating districts is "a slam dunk in terms of economic development. When a home is designated as historic, we've seen an increase in property values from 30 to 35 percent, often without even doing anything to the house."[24] Don't be surprised if such statements get your critics to do a 180° turn and hit you on the alleged consequences of rising property values.

5. ***They say: I'm not going anywhere, so this'll just raise my property taxes, won't it?!***

Taxes—a great bugbear of American politics. Challenge their per-spective.

Reframe: *Is there anyone present who'd like to buy property that's guaranteed to lose value and lower your taxes?*

We respond: *I thought so. For most of us, our property is our big-gest investment for the future. A higher selling price for a neighbor's house is never bad news.*

District designation itself isn't a direct factor in property tax rates or appraisals. Owners might also qualify for tax advantages in the district as their net worth expands—but don't oversell this possibility. Your state or local preservation adviser should be able to speak briefly to the tax issue and explain credits.

6. ***They say: Rising values will change the neighborhood for the worse!***

Issues vary. A common charge is gentrification that transforms older communities into chic enclaves for the rich or quaint mini-Mayberrys or tourist destinations. Then there are predictions that districting will displace low-income residents, put pressures on ethnic diversity, keep out younger homeowners, and increase financial bur-dens on working families and the elderly. Just whose culture, some ask, is to be preserved?

These issues have real merit, and we're giving them separate treatment in chapters 11 and 61. Here I'll focus on how our opponents use them as speculative chumming to draw in Takers and hook them on becoming victims. It's actually one of our best openings for challenging Takers to join with us to take responsibility for the future.

Reframe: *How can we be sure that the district will do what we want it to do and treat us well?*

We respond: *By everybody working together instead of just criticizing. The district is a tool. Let's fit it to our purposes. All we're saying is, let's be proactive about the kind of community that we—all of us—want to maintain, instead of just letting things happen. Doing nothing is far more likely to lead where none of us wants to go.*

What issues are you facing? Have you handled them in your practical vision for districting? As for gentrification: The wealthy—like the poor—are always with us. Do we want them isolated in suburban developments? The answer isn't simple. But isn't it better to draw affluent owners to a diverse historic district, where they'll contribute to the tax base, provide money for civic projects, develop sensitivity for urban issues, and join in local affairs as socially conscious and responsible citizens?

Districting may be used for stabilizing or reviving communities under stress. There it may halt or reverse disinvestment. In Georgia, former Historic Columbus Foundation director Virginia Peebles says, "The way to stem flight from cities and neighborhoods is for people to have good reasons for staying there."[25]

Historic districts can be democratic about who gets what. With the visibility that districting gives us at City Hall we can work for tax policy and other considerations to help maintain diversity and homeownership. Everyone in a district benefits from investment, not just folks in grand homes or businesses with political pull.

With the advantages of districting now defended, the Breakers move on to attack the historic merit of our proposal.

D. Arguments against Historic Merit

Breakers portray our choices in zero-sum terms, a kind of Newton's Third Law of Motion applied to public policy: an advance in any one policy direction necessitates an equal and opposite retreat in all others.

Thus when we say we're for preservation, they tell Takers that our plan will cost them dearly. But as soon as we assert economic benefits, they conclude that we're not serious about preservation.

They see preservation, then, as smoke and mirrors used to screen some other goal entirely. What that end might be isn't as important to them as pointing out that our claim to base the district on historic merit is a sham.

1. **They say: *This isn't really about historic preservation at all, is it? It's about property values, commercial investment, tourism—it's just about the money!***

   Variation #1: *It's about lifestyle preferences, not preservation.*

   Variation #2: *It's antigrowth. Preservation is the excuse.*

   Variation #3: *It's about taste, the snobbish enforcement of an elitist aesthetic.*

   Variation #4: *It's about . . . virtually any other interest except genuine preservation.*

   Breakers want to paint us as liars or cheats who will manipulate authentic preservation values for our own selfish purposes. Urbanist Alon Levy claims: "Let us remember what historic districts are, in practice: They are districts where wealthy people own property that they want to prop up the price of [sic]."[26] Our response will be to deny Breakers' zero-sum perspective and replace it with a positive affirmation that there are net gains for interests that are important to Takers.

   Reframe: *How do we know when preservation is working?*

   We respond: *When it saves a legacy, puts smiles on people's faces and money in their pockets. Preservation isn't just old buildings standing around. If homes aren't enjoyable, neighborhoods livable, and businesses profitable, then folks aren't going to invest in preservation. There's no hidden agenda here! What you see is what you get.*

   We want Takers to see that districting is a win-win situation for everybody across the board, except those who would profit at the expense of the rest of us. In its consequences preservation is democratic, not elitist.

   The only response available to Breakers is to deny outright that there is anything worth preserving.

2. **They say: *"Whaddya' mean, historic? George Washington didn't sleep here!"***

   We first ran into this gag line in chapter 1. Its counterpart from Newnan, Georgia, is, "No tour bus is ever going to drive down this street!"

   Variation: Critics claim that while maybe a few historic properties exist, *"There's not enough all together to justify a whole district!"*

   This will make sense to Takers because most folks have a mountaintop view of history. They see only those events and places that have risen above the lower hills and valleys of the past where our own local legacy was built. What appears deserving to us isn't to them: "These are just your basic West Philadelphia rowhouses," one insists.[27]

One of the things that we preservationists do well, given time, is open people's eyes to the history in their midst. The problem for us is not to be condescending.

Reframe: [Jokingly.] *The past just isn't what it used to be, is it?*

We respond: *Well, at least not the big-event way we all used to think about it in American History class. We're not pulling a fast one here. The district has to satisfy rigorous standards under law before it may be designated historic by the City Council.*

This is our opportunity to have our preservation specialist—or a SHPO representative—explain "historic" as a concept and clear up confusion over the criteria used for determining contributing properties.

3. *They say: Well, my property isn't historic! It should be excluded!*

This expression of narrow self-interest signals that Breakers are at their wits' end in attacking districting from a historic preservation angle. Their hope is that Takers will see the unfairness of the plan.

Reframe: *Let's cut to the chase. What you really want to know is why we don't make the district voluntary, right?*

We respond: *Because it's bad public policy. Yes, districting is about zoning policy. But people don't just opt out of zoning arrangements because they want to. Talk about fairness! That would amount to spot rezoning and policy nullification by personal fiat. And where would that leave the rest of us?! As Ben Franklin said, "We either hang together or we hang separately." We've made a legitimate case for bringing all properties into the district fold, and the courts say it's constitutional for the City to include them.*

Our affirmation of districting's constitutionality brings differences to a head and it's here that debate pivots. Breakers shift their focus from attacking districting on preservation grounds to blocking designation in defense of property rights.

NOTES

1. Jim Saltzman, "Changes to Preservation Ordinance Threaten Property Rights," www.preservationsanity.org, 1999.

2. Clara Sturak, "Historic District Opponents Rally," www.smmirror.com, March 13–19, 2005.

3. Scott Merzbach, "Need for Local Historic Districts Debated in Amherst," www.gazettenet.com, April 16, 2015.

4. Jennifer Parks, "Views Mixed among Residents Regarding Proposed Albany Historic District Expansion," www.albanyherald.com, October 23, 2016.

5. Ed Gunts, "Federal Hill Debates Whether to Become a City Historic District," www.baltimorebrew.com, February 15, 2016.

6. Jane Adler, "Preservation Haul," www.chicagotribune.com, December 28, 2003.

7. Nat Frothingham, "Majority Voices at Hearing 'Want Out' of Design Review," www.montpelierbridge.com, June 17, 2016.

8. Jason Holland, "Hearing on Historic District Tonight," *Osceola News-Gazette*, January 27, 2005.

9. Dennis Hoey, "Maquoit Bay: Property Rights vs. Preservation," www.meepi.org, July 3, 2001.

10. Martin Austermuhle, "Battle over a Capitol Hill Block Cools Off as Commission Rejects Historic District," www.wamu.org/news, October 14, 2016.

11. Alan Prendergast, "Park Hill Neighborhood Divided by Battles over Historic District, Subdividing Lots," www.westword.com, September 28, 2016.

12. Dan Haar, "Trucks Clash with History in South Windsor," www.ctnow.com, March 2, 2015.

13. Kai Sherwin, "Diane Fox, Greenwich Preservation Network Hone the Gentle Art of Persuasion," www.greenwichfreepress.com, August 29, 2016.

14. Will Doig, "Preserving History, or the 1 Percent?" www.salon.com, April 14, 2012.

15. Joseph Cress, "Selling History: Property in Historic District Can Be Difficult to Sell," www.cumberlink.com, January 16, 2016.

16. Michelle Browning, "Nostalgic Zionsville Looks Back, Then Ahead," www.thenoblesvilleledger.com, February 22, 2005.

17. Scott Merzbach, "Need for Local Historic Districts Debated in Amherst," www.gazettenet.com, April 16, 2015.

18. Cameron O'Brien, TV Report, www.wytv.com, October 30, 2016.

19. Comment by "jefnvk" following Tom Perkin's, "'It's Absolutely Despicable,' Ypsilanti Council Member Says of Bill to Weaken Historic Districts," www.mlive.com, February 3, 2016.

20. Scott Merzbach, "Need for Local Historic Districts Debated in Amherst," www.gazettenet.com, April 16, 2015.

21. Virginia Bridges, "Homeowners, Durham Rescue Mission at Odds over Historic District," www.newsobserver," August 31, 2016.

22. "Letters: A Historic District Offers Various Benefits," www.dfw.com, July 1, 2002.

23. Mark Binker, "Westerwood Residents Split on Plan," *Greensboro News and Record*, January 21, 2002.

24. Lisa Selin Davis, "Historic Preservation: Finding Room for History in the Desert," www.Americancity.org, 2004.

25. Editorial, "Milestone Year for Historic Columbus," www.ledger-enquirer.com/opinion, May 24, 2016.

26. Blog quoted by Will Doig, "Preserving History, or the 1 Percent?"

27. Valerie Russ, "Despite Landlord's Objections, Rowhouses Get Historic Status," www.philly.com, July 10, 2016.

Chapter Twenty-Three

Answering Opposition Questions II: From the "Pivotal Shift" to "Distrust of Us"

What am I doing here? I'm chasing that guy. . . . Uh, no. . . . He's chasing me!

—Guy Pearce, *Memento*

It takes but a nanosecond for Breakers to respond to our observation on the constitutionality of historic districts . . . and then they're off and gunning for us with an affirmative defense of property rights.

Passing through the pivotal shift, challenges in this chapter unfold through the following categories that are a mirror image of the preceding chapter:

- Arguments for Property Rights Merit.
- Arguments for the Desirability of Property Rights.
- Arguments for the Need for Property Rights Protection.
- Arguments Affirming Their Distrust of Us.

So take a deep breath. We're going to take pains to pay them the respect they deserve, which is to explain to Takers, our fence-sitters, why our opponents are mistaken.

Don't show impatience. But never let their accusations hang in the air, either. He who hesitates is toast. You might not think much of your opponents' arguments, but remember what the elder George Bush once said: "It's no exaggeration to say that the undecideds could go one way or another."

THE PIVOTAL SHIFT

Breakers assert that just because the courts have ruled that historic districting is constitutional doesn't mean that (1) the judges are right or (2) that politicians should enact our proposal. We can pinpoint their pivot this way: the best of them give a friendly backwards nod toward preservation, then slip us a "but. . . ."

Michigan state legislator Chris Afendoulis does it deftly: "I'm sensitive to historic preservation, *but* it has always struck me that when you're in a historic district, you kind of give up some of your rights."[1]

At the moment of the shift, others will pull out their biggest gun and claim (BANG!) that this is nothing but "a grab for power!" "The issue here is control," a landowner says in Maine.[2] An Internet blogger sums up districting as a "land grab . . . to control property."[3] Breakers then claim that the "grab" can come only with the violation of their freedom to exercise basic constitutional property rights.

Makers say:
THE CONSTITUTION PERMITS HISTORIC DISTRICTING

THE PIVOTAL SHIFT

Breakers say:
THE CONSITUTION GUARANTEES SUPERIOR PROPERTY RIGHTS

They operate under what I call the Law of Inverse Proof. When we point out that the courts don't find a conflict between districting and property rights, they claim that that fact itself proves their rights are in jeopardy. If the courts ignore property rights, they say, then it's the community's duty to honor and protect them. And once they assert that, the rest unfolds predictably.

PART TWO: AFFIRMING PROPERTY RIGHTS

A. Arguments for Property Rights Merit
1. They say: You're violating my personal property rights!
As reported in Keene, New Hampshire, Conan Salada "kept it short and sweet. 'It's a violation of property rights,'" he said about expanding a district.[4]

Variation: This is an unconstitutional "taking" of my property.

This change in direction can lead us down into the warren of constitutional theory and ideological conflict that cannot be settled in our meeting. The audience won't tolerate arguing. Our response should be quick, clean, and confident.

Direct answer: *Property rights aren't absolute and never have been in American history. Ours is a heritage of law-shape responsible use of our properties. We all know that zoning is constitutional and so are historic districts, which are part of zoning law as overlays. Whatever property rights we enjoy, and I believe in them too, they do not trump our basic political rights—including our right as free citizens to make laws about property that benefit communities. The Founding Fathers knew that. The Constitution says historic districts are fine, according to the Supreme Court, and it's time we move along.*

As long as due process is assured, districting doesn't negate existing or invested property rights. Get a preservation law specialist to confirm the Supreme Court's line of interpretation since the 1978 Penn Central case. Breakers, of course, will have none of it, not when American civilization hangs by a paint chip, as they claim.

2. *They say: No one should be able to tell me what to do with my property.*

"We must have the freedom to do what we want to do," a Michigan builder proclaims. Proportional judgment—the calculation of relative goods—vanishes at this point. A Florida couple opposed an entire district simply because it might have kept them from hanging a front door of their choice. Such folks may claim that citizens should defend the indivisibility of property rights against a tide of government empowerment that has eroded the legacy of freedom hard-won by patriots. Now they find it easy to live up to a principle saying they may do with their property as they please.

Variation #1: *I have a God-given right. . . .* It underscores the speaker's belief in the sanctity and absolute quality of this alleged right. But the subtext is always that the speaker's own human will to pursue any and every desire is inviolable.

Variation #2: It's my money and I can do as I like. "Until the historical society [sic] wants to have their own money in the game," a writer says in Michigan, "I could really care less how valuable they consider a building."[5]

Variation #3: You don't pay my property taxes, so don't tell me what to do.

Reframe: *What are the three most important words we use when we talk about rights?*

We respond: *"As long as." Example: We may exercise our property rights as long as what we do doesn't adversely affect the rights of others. We use zoning laws to define how that works in practice, regardless of who pays for what, and districting is part of the zoning code.*

Zoning is a long-established practice. The basic concept is that the government may restrict a property owner's right to use land in a way profitable to the owner but detrimental to surrounding properties. Zoning promotes appropriate uses in the future, and the historic district—which ties growth to the legacy of the past—will be a zoning overlay.

Specifically, the HPC can't tell property owners how to use their properties or what to build on them. All the HPC may do is decide that a style or alteration is incongruent based on the existing significant characteristics of the district. Thus, HPC decisions are based on findings of fact and not on the personal preferences of commissioners. A COA cannot be denied unless there is a finding of fact to back up the decision.

3. They say: This is an invasion of privacy!

In Winter Park, Florida, City commission candidate Peter Weldon avers that a democratic majority of neighbors could "compel 49 percent or less of property owners to forfeit their *privacy* and property rights."[6]

People will call "private" anything they're used to deciding on their own, even if it has public consequences. Thus, accustomed to exercising property rights one way, they are unsettled by the feeling that the district will alter what has been a private matter. It's more about feelings of independence than rights.

Direct answer: *It's out of respect for privacy that historic districts are silent about changes that take place within the walls of a property. But what happens outside, in public, can hardly be defined as private. The question of privacy hinges on your front door. Inside, you're the only one who has to live with your actions. Outside, everyone does.*

Privacy has become a hot-button topic in recent years, and the courts have found a constitutional right to privacy in certain circumscribed, highly personal areas. Doing what we want with our property is not one of those areas. Still, some folks claim a right to a blanket freedom to do whatever they wish and then say that whatever goes on under it is private. That is a pernicious notion.

4. They say: *Real preservationists should preserve our traditional culture of liberty!*

To our claims on behalf of heritage, a commenter replies: "The fact that a government entity dictates what an owner can and cannot do to their home, is the 'heritage' of tyranny."[7]

Reframe: *In what country?*

We respond: *Not in the country we live in. You will always be free to do with your property as you like up to the point it adversely affects your neighbors and intrudes on their free enjoyment of their property. That's American liberty as enshrined in the Constitution as the courts have interpreted it. You might like to read legal history otherwise, and you are free to try to change it. But until that time, the law is still the law. And our heritage is one of freedom under law.*

The Founders never thought in terms of law as the opposite of freedom. They knew that liberty without law is license, and law without freedom is tyranny. They struck the balance in the Constitution, which enables district designation.

From these arguments for the intrinsic value of property rights Breakers next turn to arguing that property rights are desirable because of what they prevent or secure.

B. Arguments for the Desirability of Property Rights

1. They say: *Why trade our rights for another layer of government?*

This basic dislike of government is usually wrapped in the garb of property rights. The "city has an overabundance of [agencies] whose purpose often seems to find new ways to tell people what they can or can't do," a newspaper editorializes.[8] "My main concern was, 'Hey, you know folks, what you're doing is giving away some property rights to the city,'" a critic says.[9] Another asks why should people vote "themselves into a control box they can never get out of" and give up "those constitutional homeowner rights that make this country special for the average person?"[10]

By defending property rights (but on specious constitutional grounds) Breakers can justify their antipathy to government. Breakers often have a very shallow concept of government, seeing it only in terms of restraining freedom. But Jefferson affirmed in the Declaration of Independence that we freely create governments to do our bidding, to serve purposes that we join together to achieve. If we're optimistic about each other, then we expect that government assists our civilized cooperation far more than it jerks our chains.

So how do we counter a fence-sitter's concern that property owners "might very well find themselves in the Homeowners Association vortex from hell?"[11] Thomas Jefferson clearly understood that good political institutions are a free people's gift to themselves.

Reframe: *Would you deny us the right to empower ourselves as a community in our relations with local, state, and even the federal government?*

We respond: *The district's review procedures will give us real leverage whenever the government—or anyone else—starts making designs on us. Let's stop complaining about how the interests of average citizens are always ignored—by big government, big money, or big pains—and decide today, right now, to do something about it! HPC procedures are strong enough to assure us respect, but the actual regulations are considerably less complicated than you might think. Your support and participation can help guarantee that we get the mix right.*

Do we want a community like Blanche DuBois in *A Streetcar Named Desire*, always dependent "on the kindness of strangers?" Texas state legislator Jessica Farrar says that "if residents don't drive their neighborhood, outside developers will."[12] An advocate in Tampa says that districting "increases neighborhood visibility with city officials" and another in Bloomington, Indiana, says it "creates an identifiable voice" in local affairs that gives a community a competitive advantage. New York City's Historic Districts Council calls itself "The Voice for Your Neighborhood." Designation also requires every federal agency, under Section 106 of the Historic Preservation Act of 1966, to take into account how any federally funded undertaking might affect our district.

2. They say: *I have a right to the highest and best use of my property.*

The argument—that we're denying owners the value in their land—depends on the propositions that (1) the value of one parcel is separable from the value of others, (2) the property owner has sole claim to it, and (3) the owner has an absolute right to the maximum return on investment. The affirmation of property rights carries the alleged promise of harvesting the largest profits from the land.

Reframe: *What is the three-word axiom of real estate?*

We respond: *"Location, location, location." Say what you will, common decency says it's just plain wrong to soak up value from your surroundings and not be considerate of others. Acceding to districting is but a small token of respect.*

Realtors who make a living off the value of property know that public and private contributions to the setting add value to a property. Historic settings are especially vulnerable to selfish grim reapers.

Besides, much public investment—your tax dollars and mine—go into creating the infrastructure that creates part of a property's value. As for "highest and best use," the courts disagree while affirming the lesser standard of a reasonable use and return on investment.

Because we remain unmoved by their arguments for the preemptive desirability of preferring rights over districting, Breakers move on to assert that we have shown that property rights need protecting.

C. Arguments for the Need for Property Rights Protection

This section contains a litany of procedural charges meant to sway Takers and public officials. No reframing here, these allegations must be met head-on and refuted.

1. They say: The district's a done deal!

Breakers claim that we're just going through the motions of public meetings since the fix is in. This, they say, is a denial of due process and a violation of their rights.

Direct answer: [With humor.] *Well now, that is good news! Why am I always the last to know?! I thought we had a good case, but I didn't know the City Council was in the bag. I guess you won't have to attend the public hearings now. We'll give 'em your regards.*

Of course, if the City Council is behind the initiative, then you might want to make a more serious affirmation of due process. But mild humor is the best way to handle a wild conspiracy theory. That brings us to the next argument.

2. They say: The district map has been gerrymandered to deny equal protection of my property rights.

Variation: *The map has changed. How can a property be historic one day and then be declared nonhistoric (or vice versa) the next?*

The charge means to tell Takers that the map is dishonest and that some properties have been included or excluded for inappropriate reasons.

Direct answer: *The map has been developed by the application of consistent criteria—which is to say by the knuckle-rappers who know the law and have kept everybody else's hands off of it! When it has been altered it has been in response to legitimate considerations.*

The map's author—preferably backed up by a SHPO official—should briefly explain its rationale and how decisions were made.

3. They say: The City's planning staff has colluded with proponents, thus using our tax dollars to support the violation of our property rights.

The goal is to convince others that our opponents have been denied equal protection of the law or equal access to what rightfully belongs to everybody. It makes us look like we've been skulking around City Hall sticking our paws into the public till.

Direct answer: *The courts have found that supporting preservation through districting is a legitimate function of government. Staff members have provided professional assistance to us and anyone else who has asked, including opponents.*

You should have the City's chief planning officer, or staff, detail the scope of the department's work on the district.

4. *They say: The district study was biased by preconceptions about how it ought to turn out.*

The charge intends to cover a variety of sins from simple bias, to ignoring facts, to targeting specific properties for control.

Direct answer: *The study is no more or less biased than a diagnosis by a doctor who is looking for the facts and is determined to provide the best treatment. The district study has been professionally carried out and its recommendations follow its findings.*

Focus on the facts that justify districting. The specialist who did the survey should have a brief, persuasive response that avoids jargon and defensiveness.

5. *They say: Community meetings have been biased.*

This is a maddening complaint that is unreasonable on its face. Next, they'll be claiming we were unfairly better organized than they, more articulate, and so forth.

Direct answer: *The truth is that bias in any meeting attaches to the better argument, the stronger facts, the clearer case. It's also true that we called this meeting to promote districting. But as evidenced by this extended Q&A, we're trying to give you every opportunity to state your feelings as well.*

Keep a detailed record of every opportunity opponents have for speaking out. If this charge becomes a serious issue, you might offer to hold an independently moderated joint meeting (see chapter 26). Whether it's held or not, the offer will be as good as gold if you have to defend yourself against having shown bias in your community hearings.

6. *They say: The proposal keeps changing on us.*

The suggestion is that we're trying to put something over on the community and can't be trusted.

Direct answer: *Changes are simply the proof you need that we're listening to you and revising in light of what we're hearing. Obviously, the district's not a done deal, now is it?*

Ask if they have any particular complaint and then explain the changes you've made.

7. They say: There will be no end to the restrictions you'll impose. This is just the start.

This kind of agitation plays up to folks who tend to feel powerless. Breakers are suggesting that designation will give the power elite the opening they need to roll back property rights.

Direct answer: *The ordinance may be amended, and guidelines expanded or shrunk in the future, depending on experience and what the community desires. As always, the best check on unwanted regulations is not to shy away from what needs to be done today, but to become involved so that the decisions will come from you.*

Don't let them get away with such a counsel of fear. It's demeaning to our political legacy of citizen boards and citizen responsibility for historic districts.

As we move through defending what we've done procedurally, Breakers begin to attack us personally for who they say we are, our qualifications, and what this means for the future.

D. Arguments Affirming Their Distrust of Us

1. They say: The district is being rammed down our throats.

This all-purpose procedural charge implies that we're pursuing designation in a damn-the-torpedoes full-speed-ahead fashion. The focus isn't on the ramming but the rammer.

Direct answer: *We've called this meeting and will have others so that the community will have time to deliberate carefully. We are exceeding the requirements of due process.*

Once again, go over the procedure so everyone knows how districting will move ahead.

2. They say: Do you enjoy dividing the neighborhood?

Breakers use this argument as a counterweight to our claim that we're pursuing districting with the good of the neighborhood in mind.

Reframe: *How can we get past this politics of blame? Surely no good can come of it.*

We respond: *Honest people can honestly disagree over issues. You don't have to make it personal. As responsible citizens, we have a duty*

*to speak out on community issues. We're all united in that responsi-
bility even though we might differ on policy. We shouldn't let anyone
take advantage of it to drive us apart and mischaracterize what this
is all about.*

Isn't it interesting that those who are most vocal about splitting the
community are the least inclined to accept any community obligations
beyond the pursuit of their own desires? If they persist, tell them you
regret that they seem determined to go their own way, but that maybe
Churchill was right: "A world united is better than a world divided;
but a world divided is better than a world destroyed."

The truth is that property rightists are unsurpassed when it comes to
alienating neighbor from neighbor. Our job is to see to it that they end
up isolating themselves on the far edge of public opinion.

**3. They say: *These are wealthy, well-educated folks who look down on
the rest of us.***

This is a transparent but potent playing of the class card and possibly an opaquely ethnic gamble as well.

Direct answer: *I don't mind lies being told about me. That's politics. But I hate inaccuracy. The truth is, I'm not that rich.* [Alterna-
tively: I'm not that educated.]

Humor is always the best rejoinder to a scurrilous remark.

**4. They say: *Nobody elected these people. They've just appointed them-
selves to tell us what to do.***

We're the "taste police," "architectural Gestapo," "cultural tyrants,"
"preservation prigs"—insults so clever you might think they came
from a distaff version of Cole Porter's "You're the Tops!"

Reframe: *Why would anybody volunteer for this kind of personal
abuse?*

We respond: *Let me tell you, it takes a lot of fortitude to get up
and do this when you figure someone's going to attack your character.
But, you know what? Volunteerism—where ordinary folks like you and
me stand up and do extraordinary things—is part of what has made
this country great. If you're civic-minded and will join us, you'll see
what I mean. If not, nothing I can say will make you any happier.*

"The community screams and shouts about a lack of leadership,"
says former HPC chair Mary Cabell Eubanks in Greensboro, North
Carolina. "Then it screams at those who take leadership."[13]

5. *They say: These people can't be trusted with this kind of power!*

The district "could lead to a form of bullying," a critic contends.[14] We hear that we'll make homeowners "jump through hoops" but "let developers do whatever they want."[15] It gets worse. Maybe you don't know it, but alleged HPC intimidation of property owners is "the same device that has been used effectively in East Germany, in Hitler's Germany, and in other similar societies in Europe, Bolshevik Russia, Red China" and now, the fellow who wrote those words warns us, in Russells Mills, Massachusetts![16] Takes your breath away, doesn't it?

Direct answer: *I couldn't agree with you more. As James Madison said, "The truth is that all men having power ought to be mistrusted." But note: he didn't say that therefore no one should have power. When we do this thing, it's going to be done right. There will be the law that governs the HPC. There will be due process. And there will be all of us watching and participating. The active involvement of all is the best check on abuse by any. You're good to be cautious, but even better to be involved.*

More mundanely, point out that all HPC meetings will be open to the public, agendas posted, and commissioners nominated and approved by the City Council in open meetings. Explain that the HPC is not a lawmaking body, that it operates under rules of procedure, and that its decisions may be appealed. Note, too, that commissioners serve without compensation and recuse themselves in conflict-of-interest situations.

Remind Takers that the alternative is to leave development to wholly unelected "self-appointed" interests—often a financial and commercial elite—whose only responsibility is to their bottom line, not the community.

If you find yourself targeted by passionate property-rights extremists, our simple Q&A approach won't work. The next chapter is designed to show you how to detect them, stand your ground, and win points with the community.

NOTES

1. Nick Manes, "Controversial Historic Preservation Reform Bill 'Indefinitely Suspended,'" www.mibiz.com/item/23571, April 26, 2016. Italics added.

2. Dennis Hoey, "Maquoit Bay: Property Rights vs. Preservation," www.meepi.org, July 3, 2001.

3. Matt Neunke, "Historic Conflicts," home.comcast.net/~neoeugenics/ historical, n.d.

4. Callie Ginter, "Proposed Expansion of Keene Historic District Still Draws Criticism," www.sentinelsource.com, October 21, 2016.

5. Comment by "jefnvk" following Tom Perkin's, "'It's Absolutely Despicable,' Ypsilanti Council Member Says of Bill to Weaken Historic Districts," www.mlive.com, February 3, 2016.

6. Tim Freed, "Preservation Prevails in Winter Park," www.wpmobserver.com, December 17, 2015. Italics added.

7. Comment by "jvh679," following Tom Perkin's "'It's Absolutely Despicable'" the former citation is note 6.

8. Editorial, www.sentinelsource.com, October 30, 2016.

9. Martin Austermuhle, "Battle over a Capitol Hill Block Cools Off as Commission Rejects Historic District," www.wamu.org/news, October 14, 2016.

10. www.users.rcn.com/landgrab/summary, n.d.

11. Daniel Ruth, "The Risks of Naming Neighborhoods Historic," www.tampabay.com, April 2, 2015.

12. Jessica Farrar, "Politics in Practice," www.archvoices.org, 2004.

13. *Greensboro News and Record*, March 21, 2002.

14. Scott Merzbach, "Need for Local Historic Districts Debated in Amherst," www.gazettenet.com, April 6, 2015.

15. Ed Gunts, "Federal Hill Debates Whether to Become a City Historic District," www.baltimorebrew.com, February 15, 2016.

16. www.users.rcn.com/landgrab/summary, n.d.

Chapter Twenty-Four

Property-Rights Extremists

I was a lot more attractive when the evening began.

—Woody Allen, *Annie Hall*

"My home is my castle, not Kafka's," a neighbor says, rising to his feet and surprising us with wit.[1] Others chuckle. We prepare to listen. Will he speak to his concerns? Or will he take a hardwired view of rights to try to shut us down? If so, then we'll have to take him on.

Fair is fair. We preservationists know how to cling to rigid views and lose. Why should we keep all of life's punishing lessons to ourselves?

EPISTLE TO YOUR QUALMS

Does that make you uneasy? Maybe you think it is uncivil to go after folks who say they care about their rights. I get it. Maybe you're afraid of taking your own side in a fight.

So here's a note to you. If you yourself are not engaged in a campaign right now but, perhaps, reading this for class, then suspend your qualms. I'm not offering this up for your considered judgment. I'm writing for folks in a real-time contest where they have to seal the deal.

This isn't about social forms of tolerance or a pretense of agnosticism about the truth of basic things. We're talking politics, where one side wins and the other loses.

If you are campaigning and you want to be respectful, then you should respect those who stand with you by winning. There are many others who need you to win but do not know it yet. Respect them by drawing out your opponents to show them the alternative. Then respect your opposition by treating their views seriously enough to isolate and defeat them.

Let's be clear. We're not opposing property rights. I hold them dear myself, don't you? I doubt anyone will be changing their views on rights themselves. We don't even need them to. We're out to alter the way they think about the *exercise* of rights we plan to leave intact.

You and I have worked through the internal conflict in ourselves between our rights and our community responsibilities, or else we wouldn't be here. All we are doing is helping Takers to decide the issue for themselves—and when they do, to break our way.

For that we need a wedge, and to know it when we see it.

COUNTERFACTUAL AGGRESSION

If you're lucky, it will be handed to you on a platter. There is no greater gift to a districting campaign than extremism in defense of rights and a pronounced distrust of government.

I don't mean by folks *in extremis*, upset with us for pushing them to think beyond their rights. No, I mean the aggressive use by some of fake "facts" to discredit us while dismissing the real-life world of our experience with rights and with legitimate self-government.

We *want* extremist types to rush at us for being Kafkaesque, because it's like in judo. An opponent charging with abandon is more easily thrown. And no one is more politically reckless than the acolyte who quickens to the distant yoo-hoo of radical ideology.

OTHER-WORLDLY TYPES

An ideology is more, and worse, than a set of held beliefs. In the field of political theory, ideologies are always meant to describe *alternative realities*. The greater their disconnection from our experiential world, the more radical they are. The greatest disconnect occurs when they are born of willful ignorance. A Turkish proverb holds that we should "fear an ignorant man more than a lion." And that is what we're dealing with.

For example: When we say districting is about making good community choices, we're told we're "idiots" not to see that "we're talking about . . . property, so anyone with a half of brain [sic] would understand that it's clearly a property rights issue."[2]

The author of that online claim should like this from another: "Historic preservation does not involve conflicts between property 'rights' and 'responsibilities.' There is never such a conflict. People have property rights and everyone's responsibility is not to violate those rights."[3]

See what I mean? The alternative mental world these folks inhabit is one in which *any* talk of property is *only* talk of rights, where rights are absolute and free from responsibilities attaching to their exercise. But you and I know better, and it's not because we're stupid. We talk the way *real people* do concretely, about property rights as interpreted by courts, and about the constitutional authority of local government to set responsible conditions for their use.

A third example from another other-worldly critic: "It boils down to your right as an American to do what you want to with what you pay for."[4]

Really? Money changing hands is the origin of rights? If you paid a penny for that thought you'd have to ask for change. Our country's Founders never uttered such, and it isn't in the Constitution. You can almost hear them say, "Pure piffle!"

All these claims are bunk. Yet saying so won't faze the self-willed ignoramuses who claim them. They inhabit the "post-truth" world of today's political climate in which, as Scottie Nell Hughes has said, "there's no such thing, unfortunately, anymore, [as] facts."[5]

In her reading of our times, something called narrative truth is said to have overtaken factual truth. The facts of a claim are less important than *who believes* the story at its core, if only emotionally. And that's what extremists prey on: the tender feelings and raw emotions on exhibit in our public meetings. In terms of facts, they are lying for effect.

OUR COMMONSENSE DEFENSE

How should we respond? We need to take extremists *seriously*, not *literally*, in Salena Zito's celebrated phrase.[6] We need to discredit them in our neighbors' eyes as hostile to their interests.

This shouldn't be too difficult. Our districting campaign would not send our opponents into paroxysms if our neighbors did not appreciate the availability of the political process to protect what they value from predation and the whims of others. That's why law exists. And that's why we have to show these extremists as having pushed beyond our nation's founding faith in *liberty under law* to a subversive *license to disparage law*, doing as they please and pleasing no one but themselves.

You'll have one sharp point to make to prick your neighbors' commonsense: These self-avowed defenders of blatant falsehoods about the constitutional relationship between people and their property are, at bottom, *indistinguishable from those strong-willed and self-absorbed individuals who, true to type in every community, simply don't like being told what to do.*

Still, there is a broadly populist subtext to their counterfactual views, a real-world fact that extremists prey on, too. It is today's kneejerk deep distrust of government, which brings us back to Kafka.

DRIVING HOME THE WEDGE

Franz Kafka's *The Castle* has entered the imagination as his central character's struggle with bureaucracy for recognition and respect, though he never stood a chance.[7] No doubt our critics feel besieged by our proposal to increase the role of local government in their lives.

But we don't live amid the ruins of the old Austro-Hungarian Empire where Kafka died with the book unfinished in 1924. So I think we can give it a happy, New World ending in challenging such views.

Let's do it in the format of our community meeting Q&A. You've already heard bits of this in the last chapter. As they worked for us back then, so they will again.

Breakers have already pronounced their extremist takes on rights. Assume we've already instructed them on Supreme Court decisions.

They'll say that they reject those decisions. See? This is their alternative reality. They are setting themselves up as independent arbiters of what is constitutional instead of recognizing the 1803 pivotal precedent set in the case of *Marbury v. Madison* that established the Supreme Court as the final arbiter of the constitutionality of law.

We'll say that nothing regarding rights stands between us and designating our historic district. We are pushing them to declare against the interests of community.

They'll say, if they're smart and quick, that nothing says we have to have the district. If they don't, we'll have to say it for them: "Or are you just against it. If so, why, besides your take on rights?"

The dialogue unfolds from there:

1. They say: *We should be taking back our government instead of giving the bureaucracy more power!*

That is, to oppress the citizenry and take away their rights. This taps into a widespread sense that distant, high-handed, and unelected decision makers have wielded too much power.

Reframe: *Why are you rooting against your neighbors?*

We respond: *The Supreme Court says you're wrong on rights. And you're wrong to try to get us to believe that property rights trump our* political rights *to do good things for our community through districting. The fact is, our historic district will give us leverage at City Hall. You say you're on your neighbors' side. But are you really ready to disempower them just to suit yourselves?*

We'll say it without rancor, yet press them hard to declare themselves as trapped by their own doctrine. We'll tell them we simply cannot understand how they can put their own biases ahead of our community.

2. They say: *It comes down to my personal philosophy and the role of government.*

With *that* we will thoughtfully nod.

Reframe: *I'm sure it is*—for you—*and thank you for saying you don't expect us to agree.*

Our response: *For us, where we stand, it's about* people, *your neighbors not philosophy, what they care about, what they hope for, and real results for them and for their families. So we appreciate your telling us what we* can't do. *But we've got real-world issues here that need* can-do *leadership and action and the community's support behind us.*

We've slipped this like a wedge between ourselves and the community. And now we'll drive it home for undecided Takers by taking the initiative.

We say: *You know, it occurs to us there's enough* mutual trust and goodwill *here to make our district possible, and enough*—we'll shrug and smile to Takers—*well, you know, of the* other sort of attitude *to make it well-advised. I think we're up to it, don't you?*

If your strike rings true, the community should split your way. If it's still only moving in your direction, there's one sure bet. Our Kafka-citing opposition won't look as good going out as at the beginning of the evening.

But keep in mind that none of this will mean a thing when you get to City Hall if it doesn't put signatures on your petition.

NOTES

1. This is a paraphrase of an actual comment that impressed me long before I undertook to write. The reference lies in some unremembered local newspaper archive in the ether of the Internet.

2. Comment by "jvh679" following Tom Perkin's, "'It's Absolutely Despicable,' Ypsilanti Council Member Says of Bill to Weaken Historic Districts," www.mlive.com, February 3, 2016.

3. Rex Curry, rexy.net, n.d.

4. Kevin Duffy, "History a Matter of Heart in Newnan," www.ajc.com, June 9, 2003.

5. Margaret Sullivan, "For Trump's Inner Circle, a World Free of Facts," *The Washington Post*, December 5, 2016, pp. 1, 3.

6. Selena Zito, "Taking Trump Literally, Not Seriously," *The Atlantic*, September 23, 2016. www.theatlantic.com/politics/archive/2016/09/trump-makes-his-case-in-pittsburgh.

7. See William Burrows, "Winter Read: The Castle by Franz Kafka," www.the-guardian.com/books/2011/dec/22/franz-kafka-winter-reads, December 22, 2011.

Chapter Twenty-Five

Petition Politics

How do I love thee? Let me count the ways.

—Elizabeth Barrett Browning, *Sonnets from the Portuguese*

Like Ms. Browning's love, sooner or later our wooing of community support comes down to number crunching. But what's the magic number that will sway the City Council? How is it derived? Well, given the great diversity around the country, that is hard to say. Examples:

- Brighton, Colorado, requires 51 percent property-owner consent by petition before either the HPC or City Council may consider districting.[1]
- Marietta, Georgia, requires 60 percent property-owner consent by HPC-generated mail-in ballot—one vote per eligible property, with unreturned ballots counted as "no"—after City Council approval of design guidelines.[2]
- St. Petersburg, Florida, sets the bar at 66.6 percent owner-consent via mail-in ballot for HPC, Planning Commission, and City Council review, with the many unresponsive absentee landlords counted as "no."[3]

In an extraordinary reversal of the pattern, Sioux Falls, Idaho, property owners received a mail-in ballot requiring no action for "yes," while "no" votes had to be notarized! Opponent Joe Hurly took a notary door-to-door, "We played their crooked game and we beat them at it," he crowed.[4]

There's an acronym for what he did. If you want to win, then GOYAKOB: "Get Off Your A** and Knock On Doors." Sitting back and letting the City run the show is your line of least resistance, but with great potential pain. The next simplest is your basic catch-as-catch-can sampling of support on sign-up sheets with hastily jotted addresses. But believe this: When you walk into decision-making hearings, you will wish you had an iron-clad petition of your own devising in your pocket. That makes what follows common to us all, regardless of local requirements or customary ways of doing things.

PROBLEMS OF MAIL-IN BALLOTING

Let's dispense with the common mail-in ballot as a favored way to go, even though it's often prescribed by ordinance. The downsides are so obvious I wonder why it's ever used. The City's over-worked planning staff should appreciate why we'll be conducting our own independent effort. Why? Because of the uncertainties of mail-in ballots:

1. We don't know if their owner-address database is precisely co-extensive with the district. Nor can we be certain that it is accurate and up-to-date with changes in our map and real-time ownership of properties, given partnership changes, marriages, divorces, and deaths. Conceivably, a recently deceased loved one may be counted as voting "no" in Marietta or St. Pete, or "yes" in Sioux City.
2. We can't be assured to our satisfaction that their methodology will fairly count multiple owners of single properties, a single owner of multiple properties, and record diversity of opinion among common owners of properties.
3. No one short on time and without a vested interest in the outcome will be as painstakingly diligent as we should like in addressing, sending out, following up, receiving, verifying, securing, collating, and then compiling ballots in an accurate and usable list delivered in a timely fashion to all decision-making authorities.
4. Mailed surveys are notoriously unreliable indicators of opinion since they also reflect such bad habits as not reading mail and procrastinating. The late Andy Rooney once said on *60 Minutes* that he routinely threw away any mail that began with "Dear Property Owner."
5. Mailings don't afford us an opportunity to engage each and every owner of a parcel as they vote. An *opponent* in Washington, D.C., says, "Getting people engaged . . . is hard, and some folks are scared to sign anything."[5] *We* know that folks will more quickly vote "no" in privacy—hiding behind an unreturned ballot—than face-to-face.
6. Will we have access to the ballots to review them to draw our own politically significant conclusions? If unreturned ballots are counted "no," as in Boynton Beach, Florida,[6] will they be reported as "unreturned" as well? That can make all the difference between victory and defeat if the vote is

close and our opponents have received a presumptive advantage by the methodology. The same goes for resident versus nonresident owners under similar circumstances. Unless we conduct our own petition, we'll be deprived of key strategic information.

Is that enough incentive for you? If not, then imagine that it is for your opponents. They can always enter hearings with their own petition survey. So how do you assure your own petition can't be bettered?

WHO GETS POLLED?

Property owners, obviously, in a clean and persuasive petition, mandated or not. No renters, no leaseholders, no live-in relatives, no store managers, no employees, no friends, no named heirs, no anonymous curbside passersby. Nothing but property owners, period, unless the City directs us otherwise.

DRAFTING YOUR PETITION

Do it defensively, imagining how your opponents might attack it. You can never be too careful.

1. **Top of the page:** What are you asking people to agree to? Be sure the petition says what you want it to say so there can be no misunderstanding. Brevity is good, but clarity is better. Don't just write a heading that says "We support the Historic District." That's vague and arguably misleading:

   - It doesn't identify who "we" are and why "we" have a stake in the district.
   - It doesn't define what "support" means.
   - It doesn't clearly convey that signers know what they're supporting.

While you consider that for a moment, let's look at how you'll handle signatures.

2. **Constructing the list of owners:** When was the last time you signed a petition? Did someone outside the grocery store hand you a clipboard with some statement at the top? Were you asked to sign on the next line? In Durham, a mass petition to exempt twenty properties for a rescue mission's plans pulled in some 2,500 signatures.[7]

Well, we can't afford to be that informal. Yet even door-to-door petitioning isn't as simple as it seems.

Suppose Tom Brown all by himself owns three parcels of land in the district: a Victorian house, a vacant lot, and an apartment building. What property is he thinking about when he signs his approval on his front steps? What if he later says he was thinking about his home, not the buildable lot and other investment property?

Now suppose Mary and Bob Smith live in an older home. He signs the petition, and later she signs on another sheet. Do they count twice as much as Tom? How do you know they own the same property instead of two or more, or whether they own them jointly or separately?

See what I mean? Our opponents will see it, and they'll say our petition can't be trusted. Any lack of clarity and rigor in our methodology is an invitation to trouble.

Our solution is to list each property in the district by its official parcel number with signature lines for all recorded owners no matter how many times they'll have to sign. Their mailing addresses should be listed with their names, along with contact information for verifying signatures.

Do not provide places for owners to check "yes" or "no." Don't share your petition forms with anyone. You'll end up doing your opponent's work for them.

Page 152 shows a sample petition page that gets the heading and listing right and is easy to use. Repeat the declaration at the top of every page, or signers may later claim they didn't see it. Now look at it.

Who are Tom Brown and Mary and Bob Smith that they should appear at the start of our petition? When you hand folks a clipboard, you want them to see right away that they'll be joining a prestigious and growing group. Let's say you've got fifteen parcels listed on the first two pages. Make sure they're owned by well-known and respected supporters from every major constituency group in the district.

Get all of them to sign before you go to the wider public. Skeptical eyes will be drawn to any gap in signatures. A solid phalanx of signatures says that the district is a good idea and well on its way to success. People want to be seen with winners.

But then how do you list the rest of the property owners? Alphabetically or by street address, for signing convenience. No one is going to care that the initial dozen or so names are out of order.

3. **Unilateral exclusions:** There are sound political reasons for leaving some owners alone. How about the local church? Talk about "dividing the community!" What about a congregation? Don't give your opponents that

PROPOSED [NAME] HISTORIC DISTRICT PETITION

We, the undersigned owners of properties contained within the boundaries of the proposed Historic District, do hereby request that our property be included in the district, to be administered under the City zoning ordinance [number]. I have been informed about historic district designation and understand how it will affect my property.

PROPERTY OWNERS IN FAVOR OF
ESTABLISHING THE LOCAL HISTORIC DISTRICT

Name/Address	Parcel No.	Signature(s)	Date
1. ROBERT SMITH	1606-273-1	_____	_____
MARY SMITH 26 Market Street City, State, Zip Code (555) 213-4567		_____	_____
2. THOMAS BROWN 564 Hill Lane City, State, Zip Code (555) 213-8901	1606-273-36	_____	_____
3. THOMAS BROWN 564 Hill Lane City, State, Zip Code (555) 213-8901	1606-273-47	_____	_____

PARCELS EXCLUDED AS COMMUNITY-WIDE INSTITUTIONS

178. SWIM CLUB   1606-273-89   <u>EXCLUDED</u> _____
20 H Street
City, State, Zip Code (555) 213-3334

ammunition. Unilaterally declare such communal places out of bounds rather than embroil them in controversy. Notify their owners with an explanation and list each parcel at the end. Explain your rationale in the executive summary you'll be sending to the City Council. If pushed, count exclusions as opposed to underscore your goodwill.

SECURING SIGNATURES

By "securing" I mean both *collecting signatures* and *keeping the originals safe*. Ideally, original signatures will be in blue ink for dependable credibility.

Don't use electronic devices that can crash, be lost, hacked, shared, manipulated, or derided for unintelligible signature scrawls. Cyber petitions—where signing is done online—are a recent and not yet generally accepted substitute for hardcopy signatures. So be careful if you're thinking that way, and clear it with City Hall and get approval in writing.

Give copies of your blank survey forms to trusted canvassers. Make sure they know not to let anyone sign for anyone else—even a spouse—unless there is good reason, and then record that reason.

Remind canvassers that, with respect to property, "leaning" counts only in Pisa. We can't go to the Planning Commission, for instance, and say we have 38 percent for the district and 15 percent leaning "yes." That will only draw attention to *why* some are hesitating.

What do we do if property owners live at a distance? We talk to them by phone and then send them copies of their signature pages to return in our self-addressed, stamped envelope. Use electronic signature only in time pinches. And if we can't catch some of our neighbors at home? District activist Barbara Fite says she made many trips from Norman to Oklahoma City to reach commuters during working hours when other efforts failed. She didn't quit till her side garnered 78 percent support![8]

Now, retain every page having an original signature on it. In the end you might have scores of original signature sheets to submit as part of the formal record. Photo copy them and then use those copies to cut and paste a final master petition that duplicates your original petition exactly. Do not remove unsigned lines. That goes to your credibility, too.

DECLARATIONS OF NEUTRALITY

There's always the chance you'll run into a few folks who just won't take sides. They're like the old Southern politician who, when asked where he stood on an issue, said, "Some of mah friends are fer it and some of mah friends are agin' it, and Ah'm fer mah friends." Get them to sign anyway as "neutral." That way, if they show up on your opponents' side you can call a foul on y'all's friend.

SUBMITTING THE PETITION

When should you submit the petition? It depends on your jurisdiction. A few cities like Brighton, Colorado, require a majority just to get the proposal on the HPC's agenda. Many don't require a petition at all. Common practice has the petition filed prior to City Council meetings. Just don't wait to make it available to the Council *at* the hearing. It won't be credible because it can't be verified.

So check with City Hall. But when filing time comes, make last-minute amendments for any intervening deaths, divorces, property transfers, or changes in the proposed district's physical borders. A typical petition takes a year or more to complete. Make sure you know everyone who must or should receive a copy, how it's to be delivered, and when. Attach your bare-bones executive summary defining your methodology. Show your final tallies.

So how do you derive them?

COUNTING AND WEIGHING SUPPORT

"How do I count thee?" Ms. Browning might ask if she managed our petition. "Let me love the ways." Let me give you some examples using table 25.1.

Table 25.1.

	For		*Against*
J. Stringfellow	4 Parcels (.5 acres each)	G. Farmer M. Farmer R. Farmer A. Farmer	1 acre 2 acres

How do we count them? One in favor of designation and four opposed? Or is it four in favor and one opposed? Obviously that depends on whether we're counting people or parcels. Here's why:

1. **Counting people:** In favor of counting people is the basic idea of "one person, one vote." In fact, we're usually asked, "How many people support your proposal?" Yet not all folks own equal shares.

   So we have another choice: Do we count each name equally? Or do we count multiple owners of a parcel fractionally? If we don't count them fractionally, then how do we deal with jointly owning couples of single properties who differ on districting?

2. **Counting parcels:** In favor of parcels is the fact that districting designates properties, not owners. But why do we assume all parcels are created equal? In Newton, Massachusetts, in 2002, a designation was resisted by Lasell College, which owned two-thirds of the property in the district. In 2004, Virginia considered adding 172 private parcels to the historic district covering the Manassas National Battlefield Park. Each parcel was assigned one vote, regardless of its size or number of owners. A county supervisor called that unfair, since a large farm could be forced into the district by a few small landholders. And consider what would happen if someone—an opponent, say, in our proposed district—were to subdivide a single large tract into several parcels in the midst of our campaign?

3. **Counting acreage:** So should we be calculating acreage and assigning proportional weight accordingly? The acreage estimates in our sample chart with J. Stringfellow and the multiple Farmers are a total wash, two acres for and two acres against. Yet given the litigiousness of some battles, do you want to defend estimates? Only if the results aren't even close and favor your side.

And that raises our biggest question: which method is going to give us the best statistical showing? So get the petition finished first. Then we'll decide how to count the yeas and nays. The word for this kind of statistical shopping is—politics!

THE MAGIC NUMBER

So don't—repeat: *do not!*—ask the City Council *who* or *what* and *how* you should count results if there is not an officially established method. You'll just confuse them. Or if you're really unlucky some bright so-and-so might stack the methodology against you for political reasons.

If there is an official methodology, follow it, as long as you have been assured it will be recognized by all decision makers. Then ignore it and do your own comparison counts. In the end, all methods are equally fudgy. Wasn't it Mark Twain who said there are lies, damn lies, and statistics?

Remember: *nothing* is ever certain or final in politics. Elected officials can still vote for or against you for any reasons they choose. They should respect you for your statistical savvy. They've built their careers on slicing and dicing numbers, too!

So in the end, regardless of stated targets, the magic number you have to reach is any number that they'll start quoting in your favor.

NOTES

1. Crystal Nelson, "Downtown Brighton Could Become Historic District," www.thebrightonblade.com, May 4, 2016.

2. Anthony White, "Residents Approve Church-Cherokee Historic District," www.mdjonline.com, May 31, 2016.

3. Daniel Ruth, "The Risks of Naming Neighborhoods Historic," www.tampabay.com, April 2, 2015.

4. Angela Kennecke, "Neighbors Fight Effort to Turn Area into Historic District & Win," www.keloland.com, December 11, 2015.

5. Martin Austermuhle, "Battle over a Capitol Hill Block Cools off as Commission Rejects Historic District," www.wamu.org," October 14, 2016.

6. Attivya Anthony, "Boynton Beach's Attempt to Create a Historic District Fails," www.sun-sentinel.com, August 4, 2016.

7. Virginia Bridges, "Homeowners, Durham Rescue Mission at Odds over Historic District," www.newsobserver.com, August 31, 2016.

8. Joy Hampton, "Newest Historic District Took Grass Roots Effort," www.normantranscript.com, October 10, 2016.

Chapter Twenty-Six

Reaching Out to the Opposition

There's only you and me and we just disagree.

—Jim Krueger, "We Just Disagree"

It's very difficult to go talk with folks who may have publicly reviled us. Still, we have to do it and *be seen* doing it without apportioning blame. No good guys, no bad guys. It's enough that we disagree. Both sides want to win. Neither has a primary interest in making peace.

But decision makers down at City Hall will ask if we've been willing to talk with the other side apart from shouting matches. From this angle, outreach is damage control.

That's for appearance's sake. Yet there are substantive advantages as well. Small compromises now can save big compromises later. And talks may help us thin our opponents' ranks.

A CALIBRATED DIPLOMACY

Our opposition is neither monolithic nor static. We have a vision and they have objections, and those objections will vary from person to person and over time.

So we need a nuanced, calibrated approach. Direct talks can help us better understand what each property owner wants. We may also be able to correct misperceptions, establish a measure of trust, make targeted offers, and split off some opponents from the diehards.

As for the rest, they simply have differing worldviews. We argue it round and they argue it flat. The best we can do is agree to disagree. But it's never really that nice.

NEGOTIATING

Outreach entails the possibility of compromise, and that means you have to think like a negotiator. The skills you'll need are more akin to those of a manager, composing differences to move forward, than those of a visionary leader setting the mark.

There are plenty of books out there on the art of negotiation. They tell you about styles—competitive versus collaborative, combative versus passive, good cop and bad cop, dos and don'ts, and even how to control your body language.

But never mind all that. Ours is a one-shot deal, not a career. At our neighborhood level, it's most important just to talk and listen. Still it helps to bear in mind three hard-and-fast rules:

- Never negotiate out of weakness.
- Never compromise vital interests.
- Be prepared.

Keep notes on specific points opponents make. Talk within your steering committee about where concessions might be made and then prioritize them. Work out fallback positions. Be clear about what is to be negotiated. Define the issues, get the facts. Think in terms of ambiguity to paper over differences. And make sure everybody on our side is onboard before sealing a deal with the opposition. We're out to thin *their* ranks, not ours!

THREE VENUES

There are three types of face-to-face meetings:

1. **Individual:** One-on-one talks are best for minor opponents who aren't leaders, who have their own issues, and who don't want to be associated with loudmouthed, abusive resisters. We can respect their differences and help them to a kind of useful neutrality.
2. **Group:** For meetings with opposition leaders in a mutually comfortable setting, make sure you are clear about their authority to speak on behalf of absentees.
3. **Community:** A community-wide meeting moderated by a mutually acceptable facilitator assures elected officials that no one has been excluded or denied a voice in community forums. They will welcome this unforced contribution to substantive due process.

Be careful, though. Do not accept *arbitration*, which means a binding settlement or judgment by an independent third party. We're talking about *mediation* here, where the facilitator helps the sides exchange views and keeps them on track.

Screen proposed moderators carefully, for some may see themselves as professional peacemakers. They may think that the goal of all politics is consensus at any price—even at the frustration of good public policy. The last thing we want is for a mediator to start finger-pointing if we're the stronger party. But a fair and balanced final report by an independent mediator that attests to our good faith effort can clear the way to a decisive Council vote.

KEEP RECORDS

Keep track of all letters, phone calls, and meetings with opponents. Note who was contacted, what was discussed, when it occurred, and where it took place. Put offers of concession in writing and always frame them in terms of strengths not weaknesses. Never say you find value in an opponent's position, sympathize with their concerns, or feel their pain—even if you do. They will turn it against you.

Get all agreements in writing and, if you can pull it off, signed by all participants. Consider it insurance against later misunderstandings. Otherwise, the safest way to proceed, politically, is to assume everyone is hiding something.

PROTECT YOUR BASE

As you continue to talk with opponents, don't take your supporters for granted. Do not water down the district to the point where it becomes:

- Inconsequential.
- A burden on property owners without real benefit.
- A benefit to property owners without serving preservation interests.

The more things you concede the greater will be the potential threat to your leadership. On the other hand, solid progress can come as a relief to anyone who has reluctantly stood with us.

So keep your base well-informed. There might not be any truly bad guys around, but there are good guys for certain. We need to be most careful of their interests and keep them close.

Part IV

MANAGING THE FORMAL
DESIGNATION PROCESS

Chapter Twenty-Seven

Moving on to City Hall: Preparing for Commission Hearings

Our similarities are different.

—Dale Berra on his father, Yogi

We've done it all.

We've learned to strategize. We've looked around our neighborhood, read the lay of the political landscape and crafted a practical vision. We've gained confidence and public support in community meetings. We've brought forth a vital sense of community in the midst of continuing conflict over districting.

Now we've got to do it all again, but differently. It's time for us to take our show on the road and win the day at City Hall.

Keep in mind that we are using our Wilmington model where we have a three-stage approval process starting with a HPC and Planning Commission ending with the City Council. In what follows, I will be introducing mayors and city managers into the mix.

Our task now is to translate our community successes into votes for designation in public hearings. We'll prepare in stages, starting with the appointive commissions and understanding the constraints under which we testify.

DUE PROCESS

First, let's consider those constraints. As we do, bear in mind that they will be applicable also before our City Council.

In all three public forums we'll be dealing with people who have interests and responsibilities different from those we've encountered in our community meetings. The public hearing format will be different, too.

163

We will no longer be in charge of setting meeting agendas and managing discussions. In fact, there will probably be no interplay at all between those for and against districting—just separate presentations from the floor.

That's because we're getting *procedural due process* and nothing more. This is our constitutional right to be notified of an impending action and be heard on it. But once the meeting is gaveled to order, the give-and-take between citizens and public officials is mainly a one-way street. We give testimony, and they take it. What they do with it is up to them.

So what will we tell them, and how will we say it? We don't want to be like the cuckoo in Shakespeare's *Henry IV*, "Heard, not regarded."

Do we tell them why we want a historic district? Yes, by all means. And our opponents will say they don't want it. So how will decision makers decide the issue?

The answer depends on what commissioners bring with them to the hearings. So it's a good idea to do whatever we can *now* to influence their preparation. If you agree with me—and I'm sure you do—then we ought to think about a strategy for working with the planners who act as HPC and Planning Commission staff.

ACTING THE LEADER

Do you remember the first time we walked into the Planning Department to ask about districting? We represented only ourselves and a few others then.

Things have changed. Now you speak for a large portion of our community. You've attained the stature of a recognized leader. You've kept planners informed of your progress. They've been invited to attend our local meetings. They've watched you gain popular support for designation. Your success should make you their dependable partner.

So what does it get us? Can we parlay our status into an advantage?

That is a delicate question. Planning staff will be—as they should be—protective of their prerogatives and responsibilities. We don't want to compromise their standing with decision makers. And we certainly have no interest in jeopardizing their willingness to work with us.

But by now they also have a professional stake in our success. They've been working on the official side of the designation process. They've put together the districting proposal, shepherded the study through SHPO and worked on the text of the legislation to be approved. They have coordinated the Planning Department's effort and probably brought it to the attention of the City Manager and other administrators.

It's in our interests to work collaboratively together from here on out. Yet we want to avoid the appearance of improper collusion. What we ask of staff has to be within the scope of their legitimate functions. Our main interest is seeing that commissioners are well informed about the district proposal and their role in recommending it to the Council.

We also need to guard against procedural glitches or irregularities. If you live in a town where overworked staff could use some help, you might act as de facto project manager, keeping track of everything that has to be done, by whom and when. But no matter where you are, I suggest you get staff to help you put together two "maps" for your own benefit:

1. An organizational chart of every City office—with personnel appended—that will be involved in designation.
2. A flowchart of the approval process down to the last detail of who signs off on what and when, with drop-dead dates for submissions highlighted.

The simple act of putting them together can be a useful exercise even for planning staff who have done it all before.

Check from time to time to see that everyone is on track, signing off on every detail, scheduling every meeting, meeting every deadline. Do it with a light touch, though. Treat everyone with courtesy and respect. Make regular friendly visits to the Planning Department. Don't take doughnuts: those will be a bribe in the eyes of an opponent who sees you do it.

Offer assistance. Many departments don't have a preservationist on staff. Your own specialist might contribute to the background information packets that should go to commissioners. But make certain that there's a firewall up between what is done for you and for the City, one that can sustain reasonable scrutiny about a conflict of interests.

DEVELOPING BRIEFING PACKETS

While I'm on the subject, we should be preparing to send our own information to commissioners. But there is a difference between what we mail out and what staff provides.

The Planning Department's packets should contain *documents* and *factual materials*: copies of the draft legislation, the district map and survey study summary, the criteria by which the district was drawn, perhaps a compilation of relevant court decisions, and any number of brief statements on such technical matters as what a "zoning overlay district" means and how design guidelines function.

Whatever isn't covered by the Planning Department will have to be added to our own packets. Avoid overlap and anything at variance with their information.

If you're able to contribute, do what you can to make their information packet *brief* to invite reading and *comprehensive* to be sufficient. Be deliberative. Don't just think "guidelines!" and toss some photocopied pamphlet into the mix. Find the best source to define and convey what guidelines are. Edit or summarize it. Don't expect commissioners to wade through more than what is absolutely on point. They'll just lay it aside.

Our own packets should make our *political points* in a brief and common-sensical format. But how can we know which points to hit?

PROFILING COMMISSIONERS

We'll first need to know everything political about anyone who is going to weigh in on designation. If you haven't found a political insider as I suggested in chapter 8, then you'll have to do your own spadework.

Start with the HPC. Ask staff about the chair and other commissioners. They may be reticent until you explain that you're not asking them to reveal confidential information.

- How do they see the commission functioning in public session?
- Who takes the lead in discussions?
- Are there policy or personality cliques?
- Who tends to agree with whom?
- Are there any outstanding issues that regularly arise—say, of a budgetary, personnel, or program priority nature—that can affect our interests?

Next, cross-reference what you've heard with a former commissioner or two if you can. A local preservation organization that's taken an active role in commission proceedings can be a good source of independent insights. The same thing goes for architects or contractors who've made regular appearances.

Analyze HPC minutes for the last year or so. Check your local newspaper archive for informative stories. While you're at it, pay attention to bylines. We're going to be looking for a reporter in chapter 29.

Put together a political profile of each member and double check their terms of office. Someone might cycle off the HPC before you get there.

Now do the same thing all over again for the Planning Commission.

Once you've researched the book on them, go see the movie. Attend as many HPC and Planning Commission meetings as you can squeeze in. You might not learn much new, but you'll start getting comfortable with the setup.

And keep your mouth shut! Resist speaking out and messing things up. Your dog's in no one's fight but ours.

Now that we've established our presence in City Hall and gathered passive intelligence, we're ready to move over to a more active role. Next we'll be working behind the scenes to develop the information we need for plotting the next stages.

Chapter Twenty-Eight

Behind-the-Scenes Intelligence

All rising to a great place is by a winding stair.

—Francis Bacon

Now to the obvious question: Why don't we just go and talk with each commissioner face-to-face? Your local jurisdiction might not permit direct, so-called *ex parte*, contacts outside of advertised meetings. Normally, that's the case when commissions are acting on permit applications.

But our situation is different, isn't it? The district proposal also isn't ours, technically. The Planning Department is bringing the proposal forward, albeit on our initiative. We are supporting new legislation, not asking if a project conforms to existing laws.

So get a ruling from the City Attorney or your local ethics commission. Make sure everyone knows the answer. We want our opponents playing by the same rules and no misinformed accusations flying about.

If you *can* meet one-on-one, show them what you're made of. A private meeting is in a class of its own when it comes to taking another person's measure—theirs and *yours*.

Don't go in expecting straight talk. You might get it, but private citizens serving on commissions tend to be less open than elected officials who are used to talking about legislation. To discover what they're really thinking, we want to draw them out with their guard down. Just like in chess, we'll try to catch them looking the other way.

A PROCEDURAL GAMBIT

Anecdotal evidence—but a ton of it—suggests it's the rare member of any commission who has ever read through its enabling ordinance and rules of procedure. But *you* ought to read them. Then open your gambit by asking planning staffers to explain to you specifically how the commissions will function in the designation process.

That innocent question might get you a blank stare. Why? Because our kind of hearing is unusual in most localities. Even staffers might not have thought about it much.

Appointed commissions mainly *interpret and apply existing ordinances* to applications that come before them. Most have little experience in *advising on making laws*, and practically no institutional memory from case to case apart from long-serving staff. Each sitting board tends to make up its own interpretation on the fly—and does so for better or worse.

Commissioners just can't seem to resist acting like policy makers, not advisors. Instead of passing on how the district will affect preservation and planning, they'll presume to decide what's good for the community by their own lights. Take this, for example, from a Planning Board chair talking about the opposition:

I don't blame them. I wouldn't want my house in a historic district either. It's another layer of bureaucracy. I'm not dead set against it. But the more I think about it the more I am. It's ridiculous to have to get a permit to [replace] porch flooring. . . . Just think if they had that mentality of not wanting change back when they started putting bathrooms inside houses. If you wanted to keep everything like it is, we'd still be using outhouses.[1]

This is risky business, from our perspective.

Never mind his house isn't in our neighborhood; that even as a commissioner he's unwilling to consider community interests beyond his front porch; that there isn't the slightest inkling here of an understanding of what it means to be a neighbor; and that he hasn't been present at the meetings where we've convinced many of our neighbors differently. It's enough that he seems to think he is allowed to step into the shoes of an anonymous homeowner in the district and, unlike the rest of us, be able to vote a commission position—and vote his prejudices.

So our next move is to ask staffers to give each commission an up-to-date briefing on its *advisory role* in the process, detailing the scope of what they're to cover and what the City Council is looking for in their recommendations.

How the briefing takes place is unimportant. It might be at an administrative meeting or special workshop. Leave it up to them. Just don't settle for a briefing by memo. If you encounter resistance, point out that it'll also be an excellent opportunity to walk commissioners through the documentary and technical materials they'll be receiving.

In fact, insist upon it. This will test your relationship with staff. But if there is ever a place to test it, *this is it.*

Experienced staffers are well aware of how routinely commissioners come to meetings well-intentioned yet less than adequately prepared—and then turn around and blame staffers for their own mistakes. Staffers should jump at the chance to cover their bases.

Besides, we have a right to a fair and proper hearing. Testifying before ill-informed commissioners is like striking matches on soap.

AN UNGUARDED WINDOW

Our angle is simple. Any effort to set commissioners straight should get them to reveal their current thinking.

How? Staffers have to prepare for the briefing. Don't you think they'd benefit from getting each commissioner to send in questions or comments in advance? Nothing particularly well-informed, you know, just whatever comes to mind.

And why not? It makes staffers look solicitous and responsive. It's protection, too. They can't very well be blamed for giving the commission what it requests. It will also insure them against surprise questions in public, especially ones that put them in a bad light.

These submissions will be as unguarded a window as we're likely to get into commissioners' attitudes toward districting. And that, my friend, is invaluable intelligence.

Whatever they submit will be a matter of public record. If a staffer is uncomfortable sharing it, then suggest they compile the responses in a memorandum for the commission and make it available for public review. Still, do your best to find out *who* is asking *what* questions.

I have one such memo from a planning commissioner. In summary, he asked:

1. Has the process been tainted and biased by proponents and planning staffers?
2. Has the public been provided copies of all relevant statutes and policies?
3. Can individual owners ask to be excluded under existing state and local law?

4. What criteria determine historic significance?
5. Who determines the boundaries and by what authority is that power exercised?
6. Have any proponents or staffers made incorrect or misleading statements?
7. Has the planning staff been fair and evenhanded in dealing with all parties?
8. Why haven't proponents been willing to compromise?
9. Is any other self-appointed group studying other districts without public knowledge?

The background check showed him to be a real estate broker and property rights advocate who *always* voted against regulation. Those questions—mostly accusations, some offensive—could smother us if we met up with them at the hearing for the first time. I think staffers would feel the same way, don't you?

A swing voter on the same commission summed up his central concern: "Can we encourage designs that have historic significance and not unrealistically burden the property owner?" Still another said the majority was taking advantage of the minority and wanted a compromise. A third could find no justification for excluding opposition owners, while a fourth was uneasy about designating property over owners' objections. Coming out of the same meeting, the chair concluded that key issues for most members were:

1. Whether a historic district is a public taking of private property.
2. The "another layer of bureaucracy" argument.
3. Whether design guidelines were onerous procedurally and financially.
4. The impact of guidelines on noncontributing property.
5. Whether districting concealed an antidevelopment bias or other hidden agendas.
6. Map boundary issues.

Now you might say these issues aren't new to us, that we've seen them in one form or another in our community meetings. And I'd say you're right. But do I have to spell out the advantages for you? Just think:

- We know we've been on the right track in anticipating questions all along.
- We can do subtraction and see which issues we might set aside now.
- We might detect how well our opponents are doing in getting their points across.
- We can gauge how the vote is shaping up before the hearing.

This kind of intelligence will keep us focused on what's important. We can use it in drafting our own mailings. And when the time comes for our testimony, we will have a fair assurance that commissioners who've raised the issues we address will be mentally, not just bodily, in attendance.

And what if the planning staff won't play ball? Well, it's good to know it early on, too. In that case, it'll be up to us to get some kind of clarity about how the meetings will be conducted and the final report crafted.

SETTING THE GROUND RULES

Speak with the commission chairs directly about how they plan on conducting their hearings. This kind of procedural query does not fall under *ex parte* restrictions.

Does the chair plan on taking public sentiment into account? If so, find out whether he or she will be looking for a petition, or will the sampling be broadened to invite any and all comments from the floor? Of course, no chair is likely to rule any citizen's testimony out of order. But the chair may define what is germane, ask the public to stick to it, and instruct fellow commissioners on what's under consideration.

It's a question of the hand on the tiller. Will the chair pursue the most direct course, or will the hearing be allowed to wander wherever public opinion blows it? We ourselves knew to take a firm line in our community meetings. But we shouldn't assume commission chairs will be as clear-sighted and determined.

Of course, any chair may say one thing before the meeting and behave quite differently in the event. This is especially true if opponents toss legal or procedural sand in the commission's eyes. Then, too, a handful of demanding opponents can start the commission backpedaling.

STRATEGIZING OUR PRESENTATION

So even if the chair promises to keep the hearing focused on a narrower range of considerations, it's a good idea to go in prepared with a Plan A and a Plan B:

- **Plan A:** We will develop a presentation keyed to all specific directives and criteria in the commission's charge as explained to us by the chair.
- **Plan B:** We will be ready with a full-blown response to anything our opponents try and the chair permits.

In short, we don't want to get caught carrying the proverbial knife to a gun-fight.

But we have a potential problem, depending on how testimony is taken. If we proponents are to speak first, then we need to know in advance if we have a right of rebuttal should our adversaries take off in another direction. If not, then we need to use our testimony to:

• Lay out what we've prepared for Plan A.
• Throw a rope around our opponents.

We'll do this by stating unequivocally what the hearing is about, what is prescribed for consideration by the commission's terms of reference, and *what the chair has specified to us in those terms.* This is the way we interject our own leadership into a proceeding where the commission's leadership may need stiffening.

But be careful: Do it as addressing the audience and stay clear of the political faux pas of reminding commissioners of their duty.

As for *how* to arrange your presentation, let me send you to chapter 36. That chapter is about preparing for the City Council hearing, but its basic advice is applicable here as well.

WINNING COMMISSION ENDORSEMENTS

Much is riding on these commission hearings, but not everything. With the skills you have developed in community meetings, winning HPC approval should pose few problems. The same goes for the Planning Commission, so I'll leave winning both to you.

Still, losing the Planning Commission is not a death knell. The City Council has the final say, as long as your local law allows the proposal to move forward. The Council may agree or disagree with its advisory commissions. Still, we want the two endorsements, and we value the sense of momentum that favorable votes give us in these first hearings.

Momentum attracts attention. We want Council members to take us seriously. We can't be sure they'll read what we send them in briefing packets when the time comes. But you may be sure that every one of them will read the local newspaper, and success pulls in the press.

NOTE

1. From private files, not for attribution.

Chapter Twenty-Nine

Working with the Press: Guidance from a Reporter

There is nothing more deceptive than an obvious fact.

—Sherlock Holmes

People say they don't believe everything they read in the newspaper. But have you ever noticed how a news article will influence the way they see an issue and the questions they ask?

And what's not to believe? The facts? In my experience, reporters usually get facts right. But like the smile on the Mona Lisa, an obvious fact is incomprehensible out of context.

No political issue is ever just about facts. No one more fact, once found, can ever settle a political difference. As we know, politics is about conflicting interests, contesting perspectives, and competing influence among contending parties.

That's what good newspaper stories are about, too. Nailing down a story is like jumping on a moving train: the facts are easy. It's the dynamics that can put you in the hurt box. Reporters know it. When the time comes to move on a story, they have to go with what they know and trust their own judgment.

So each reporter will catch hold of a story from a different angle. That's not bias, per se. It's just the way it works when we try to get a grasp on complex passing events.

Reporters are keen observers and far less likely to be biased than we are as participants. That's why politicians—if they're at all serious—prefer to look to the press to tell them what's going on before they listen to us. Their introduction to our districting effort can't help but be seen through the eyes of the reporter's take on the contest.

So when they read an article on districting, we want it to portray the issues as we see them. We want it to raise questions in their minds that will latch onto our answers.

In brief, we want good press. The only thing worse than bad press isn't getting no press at all. It's realizing too late we could've done something about it.

A REPORTER'S INSIGHTS

I've arranged for us to have lunch with Jeff Horseman, a longtime city reporter for *The Capital*, a midsized daily here in Annapolis.[1]

Jeff has interviewed me for several preservation stories, and I've learned to trust his fairness and accuracy. So I was pleased when he agreed to speak to us about talking to a reporter to get our story out.

Me: Thanks for taking time to talk with us at lunch today, Jeff.

Jeff: So we're going to turn tables here. I like the idea of being the one who gets interviewed for a change!

Me: How open are you to calls from local activists who want you to do an article on their cause?

Jeff: It depends on how it's presented. I think my best ideas for stories are the ones I find on my own, not those that come from people calling in who want me to do this or that for them. But if we can sit and talk about your concerns, I'm more inclined to be receptive.

Me: Would it be hard to interest you in our districting campaign?

Jeff: I think a historic district initiative is a pretty easy thing to get your average local paper interested in. It's a compelling story. It's very emotional. Property rights are fundamental in this country. People will say, "I paid money for this land and I want to be able to do what I want."

Me: What kinds of mistakes do people like me make at the start?

Jeff: There's a common misconception that we're spouting information out, that we're just collecting information to give to the public.

Me: You're not?

Jeff: The best newspapers do stories about people and communities.

Me: What do you look for?

Jeff: The key to a good story is what I call "the central conflict." The real issues confronting neighborhoods—things like that. Many people don't realize that a paper is a business. If people aren't interested in what we write they won't buy our paper. I want to write stuff that people will read, so I look for a compelling story, stories that people can relate to.

Me: But people look to you for information, too.

Jeff: The reality today, with the Internet and cable news, is that we're not going to be providing breaking news. We survive by putting information in context— writing about real people in plain language to grab attention.

Me: What do you say to the charge that reporters care only about controversy?

Jeff: I hear it all the time. This is what I say: Look, I'm not creating it or trying to stir it up. It's out there. My job is to get it right, be fair, and help people understand it. I want to deliver the story in a way that helps the reader understand the world they live in.

Me: And try to help solve the conflict?

Jeff: If what I do ends up helping, then fine. But if I get involved it jeopardizes my objectivity. It's not that I don't care. But if I advocate one way or another it violates my objectivity and makes me part of the story. That's the last thing I want to do.

Me: So how do you deal with it?

Jeff: I try to be open and receptive. I want to get the story right and be scrupulously fair to the people involved. And accountable—to everyone.

Me: Let's talk about balanced reporting. When you talk about doing a balanced story about a controversy, do you mean by balance that there are two sides to the story or two groups of roughly equal size? What if there are two points of view split, say, 70 percent for one side, 15 percent neutral and the rest on the other side in the community?

Jeff: It's a tricky issue to say how many are on side A and on side B. If it's a ninety–ten split I don't want to say it's fifty–fifty. On the other hand, I don't want to ignore the fact that other people may have different opinions.

Me: So I ought to get you reliable statistics.

Jeff: I want to see a poll, something quantifiable. But absent that, I have to be careful about accepting your word that "most people" are on your side. I have to see the evidence with my own eyes. For instance, I might go to a hearing and see where people stand. But if you say to me, "You know, Jeff, most people want the historic district," you might be right but I have to be careful about writing it. Some people get upset with reporting the other side. They say it clouds the issue or shows bias. But it's not my job to be referee or declare a winner.

Me: Would you trust our petition as evidence of our support?

Jeff: In journalism, there's an old saying. If your mother says she loves you, check it out. I think a reporter would call up a random sample and say, "Hey, this is Jeff Horseman at *The Capital*. I just want to make sure, did you sign this petition?" And find out why. I'd want to make sure I wasn't given phony names and street addresses. It happens. You don't want your evidence in a story to turn up fraudulent and backfire on you. Just make sure your petition is verifiable.

Me: Let's say a group of us has a districting proposal ready and now I'm picking up the phone to call your paper. I want to get our story out. What happens next?

Jeff: The switchboard will probably pass you to the newsroom. Every newspaper operates its own way. You might get the city editor, or the assistant metro editor or you might be sent directly to a reporter. An editor will talk with a reporter later, or the reporter will go to the editor who'll say "go ahead" or "nah, this is part of a larger story we'll do differently."

Me: What if I've read your reporting and liked it? Can I just ask for you?

Jeff: Of course.

Me: What can I say to get you to do the story?

Jeff: Try to put some salesmanship into it. Think about how a reporter has to tell readers, "This is why you ought to care about this." You need to realize that what's important to some people is not necessarily important to a larger group of readers. It's like broccoli. We know we ought to care, but do we?

Me: So how do I pitch it?

Jeff: Don't use big words. The key is simplicity. People want to sound impressive so they'll sound like they know what they're talking about. But I strive every day to kill the jargon. If I hear about—

Me: —"preserving the integrity of the built environment."

Jeff: Yeah, if I hear that, I start mentally checking out—"Oh, no, here we go!" Some people say we dumb down the news by avoiding big words. But I think it's the opposite. When you use one-syllable words you do a better job of explaining to more people.

Me: And they take up less space.

Jeff: I might write twenty, thirty-five, or forty inches for a story and my editor says cut it, condense it. I want to leave crucial information in. And what about this great quote I have? People don't understand this. They complain that I took a complicated issue and oversimplified it. They don't understand that I have to appeal to a broad audience that doesn't care about the details like they do.

Me: So what you're saying is that if we think it's important we should tell it to you in the simplest, most straightforward way possible.

Jeff: With a lot of interesting detail and a lot of simplicity that will hook the reader from the beginning to the end.

Me: Say I've got you interested. Do you want me to send you materials before we talk, or talk first?

Jeff: Charts, graphs, testimonials—they're helpful once I decide to do the story. First we'll talk. I like to do my interviews face-to-face. The people I interview are more comfortable with me in person. The phone is too impersonal. I always, always want to go knock on doors.

Me: Do you expect a press release from us? If we don't have one, will we look amateurish? If we do, will we appear too slick?

Jeff: I don't expect anything. A press release, prepared statement, whatever, is no indication of your credibility or standing. As a journalist in my community, anyone can call me and I'll treat everyone equally. There's an ethic here that Joseph Pulitzer stated well. He said that we should be a voice for the voiceless. That means to tell the untold story. Representing all aspects of the community is part of the creativity and satisfaction of the job.

Me: Do you think reporters favor the underdog? If we're fighting big property developers, are we the underdog, or is the underdog the retiree who's afraid of historic districting?

Jeff: I try to present the whole picture. It comes down to communication. I'd be off base if I tried to talk only about the big, overarching issues that don't seem to affect anyone in particular, or if I only wrote about the little grandmother being pressured by preservationists.

Me: When we meet, do you want a presentation from me, or do you want an interview?

Jeff: A conversation. I'll probably start with, "OK, tell me why you're doing this." I want you to do most of the talking.

Me: Would you prefer to talk with two or three of us to get varying interests and perspectives?

Jeff: Every reporter has a preference. I prefer one-on-one. It all depends. A conversation is harder to do with more in a room. A panel discussion bouncing ideas around can be good, too, if a reporter can stay with it.

Me: What's the ideal interview, or conversation?

Jeff: It's one in which you can get someone away from pat, safe answers and move to the heart of the issue. So I want to do my homework and ask insightful questions. When I do this, some people think I'm trying to trick them into saying something offensive. No, I'm just trying to find out where they're coming from and get an honest story.

Me: What's your pet peeve?

Jeff: "I want this to be a positive story." If you say that, it indicates to me you don't understand my job. But people often tell me they want the story to make them or their program look good. We're not in the business of making people look good or bad, building up or tearing down. My job is to look for the truth, get the facts, be comprehensive, and write it in a way that's easy to read. I want to be able to say, "OK, folks, this is your world."

Me: Let's assume then it'll just be the two of us in the conversation. Do I talk off the record or on?

Jeff: Assume I'll use everything you say.

Me: But what if I don't want my name in print?

Jeff: It'll hurt your case. If you have the courage to call up the paper then you should stand up for the article. People have this idea that reporters use lots of anonymous sources. We don't like them. If someone says they don't want to be quoted, I get skeptical. "Well, why don't you?" I think. If you've got a good reason, like a boss's policy, I can work with that. Talk to me on background, then, but direct me to people who'll talk on the record. It's not all or nothing.

Me: What else do I need to do?

Jeff: Preservation is a good story. It's not hard to sell it to an editor. It's very emotional. It deals with interesting problems in a community.

Me: What if your editor has already taken a position on the historic district? Is there pressure on you?

Jeff: None whatsoever. My newsroom editor isn't the editorial page editor. Editorials are usually written after the story appears. My job is to tell the story. An editorial is to get the debate started.

Me: So how should I time my call? Just before a hearing, or sooner than that?

Jeff: An upcoming hearing in a couple of days will be a point of interest to readers. We tell them about the hearing and tell them what it's about. But a longer lead is a good idea—a week or longer. You've got a chance at being a front-page Sunday story. People can read a longer story and get a better base of knowledge.

Me: So something doesn't have to be happening right now?

Jeff: The more time you can give a reporter the better the story will be. You need to realize that reporters are juggling two or three or more different stories on deadline.

Me: Let's say I give you a long lead. What if you want to call the Mayor or members of the City Council but I'm afraid they'll stake out a position before I've had a chance to influence them?

Jeff: You need to be very clear if you want me to keep it under wraps. I want to write this story and I'm not going to let anyone tell me when. But I might agree to hold off if you give me a good idea of when we can run it. But you can't say, "Write on this, but don't call that person." No editor would agree to that. And I won't agree to let you see a copy of it before it goes to press.

Me: We have three hearings coming up. Can I get three stories, one before each meeting?

Jeff: All depends. "Can we get three?" That's not the approach. Toss your ideas out and let the paper decide if it's worth a second or third story.

Me: Will you be telling me if you're talking with the opposition and give me a chance to rebut?

Jeff: Not necessarily. You have to expect I'll try to get the other side. If you ask me, I'll tell you. But don't expect me to call and tell you who's getting interviewed. If some developer calls you a NIMBY [not in my backyard] moron and I might use the quote, it's a courtesy to tell you first.

Me: If I ask will you tell me what the opposition is saying and doing? Can you be a source of intelligence about them?

Jeff: You mean, like what a developer says? I don't mind telling you what's common knowledge or on the record. But if you want me to predict what's coming down the road, that sort of thing . . . I'm more reticent.

Me: How about what you know about the City Council or one of the commissions? A little quid pro quo, you might say. When I'm talking to you about our plans, would you answer questions I have about what you've seen, who is who, how they might respond to our issue? Can we have a two-way conversation?

Jeff: The last thing I want to be seen as on my beat is a power broker. If I wanted influence I'd run for office. But I might respond to specific questions as long as I'm not burning my other sources and you're asking about public knowledge. But basically, ethically, I can't get involved.

Me: How much do you think local officials are influenced by your articles?

Jeff: [Smiling.] I've been told we have a lot of influence. But reporters aren't deliberately trying to influence City Hall. That would affect their credibility. Officials read the paper to find out what's happening.

Me: What kinds of mistakes can I make with you that'll hurt me?

Jeff: Shopping the story around to the competition. That strikes me as manipulative, playing people off against each other. Of course, if I think a competitor might print it first, I might want the story. But it's not a good idea to try it.

Me: What else?

Jeff: If you don't like the story I write don't call and say, "Jeff, you idiot! This is totally wrong!" You can catch more flies with honey than vinegar. I'm going to be much more receptive to working with you if you say, "Jeff, you missed this point. Let me explain how." If you come in with guns blazing I'm not going to be receptive. Reporters are people. The more you're aware of the pressures they face, the more they'll work with you.

Me: And?

Jeff: Don't lie. My credibility is important. If I find out I've been snowed, if you've handed me a lot of BS, I'm not going to believe you again. Every day I put something with my byline in the paper, people are going to judge me. There are a lot of people out there who like to see reporters get screwed.

After that, I figured I couldn't very well stick him with my lunch tab. So I thanked Jeff again, said goodbye, and picked over my tortilla chips along with something I'd heard. Once the story appears, an editorial may follow. So once you've put your story out, go see the folks at the editorial page and sell them on your civic vision.

NOTE

1. Since this interview Jeff has moved to another paper.

Chapter Thirty

A Civic Vision

There is no substitute for a clear vision and a decisive direction.

—Dick Morris

As a reporter, Jeff told us that he looks for the "central conflict" in a community story and aims at being "scrupulously fair to the people involved." That's balanced reporting. So we have to wonder: How will we come across to his readers—on balance?

Imagine what will happen when Jeff goes after the story. Our opponents will stress their pivotal issue: property rights. And what will we do? Take him on an eye-opening walk of the neighborhood? Of course we will. And he'll report it as he sees it.

So what will official decision makers take away from his story? Next to property rights, our issues may sound a bit precious. These days, like it or not, rights talk is presumptively, well, right. If we're to win them over, we should give Jeff the story of grassroots leadership that has forged a new sense of community in the midst of conflict.

"JUST AUTHORITY" AND THE PUBLIC GOOD

Columnist David Brooks of *The New York Times* points the way. He has affirmed that good government is about more than liberty. It is about *just* authority.

What does that mean to us? Well, obviously the historic district will establish a new *authority* over how we exercise our property rights as free citizens. We know that this authority is *legal*. But what is it that makes it *just*?

When we put together our practical vision we took pains to justify district designation in terms of property owner interests. That is no longer enough.

Our target audience has changed. We have to assume the decision makers we seek to win over don't have property-based interests in the district. If they do, then recusal will be a matter to address according to our interests and official ethics.

Of course they'll want to know, and we should tell them, why a majority of property owners sides with us. Still, numbers aren't enough—and for a good reason. A majority calculating their own interests can be wrong-headed. Our form of representative government holds that elected officials are better situated than the self-involved people themselves to judge the connection between self-interest and the public good—and to protect and advance the latter.

So what is it about the historic district that is in the public good—and thus just—beyond our practical vision? What can we say for it so that it can hold its own against property rights claims?

ECONOMIC DISTRACTIONS

A great deal of useful investigation has generated much interest and literature about the value of preservation to local economies. In the field of who does what, consultant Donovan Rypkema tops the list.

Making an economic case for a historic district is advisable. But your districting challenge isn't reducible to money. During a campaign in Norman, Oklahoma, resident Steve Davis observed that the district "will enhance our property values, although I don't think that is the primary motivation."[1] That's not all the story in every district: there are advantages to be found in business prosperity, niche job creation in construction, lower costs in adaptive reuse, and so forth.

Just don't count on using reverse alchemy to turn gold into votes.

Your opponents may talk in money terms. If you follow them down the rabbit hole of economic statistics in a public hearing, they will go after you like a ferret. They might even quote that old Mark Twain lie about there being lies, damn lies, and statistics.

While elected officials might be intrigued by what you say in general, they'll hear it as checking a box. *Everyone* who comes before them on zoning-related issues makes an economic argument. They've learned to see it as a gambit.

Besides, your opponents' real interests aren't economic, even if they make a free-market economic case against you. Their main thrust is antiregulatory.

We need a new sort of vision—a *civic vision*—that ties the *political* interests of City leaders to what we've already achieved in our community. Instead of simply advocating preservation and its benefits, we'll be giving them a *leadership investment* in our initiative and make them complicit in our success.

SEEING THE CIVIC COMMUNITY

Now let's get reporter Jeff back in here. A great thing about reporters is they don't like getting bogged down in details. We can tell him about the "preservation-plus" approach we've used and avoid the quicksand of technicalities. Those details, we may confidently say, are well-known and accepted by our supporters. We've got their signatures to prove it.

So have our allies all become preservationists? No. Our message is that they have become *pro-district.*

"Ahh," comes the response. "They're in your chorus now, but when the time comes for the regulations to apply to them they'll be singing a different tune. That's what I'm hearing at City Hall."

And that's a most dangerous critique, if it's coming from appointed commissioners or elected officials. As they see it, we're asking them to make law on the basis of an insubstantial and transitory confluence of interests. Oh, they'll accept that everyone is pro-preservation after their own fashion, at least for now. But experience has taught them to doubt that our neighbors really, truly want more regulations. "They ought to be careful what they wish for," they'll say. And public officials know they'll be the ones to take the fall if folks turn on the district later on. Can you blame them? In the land of electoral politics and political appointments, it's always CYA time.

We haven't come this far to smile and say, "But that's what they want, Scout's honor." So let's go right into the teeth of their argument.

We want to make it crystal clear that we're talking about *districting* here, not just *preservation*, and so are our supporters. Our reporter has probably heard Breakers claim that there's not much around here worth preserving, or something like that. Well, we disagree. But that's not where the real story is. And that's surely not the only thing our City leaders should be looking at. So here's our pitch.

The truth is, in most of our communities, *what's preserved isn't nearly as impressive as the rare quality of civic life seen in the very fact of citizens caring for a legacy*—any legacy no matter how common.

Here's how I see it. The outward appearance of a historic district reflects the internal health of a community. Long-standing features of the built environment are touchstones of civic memory, reminding us that what we do lives on after us. A community that cares for its past by districting, then, is a community dedicated to being responsible for its own future. A historic district says to us, "This is a place to invest our lives, to raise a family, to grow a business, to retire in security."

Getting to the point where a community petitions for district designation is quite a civic accomplishment. Isn't this, we should ask, the ideal toward which all political leadership aspires?

That's it, then. Three short paragraphs to refocus attention from conflict to what visionary leadership can achieve in community building.

SHARING OUR SUCCESS

We know that ideological fights over property rights can make decision makers shy. So we need to stand firmly for action, not talk, deeds and not principles that lead to a better community.

Our basic conviction is that sound communities can't be achieved by standing on abstract principles—especially if those principles give folks an excuse for acting irresponsibly. Principles of freedom are the foundation of free government. And free government holds that *when the citizenry is self-governed enough to do good things, those things should be encoded in law and supported by institutions equal to the task.* That is how just authority arises.

Leadership is about context, then, about inspiring and facilitating good acts and securing them in public practice. Ronald Reagan understood the point. He told *60 Minutes* that "the greatest leader is not the one who does the greatest things, but the one who gets the people to do the greatest things."

Public officials should be satisfied that our neighbors see the historic district as a great gift to themselves. *And they should be proud that it has taken place on their watch, at the time of their leadership.*

So everywhere we go, every public chance we get, let's congratulate them. I mean it. Look them in the eye. Shake their hands. Thank them for having nurtured a community in which average folks like you and me have been inspired to bring a winning proposal like ours before them for ratification. Let's speak in celebration of the opportunity to join together with them in the final stages of this exceptional achievement.

Make it a main theme in what you say to your reporter, what you put in a guest column, and what you submit to editorial writers. Put it on your website. Emphasize it wherever you speak and *make sure your City leaders know it.*

Our goal is to raise the level of discourse in the community. Reporters' good instincts may seek out the "central conflict." But don't let them miss the new and vital awareness of community that we've brought out of that conflict.

The big human interest story isn't about the penurious resident who fears districting. The real story is about how regular folks around the corner got off their duffs and inspired their neighbors to uncommon accomplishment.

Back when we put together our *practical vision* we joined the particular interests of individual neighbors with our own. Our *civic vision* now proclaims that the sum is greater than its parts: The historic district is in the common interest of everyone even if some individuals with particular interests don't acknowledge it. If the concept of the common good has any validity at all, then it's to be found in that kind of public policy.

You won't need to remind decision makers that this is about more than public policy, either. We're not just designating a district here. To deny the district would be to deny the best in us—their constituents—and cheapen their records. They should see there's no future in going there.

That's not just a civic vision. That's a promise.

FOCUSING OUR EFFORT

Will decision makers recognize the public good when they see it? And seeing it, will they know what to do with it, with the political courage to see it through? Those questions matter the most with respect to elected officials. It's time for us to take a look at who among them matter most.

NOTE

1. Jane Glenn Cannon, "Norman Neighborhood Seeks Historic District Designation," www.newsok.com, October 10, 2016.

Chapter Thirty-One

The Top Tier of Local Government

All animals are equal.

—George Orwell, *Animal Farm*

"But some animals are more equal than others," right? The difference depends on their power over others. When Aristotle dubbed us all "political animals," he set the stage for Orwell's allegory. Given the tremendous impact local government has on our daily lives, you'd think we'd be as well-informed as Orwell's barnyard critters about who it is who rules our roost.

We aren't. Local government is so little understood by most of us that, like Orwell's imagined farm, it might as well not exist at all. We can move from farm to town, town to city, state to state and never even think about how our governmental situation changes.

Under the unspecified powers reserved to them by Amendment 10 of the Constitution, the fifty states have been amazingly inventive in authorizing local forms of government. Take mayors, for example. If you live in a place that has one, you might be surprised to learn that others don't. Yet most do. Even then, new to you may be the varied types of mayors you'll find from place to place.

Why is this important? Your Mayor's support can either make *a difference* or *all the difference* to you, depending on your local form of government. So while we started working with Wilmington's model in chapter 4, we ought to take a moment to consider the ways your local governmental setting may differ.

MAYORS AND TYPES OF SYSTEMS

There are "weak" and "strong" mayors. Neither has to do with character, but systems. Though there are many local permutations, local systems tend to break into three main forms.

The mayor-council form: Here the "strong" Mayor comes to office through a city-wide election. The Mayor presides over an executive branch while the City Council serves as the legislative branch. The Mayor usually has veto power, proposes budgets, has the authority to hire and fire administrative department heads, and thus enjoys considerable independence. Some mayors will appoint a chief administrative officer responsible to them.

   Note: In some places this system has a "weak" Mayor whose policy and administrative authority is largely subordinate to the City Council.

The council-manager form: Many municipalities outside of larger cities have this form of government. Their typically "weak" Mayor often is an elected member of the City Council appointed by the other members, or elected at-large, to what is largely a ceremonial position. Executive authority resides in a professional manager responsible to the Council, hired to oversee administrative operations and to advise the Council on policy. Many smaller towns, however, can't afford a manager and have few (sometimes no) administrative employees. In these cases, the Council is responsible for administration.

The city-commission form: Commissioners gain office in an at-large, city-wide election based on the plurality of votes. The Commission combines both legislative and executive functions with individual members appointed to administrative functions. The "weak" Chairman or Mayor chairs meetings without enjoying powers not accorded to other commissioners. This form of government is common in counties as well.

The support of "strong" mayors is absolutely critical to your eventual victory. But you should also take special deferential care with "weak mayors." They are likely to exercise subtle power while using his or her personality to attain desired outcomes. The same goes for chairs of county commissions.

ABOUT CITY MANAGERS
AND CHIEF ADMINISTRATIVE OFFICERS

These designations are often interchangeable. You will want to talk with—not lobby—your professional administrative manager, if your jurisdiction has one. What you say is based on several understandings:

1. Their interest in giving technically accurate policy advice about the district plan.
2. Your need for them to understand the merits of historic districting.
3. Their interests in the budgeting and personnel implications of administering a district.
4. Their personal concern with weathering the politics of districting before and after designation.
5. Their need to be well-briefed about what you have done in the community and plan for City Hall.

A persuaded manager may bend the Mayor and Council members your way and go to bat for you against misrepresentations. The same holds true for the lead commissioner in the city-commissioner system who will have executive responsibility for the administration of the historic district after designation. These administrators will be all the more inclined your way if your opponents have ignored them and you have won their trust.

ABOUT YOUR OWN CITY COUNCIL REPRESENTATIVE

It's a good idea to put special focus on your own district representative on the City Council (or County Commission). The member's ability to influence the outcome of the vote may be enhanced by common practices.

In a few locales there is what's called a "councilmanic prerogative," founded in tradition rather than in law. Taking Philadelphia as an example, the assumed prerogative means, as reported by the Pew Charitable Trusts, that "individual City Council members make nearly all of zoning and overlay decisions in their jurisdictions."[1]

Even in localities where such a prerogative isn't acknowledged, Council members may routinely defer to one another on such matters. The practice is controversial. The good news for us from the Pew report is that it is used "most often in response to neighborhood concerns" to make zoning-related decisions "more palatable to neighborhood groups."

The bad news is that it's also good news to our opponents. As always, the question is who will gain advantage? Unluckily for us, City Council proceedings are not well designed to produce a distinguished outcome, as now we'll see.

NOTE

1. The Pew Charitable Trusts, "The Philadelphia Councilmanic Prerogative: How It Works and Why It Matters," July 23, 2015, www.pewtrusts.org/en/research-and-analysis/reports/2015/07. To see the full report, including how the prerogative is used in other major cities, go to www.pewtrusts.org/~/media/assets/2015/08.

Part V

WINNING THE
CITY COUNCIL VOTE

Chapter Thirty-Two

The Politics of Public Hearings

Everybody lies, but it doesn't matter since nobody listens.

—Lieberman's Law

City Mayors and Council members aren't disinterested judges of merit. They are for the most part biased listeners who have been rewarded for their biases by getting elected. Most of them want to do it again next time.

Can you blame them? The electoral process being what it is, they have to be creatures of interests—their own and others. They don't want to know about the historic district nearly as much as they are attuned to a question as old as politics itself: *Cui bono?* Who benefits?

You and I already have an answer. It's all to the public good, we like to say.

But the common good, the public interest, is hard to see from where they sit. Of course, not every public official is nearsighted. Some are truly devoted to doing the right thing. They're the ones who take time to listen and study. They ask good questions and sift through the evidence. They engage their colleagues on substance. Such officials do exist. I hope you'll find one or more on your City Council. If you have a majority, call *Ripley's Believe It or Not.* Even then bear in mind that the public hearing format of Council meetings isn't conducive to taking the longer view of things, either.

These meetings are very much in the moment, with all the emotionally charged *Sturm und Drang* of community fights—though with much of the feeling of community stripped away by the proceedings. Testimony is a rat-a-tat-tat of rights versus regulations, "he said," "she said," "ifs," "ands," and "buts." Time presses, and there's likely more on their agenda than just us. They are perhaps perturbed that we haven't settled this thing on our own. They wonder how they can solve it if we can't.

A QUESTION OF LEADERSHIP

"We don't have a clear mandate" for designation, the Southern Mayor concluded at the end of a hearing described as "both tedious and confusing."

And whose fault was that? Long months of hard work were lost because historic district proponents failed to exercise the leadership needed to get the vote. In a hard-fought districting contest, winning the vote depends on creating a political environment in which decision makers are motivated by their interests to vote with us.

So what's this "mandate" thing about, anyway? Think a minute. When did you last hear a politician use the word *mandate*? I'll bet it wasn't to say, "I don't have one. My hands are tied." We're used to hearing mandates claimed on the thinnest of pretexts, aren't we? Sure we are. *Leaders* claim mandates and then spend whatever political capital they have to press ahead with favored legislation. What the Mayor was pointing to wasn't the absence of a mandate. It was the Council's own *lack of a will to lead*.

Elected officials prefer to be pushed toward a decision that finds general favor. "We want something everybody can feel good about," a Council member said in similar circumstances. But if the Council is looking for a mandate in "feel-good" solutions then they're not thinking in terms of public policy. They're looking for palliatives. You and I have to lead them to a better result.

AN INAUSPICIOUS SETTING

Here's how a City Council typically proceeds. The chair of the HPC or the Planning Department presents the draft proposal. The floor is opened for sworn public comment from anyone wishing to be heard. Public testimony is then closed and the question is turned over to Council members for an exchange—rarely a real discussion—among themselves leading toward a vote.

When it's our turn to speak in the process, we are asked to give our name and address for the record and then state our interest. That's it. No prologue, no follow-up. We get to say anything we want. And, too bad for us, our opponents usually do.

Any progress we might have made on issues in our community meetings doesn't help us much here with the opposition. Once the hearing begins they will revert to the same canards, the same red herrings, the same distortions—that is, the same discrediting tactics that they started with on day one. They'll try to flood the hearing with accusations, complaints, and appeals to property rights. Their goal is to create the appearance of an unholy mess of disagreements in the community.

So now what? Do we have to fight the fight all over again?

That's why Lieberman's observation is a comfort. It tells us to take it easy. Sworn testimony or no, everyone knows our opponents are lying—or playing fast and loose with the truth. But then everyone assumes that we are, too. Still, no sweat. Nobody's paying attention anyway.

Is that so? Don't just take it from me. A past county commissioner suggests I title this chapter, "The Art of Not Listening." Former Missoula mayor and speaker of the Montana state legislature Daniel Kemmis has written in *Community and the Politics of Place* that public hearings "are curiously devoid of that very quality which their name might seem to imply."[1] So remember: *Not much hearing goes on in public hearings.*

The right of every citizen to be heard is also an equal right to be ignored. Those who testify have no obligation to respect, much less engage, each other's views or ours. And once public testimony is closed, Council members will generally care less for puzzling through what is said than for finding some way out of the impasse before midnight. Talk is about policy. That's on the surface. But calculating political interests is far easier for elected officials than sorting out and weighing conflicting testimonies.

We are not strangers to the sway that interests hold over ideas. We rose in stature as community leaders by drawing our neighbors' interests into our practical vision. But we may feel mighty puny as we arrive at City Hall, where other leaders with other interests rule, and the reality of the hearing room sets in.

Matt Damon's freshman trial lawyer in *The Rainmaker* knows the feeling. He has the law, his case, and the evidence down pat. And still, on that first day he tells us, "I look around the courtroom and I know I haven't even been born yet."

CHANGING OUR STRATEGY

The way Council procedures are supposed to produce policy reminds me of what Woodrow Wilson once said about golf. What we call golf, he said, is a game in which you try to put a small ball in a small hole with instruments wholly unsuited to the task.

So what can we do if the Council is going to give us a sub-par round? We can't refuse to play the game, and they're not going to change the rules just because we ask them. You play your ball where it lies—but you're not without options. You may change that one part of the proceedings that you control: your testimony.

Council proceedings are set up for us to testify to our interests. Changing our testimony means changing the interests that we want the Council to consider. What I have in mind, then, is a significant change of strategy. We will speak to the *Council's own interest in finding their way to a defensible vote.*

We will, of course, advocate the district. It would be disorienting if we didn't. But we're not going to engage our opponents and argue it from scratch. We've been there, done that, got the T-shirt. We have already brought our neighbors to a decision that is as good as it gets. So let's give the Council that decision, back it up with our testimony, and show them the style of leadership that will enable them to make it their own.

OUR TESTIMONY

We'll speak their language of partnerships and alliances and show them the coalition of supporters we've put together in the district. We will talk, too, about synergies between the district and the larger community—the symbiotic interplay among historic resources, private and public places, business interests, nonprofit activities, cultural and recreational opportunities. All this will put them on notice that they'll be disappointing a broader coalition of interests than just ours in preservation if they fail us.

That is the lead-in to our other argument. We will assert that the community itself has done all the sorting out, the balancing of interests, the brokering of agreements that may be expected. On our own, we led our neighbors through an open, inclusive, and fairly conducted decision-making process. Call it an exercise in direct democracy, if you like. Property owners have met and talked, contended and reasoned together in different venues.

Along the way we established a practical vision that succeeded in quickening a new civic sense among many of our neighbors. We found common ground as we worked together, and together we took responsibility for our neighborhood.

Many who joined our campaign have become newly optimistic about local government. Try as we might, we'll say, we could not persuade everybody that politics is about more than just isolating themselves from the public interest and defending themselves from government.

As it turned out there was enough community feeling to make winning the decision for districting possible and enough of its absence to make designation necessary.

The results of our efforts, like votes, are registered in our petition. This long, deliberative process has produced a responsible decision that—with all due respect to the Council—is quite likely a better decision than any that might be reached in Council chambers in an hour or so.

THE SOLUTION

Our strategy, then, will be to insist—with all the influence that our standing in the community gives us—that the political question before the Council isn't whether the historic district should be approved. The real question is *whether the Council is going to accept and validate the community's decision.*

And what are the Council's interests in this? Right now, we are offering them something that is as close to a mandate as they are likely to find. It is the solution they are looking for to bring the proceedings to an efficient close with a show of decisive leadership.

Our solution offers them a ready-made, uncomplicated way to justify their vote to anyone who may pick them apart later. *Justify,* not simply explain. A vote for the district is more than a vote for one side over another. *It is a vote for community in the midst of conflict.* It is a vote for the public good as the public—the people—have come to see it. So it is also the right thing to do.

ACTING IN ADVANCE

We have one issue left to address: timing. Council members will have at least a fair idea of how they'll vote before the hearing begins. And a made-up mind is a terrible thing to chase.

So how do we get to them first? Through lobbying. We don't know, until you find out, whether you can meet one-on-one with HPC and Planning commissioners. But you should be able to speak to each Council member. Pay special attention to the Mayor and the Council member from your own district.

Assume what you say will get back to our opponents. But if we hold off till the public hearing, we run the risk of saying too little too late.

Just keep in mind that you don't get to take a mulligan, to call do-overs in politics. So before you head downtown to talk with your elected officials, let's get some pointers on how to do it from a successful lobbyist.

NOTE

1. Daniel Kemmis, *Community and the Politics of Place,* Norman: University of Oklahoma Press, 1990, p. 54.

Chapter Thirty-Three

Lobbying City Hall:
A Conversation with a Lobbyist

Here's to plain speaking and clear understanding.

—Sydney Greenstreet, *The Maltese Falcon*

We are sitting in the back room of a political speakeasy on the outskirts of Washington, D.C. Just the two of us in comfortable chairs, drinks in hand, talking politics.

He's a successful lobbyist who has agreed to talk about his craft. He prefers to remain anonymous so he can be candid. I'll just call him "Sam."

Like many lobbyists, Sam has also had a career in law. In recent years, though, it's been politics. He has spent twelve years lobbying and three and a half being lobbied. Walked both sides of the street in fair weather and foul. His conservative credentials are sterling and he has lived in a historic district. Liked it, too. Mostly.

I set the stage by explaining that we're expecting a Council fight over our historic district. We think a little lobbying is in order and would like some pointers.

In the momentary silence that follows as he gathers his thoughts, I swear I hear Sydney Greenstreet say to Bogie, "Now, sir, we'll talk if you like. I'll tell you outright, I'm a man who likes talking to a man who likes to talk."

THE CONVERSATION

Me: What's the best way to approach an elected official?

Sam: Find someone to make an introduction for you. Let them send a note and say, "My friend Bill is going to call you and wants to come by and really needs

198

to see you." If you want to see the Mayor, that might get you a "Hi, Bill. This is Mary, my assistant. I wanted to meet you but I've got another meeting. She'll take notes and brief me today about what's going on." Where there's no staff, just the official, it's harder for them to give you the slip.

Me: Are you saying they'd just as soon not meet with me?

Sam: It's really all about maximizing their time. It's like this: staffers or other people I trust are extensions of me. They help me see and talk to more people and accomplish more of what I'm supposed to be doing.

Me: So what do I say when we meet?

Sam: Lobbying to me is a matter of priorities. Know your subject backwards and forwards. If you're going to give them printed material, know and be able to explain every word in it.

Me: And second . . . ?

Sam: Know this person so you can walk in and say, "Well, Alderwoman Smith, I saw your last three votes on the environment and that was a good piece of work." They love that, you know. Visit their websites. Find the topics that have made these people jump up and do things.

Me: So you're telling me to schmooze them!

Sam: If you come in the door and start saying, "We've got a historic district pending," their eyes are going to glaze over. They'll say, "OK, just give me your literature and I'll see you later." But if you walk in the front door and say, "I understand you had a charity golf tournament the other day? How did you do?" "Aw," he says, "I just go out and have my picture taken with the donors and hit a few balls. But I can tell you I came that close to a hole in one." And now you're in. Call it what you want, but we're talking by that point.

Me: What else?

Sam: If you walk into an elected official's office and don't know how they've voted in the past, *shame on you*! If he's voted against your issues, you want to be able to say, "I know your record and it's important to me to know why you voted that way." You'll find out pretty quickly where he stands with you.

Me: Then what do you do?

Sam: You're getting to the point where you can say, "Let me tell you what makes our proposal different." Talk about substance, and address how technicalities might get worked out. If that doesn't move them, then say, "If you can tell me something we can fix, something we can make better that would bring you onboard, that's what I want to hear. Let me try to work with you on this." If you go in there with this completely adversarial "you and I don't agree and you've always voted against us" attitude, then don't waste your time. You'll just make them mad. But if you go in there with the idea that you really want to figure out what the problem is, then *that* makes you a very valuable player in their eyes.

Me: What do you do if they agree with you but still say they can't vote for you?

Sam: They can say that you make perfectly good sense. But then, if they're candid, they might tell you they have other commitments and can't vote for you. It's not easy for them to look you in the eye and tell you no. When that happens, I say, "Thank you for being direct. I admire your refreshing candor. It's been a pleasure." Stand, shake hands, and leave.

Me: Just like that, it's over?

Sam: Sometimes you just have to know you're going to lose that vote and have to move on. But never burn a bridge. Treat them well and with respect, and they'll know they owe you one.

Me: Do you ever lean on them, threaten them with political repercussions?

Sam: If you're part of the Soprano family you shouldn't be a lobbyist. That's just not going to get it. Still, you have to show them why it's in their interest to vote with you. Have your statistics perfect—that impresses them. If you can tell them how their vote will affect them, they'd be fools not to listen to you. I have seen people with steam coming out of their ears talking to people they wouldn't choose to talk to, yet saying to themselves, "I need this. This is an education. I'm listening to another portion of what's going on in this town and I need to understand it."

Me: What mistakes can I make?

Sam: Never lie. Never tell any elected official anything that isn't absolutely true. You have only one chance in this business, *one lie*, and they'll never listen to you again because they can't depend on you. And nobody will be able to repair the damage you do to your cause.

Me: Do we talk about our opponents or just stick to our message?

Sam: You need to tell the person what the opposition to your proposal is going to be, and you need to be deadly honest with them. No sugar coating. If they end up getting hit in the back of the head when they're not looking by something you didn't tell them you won't be welcomed back.

Me: So we show them the downside, too.

Sam: You go in and say, "I want you to do A, and if you do A you're going to be hearing from this group of folks. They're going to come in and yell and scream at you. But let me tell you why you're going to be better off in the long run for being with us on this issue."

Me: What should I take in with me?

Sam: Suppose they say, "That's a very interesting point. Do you have any facts you can leave with me?" I usually go armed with one-page talking papers on major topics that I can put in their hand.

Me: How detailed?

Sam: Short. Bulleted. This is a one-shot deal. Not even complete sentences. Less than one page. My phone number on each page at the bottom. "Call me," I say, "and I'll give you a blowout on it." If I can get a screwdriver under the lid of the paint can and start popping it up—enough so I can slide some fact papers in there with them—now I'm doing something.

Me: Will they tell me where they stand before I leave?

Sam: Most of them—the smart ones—will never tell you they're going to vote one way and then go and vote another. They'll simply not commit while you're there. You'll hear "Thank you and now let me go back and look at this." That gives you a perfect opportunity to say, "Well, let me help you. Give me an e-mail address where I can send you more information if you need it."

Me: Does money buy influence?

Sam: Not since campaign contributions have been restricted. So I've got to be a good talker, a good presenter.

Me: What defeats you?

Sam: Sometimes I watch the vote and wonder how that person could vote against me. They can be sincerely with you, yet vote where their constituents are. If you let yourself get upset about that, then you'll end up against our whole system of government. They're just being smart. That clue tells me that when I walk in their door, at the very least I have to know something about their constituents.

Me: But our historic district is probably going to be limited to the geography of only one Council member's district.

Sam: You'd be surprised. Put together some "well whaddya know?!" facts. A historic district in one place might be the balance needed to secure rezoning for business in another. If you can make that kind of link, you can go in and say, "Hey, this will be good for you, too." Be specific. Use examples from other cities if you have to. Get them thinking that there *are* advantages for them, too. "By golly," they'll say, "I can vote for that."

Me: Why do they always seem to want a compromise?

Sam: That's the way politics works. They know that policy differences never get fully resolved. So pulling to the middle is what it's all about. If you get to the middle you win.

Me: Do you go in alone or take others with you?

Sam: Depends on the situation. If it's a technical issue, I'll take a specialist along. I don't want to be caught talking about something outside my area of expertise.

Me: Do you ever coordinate with other groups or associations?

Sam: Good question. I handle what I can do best. If I anticipate prejudice against me because of my client or my issue, I might ask someone else, like the Chamber of Commerce, to go in with me and speak to our issue. I'll be a follower and they'll say this isn't just about preservation. There are other interests involved, and they're here to talk about them.

Me: How do I know when to leave?

Sam: That reminds me. I've got a trip to Texas tomorrow and I still haven't packed my bags. . . . See? You'll know when it's time to go. *But don't you push it.* Don't pop in and pop out again. Don't just say your piece and leave. They'll wonder, "What was *that* all about?" Maybe their questions don't get answered. Maybe they don't even know what those questions are when you walk in the door. Give them time to think while you're there. Look, if the guy seems to be in no hurry, then spend some time getting to know each other on a personal level. It puts a human face on your issue.

Me: How soon do we go see them?

Sam: As early as possible. Get them your materials. Start telling them why this district is important to them. Give them time to get a handle on the pros and cons and then go back again. *Get that door propped open for further contact.* Ask them, "Where do we need to go on this? What do I need to do to make you comfortable with this? Can you give me some direction?" That way, you're taking them seriously *and* getting yourself invited back.

Me: How likely are they to make up their minds before the public hearing?

Sam: Some won't have their minds made up. But the ideal of the hearing, where ideas and positions are exchanged and decided, is not the way it works in America today. Everybody has access to all the information they need without having to listen to speeches. If they like what they hear from you they'll be repeating it at the hearing.

Me: How important is good press?

Sam: Everyone reads the paper, maybe has a clipping service. If there's an article on a meteor falling in Farmer Jones's field today, tomorrow there will be a hearing on "Meteors: What We Can Do about Them." The news is of critical importance to them.

Me: Final thoughts?

Sam: Do you know the movie *The Music Man*? It opens with a train coming into River City carrying traveling salesmen singing about selling. They all agree on one thing. As the train comes into the station, they're singing in rhythm with the slowing pistons, "You've got to know the terr-i-tory." Well, you have to know how politics is played. It takes a lot of effort. You can't just jump up, jam your finger into the air, and say, "I'm going to change this!" Folks will come down on you like a ton of bricks. It takes knowing how the game is played. And if you can't play the game you've got no business doing this.

Me: So we've been told.

With that he says he *really* is going to Texas and has to pack. We put away our glasses. We step out into the night. A chill mist has blown into town. As we shake hands I can't help but think, "So that's the stuff that votes are made of."

Chapter Thirty-Four

Speaking Mayor to Mayor: A Dialogue with Charleston's Joseph P. Riley Jr.

> That some achieve great success is proof to all that others can achieve it as well.
>
> —Abraham Lincoln

Mayors are special cases when you lobby City Hall. Whether they are strong executives or conveners of the Council, they know that they will be personally identified in the public's mind with the historic district vote.

Whatever we say to them about the merits of district designation and what it means for them politically, they will hear it as *our* views, those of biased citizens. So what can help our effort better than hearing from another mayor uniquely suited to inspire?

Here's the plan: I've written what follows as a letter to your mayor. Use it as you wish.

A SPECIAL MESSAGE FOR YOUR MAYOR

Your Honor,

With respect, I have taken the liberty of suggesting to your constituents that they submit this interview to you in support of their historic district effort.

To see how a district can work to great effect, you need go no further than Brian Hicks's *The Mayor: Joe Riley and the Rise of Charleston*. In the meantime, join me if you will on a trip to South Carolina to meet the man the *New York Times* has called perhaps "the most loved politician in America."

Charleston's local historic district, the nation's first, was founded in 1931. Some forty years along, in 1975, Joe Riley became the city's mayor for another visionary forty years. He's now retired from politics, but far from disengaged. He has generously agreed to talk through me to you about your pending district vote.

Christina Mortti, so very helpful in arranging our interview, greets us in reception. Moments later, the former mayor comes through with expected Southern charm, and I shake the hand that had so deftly levered power for so long.

Now inside his office, I win the first of many smiles by quoting Lyndon Johnson, although a tad inelegantly: "By the time a man scratches his behind, clears his throat, and tells me how smart he is, we've already wasted fifteen minutes." Still, I launch into a prologue. I tell him that I want to help you see your way through the contentious issue of supporting a new historic district.

Joe Riley: Good for you. Fire away.

Me: Let's assume I'm the mayor. Besides the district's backers, I've got folks just as set against it. The way I see it now—it'll be the first historic district in our town—I can go either way.

Joe Riley: [Without hesitation, firmly.] Mr. Mayor, it's unlikely you will do anything more significant in your tenure as mayor than assisting your citizens in creating a historic district. It ensures that twenty-five or a hundred years from now, the character of your town, its scale, its history, its lessons, its buildings speak to you. You keep your town from being any place, anywhere, by assuring its distinctiveness. You make it a more desirable place for people to live. The historic district strengthens and enhances the economy. Because, let's face it, Mr. Mayor, there are lots of small and medium towns in America, many faceless, all the same. In every community that has engaged a historic district to preserve its past, it has differentiated itself.

Me: You make the choice sound easy.

Joe Riley: If you go for it, the road will be bumpy. A lot of decisions won't be easy ones in the process. You do the best you can. But if ever you err, err on the side of preservation, because you're doing it for future generations.

Me: By keeping things the way they are?

Joe Riley: Well, Mr. Mayor, preservation is a very futuristic kind of thing, for lack of a better word. Because you're not freezing a community. In a democracy, a city or a town is about its citizens, and new buildings will get built and there will be adaptive reuses of older buildings. So there will always be new energy that citizens will bring. But if you have the fabric and the scale of another time, you've given your town a character, a style that can't be recreated, and that is what you build on.

Me: Okay, but the devil's in the details, right?

Joe Riley: The new is very important, and this, Your Honor, is very contro-versial. It's very important that you have design review. Get it with a historic preservation ordinance. Get it any way you can.

Me: It's *that* critical?

Joe Riley: The reason why design review is important—if somebody owns a building, has a lot, and you give them some guidelines and they say, "You know, this trouble is going to cost me money," what you say is, "Mr. Citizen, let me tell you something. You know that vacant lot next to you? What this ensures is, something worthwhile gets built there. Your property values are going to be protected." So in the design of the new, that's where a board of architectural review [his BAR, our HPC] has input. You want good people advising because you don't want to try to copy something, or build something that looks like its seventy-five years old. On the other hand, you don't want an architect saying, "Aha! I've got this historic district and I'll show them what I do!" A new build-ing can be of its current time, but it shouldn't show off. And you've got to keep the junk out.

Me: The junk?

Joe Riley: [Smiling.] That's right.

Me: You know, some of the opponents I've heard from basically agree with you. As good Americans, they say, they're just opposed to excessive regula-tions. So I'm thinking, what if we got design review, but made it voluntary?

Joe Riley: What I'd say to them is: "If you ever get a chance, go to Charleston, South Carolina, because there you see new buildings subject to stringent design review. The buildings are compatible and the city's economy couldn't be stron-ger, and so it's proof in America that it works."

Me: But folks resist government intrusion by bureaucrats and unelected boards.

Joe Riley: [Smiling.] Well, it's not some foreign power or the national govern-ment telling you in a historic district what you ought to do. In our democracy, it's local citizens who have input, say-so. The owner and the BAR, preservation-ists, and everyone who has an interest. It's good American give-and-take.

Me: Still, they stand on property rights.

Joe Riley: There's a fine phrase, Mr. Mayor, and that's the "public realm." That's not just some public park, court house, and so forth. It's the collective, the *tout ensemble*, of what has been created. It's reasonable that you take into consideration that greater value in your town. So if I'm engaging in a project and I'm having my plans reviewed, and getting input, and people guide what I do—not some bureaucratic entity from Washington, D.C., but local people, all good fellow citizens, you know—it'll all work out.

Me: So what are you saying? That if we get this district up and going, the politi-cal turmoil will just settle down into an administrative process?

Joe Riley: [Laughing.] Well, if it ends right now, you'll miss out on a lot of fun.

Me: [Caught off-guard and laughing.] A lot of *fun*? That's terrible!

Joe Riley: [Speaking through his laughter.] No, no, it's okay. It's like a robust family discussion about something where everybody cares about each other. And you can get some pretty feisty arguments around the dinner table. So with your district, there will be some discussion. That's good. It isn't over. But it's okay. It means, you know, if you're the artist you produce good art, if you're a writer you produce better writing: it's like the arguments you have with yourself. It's the same kind of thing. It's okay, Mr. Mayor. Don't worry about that.

Me: Don't worry? It seems to me it's one thing to listen to everybody, and another thing to pick a side. When I do—it's tough. Some will be rewarded and others disappointed.

Joe Riley: Well, you do the best you can. You do as much work as you can to make sure your decision is correct. You listen to people whose judgment you respect and have confidence in, and listen to those with whom you disagree. The thing is this: Do the best you can, but remember that this may be a hundred-year decision. Keep in mind that long after you are gone somebody will be visiting your town. If what could have made it great has disappeared, they might ask: "Why in the world did they let that happen?" Or you'll hope they'll say: "This is really great, what they did." [He smiles.] So do the best you can.

I sit back and look at him. This is what we came for, brief and to the point. I glance at my recorders. "You were smart to bring in two," he says. "Didn't want to miss a thing," I say. And yet already I am sensing my transcription will sound flat compared to what's transpired.

In black and white upon the page, the points he made on merit may sound to you like arguments. The way that he delivered them—his tone, his style, his eyes, his smiles, the gestures with his hands—they came as opportunities for you to forge a legacy.

More important still, he's spoken to you mayor-to-mayor, facing your uncertainties and sharing his experience. He was not a one- or two-term mayor, but ten. If the district could have turned on him, it would have done so long ago.

Not all of it's been smooth. He took some lumps along the "bumpy" road he mentioned only once. But look again and listen to his many small encouragements: "don't worry," "it's okay," "it'll all work out," and his oft-repeated charge to do "the best you can," that is, that it will be enough. Spoken reassuringly without a second thought, they have the ring of truth from his forty years in office.

They, then, are our takeaway. He wanted you to know that once you have your district, you *will* find its politics more buoying than threatening, rewarding—even fun if you embrace them.

The choice is yours to make, of course, and I don't envy you your job. Nor did Lyndon Johnson. At the end of the interview, I quote from him once more: "When the burdens of the presidency seem unusually heavy, I always remind myself it could be worse. I could be a mayor."

This earns a parting laugh. I thank Mayor Riley for his time. He shakes my hand and thanks me for my service. Does he mean me—*or you*, the mayor I've represented?

I wish you well with your decision, and I thank you for your time.

A FINAL THOUGHT

Back out on the street and walking through the district, again I think of LBJ. He knew his limitations. As I pause and look around, I'm glad to see Joe Riley never met his own.

His example is inspiring, just like Lincoln said. The irony escapes me not, as I head off to The Battery to glimpse Fort Sumter from the park.[1]

NOTE

1. References omitted from the text of the "Message for Your Mayor" are: Brian Hicks, *Mr. Mayor: Joe Riley and the Rise of Charleston*, Charleston: Evening Post Books, 2015, with a forward by Pat Conroy; and Frank Bruni, "Is Joe Riley of Charleston the Most Loved Politician in America?" www.nytimes.com, July 5, 2014.

Chapter Thirty-Five

A Checklist for One-on-One Meetings

Come, give us a taste of your quality.

—William Shakespeare, *Hamlet*

The moment has come to keep your appointments with our elected officials. This is your best chance to show them who you are. So are you ready?

Here's a checklist to help you get squared away. Most of it should be obvious by now.

1. **Work your contacts.** Have your reputation precede you. Get the introductions that will make the Mayor or Council member look forward to meeting with you. Ask a well-connected supporter or shaper to place a phone call. Check with national, state, and local preservation groups for influential intermediaries.
2. **Know the territory.** This is the land of politics. You will be having a political discussion that has political objectives. Don't push them to agree with you on preservation if they'll vote with us for other reasons.
3. **Suit up for the game.** Become them. Dress as they dress. Look and act the part. There are two kinds of intelligence: the kind you *gather* and the kind you *show*. You want them to say to themselves, "Well now, there's more to this than I suspected. Maybe this can work for me, too." Intractable issues are sometimes decided on the basis of personalities. The more appealing party can get the vote.
4. **Go with others.** As Clint Eastwood said in Pale Rider, "a man alone is easy prey." Especially if you're a political novice. Take along two or three people who know which end is up. Divvy up the presentation and rehearse it. Be ready to bail each other out of tight spots.

5. **Know your subject.** Think inside the box and *know that box*! You're looking for fluency in focused arguments. Stay on message. No invention and no speculation. Don't talk about what you don't know. Remember Molly Ivins's advice: If you get in a hole, stop digging.

6. **Don't personalize issues.** By now the politics of personality are in full swing. Don't use opponents' names to characterize issues. It will make them memorable and make you sound petty.

7. **Know your policy maker.** It's smart and courteous to know your host. Assess the relative influence of the Mayor and each Council member. See where the likely swing votes are. Find out what is important to them and focus on that. Engrave on your memory any comments pointing to intramural Council politics that you should avoid or might exploit.

8. **Look them in the eye.** Watch how they respond to you. See when to move on. If you get stuck, island-hop. Move on to the next topic. What was a sticking point may be resolved in the process.

9. **Listen.** Don't just tell them what you think is important. Make sure you understand their point of view. They know best where the levers are to move the vote.

10. **Be positive. Expect to win.** Reframe negative questions and comments in constructive manner. Don't blame others and don't make points at someone else's expense. Be for, not against. Talk of possibilities, not problems.

11. **Focus on their interests.** What does the historic district mean for them as politicians and as elected officials? What does it mean for the City at large? Don't leave them thinking you don't appreciate their needs. Explore compromises.

12. **Keep your rhetoric cool.** Lose your temper and the district will flicker out like your last match on a windy night. Don't rise to incitements and don't debate—you can't win. Say nothing you'll regret the next day.

13. **Be brief.** You have a perishable claim on their attention. Dick Morris says that any political idea can be conveyed in thirty seconds. Even a minute is no time for minutiae. Make a point and then move on to the next one.

14. **Avoid jargon and technicalities.** Don't show off what you know about preservation's more arcane concepts. Speak simply and clearly to sell the district.

15. **Have your talking points ready.** Talking points should be dual use: to convey *content* and to have the desired *political effect*. Give them concepts and facts to side with you. Supply them with the words, phrases, and statements that they can use.

16. **Have one-page position papers in hand.** Preface them with an executive summary of the origins of the effort, main objectives, points of

contention, community meetings and due process, and reasons for voting yes. Have briefing papers ready on such basics as:

- The legal basis of historic districts.
- A glossary of regulatory terms—list of work activities, design guidelines, certificate of appropriateness.
- Justification of the district's geographical boundaries.
- The chronology of our community notifications and meetings.
- Documentation of outreach to our opposition.

Coordinate your materials with other briefing packets (see chapter 27). Include a copy of the FAQs document you distributed in the community. Have your contact information on every page, including your website.

17. **Tell them your story.** Brief them on how we reinvigorated a sense of civic pride and responsibility in the community. Show them how voters have come to say "yes" to districting.

18. **Give them a heads-up on the downside.** Help them reduce their exposure and manage negative fallout from voting for us. Tell them the juice is worth the squeeze.

19. **Invite them on a tour of the district.** Put a face on your district, a living dimension to your proposal. This will make an abstraction a concrete reality for them.

20. **Put a hyphen in your conversation when you leave.** Don't expect a commitment yet. Keep the door propped open. Find a way to stay in touch. Then follow up.

21. **Thank them.** As we'll hear in the next chapter, few people remember to thank politicians for their work. Be the exception, and make it sincere. After all, the words *polite* and *politics* share the same root, as do *civil* and *civics*. Being polite is politic, and civil the key to civic accomplishment.

Bear in mind that their time is valuable. Follow Big Dan Teague's rule in *O Brother, Where Art Thou?* "The one thing you don't want is air in the conversation."

Chapter Thirty-Six

Our Public Hearing Presentation

I'm always a nervous wreck, or I wouldn't be in politics.

—James Carville

A public hearing is like a trial by ordeal. It is less about a search for truth or the facts in evidence than how we survive it. So let's plan to get it over with quickly.

I don't think the City Council is looking forward to it either. They are used to presentations running on and on as citizens parade to the microphone to say their piece one after another. You can be sure that if we discipline our presentation they'll be grateful.

What's there to lose anyway? As a practical matter, we may assume that most opportunities to win their support will have been seized or missed before we walk into the Council chamber.

We've met one-on-one with Council members and the Mayor and given them information packets. We've invited them to tour the district. We have, I trust, favorable reports from the HPC and Planning Commission. The newspaper has covered us. Letters and e-mails have been written and phone calls placed.

What better way is there to demonstrate our leadership in the community than to exercise it now in the public hearing? We can do this briefly and, so, impressively.

GETTING TO BINGO

As I'm considering this I run into Bob Agee, our City Administrator, and he couldn't agree more. "Always do that," he tells me. "Avoid redundancy." He has spent years in Council meetings and says that "the one thing that'll just drive you crazy is hearing the same thing over and over and over again. Soon you stop hearing anything, even when new points are interjected."

The core of our presentation must be a unified message delivered in a political narrative that quickly puts on the record:

• This is why the district deserves overlay protection.
• This is the practical vision that's won over property owners.
• This is the civic community that has arisen in the midst of conflict.
• This is what the district will mean for the rest of the City.
• This is what it can help Council members do.
• This is what they can do for it: *vote yes.*

That's your outline. Mix in whatever specific issues motivate Council members. They'll be ticking them off as you speak. You want each of them to get to "Bingo!" as fast as possible.

I'll leave the details to you and your steering committee. You've become the masters of your local situation.

And that's the way I want you to present yourself to decision makers. When you speak to them speak as leader to leader. Show them you know what you are doing, that you've grown accustomed to success in the community and that you expect to win.

PROCEDURAL QUESTIONS

Check out how the City Council conducts hearings. Will we have to sign up to speak, and when? In what order will speakers be taken? First come first served? Or will it be proponents first and opponents later? What is established Council practice?

Will there be any changes in procedure, perhaps because of expected turnout? Will there be unusual time limits on individual presentations, for example? Don't accept secondhand assurances. Call the chair—if not the chair, then the Council secretary or the City Attorney—nail it down and ask to be informed if things change.

While you're at it, ask how the Council will gauge support. Will folks be asked to stand in support or opposition? It's important to paper the room with our supporters anyway. But we still want to know how the Council will distinguish between property owners and others in attendance.

This is where we need to make our case for our petition. After all, it's easier for a nephew to stand with an uncle against us—regardless of what

214214214214214214214214214214214214214 214214214214214214214214214214214214214214

Be forward looking in your conclusion to underscore the compatibility of historic districting with community development and change. Once more stress the core of our civic vision, that we are taking responsibility for our future as well as our past.

We've been down that road so many times by now that you should be able to speak from your heart instead of from notes. And as FDR once advised, "Be sincere, be brief, be seated."

CAUTIONS

Bob Agee thinks this take-control approach will stand us in good stead. But he's also eager to share some cautionary perspectives from his experience. So we follow him back to his office for a chat.

Bob: You want to be careful in several areas. When you get to the Council chamber, be aware that there may be personality conflicts up there between elected officials. Don't get caught up in their likes and don't-likes. Be dedicated and firm about your cause, but don't be overly defensive or irritated. Don't be impolite, rude, and obnoxious. Don't allow yourself to be pulled in and pulled down by someone else's lack of courtesy. Just extend courtesy even when it's not extended to you. At the end of the day, even if you can scream louder and scream more points at an elected official, that person *has* a vote and you *don't.* [Laughter.]

Me: That seems commonsensical. We're going to work hard at presenting our case in a respectful and responsible manner.

Bob: But don't just assume people are working on a subject in good faith with the idea of trying to come up with a reasonable solution.

Me: [I give him my best interviewer's surprised well-why-not? look.]

Bob: Think about election cycles, for example. If members are wanting to get reelected, that can make everything different. Maybe someone is looking for an issue to make a campaign point, something to rally people around. So you may be in the unfortunate position of having a Council member who has decided to start a fire with the district issue—and pouring kerosene on it will help him get reelected. It might be that they want to keep someone else from getting elected. So they end up taking a position that has nothing to do with the subject matter of the issue. It just has to do with their own political survival in that case.

Me: Now you've got me thinking about the personality issue again. How should we be thinking about the interplay among Council members?

Bob: All of us have relationships with people we have confidence in. If a seat-mate is expert in an area and I'm not, I might just follow her lead. The Council is just a group with the usual group dynamics. And there are people who are going to go against what someone else wants out of sheer spite. If the other guy is for it, they're against it. It's as simple as that.

Me: Which seems to caution against being identified too closely with the wrong official.

Bob: You want everybody's support. But another might then tell you, "I understand what you want. I don't have any problem with it. But you've got sponsor problems." That is, someone you might have as your champion is a pariah. The result is that you've encumbered that person's baggage. That's the unpleasant part of what is a dynamic political process.

Me: How can a political novice keep from blundering into that kind of political minefield?

Bob: Do your homework. If you don't know what to expect, you're already behind the eight ball and probably aren't going to get anywhere.

Me: Maybe we ought to hire a professional to handle the hearing for us. [Pause.] You don't look so sure. . . .

Bob: You have to be the judge of what you need. But I'd caution you to be careful that your speaker speaks to the right audience. I've seen it happen. You think they're doing just a great job and you love everything they're saying. But up on the dais it's not going well with the Council members at all. What's happening is that your speaker is following his paycheck. He's talking to *you*, the audience that is behind him in the chamber and not the audience up in front that's going to make the decision. He—or she—doesn't need to convince *you*; they need to be convincing the *others*.

Me: And if we do it ourselves? Is there a secret to success?

Bob: Be firm but polite. You want to make it hard for them to dislike you. And don't forget to say "thank you." Say: "We really want to thank you for your interest and support on this. And at the conclusion, whichever way it goes, we appreciate your time." Politicians get blamed a lot. When you like the result, it's because the cause was good and it should have succeeded on its own merits. But if it doesn't go the way you want it to, then it's because "those people are dumb, incapable, and corrupt." The simple act of giving a little credit means a lot. It's probably the most powerful and underused weapon you have in getting where you're trying to go.

Me: But is that really going to win votes for us?

Bob: You don't want to *lose* votes. You have to know how to count. You need a majority. If you have eleven Council members, you need six. It's that simple. If you've got six or seven going in, you can feel great. But the only thing that's certain in politics is uncertainty. All of a sudden something comes up—a group from the audience surprises you. You look at the dais and see things are falling apart.

Me: Then what?

Bob: I have a saying: Never go into a room that doesn't have another door.

Me: Can we ask the Council for a postponement?

Bob: You can ask, but it doesn't mean you'll get it. The other side will object. Suppose you count seven votes before the hearing. Then one member comes down with the flu. That leaves you six. In the middle of the meeting another rushes out because of a family emergency. That's politics. If you're a general in the field and a general on the other side has something unfortunate happen, are you going to say, "Oh, give them a time-out!?" No. You're going to push the battle.

Me: So what kind of second door do you mean?

Bob: Remember the old saying: The perfect is the enemy of the possible. You might not be able to get 100 percent of what you want. Don't reject all amendments as hostile and out of hand. Now, sometimes they *are* hostile. Sometimes they are meant to cripple. But don't be afraid to deal with amendments and take less than what you regard as the best. That's when you might get a delay, too. Thank them for bringing up "some good points." Say that you'd like to work on language with their staff that will satisfy their concerns. Still, if you have eight or nine votes you can count on, you can be less attentive and push things through.

Me: So how would you tell a friend to prepare for the hearing, to feel composed?

Bob: You mean you? *You* I'd tell, go have a good stiff drink and relax!

His smile said no hostility there, and I made sure to thank him for his help. We spoke briefly about the next chapter. I told him we'd be looking beyond tactical amendments to the far more serious question of responding to compromise pressures that might win the vote but gut our proposal. He gave me a look that said "good luck."

Chapter Thirty-Seven

The Politics of Compromise

The middle of the road is for yellow lines and dead armadillos.

—Texas Representative Jim Hightower

And it's a long and winding road that brings us back to Newnan, Georgia. It's more a land of possums than armadillos, but the center lines are just as yellow.

You remember Newnan, don't you? That's where the Planning and Zoning Department authored the fateful last-minute, center-of-the-road compromise that made their guidelines voluntary. "That's like making the speed limit voluntary," an observer said as politics ran over them.[1]

Can we avoid their fate? The hour is late. Our City Council hearing has been difficult and wearing. We have stood for *firm principles vigorously defended* and *practical results resolutely pursued*. How should we respond if the Council broaches compromise to satisfy our opponents?

We'll need to keep our wits awake to accept the challenge on our terms to keep our plan from being DOA.

WHAT OUR OPPONENTS WANT

When Breakers talk compromise they want changes to our proposal that add up to no district at all. Their bottom line typically is that there needs to be "a way to opt out" of the district, as a Simpsonville, South Carolina, opponent said in their designation battle.[2]

218

The three most common offers are:

- To exempt their individual properties—the so-called Swiss cheese option.
- To make the district's design review procedures voluntary, as in Newnan.
- To have design review be mandatory, but compliance voluntary.

They all say the same thing politically: "Here's my compromise. I'll shut up about *your* district if I can do what I want with *my* property."

Such has resonance in Council chambers. In Durham, North Carolina, Councilman Eddie Davis was reported as saying "he supports people's freedom to want to live in a protected district, but he also supports the right of property owners to do what they want to do with their individual properties."[3]

THE PERIL OF LEGALISM

Each option raises a variety of legal issues for the Council. Nothing derails a hearing faster than legal uncertainties. So if any of these alternatives looks like it might figure in your hearing, you'll be wise to have a preservation law specialist ready to respond authoritatively. Speak in advance with the City Attorney as well, so that the Council gets good advice.

But don't get legalistic, as if law can save your grits. The City Council can pass any ordinance it wants, regardless of advice. The courts might overturn it later. But that won't put us any closer to designation, and our political moment will have passed.

Legalism is the intellectual error of thinking that law does or should govern politics. Actually, the power flow goes in the opposite direction most days. Let's take care of politics now, and sound, enduring law will follow.

DIAGRAMMING COMPROMISE

So where do we go with compromise? Most folks think that compromise is a matter of meeting each other halfway. Ask them to sketch out an issue and they'll draw a line with two opposed parties at either end. Somewhere on that line—in the middle, they'll guess—lies the point of compromise.

Let's put it to the test. Take a look at figure 37.1 with the center line marked. I've placed Breakers—our inflexible can't-tell-me-what-to-do opponents—on the far right-hand end. Now write *us* in. Where do we go? On the far left-hand side? We do only if we are equally inflexible save-it-at-all-costs preservationists. *But you and I are not on that end.*

| breakers

Figure 37.1
Created by the author.

Maybe we started out there a long time ago, but we know better now. We're practical preservationists. We've accommodated our vision to our neighbors' interests with just about all the compromising we can do. That got us our quotient of support that translates into a majority consensus for designation.

We and our coalition now occupy the vital center ground in the diagram right where we want to be. So we'll be happy to talk about compromise if that's what Council members want. But we'll talk about facts, not wishes. And our starting point will be: *the historic district* is *the compromise*.

HOW WE SEE COMPROMISE

That is an arresting claim. It should halt any headlong rush to find some—any—concession that'll paper over differences. We won't get much time to explain ourselves. Given a chance, I'd say something that more briefly tracks along like this:

1. The District as Our Compromise

I'd start by saying that the district is about far more than preservation. It's about forward-looking community development. It's an agreement we've negotiated with many of our neighbors who don't share our passion—the passion of preservationists—for our common historic legacy.

We ourselves would like to do more—perhaps a lot more—for preservation and its role in our community. But we've taken a "preservation-plus" approach. We've fitted together a diverse group of personal and community interests that now support designation.

Our coalition's strength is seen in what each of us has given up. The district squeezes us as preservationists to work constructively with forces for change, and it squeezes those who advocate change to build upon the past. Its mandated procedures squeeze all of us as property owners, too. Yet each one of us for our own reasons has come to the conclusion that, as we say, "The juice is worth the squeeze."

And you know what? That's as fine an expression of how compromise works when it works well as you're likely to find anywhere. It's our opponents who have placed themselves beyond accommodation.

2. The District as Streaming Accommodation

Is it reasonable to ask the community to compromise this core compromise for the mere appearance—but not the substance—of agreement with Breakers? No, of course not.

Compromising the district's arrangements will get us *nowhere*. And that's precisely where our opponents want it to go.

That's not surprising. The district will create a new political process for dealing with conflicting interests. It's always the case that such new arrangements are never welcomed by those whose interests get bigger play without them.

We're not singling out our opponents' interests, either. We've said from the beginning that everybody—including us—has interests that run into everybody else's all the time. When those conflicts affect the public interest, accommodations have to be found.

We're willing to work on our differences within a framework of the district's future guidelines and procedures. Our opponents are not. *We* talk about compromise and accommodation, and we put our money where our mouth is. *They* talk about compromise and they want to take a walk.

So what's the Council's responsibility? Is it to make the naysayers happy? Let's say it again: of course not. It's a *fundamental axiom* of democratic institutions—and our long-standing mantra—that there only has to be a majority of cooperating interests to make them *possible* while dissenting minority interests may show why they are *necessary*.

We and those on our side have agreed that our community needs a forum for a continuing conversation—*punctuated by authoritative decisions*—in which the community's interests in keeping historic resources in play will engage the widest array of other interests. That process may best be described as *streaming accommodation*.

LOOKING DOWN THE ROAD

Streaming accommodation means that over, say, the next ten years, scores of projects will be vetted through the HPC's procedures. Each review will aim at fitting preservation to the interests of the property owner and, conversely, the interests of the property owner to preservation. Each outcome, one after the other, will be a partial installment on our future.

Can't these arrangements be voluntary? Wouldn't that push the HPC to find accommodations rather than issue edicts? A good preservation commission will always work to get to "yes," but law is necessary. Without it, there will be no incentive for property owners to reciprocate. If the process fails, the Council can appoint new commissioners or revise the ordinance.

The district won't solve all our problems, nor is it intended to. Differences over teardowns and "McMansions," adaptive reuse and new construction, repair and replacement, traditional materials and new technologies will continue to confront us daily as our community evolves, pushed this way and that by competing interests. Yet that doesn't mean we shouldn't try to reach proximate settlements and, trying, find a practical way to move on down the road together.

IN THE COUNCIL'S INTEREST

So what's the Council's own interest in this? Its vote won't settle our differences with opponents. *But the vote will determine how and where those differences will be played out in the future.*

If we don't get the district, then we'll be back to fighting out our basic differences over and over, issue by issue, and project by project—and all without benefit of guidelines or ground rules. And guess where we'll be doing that on big-ticket issues?

I don't think I'd look forward to that prospect if I were on the City Council, would you? I'd much rather have the HPC play its role than to have the struggle over the future of the neighborhood dragged out before me, again and again and again.

Council members shouldn't start down that road. But if they do, then now's the time to cross their path and stare them down. It won't be easy. It takes a tough bird to play chicken. But then every kid in the South knows why the chicken crossed the road. It was to show the possum it could be done.

NOTES

1. Kevin Duffy, "History a Matter of Heart in Newnan," www.ajc.com, June 9, 2003.

2. April M. Silvaggio, "Debate Heats Up over Simpsonville District," www.greenville.com, August 8, 2004.

3. Virginia Bridges, "Durham City Council Approves Cohesive Golden Belt Historic District," www.newsobserver.com, September 7, 2016.

Chapter Thirty-Eight

Winning the Vote

It's the end that crowns us, not the fight.

—Robert Herrick

World War II, North Africa, at your local cinema. George C. Scott in *Patton* is crushing Field Marshal Erwin Rommel's panzers. "Rommel, you magnificent bastard!" he exults. "I read your book!"

The lesson? Know your opponents as they know themselves. I've kept that in mind. Just as Rommel's prewar writings gave away his strategy, so might mine to our opponents.

Generally speaking—if you'll forgive my pun—I doubt you'll run into any Pattons in your neighborhood. But you never know. Even if you do, and they gain some advantage here or there, we'll be better off for having had the preceding discussions among ourselves.

SEIZING THE BRASS RING

Still, our strategic line might not be sufficient to win the vote for designation. I want to prepare you for that eventuality, too. So it's time to think outside the box and prepare to do the unexpected.

Be brilliant! Catch your opponents off guard, move the Council, win. I can point you in the right direction. But it wouldn't be smart to show all our cards in public, would it?

And now at last congratulations all round! The vote is in. We've won the district. "So," as Othello said, "they laugh that win."

AND NOW?

What's next for us? Do we follow the lead of Cincinnatus, the Roman citizen-politician, and return to our plow now that the public's work is done? Not on your life, unless you want to give our opponents the last laugh.

At a time like this, you should heed Winston Churchill's timeless observation: "The problems of victory are more agreeable than those of defeat, but they are no less difficult."

You've already run a campaign and made promises. It's time you kept them. So get yourself back down to City Hall, see the Mayor, and offer to serve on the HPC. The district is going to need your continuing leadership.

Heaven knows, you've already been sworn at. Now step up, raise your right hand, and be sworn in.

Part VI

THE POLITICS OF ADMINISTERING
THE HISTORIC DISTRICT

Chapter Thirty-Nine

Our Transition to the HPC

The greatest danger occurs at the moment of victory.

—Napoleon Bonaparte

Thrilling, wasn't it, our political baptism by fire, even if it was unnerving at the start? What didn't beat us made us wiser, tougher.

Some may judge our victory flawed. They'll say we should have shown more zeal for our ideals to put our historic district on a less political footing. They may criticize us for abandoning our finest principles to find a way to win.

THE SECRET OF OUR SUCCESS

Well, if it was a simpler thing we did, it wasn't easy. We confined ourselves to getting what we could by manipulating the forces that constrained us. We schemed to win the vote to change the law by drawing other interests to our side. We inspired, negotiated, and hedged our bets to get agreement. I don't remember giving up our principles, do you?

Elsewhere, others who have aimed first at changing hearts and minds for heritage, and only then the law, have failed. The hard-nosed fight we fought was by result more moral. By aiming low, we got more. We won the district vote at City Hall; at home we built community.

And now, like the dog that caught the car, we have a district to administer.

OUR JOLTING START

How quickly now we pass from leading our community to reviewing applications for COAs. This startling shift from action to reaction alters how we think of change. It's mainly out of individual owners' interests—not our campaign vision—that the future of the district is being shaped, often as it seems by random chance, by who wants what and when and where.

So here we are fresh from making history, now enmeshed in a project-driven process in which the future comes at us piecemeal, application by often-numbing application for windows, doors, and rooftop changes. These get shuffled in with plans for rehabilitations, restorations, adaptations, new additions and in-kind repairs, as well as public projects and large-scale new construction.

We drop our eyes to what's at hand, and then we get surprised. "We're standing on sand," Gary Prolaska told one of my Wisconsin workshops as he described the plight of his Platteville HPC. "Things are happening and we don't hear about them until the eleventh hour and then we have to deal with it."

The problem for us now is what Gregg Easterbrook, in *The Progress Paradox*, has called the "tyranny of the small picture."[1] A Cleveland preservationist worries about approving a tear-down for a freeway: "It's a 'bigger picture' than just one building that really matters."[2] The political impact of our work is easily overlooked when we focus on a single project. "Frankly I was stunned by the level of useless nit-picking that went on," a critic told the Jackson, California, City Council about a HPC hearing on a hotel restoration. He, too, said that commissioners had "lost sight of the big picture."[3]

Vetting COAs is simpler than campaigning. "Mistakes are always made when people get to the easy places," wrote the Buddhist monk Kenko in fourteenth-century Japan.[4]

COMMISSION TRAINING

In a perfect situation, we will have undergone commission training before we begin reviewing COAs.[5] I have sat through several sessions that center on "best practices." The overall goal is defensible decision making in a transparent, consistent, and predictable COA review process. You'll typically start with general concepts like understanding your ordinance, guidelines, and due process. Then you'll move on to such specifics as procedure, conforming projects, and how to conduct yourself in hearings.

You may work for better outcomes, but you'll be advised you must approve any project that even barely fits inside the envelope of your ordinance and guidelines. As a matter of priority, you'll hear that getting to "yes" ASAP is highly prized. While mastering the material we learn to discipline ourselves, our expectations and behavior.

And why is this important? Because, still thrilling from our triumph, we may overreach for preservation. As Thucydides said of the Athenians in the aftermath of battle, "their extraordinary success made them confuse their strength with their hopes."

THE IMPERMANENCE OF LAW

Our administrative strength is in the law. It enshrines not hopes, which know no bounds, but rather the distribution of influential interests at the moment law is made. Because those interests keep changing, the law is never stable as we proved in our campaign.

In fact, the model way we changed the law may now be used against us. In Wisconsin, the Madison Trust's Jason Trish described the way a development company got the Common [City] Council to overturn the denial of a hotel rehab and expansion project. "Sell the project to city officials," he wrote, "and as many Council members, neighbors, and members of the public as will buy it, and the codified zoning restrictions, including Historic District requirements, are up for negotiation."[6]

THE PERMANENCE OF POLITICS

Do you see the lesson? After designation, politics only seems to stop at the threshold of administration. The truth is that it doesn't.

"They are wrong who think," said Plutarch, "that politics is like an ocean voyage or a military campaign, something to be done with some particular end in view, something which leaves off as soon as that end is reached. It is not a public chore, to be got over with. It is a way of life."

What does that tell us? We have to gird ourselves anew with politics to fit our present situation. If we are to keep our law and make it work, we have to shift our thinking from the politics of victory to sustaining what we won.

EMERGING DISTRICT DANGERS

Our districts will face many threats. Some are *avoidable*, and have to do with us, as we will see, and some are *inevitable*, no matter what we do. Through them all, the most important factor in our future will be *keeping with us* those who *can undo us*.

We do this by being faithful public servants of the many varied interests that got us where we are.

NOTES

1. Gregg Easterbrook, *The Progress Paradox*, New York: Random House Trade Paperbacks, 2004.

2. CraigB, "More Local History to Be Lost for Freeways?" www.preservation-sanspolitics.blogspot.com, May 8, 2006.

3. Scott Thomas Anderson, "Public Rallies for National, Jackson Leaders Bypass Planning Commission," www.ledger-dispatch.com, June 28, 2011.

4. Robert Greene, *Power*, New York: Penguin Books, 1998, p. 414.

5. This will be my shorthand way of saying "reviewing applications for Certificates of Appropriateness." Some prefer "design review," though not every COA, such as those for extensive maintenance or in-kind replacements, involve design.

6. Jason Tish, "Edgewater: Losing the Preservation Argument," Executive Director's Blog, www.madisonpreservation.org, June 10, 2010.

Chapter Forty

On Public Service

We don't have time for your damn hobbies, Sir!

—Captain Jack Aubrey, *Master and Commander*

As the federal agency tasked with preservation, the National Park Service invites you to explore preservation "as a career or a hobby."[1] Where does this leave volunteers like us on HPCs? I hope it was an oversight.

This much I know: If you've engaged preservation as a "career or hobby," you leave *your* own interests at the door when you enter public service. You don't scrub your mind of them. But the HPC is not the place for them, nor has it got the time. Once the proper business meeting starts, you serve the *public*'s interests, not your own.

PUBLIC VIRTUE

This isn't always as clear as it should be. Most local governments expect their HPC commissioners to have personal preservation interests in their career or hobby backgrounds. Because those interests lead to their appointments, such commissioners may think themselves anointed to pursue them on their HPCs and—attention, please!—*that doing so is virtuous*. Those who think this way are wrong.

Okay, maybe just confused. They want to do the right thing, sure. But they are conflating different virtues:

1. A *private virtue* that has inspired their *preservation* interests.
2. A *public virtue* that must inform their service to the *district*.

Let me lay the difference out:

- As *private* citizens, we may pursue our preservation interests and pay the price alone when our actions don't pan out.
- But those who have a *public* trust may not.

As HPC commissioners, we sacrifice the district's *credibility* when we use our *capability* in decision making to elevate our preservation interests above the business of the citizens we serve. An ability to discipline ourselves to the success of our HPCs is always and everywhere a sign of political maturity.

But note: Expertise is welcomed. In Portsmouth, Maine, HPC members have caught the difference. Touting the diverse professional makeup of their board, they wrote that without it "we would be making decisions based on personal likes and dislikes rather than on the accepted principles of those fields. . . . [We] have a wide variety of opinions and no agenda other than the safeguarding of our Historic District according to our ordinance."[2]

Maybe George H.W. Bush inadvertently set the standard for us in keeping the personal and public separate: "I have opinions of my own—strong opinions—but I don't always agree with them."

Each time you walk into a commission meeting, you would do well to mentally recite something David Brooks has said on the *NewsHour*: "You leave private life behind when you go into government."[3]

OUR ROLE AND GOAL

Public service is a *role* we play on behalf of others: our former foes and backers and those who didn't take a stand during our campaign. *They* may come before the HPC and testify according to their interests. But *we* commissioners are pledged to decide things on their merits according to our ordinance.

Still, it's morally small of us to think that administration is just about conforming projects to the district's law and guidelines.

James Madison, who was the wisest thinker of his age, sets us straight in *Federalist 62*: "A good government implies two things: first, fidelity to the object of government, which is the happiness of the people; secondly, a knowledge of the means by which that object can be best maintained."

The second is the aim of standard commission training. The first is up to us, to put smiles on people's faces. This doesn't mean that every applicant must leave our meetings grinning. But it does mean that the community at large should be secure in their belief that we are serving them.

OUR ESSENTIAL TASKS

No legacy I know is as rich as committed public service. Our administrative challenge as HPC commissioners is to make sound decisions when vetting COAs. More generally, we are responsible for upholding the political good order of our districts. In doing so we must sustain the public view that:

- our essential administrative tasks are being fulfilled,
- our process runs smoothly according to the law,
- we are respectful of all interests,
- our decisions are just and prudent, and
- we pay heed to criticism.

Yes, that too.

CREDITING OUR CRITICS

Back in our campaign our critics were a challenge, and so they will remain. Then, we pitched our district to our neighbors, and now they're hurling beanballs back. "We're not anti-preservation, we're anti-HPC," we hear in Frederick, Maryland. "Trying to deal with these folks is something more than you can bear."[4]

Has that been said of you? Well, my friend, it will. In fact, you'll find such barbs so common as to be considered *de rigueur*. But what if dismissing them as such is *de rigueur* with us, and we miss important insights into how we're doing?

Michael Gerson has written on how hard it is to see "the wheel on which we turn," to see ourselves as others do when we are on the top—and they are not. That takes "empathy," he says, "the ability to imagine oneself in a different social circumstance, to feel just a bit of the helplessness and anger" others feel. "And it calls upon moral imagination—the capacity to dream of a better future."[5]

We once dreamed of better futures for our communities. If we're not putting smiles on people's faces, then we should pay attention to their frowns.

TREATMENT OF OUR ILLS

This requires a healthy self-examination of our links to the community right down to individuals. I don't know your community, can't point to particulars that need addressing by your HPC. Even so, I have looked across the country to detect some common ills.

If you are truly well, then fine. But you might treat the problems I'll be raising like the medical history you fill out before your annual physical. As you check them off in the following chapters, I hope you'll say, "Not me, not me, not me."

Still, you don't want your doctor taking your word for it, do you? You want a medically aggressive examination. It does no good to hear, "Well, since you haven't noticed that thing on your back I'll see you next year." You want the doc to assume the worst, biopsy what you failed to see, and then decide on treatment.

OUR WORST CASE SCENARIO

As I've checked the health records of historic districts all around the country, I've looked for signs of trouble. I have selected the best examples of the worst cases and lumped them together in "our" district.

It amounts to a rather glum diagnosis. But I want you to take heart. I doubt any real historic district "presents" them all, as doctors say. My own doctor- ate is in politics. By pointing out to you what *can* happen, I mean to interest you in wellness.

FORESIGHTFUL SERVICE

Beyond our essential tasks, the wellness of our district rests with us. When we fought for designation we knew that the worst thing in politics is to be right and to lose. And now, the second worst thing in politics is to win then fritter away our victory by neglecting the compact with our neighbors that brought our plans to life.

NOTES

1. Jenny Parker, "Learn How to Be a Preservationist," www.nps.gov/subjects/ historicpreservation/learn.

2. Letter to the Editor, "HDC Members Want Almeida to Remain Chairman," www.seacoastonline.com, July 26, 2016.

3. Public Broadcasting System, *NewsHour*, December 23, 2016.

4. Erika L. Green, "Historic Preservation Commission Criticism Not Supported by Numbers," www.gazette.net, January 22, 2009.

5. Michael Gerson, "From Selma to Ferguson, *The Washington Post*, March 10, 2015, p. A17.

Chapter Forty-One

Our Community
Compact for Rooted Growth

History is the myth we live, and in our living, constantly remake.

—Robert Penn Warren

In the post-campaign euphoria of victory you'll find yourself wanting to visit other historic districts. Each will have an ordinance and most will have a set of guidelines mapping out the scope of its regulatory intent. Some will care for a bare minimum, reflecting political realities and Bill Clinton's maxim, "If you can't get a dollar and you can get a dime, take a dime every time." Others will be quarter, half-dollar, six-bit, or even pricier districts.

If you're like me, all the streets and buildings will begin to blur together. But everywhere you go you'll find that commitment to *community* is the prevailing district ethos. The "days are gone," Richard Moe once said at the National Trust, when preservation simply aimed at protecting buildings. "Preservation is in the business of saving communities and the values they embody."[1]

THE COMPACT

Well, yes, except that is not the way it works. Those of us who have actually led districting campaigns know that we create *communities and value* by forging common interests into a shared vision of the future in which preservation finds its place.

The result is a tacit compact with our neighbors that aims at what I think we ought to call "rooted growth."

ROOTED GROWTH

If the term is new, the concept isn't. It's what we argued for when we campaigned on "preservation-plus." We knew that district designation would *not* be preservation's triumph *over* change. Rather, district designation ensures a place for preservation *within* on-going change as our neighbors bring their projects in for our review.

Now that we have our district, "rooted growth" does a better job than "historic preservation" in describing district goals.

- "Rooted" speaks to our neighbors' interests in security against haphazard change, and it relates to our own concern for protecting historic resources.
- "Growth" points to their interests in improving their situations, while it captures our own stake in community vitality for securing historic resources.

"Rooted growth" agrees with novelist Ellen Glasgow's observation: "All change is not growth, as all movement is not forward." Growth as change that we support is qualitative. It covers new construction, yet also stabilization, rehabilitation, restoration, and adaptive reuse of historic resources.

It cannot countenance demolition by neglect, which Michael Young in Salisbury, North Carolina, calls "a colossal short-sighted lack of imagination. . . . Jobs and growth do not come through demolition and the degradation of our downtown historic district."[2]

Adopting "rooted growth" assures us of a steady tone with a historic vision, a firm commitment to the past wedded to a sense as well of how our district changes.

SEIZING AN ADVANTAGE

If "growth" makes you cringe, then "rooted change" might do. But why cede half of our advantage at the outset?

As San Franciscan Tim Redmond has pointed out, "change and growth" are "key words that anyone who has followed local politics knows are the mantra of developers who want to get rid of historic landmarks."[3]

"Growth" is the high ground in this recurring contest. By putting it at the center of our message, we can steal the rhetorical thunder of developers and get other decision makers, from property and business owners to elected officials, to think about us differently.

"Rooted growth" also better represents the way our backers think if their main interests aren't in preservation but in, say, retail business, real estate, or tourism.

This doesn't settle *how* rooted growth takes place. Here in Annapolis, a guest columnist observes that "Residents, merchants and developers regularly contend over views of stewardship of the historic district (our national treasure), promotion of the city as a destination for tourism and sailing, and the encouragement of diverse downtown businesses."[4] That we "contend" is true, but there is an overarching effort to make them work together.

AVOIDING "BALANCE"

HPC decision making is always fretted by the question of *what to save* and *what to change.* Typically we hear, as Jenn Stanley has observed, that commissioners are seeking "balance" between "*remembering their roots and promoting progress.*"[5]

But by itself "balance" is no guide. It conjures up the image of a seesaw with equal weight on either side. Take the recurring issue in our districts of embracing new materials in repairs. Are we aiming at *in-kind* changes, *similar* repairs, maintaining a historic *look*, or salvaging the *integrity* of historic materials through heroic effort? If the choice were truly one of "balance" between what is saved and what is changed, then shouldn't every district look the same?

They don't look the same because every community puts its own thumb on the scales. An Illinois city planner says the Lake Forest Preservation Foundation (LFPF) partners with the city "to make sure we strike the *right* balance between preservation and change."[6]

But what does "right" imply? Look, I'm not splitting hairs. Folks will use "balance" to attack us when they want to. "I thought you wanted balance," they might say, "but now you're saying no to my commonsense repairs."

Elected officials will use it that way, too. I recently received this email, for example: "'Property rights' isn't in [our] ordinance, but even the mayor claims we need to find a 'balance' between preservation and property rights so she's allowed several important structures . . . to be demolished."

If we speak of "rooted growth," we avoid such shifty notions and change the conversation. We have our bases covered with an image of a tree.

LIKE A TREE

We expect trees to grow and change with loss and gain. We look forward to new spring shoots while cherishing their moss-backed bark. We protect their roots and prune as needed.

That's the way it is with districts, too. We protect their life-sustaining roots. Then when new growth comes, we want to see it connected to sturdy branch and gnarled old limbs and a broad, strong trunk with roots running deep and smelling richly of *our* soil, and not like someone else's from some other place.

To that we have agreed and pledged ourselves as a community. If not to that, then nothing.

OUR COMPACT AS A MYTH

That, then, is our compact. You won't find it spelled out in your ordinance, except perhaps for hints of it in the prologue that we often skip.[7] Otherwise its absence is no evidence against it.

As Pablo Picasso told Gertrude Stein, "You paint what you know is there, not what you see." It's like the difference between a portrait and a photograph: one reveals the essence that the other cannot see beneath the surface details.

The surface details of our district are the institutions of the HPC: its law, its guidelines, and its procedures. But underneath and giving life to them—what makes them work—is our community achievement in winning our neighbors over to district regulations.

That was *the* great victory of the citizen activists who led the fight for districting, which the concept of a compact perfectly enshrines.

As we tell the story of our district, we should remember it as myth. Not a falsehood, mind you. The other kind of myth: a sanctifying, justifying, self-explanatory, decision-guiding legend abstracted from our origins, reminding us of who we are vis-à-vis the public. If our district fails, if folks lose faith in us, it will be this compact that has broken.

So now don't you think that hard-won compact deserves protection as much as any other legacy addressed by preservation? If you do, then good for you! You are already thinking like a "districtist."

We'll turn to what I mean by that in just a moment. But first we need a sidebar on drawing up the guidelines that will define the shape of rooted growth.

NOTES

1. Quoted in "Editorial: Aledo Embracing Its Past to Ensure a Better Future," www.qconline.com, January 15, 2016.

2. Michael S. Young, "Razing Property Is Short-sighted, Lacks Imagination," www.salisburypost.com, October 2, 2016.

3. Tim Redmond, "Historic Preservation Fight at the Board," www.sfbg.com, January 25, 2011.

4. Larry Claussen, "Reorganization Plan by Mayor a Step Forward," www.capital-gazette.com/opinion, March 17, 2017.

5. Jenn Stanley, "Southern Rivals Struggle to Balance Historic Preservation and Modern Architecture," www.nextcity.org, June 1, 2015. Italics added.

6. Mark Lawton, "Lake Forest Preservation Foundation Celebrates 40 Years: 'There Is a Comfort to the Beautiful Old Buildings,'" www.chicagotribune.com, June 7, 2016. Italics added.

7. Our prologue in Annapolis includes this: "It is the further purpose of this article to preserve and enhance the quality of life and to safeguard the historical and cultural heritage of Annapolis by preserving . . . districts . . . to strengthen the local economy; to stabilize and improve property values . . . ; to foster civic beauty, and to promote preservation and appreciation of historic sites . . . for the education and welfare of the citizens of the City." Ordinance 0-1-04 Revised (part), 2005.

Chapter Forty-Two

Drawing up Our Design Guidelines: Tackling the Problem with Consultant Peter Benton

History provides no precise guidelines.

—Douglas Hurd

We may revere our rooted past, but the landscape of our community can't tell us very well what to do when addressing change. For that, we're well advised to develop a rather precise set of design guidelines.

I've asked Peter Benton of Heritage Strategies to take us through the process. He is an architect and planner who has worked for forty years in historic preservation.

My main goal is to show you what's involved. Other matters should capture your attention. One is how guidelines draw upon preservation standards, yet reflect local conditions and what specific regulations the community will support. Another is his view that, at bottom, guidelines aren't about historic resources. They are about individuals as they are writ large in community, a view that dovetails with our ethos.

THE DIALOGUE

Me: Let's say we've just met at a preservation conference. We recently got our historic district designated, our HPC up and going. We've been working with the Secretary of the Interior's Standards and find—well, the job of reviewing COA applications is more difficult than we imagined. Why's that?

Peter: Because the Standards can be applied with different degrees of flexibility. They're a set of "best practices" for historic preservation that have been worked out by preservation professionals over a long period of time and they can serve as the philosophical and policy basis for your reviews. But more detailed design guidelines are needed to understand how to apply the Standards in supporting good decision-making under the particular circumstances and characteristics of your community.

Me: What can a professional group like yours do for us in developing those guidelines?

Peter: Basically, we try to emphasize strengthening historic community character through preservation planning and guideline writing.

Me: Where do you start?

Peter: With good planning. The specific guideline tools depend upon what the community is interested in and willing to accept and the nature of its historic resources. We work with the community to help them identify the issues, identify the options, and figure out what is best, given their particular circumstances.

Me: When do you usually get called—by whom, specifically? Our HPC?

Peter: The HPC usually decides that they need to prepare or update design guidelines for their districts. They then put out a Request for Proposals through their municipality and firms like ours respond. A consultant is then chosen through a selection process.

Me: What point in time is optional?

Peter: As you've discovered on your own, it's best to have the set in hand as soon as you begin design reviews. They help property owners and designers understand what to expect in the review process. It is critical that the review process be as clear, efficient, and expeditious as possible. Avoiding a bad and inconsistent review process is essential if the historic district is going to be viewed positively by residents.

Me: The alternative, then, is—

Peter: Inconsistency, differences of opinion, lack of understanding about the process, contentious meetings, bad outcomes. Design review isn't easy. It is hard enough when things are going well. Projects coming before the review board often raise difficult and compromising issues that are not easy to address, even in the best of circumstances. The use of design guidelines is very important to establish a clear set of goals, standards, and criteria based upon your particular circumstances. They professionalize the process and make it smoother.

Me: Once the City has retained you, what happens?

Peter: The process of developing the guidelines is pretty standard to community planning.

Me: What do you ask communities to do before you arrive?

Peter: The community should pull together background materials about the historic district and the surrounding community context. We would be interested in historic resource inventories, nominations, context studies, past design guidelines or preservation plans. And of course the ordinance. We'll study the history of the community, look at maps and photographs. Zoning is important. So are comprehensive plans and other community planning materials.

Me: What about demographics?

Peter: We'll be interested in the people living within and owning district properties. Who are they? What is the percentage of ownership versus rental? What are their interests, motivations, and capabilities?

Me: Who do you work with?

Peter: Usually the community's professional planning staff, if they have them, or else some other community staff member, like the town manager. We usually work directly with the HPC, but we often ask that a separate Steering Committee be established that includes some HPC members. But it will also include other key stakeholders, such as property owners, business leaders, realtors, or others, depending upon the situation. The purpose is to get the best advice during the process as well as buy-in from respected leaders.

Me: What are the typical stages in developing the guidelines?

Peter explains the process. It is the same one we will see in chapter 72 when I speak with his colleague Elizabeth Watson on developing a broad preservation plan. What follows are edited extractions from the present discussion.

Peter: We conduct an initial meeting between the planners and the staff members responsible for managing the process to go over the work and background information. We'll have the staff and a few key others give us a tour of the historic district and community to show us conditions and issues. The issues can be complicated. Often, buildings have been subject to successive periods of change and alteration. During the field review, we try to anticipate the kinds of issues that will come before the HPC and how they will be approached.

Me: Is the community involved at this stage?

Peter: Yes, reaching out to stakeholders is important to gather input from those who will be using the design guidelines in developing their project applications. This could be done with a series of personal meetings and/or focus groups. Those involved are residents and property owners, local architects, business leaders, and others as appropriate. We'll conduct a public workshop open to anyone to go over the purpose of the project, to clarify the planning process, and to gather input.

Me: What about other officials?

Peter: It is important that those of us working on the project meet with official decision-makers—from the Mayor on down—to gather their input and support.

You don't want to get to the end of the process without having built their support for the result!

Me: What comes next?

Peter: We return with our general recommendations for the scope of the design guidelines. This involves a detailed outline of the proposed document on which we hold a discussion with the HPC and/or Steering Committee. As is standard in public planning, we will hold another workshop and touch base again with key community leaders. Then we work with project leaders to draft the guidelines based on what we've heard. This may take some time, but should really only be done after we've had a thorough public airing.

Me: Break it out for me. Who, what, and when?

Peter: The draft design guidelines should be reviewed by the staff, Steering Committee, and/or HPC and any desired revisions made. The revised draft is then presented to the community leaders, stakeholders, and public for their review and comments. This can usually be done with an electronic copy online. In the final stage, after public review and comment, the design guidelines are finalized and formally adopted by the HPC and, if necessary, the City Council.

Me: Okay, I understand that's the standard planning process. When you first arrive, do your clients have a strong sense of (a) what they want, and (b) what the community will support?

Peter: Usually. A lot often depends upon personalities and past issues and conflicts. The project planners need their help to work through any issues. You have to work with the realities on the ground.

Me: How much politics is involved in dealing with the community?

Peter: Basically, it's reading the personality of the community. Politics is part of it, and if there are political issues, they need to be addressed early or the whole project could collapse. Most communities have issues that need to be worked through. For touchy political issues, you need community leaders—champions—who will run interference, build support, and carry the project through.

Me: I assume one size doesn't fit all. What are the typical differences among communities? Are there any broad-brush types or categories, or are the differences really more of minutiae?

Peter: Every community is different. Every historic district has different types, ranges, and conditions of resources. While the Secretary's Standards provide a common philosophy and policy approach, the design guidelines need to be customized to the actual conditions in the field and the issues that are likely to be faced.

Me: In addition to the guidelines themselves—the wording—do you offer illustrations?

Peter: Many design guideline documents use line drawings to illustrate "do's" and "don'ts." These are fine, but they often tend to simplify the issues. I like to use actual photographs of buildings in the historic district that can be used to illustrate the complexities that are likely to be faced, such as multiple styles and changes within an existing building. Showing bad examples helps, but if you use photographs, then it's a good idea to use bad examples from another place so you don't offend local property owners.

Me: What kind of basic advice do you give at the start with respect to practicality—local workability?

Peter: I encourage flexibility, adaptation, and understanding of the underlying goals of the guidelines. We are trying to strengthen the community for everyone's benefit. It's not an academic process. There are real results of community and quality of life at stake.

Me: Let's go back for a moment to who actually defines your policy framework. I'm interested in whether the Planning Department or the HPC is leading.

Peter: It depends upon the community. The Planning Department usually has the best grasp of the situation and can help strategize. HPC members may vary in their interest and capabilities, but usually there are one or two leaders that can provide real leadership. As I noted before, you need to get government decision-makers on board. You need to understand, include, and support the interests of community leaders in order to make things happen. However, they seldom want to get too deeply involved in the details of the planning process.

Me: What kinds of directions are you typically given? Do you find that the folks who retain you press their own views on preservation?

Peter: Not really. Folks who retain you are usually looking for professional leadership and advice. They usually appreciate the fresh eyes that outside consultants bring. Often there are insiders with agendas—property owners, developers, realtors, designers. That is what the stakeholder process is for. But they are not usually the ones who brought you in.

Me: Whoever leads, and outside your standard information collecting, do they regularly want to tell you about what the community has generally agreed to in supporting designation—or has let them know since then?

Peter: Those you are working with need to absolutely tell you what the community is interested in and capable of supporting. But we'll test this during the stakeholder process. We're gauging their interest and capabilities and trying to build their support for the guidelines by educating them about historic preservation principles and treatments. This is an important part of the public outreach.

Me: Do you ever find you have to mediate among contesting parties?

Peter: Yes. But you need to be able to identify the local leaders and champions who can help you work things through. Our job is to provide a professional perspective to help resolve such conflicts.

Me: Do you ever find that the process involves re-fighting the designation campaign, even years later? That is, do contentious oppositional interests play into it?

Peter: Yes. Again, it depends upon the community, but bad experiences from past design reviews tend to get rehashed and used as obstacles to progress. We need to hear these but keep from getting bogged down in them. Sometimes issues brought up are symptoms of other underlying issues.

Me: Do locales ever want you to work in particular guidelines for, say, businesses versus residences, low-income housing, et cetera?

Peter: Absolutely. If they don't, project leaders should. That is one way in which the design guidelines need to be customized to the conditions in the field. Another is the nature and condition of the resources themselves.

Me: The NAPC *Code of Ethics* advises HPCs to work for the overall goals of preservation *and* provide substantial justice for everyone. How does social justice play into guideline development?

Peter: The real social needs of the community must be taken into account. Sometimes, the issues that need to be addressed are not related to historic preservation. To be successful, the guideline process must recognize this and take it into account. Design guidelines won't solve underlying social issues, like poverty, crime, drugs, jobs, and education. But they support neighborhood revitalization, which is part of the larger community program.

Me: Do you find gentrification concerns relevant to guidelines? How can they be worked in?

Peter: Yes. In poorer and/or culturally diverse communities, we are generally trying to support a larger neighborhood revitalization strategy. That includes increasing home ownership versus rentals as well as basic maintenance and upkeep of homes and yards. Design guidelines show homeowners how to maintain their historic homes. They need to be sensitive to cultural differences and sometimes accept or adapt to them in lieu of strict preservation treatments. Strong, stable neighborhoods are the goal, not gentrification and displacement. That said, gentrification will happen as communities change. That can be good as neglected neighborhoods are rediscovered. The community needs to understand what is happening to and support those who might be displaced.

Me: Can you comment on any typical mistakes communities make in addressing guidelines?

Peter: I'd just like to say that the broader goal is building a healthy community. What does that mean under different circumstances? History will judge us by what we do and how we answer that question. It's not about "things." It's about people and the environment.

Me: Thank you, Peter. You've coached us well.

Afterwards, something I remembered Brandi Chastain said. I looked it up: "Ultimately, what I tell the kids," the soccer icon said, "is coaches can give you information, they can give you guidelines, and they can put you in a position. But the only person who can truly make you better is you."

And now it's time we turn to learning to think better, in order to improve ourselves as servants of our district.

Chapter Forty-Three

Fusion Preservation: Thinking like a Districtist

The reward of one duty is the power to fulfill another.

—George Eliot

"What's a districtist?" you ask. Think about it. Our core political understanding about district preservation in terms of rooted growth can be represented as:

P > HD > P

Preservation (P) is about a great deal more than historic districts (HD), and historic districts are about considerably more than preservation (P). This formulation helps us to discern why some folks work with us and others don't.

Many preservationists won't rank the workings of our districts high among their priorities—and yet some do. On the other hand, there are many other folks who care less about preservation than for what districts can do for them through rooted growth.

So what are we to call all of those who share an interest in our district?

"Preservationist" just doesn't fit. It's too big here, too tight there. What about "district activist," "advocate," or "supporter?" Can a city planner be a partisan while working with a HPC? Not and keep the job.

To get around these problems, I've coined the simpler term of "districtist."[1]

Still, if you already self-identify as a preservationist, I'll understand your reticence to change.

"I don't want to lose my name because that's how I know myself," says Frank's daughter, Moon Unit Zappa. "There's a legacy here."

Yes, Moon—and so do you, as a preservationist. But as districtists, our legacies are *two*.

TWO LEGACIES, TWO TRUSTS

As we begin our service on our HPC, we ought to be acutely aware that we have two distinctive legacies:

1. Our architectural and cultural heritage.
2. Our political victory in district designation.

And so with these two legacies come two distinctive trusts:

1. A stewardship trust for preserving the *historic resources* of our community.
2. A public trust for sustaining the *political resources* in our community that underpin the district.

We have to tend to both. With continuing political support, we may accomplish much. Without it, little that we do will last.

THE LINKAGE

These two trusts reflect the two essential yet competing promises we made in our campaign. They formed the structure of our compact with our neighbors in support of regulations and committed us to rooted growth:

1. To *work for preservation*, and
2. To make *preservation work for* the community.

When we think politically about discharging our two trusts, the compact that we won remains the link today between our caring for our heritage and the interests that support us.

A MATTER OF INTEGRITY

Abiding by our promises is a matter of integrity. Not in the sense of honesty, though that is in them too. I have in mind integrity in the sense of its other meaning, as a *basic soundness and completeness*.

If you've been around preservation for any length of time, you will appreciate the way we commonly apply "integrity" to individual properties and to their combination across the district's landscape. If an owner removes character-defining architectural details, a building is said to lose its integrity. Then as entire structures disappear, the district as a whole loses its integrity.

That's how we talk as *preservationists*.

As *districtists*, we also strive to maintain the integrity of community support for the work of our HPCs. We can talk about this support in terms of individuals, person by person, as well as in terms of various combinations of people across the whole political landscape of intersecting interests. In losing the confidence of individuals or groups in the HPC, our district suffers a loss of its political integrity.

When we attend to both concerns, our compact with our neighbors achieves its own integrity, complete in its two parts.

INTEGRAL DISTRICT POLITICS

We see this double-barreled approach wherever historic districts are working well. There, attentiveness to sheltering historic resources is matched by a decent respect for the good opinion of our community *and* elected officials to keep our compact safe.

We see the evidence of this way of thinking most vividly *by its absence* in our HPCs.

Take the commissioner—please!—who said in a hearing that her job was preservation and it was none of her concern whether the applicant's commercial business—the issue was signage—succeeded or failed. Then there was the state historic preservation officer who was incensed that folks might think differently. "I defy anyone to show me," he said, banging his fist on a restaurant table, "where it says in state or local law that we're responsible for economic outcomes."[2]

He might be right on law, and sometimes we *are* unfairly blamed for other people's failures to tend to their own businesses. But shouldn't we be good for business and business good for us?

That's what your average neighbors think, and so did we in our campaign. To them such statements lack—what? In a word, *integrity*.

TWO WAYS OF THINKING

Integrity comes with thinking two ways simultaneously when taking a position on, say, a controversial COA application. You have to ask yourself two questions:

1. How will what I do and say *comport* with district law and guidelines, which define our preservation trust?
2. How will what I do and say *affect* support for regulations, the public standing of the HPC, and the district's future prospects?

These are often tense occasions. If you've sat on a HPC, you know the difficulty of what Chicago mayor Rahm Emanuel has said about the challenge of "knowing how to constantly weigh policy and politics and public relations."[3] If not, then let's go back to Madison, Wisconsin, and do a little role-playing.

POLITICAL TENSION

We are picking up the story Jason Tish started for us in chapter 39. Imagine you are on Madison's Landmarks Commission and considering the plans to revive the historic 1947 Edgewater Hotel at the price of a new tower block exceeding height limitations, among other issues. The neighboring community has folks supporting each side. The Common Council is waiting, watching. This is big-time decision making, and you are about to vote. The room is packed, the press is there. All eyes are turned on you.

Do you feel the pounding in your chest? That's the beating heart of politics, quickened by the living spark that plays along a line between two poles, one bidding you to "do what's right," the other one advising you to "be careful" of the political fallout. To act at all takes nerve.

TENSION AS INTEGRITY

Our notion of a compact puts this tension at its core as we tend to our two legacies. But it isn't a tug-of-war between our political and preservation trusts. Neither trust is diminished by our duty to the other.

The best way to think of the interplay is like yin and yang in Chinese philosophy. They are not opposing forces akin to good and bad. Instead, they are contrary and complementary tendencies, interconnected and mutually dependent. The tension between the two actually acts as a bond between them, holding them together.

And so within our compact, as Buckminster Fuller said of architecture, "Tension is the great integrity." Without it, the political architecture of our district starts to fall apart.

FUSION PRESERVATION

We districtists face two challenges that fuse together in our approach to district operations:

1. To combine stewardship for historic resources with care for the political resources of district institutions, and
2. To take responsibility for the community's past and future in working for rooted growth.

We demonstrate we're keeping to our compact for rooted growth and discharging our twin trusts by delivering good government.

NOTES

1. Preservationists are used to inventing words. "Preservationist" itself wasn't recognized by *Webster's New Collegiate Dictionary* fifty years ago.
2. In these two examples and elsewhere, I will occasionally quote individuals or summarize their views without attribution, understanding that nothing is gained by calling public attention to them by name.
3. Interview on Fahreed Zakaria's *GPS*, CNN, June 25, 2017.

Chapter Forty-Four

Political Maintenance: Delivering Good Government

What government is best? That which teaches us to govern ourselves.

—Goethe

The greatest long-term threat to historic resources isn't the sapping of our will to save them. It is our neighbors' loss of trust in us when we become undisciplined in tending to their interests.

This is almost never a one-time event, which once occurring may be corrected. It is instead a soft sediment of sentiment piling up because of what we do or our omissions.

It is ever a paradox: it is easier to govern good people than it is to govern well ourselves.

THE HIGHEST MORALITY

Benjamin Franklin said that "there is no form of Government but what may be a blessing to the people if [it's] well administered." But what is good administration? For that, I think we ought to take our cue from Robert Kaplan's observation: "the belief that *making the system work* constituted the highest morality" in ancient regimes from Mesopotamia to China.[1]

That sounds like great advice today when all manner of public institutions are held in low repute. *The Washington Post* reported in 2010 that a mere 26 percent of Americans were optimistic about the future when "thinking about our system of government and how well it works."[2]

So pause and take a bow. We beat those numbers soundly back on our campaign. We convinced a solid majority of owners in our district that we would make the district work to their advantage.

And now all around us, what? Twenty-six percent or likely less, with new waves of attacks on the "administrative state?" Whatever others may be doing wrong, we can't. Not if we are to keep our neighbors and elected officials with us for the long haul.

JUDGED BY POLITICS

As servants of the people, we are not the final arbiters of what works and what does not in delivering good government. Our property-owning constituents are, as well as others with important interests in the district.

As we campaigned, it was easier to read owners' verdicts on our efforts by their signatures on our petitions. Now their "vote" is a good deal softer. It's not much more than vague feelings that accumulate in either a general culture of compliance or one of resistance and complaint.

Not only must we make the system work, it must be *seen* and *felt* as working in our communities, on Facebook walls and Twitter—anywhere that people meet. The repeal of the twenty-year-old Monterey historic district in Virginia was supported by a majority of residents who were, as described by a celebrant, "fed up with what they called 'arbitrary decisions,' 'ego clashes,' 'arrogance,' and 'bureaucratic restrictions.'"[3]

Politics created our district and politics will judge it. Whether such views are accurate or not, perception is everything in politics.

COMMUNITY ATTITUDES

We know that folks in our community won't take to HPC procedures with affection. Complying with district regulations is rather more like Samuel Johnson said of reading Milton's *Paradise Lost*, "a duty rather than a pleasure." In Montpelier, Vermont, Leslie Watts is reserved. Speaking with candor on bringing more properties under design review, she allowed that "not everyone is going to love the proposal," but hoped "they can at least live with it."[4]

Happily for us, most of our neighbors want us to succeed after designation. As for the rest, as we told the City Council, those who stand apart may need to feel the HPC's authority in compelling their compliance.

Still, bringing them to heel is never easy, if we have to do it. There is a considerable difference between our delegated authority and our ability to translate it into results. Why? Because *authority* is not the same as *power*. You need to know the difference if you're to govern well.

AUTHORITY AND POWER

So what is power? It isn't a commodity. We can't actually hold power, store it up, add to it or deplete it outside of action. Power is just a relational concept between people. We don't even know if we have it until we try to use it.

We might have a lot of *paper power* on the HPC. Some commission chairs are ordinance thumpers. Margaret Thatcher spoke to them. "Being powerful," she said, "is like being a lady. If you have to tell people you are, you aren't."

To lay claim to power, it must be recognized by others and move them as we wish.

- *Hard power* rests with our district law and its enforcement to inflict pain on miscreants by fines and project re-dos.
- *Soft power* to shape behavior conforming to the law depends on our neighbors' continuing trust in us as we keep faith with them.

No matter our authority, we will be seen as powerless on either count if we can't achieve our ends. Power is like the wind: it is known by its effects.

Overreaching our authority alienates our neighbors. But underachieving for our preservation trust carves away at those who share such goals. In New York, novelist Tom Wolfe described the city's Landmarks Preservation Commission (LPC) as a "defunct" board, "a bureau of the walking dead."[5] Unless you're into zombies, that's something to avoid.

POWER AND GOOD GOVERNMENT

Governing well is, if nothing else, *the fruitful exercise of power*. So we won't find good government lodged somewhere in the institution of the HPC itself, in the excellence of its goals and law, or the brilliance of its guidelines.

As commissioners and staff, we may even achieve a process that we assure ourselves is transparent, consistent, predictable, and efficient. Yet if it isn't also *effective* in getting good results, it won't be supported by the public or elected officials who entrusted it with us.

NURTURING COMPLIANCE

Our condition is unique. We are acutely aware of the fragility of historic resources. When the law is broken, it may be repaired by imposed fines and other penalties. When an original broken window gets ripped out and trashed, it's gone forever.

Do you see what this means? Saturday's do-it-yourselfer has more power over historic resources than Monday morning's enforcement officer. What we need more than law itself is the sort of action on the part of the HPC that fosters and sustains a public *culture of compliance.*

So we ought to ask ourselves, why do folks obey the law?

Of course there is the fear of punishment. But we need folks' cooperation, not obedience, or else our district rests upon compulsion. Politically, that's deadly.

What else keeps them respectful of the law?

Is it true, as historian Arthur Herman says, that "the better ordinary people understand the law, the better the law?"[6] Possibly, unless familiarity breeds contempt.

But let's not kid ourselves. No one really *reads* our ordinance—have you, from start to finish?—or cares as much as we do about mastering our guide-lines. Most folks know and care about the law only as they *experience* it.

You and I: *we are the law.* Or so folks come to know it by going through our process. The better their experience is *of us,* the stronger is our district law and their respect for it.

So we want to comport ourselves in such a way that our district operates as though based on *voluntary* compliance. The fact that it's enforceable by law, we'll save for when we need it. Success in getting good results will give us power when we need it for enforcement, and our restrained exercise of authority will appear to most as just.

For example, my former neighbor, Matt Herban, was restoring a house in Worthington, Ohio. I asked him what their guidelines were like. He responded by telling me "what a pleasure" it was going through the process. *That's* what I'm talking about.

On the other hand, a couple moved to Evansville, Indiana, to open a B&B. They sued the local HPC in Vandenburgh Superior Court three years after purchasing their property, having gone round and round on approvals. "To go back to the Commission would be futile," the owner said. "They called me an outsider and were extremely contentious. We would rather have a [court-room] jury of our peers."[7]

Which brings up something else. We once had an applicant in Annapolis who doubted our credentials to review his architectural plans. Some members were offended. It was only when I got to know him that I understood the real reason for his charge: he himself wanted to be valued.

Common wisdom says: "The government that governs least governs best." Some use it as an antiregulation slogan. But what it really means is this: *The government that governs best is the one that governs with the least compulsion to the best effect.*

In the end, the burden of creating a ready culture of compliance falls on us. Whatever our authority—never mind our power—the key to successful administration lies in facilitating COAs while respecting each and every applicant.

FACILITATING APPLICATIONS

I recently met a Texan who's been involved in local districts. She said she was always taken aback when someone said the likes of, "So *you're* the one who tells me what I can and can't do with my property." I said to smile and say, "Oh, that's 'Joe.' I'm the one who helps facilitate your project."

And that is in our interest. As Alan Kay has said, "The best way to predict the future is to invent it." In our case, the best way that we can shape it is by accommodating other interests.

Some may call it compromise.[8] It's not.

Do you recall in *The Godfather* how Marlon Brando looked around the meeting of the Five Families and asked the other dons, "When did I ever refuse an accommodation?" Would Vito Corleone *compromise*? Fuhgeddaboutit.

- *Compromise* is giving up to get.
- *Accommodation* is mutual fitting in.

Accommodation finds a place for preservation in other interests, while finding room for them in preservation. It involves adjustment and adaptation. We expect architects, for example, to accommodate our guidelines to their clients' plans. And the language of our guidelines—the very "shoulds" and "shalls" and "mays" instead of "musts" that make them *guidelines*—anticipates reciprocity from us within the terms of our discretion.

DISCRETIONARY DECISION MAKING

Our local ordinance and guidelines are the banks of the channel through which accommodation flows. The width of our discretion depends upon their terms and the exactness of their language.

Within those banks, HPCs develop interpretive practices. Some keep closer to the side of a strict reading of their language. Others show more latitude. The choice is politically significant. The greater the latitude, the easier is the process of accommodation. "There is an interest in having more wiggle room," said Bill Henry, Baltimore City councilman and HPC commissioner in 2015.[9]

Chair Ginger Grilli in Salem, Ohio, has talked about her Design Review Board's practical approach, as reported: "She said they try to work with people and if [Board members] say no to what a person is requesting, they try to find an alternative they're willing to approve."[10] That's accommodation.

By exercising creative discretion for everyday COAs, we conserve our power for handling major problems. In Amherst, Chair Tom Ehrgood observes that HPC members "are flexible and accept imperfection" while their "goal is to catch big issues" before they blow up.[11]

THINKING BIG AND SMALL INSIDE OUR HPC

That's the right approach. "You've got to think about big things while you're doing small things," Alvin Toffler said, "so that all the small things go in the right direction."

Working for the greater good through accommodation, holding to our promises, administering for happiness, crediting our critics, and nurturing compliance: this is thinking big inside the small box of our HPCs as we process COAs.

Think of it as political maintenance of our compact. As with all historic resources, the opposite is demolition by neglect. We get off track when we think small. We fall into error if we:

- become overzealous in gatekeeping change for the sake of preservation,
- trap ourselves bureaucratically in a legalistic approach to applying our ordinance and guidelines.

These separate but overlapping errors are matters of our own devising. As we turn to considering them, you should be aware that they are the most common obstacles to our being the well-respected, successful servants of our districts that we intend to be.

NOTES

1. Robert D. Kaplan, *Warrior Politics: Why Leadership Demands a Pagan Ethos* (New York: Vintage Books, 2002), 139. Italics added.

2. *The Washington Post*, March 20, 2010.

3. L. M. Schwartz, "Precedent-Setting Victory for Property Rights: Local Historic District Abolished," www.prfamerica.org, September 8, 2004.

4. As reported by Gina Tron, "Design Review Meeting Long and Emotional," www.timesargus.com, June 10, 2016.

5. Tom Wolfe, "The (Naked) City and the Undead," www.nyt.com, November 26, 2006. Judge Marilyn Shafer's ruling in 2008 was critical of the LPC's performance, including failure to make timely decisions. Allowing applications "to languish is to defeat the very purpose of the LPC," she said. Historic Districts Council, www.hdc.org/blog, November 26, 2008.

6. Arthur Herman, *How the Scots Invented the Modern World* (New York: Three Rivers Press, 2001), 265.

7. Kristen Tucker and Sandra Hoy, "Price of Preservation," www.evansvilleliving.com, March–April, 2002.

8. No author, "History Should Never Be Compromised," www.valdostadailytimes.com, May 8, 2016.

9. Natalie Sherman, "Historic Districts Proliferate as City Considers Changes," www.baltimoresun.com, March 14, 2015.

10. Mary Anne Greier, "Proposed Design Board Changes Referred to R&O Panel," www.salennews.net, November 18, 2016.

11. Scott Merzbach, "Need for Local Historic Districts Debated in Amherst," www.gazettenet.com, April 6, 2015.

Part VII

POLITICAL DEMOLITION
BY NEGLECT

Chapter Forty-Five

Dispositional Gatekeeping

Change is inevitable—except from a vending machine.

—Gallagher

And maybe HPCs? A recurring problem that I hear in sessions I conduct is that of HPC commissioners for whom dispassionate public service has not contained their passion for historic preservation. Good government for them is whatever best protects the historic resources as they care about. They dislike change, and they see themselves as gatekeepers.

A LEGITIMATE FUNCTION

Mind, gatekeeping properly understood is an important HPC function as we accommodate applications. "You have to go through me," says Sag Harbor's Anthony Brandt, who chairs their BAR.[1] That's a legal fact.

But gatekeeping is also an *attitude*. Those who are *dispositional* gatekeepers believe the best way to discharge our preservation trust is to keep a tight hold on the latch.

DISPOSITIONAL GATEKEEPING

For some, their mental gate stays shut. One fellow at an Annapolis preservation luncheon told my table, "My grandchildren ought to be able to experience the historic district exactly as I did when I was their age." Most HPC commissioners aren't that silly. Their image of the past isn't some nostalgic slice of time. They base their work on the documented record of what existed at the time of district designation.

Still, every one of them may be haunted by a sense of loss in which vetting change becomes a zero-sum affair. As they see it, every project involving change, major or minor, may be calculated as subtracting from our fixed supply of historic resources and their context.

Even *new additions* to our physical surroundings may be seen by some commissioners as subtractions in their calculations of our historic resources.

Guidelines themselves are rarely found to be satisfactory by dispositional gatekeepers. Some fall back on the Secretary of the Interior's Standards as controlling because their broader formulation, ironically, eases their strictest application.

Alternatively, an effort might be undertaken to revise local district "rules," as former Tampa property owner George Meyer called them, to make them "tighter and tighter" and eventually "unreasonable." After restoring a house in the Hyde Park district, he moved out.[2]

The impulse toward divesting the HPC of decision-making latitude also arises from worries about alienating our "preservation base." But, with rare exceptions, this private-sector "base" is largely absent from our meetings. Whatever, giving special weight to anyone's interests because of who they are or whom they represent is both contrary to substantive due process and politically untenable.

So is the nasty tendency to denigrate applicants who have priorities other than historic preservation. One commissioner said her job was "to preserve the special character of our town," adding: "Not all of our applicants demonstrate this concern."[3]

But should they have to? Isn't it enough that they go through the COA process to comply? She would probably agree, and yet her tutelary attitude is telling. By calling them "*our* applicants," she has turned them into supplicants. Well, so much for public service, right?

THE SEPARABILITY-PRIORITY THESIS

The seductiveness of such a narrow approach to gatekeeping is helped along by the way that HPCs work on a *separability-priority* basis. We require applicants to split off the design aspects of their projects and submit them for review prior to getting building permits and beginning work. It's a functional arrangement. There just isn't a better way of doing design review.

Yet staunch gatekeepers will take this practical arrangement a long step further. They let themselves believe they *should* go on to separate historic resources *from all other interests* and secure them *first*.

A tantalizing notion, isn't it? It encourages a false sense—a sense of vindication—that the way our district works *procedurally* confirms a belief that our heritage resources are so special that they need shielding on their own. What's more, our neighbors and elected officials must have known it too, deep down. They approved the system, after all. What we did in our campaign by playing up to other interests was *clever*, really nothing more. Now we're through with that: Our opponents are defeated, the district is established, and all we have to do is administer the district to protect our fragile built environment and cherished open spaces.

This reshaped story line is what's left after we subtract our hard-won political experience in campaigning from district operations. It captures how we think and act *when we behave as though we won the district by advocating preservation* rather than through politics and the pulling in of other interests.

POLITICAL FALLOUT

A few years back, San Franciscan supervisor Scott Wiener took steps "to rein in . . . heavy-handed preservationists before they stamp out important development." As reported, he believed the HPC "in its effort to preserve the past . . . might just be hindering the city from having any kind of real future—one with affordable housing, good transit, and healthy redevelopment."

He took a dim view of the City's mandate that six of the seven HPC seats go to preservationists. "If we have a commission made up exclusively of advocates for historic preservation—only advocates—that is a problem." The problem, he said, is that the HPC is "unbalanced."[4]

The lesson Wiener offers is that change-resistant gatekeeping is politically unsound:

* Unsound from the ground up, among property owners.
* Unsound from the top down, among elected officials.

His complaint is a common one of bias. But packing HPCs with a team of rivals is no solution to a charge of bias levied against hard-line preservation advocates. It can't guarantee more inclusive perspectives, only other points of view. Builders, developers, and realtors—no less than, say, preservationists or architectural historians—can be just as obdurate for their own positions, too.

What we need are vetted *districtists* to work for rooted growth through accommodating COAs while performing on their preservation trust. What's more, they have to be seen as doing both. That's the antidote to dispositional gatekeeping and another form of political, one that I term "administrative legalism."

NOTES

1. Kelly Zegers, "Sag Harbor's Historically Black Communities Eye Cultural Recognition," www.27east.com, September 5, 2016.

2. Cindy Rupert, "Historic House Divided," www.sptimes.com, February 22, 2002.

3. Name withheld, e-mail on file.

4. Erin Sherbert, "Supervisor Scott Wiener Says Historic Preservation Is Overbearing," www.blogs.sfweekly.com, January 25, 2011.

Chapter Forty-Six

The Temptation
of Administrative Legalism

I know when you make up your mind you lose your head.

—Peter Lorre, *Arsenic and Old Lace*

Dispositional gatekeepers have one clear advantage. By keeping a firm hand on the latch, they gain relief from the uncertainties of protecting historic resources while facilitating change in tandem.

The rest of us want to know with confidence but cannot know two things:

1. Are our decisions the right ones for the projects we review?
2. Will our decisions reflect well upon our HPC as we work for rooted growth?

Shakespeare understood our plight when he had Banquo tell the witches in *Macbeth*: "If you can look into the seeds of time, and say which grain will grow and which will not, speak then to me."

We'd give anything for just a bit of certainty. So what happens? We may fall into the trap of what I call "administrative legalism." That's when we end up seeking *dependable answers* to what we should approve or not in the details of our laws and guidelines. It's then we lose our heads.

SELF-DELUSION

I'm not suggesting for a moment that we aren't sworn to follow procedure and apply our ordinance in conjunction with our guidelines. The opposite is damning. In 2016 the Beckley, West Virginia, Common [City] Council was considering the dismantling of the Historic Landmarks Commission. Looking toward reforming it, the director of the Preservation Alliance testified that, "We examined the law and guidelines and found that all that was needed to save the district was for its Landmarks Commission to begin to follow the law."[1]

Administrative legalism is not about holding to our law and guidelines, but how we grip and use them in resolving issues. The NAPC's *Code of Ethics* advises us to "seek compromises or search for alternatives where necessary to achieve overall preservation goals *and* provide substantial justice for citizens."[2] Merely by its spelling, "justice" is more than dotting "i's" and crossing "t's."

A passion for the law is commendable, but our district needs our judgment within the boundaries of discretion. We delude ourselves by thinking that reviewing applications by the strictest reading of the letter of the law is all there is to duty.

THE TEMPTATION

But it sure is tempting, given who we are. Most of us are new to public decision making. When I joined our HPC, I took to heart Edgar Watson Howe's observation: "The average man's judgment is so poor, he runs a risk every time he uses it."

How much easier it would be to stick to the letter of our law and a close interpretation of our guidelines. If things work out—then great! If not—well, we'll just go home, put our feet up, say we did our best, and let the Devil take the rest.

POLITICAL DEMOLITION BY NEGLECT

This approach has great emotional appeal. But like all seductive notions, it subverts our real-world interests. It turns us into the very bureaucrats our districting opponents warned others we'd become during our campaign.

Who else but a bureaucrat could write this confidential e-mail? Barraged by nonconforming applications and subsequent complaints, a preservation planner wrote: "They're a bunch of spoiled yuppies. There's a law, and they're just going to have to get used to it."[3] There is no evident interest in what these property owners want for themselves. All the writer cares about is that they toe the line.

This is quintessential administrative legalism. And it can't but lead to political demolition by neglect.

THE GATEKEEPING OVERLAP

Those who think this way see the law as closed. The way they see it, the law has already decided where we're going from the get-go. For dispositional gatekeepers who buy into this interpretation, the law embodies the well-preserved community as potential.

To see it as they do, imagine the law as being pregnant with preservation. If we can deliver on the law, we can deliver preservation. The more intent we are on preservation, the stricter we are about the law. And the stricter we are about the law, the less are we inclined to think about the greater good as involving other interests. What's more, compliance with the law can take place without understanding or acceptance of its purposes.

The brief against this attitude is that it's Procrustean. According to the legend, Procrustes lived beside a road outside of ancient Athens where he offered overnight lodging to weary passersby. Those too tall to fit his bed he chopped to size, and those too small he stretched.

IMPOVERISHED EDUCATION

When we treat law this way we impoverish district education. After all, we think the law's the law. We don't really need to win folks to it, just instruct them in it. Simple promulgation of our districting arrangements—printing them up, getting them out, putting them online—takes the place of engaging our neighbors about their interests and how the district serves them.

We see it at our hearings, too. "Have you read the guidelines?" asked a commissioner. "Yes, but . . ." began the applicant, as he pressed a point of interest. The commissioner interrupted testily, "I'm not here to argue with you."

Holy cow! That's *it*? Not even an explanation, much less an invitation to accommodation? That's government behaving badly. "If that's the eye of the law," Dickens said in *Oliver Twist*, "the law is a bachelor."

Well, perhaps we aren't the suitors we once were. We vowed at designation to be faithful to our neighbors. Now we may find ourselves back before a City Council neglectful of our interests.

NOTES

1. Wendy Holdren, "Preservation Alliance Says Beckley Historic District Can Be Saved," www.register-herald.com, January 12, 2016.

2. National Alliance of Preservation Commissions, *Code of Ethics*, napc.uga.edu/programs/napc/publications.

3. Name withheld, e-mail on file.

Chapter Forty-Seven

Municipal Neglect

Now a promise made is a debt unpaid . . .

—Robert Service, "The Cremation of Sam McGee"

We set ourselves up for trouble when dispositional gatekeeping and administrative legalism fail to reach accommodations.

A dispute pitting church officials against preservationists in Peoria, Illinois, led an observer to comment on "the philosophical divide between the two groups" in HPC deliberations. Former city council member Jim Bateman, then president of the Central Illinois Landmarks Foundation, said, "There is no easy middle ground." Attorney Brian Meginnes concluded, "I think it's inherently a political question that needs to be addressed by the Peoria City Council."[1]

Meginnes may be right. But in ceding our authority to our City Council because we cannot reach accommodation, we jeopardize our compact with our neighbors. This is not to say we cave to every interest. But we also swore before the Council to take such matters off their plate with district designation. Are we saying now we can't?

How is that good government?

Besides, we can't count on the City Council to help us out just because we are part of municipal administration. Councils can be as inattentive to our HPCs as we are to those we serve. Outside of decision making, we experience their neglect of us in several ways.

NEGLECT BY HPC APPOINTMENTS

A major problem is poor or hostile appointments to our HPCs. After more than a year, one commissioner, a former state senator, asked, "What are these guidelines y'all keep talking about?" He had a copy, never read them, and came to meetings unprepared without previewing applications or visiting project sites.

Another time, a property owner who had been found in violation for altering a driveway's retaining wall applied to serve on the local HPC to counter preservationists. After his appointment, his default attitude was that owners should be given COAs just for filing applications. It was how he rolled, like a bad wheel on a grocery cart.

Poor appointments lead to poor attendance. The Alexandria, Louisiana, HPC reportedly was "hampered by trouble gathering a quorum."[2]

Elsewhere seats go begging. In Connecticut, the Canton Center Historic District in 2016 had one member on its board. Talk of revitalizing versus dissolving the HPC led David Leff to say he thought it was "important that some kind of protections in the district be maintained."[3]

NEGLECT BY DEFICIENCIES

Cultural memory is geographically deep in historic districts, yet thinner past their boundaries and especially at City Hall. Elected officials are happy to have the aid of HPCs for revitalization or tourism projects. They are less interested in delegating scarce resources to sustaining districts when it looks like stasis.

The National Park Service concludes that "there are troubling hints that in many communities existing [HPCs] do not (*because they cannot*) do an adequate job of protecting local resources."[4] Among contributing factors we find:

- Inadequate staff support for shepherding COAs, advising HPCs, and monitoring approved projects.
- Inadequate budgetary support for effective commission training.
- Lack of dedicated legal support from city attorneys.

Many of us have also found serious deficiencies in City offices that handle permits, inspections, and enforcement. Personal biases or a lack of direction by superiors may lead to conflicting advice on COA applications and neglect of project oversight and enforcement.

Then there are the turf wars. When the owner of a colonial residence in Annapolis tried to remove a fireplace mantel, the two-story brick wall began to fail. Inspectors closed the street. I rushed over to verify that appropriate steps were being taken. When I identified myself as chair of the HPC, the inspector narrowed his eyes and curtly informed me that my jurisdiction was limited to outside of buildings. I pointed out that if the interior side of a solid wall collapsed it would take the outside with it. Geez!

SHOULDERING THE BURDEN

I am awed by commission chairs who say they do everything themselves, from taking applications to enforcement. The Park Service advises that "help for these commissions will require some careful political groundwork over a period of many months or even years" until a HPC has "proved its worth."

And yet after four decades, HPC commissioners in Ypsilanti were still tasked in 2016 "with patrolling the neighborhood" for violations that could only be addressed by taking the owners to court. Claiming their interpretations of guidelines in finding violations were "inconsistent," City Council member Brian Robb opposed a bill to authorize the HPC to levy fines. That was after supporters weighed in saying the district "has done exactly what its designers hoped it would—safeguard historic structures and character from demolition or alteration, and boost property values."[5]

From a preservation perspective, it is unfortunate that proof of worth does not rest alone, or even mainly, on HPC job performance and fulfilling promises. Who can help but sympathize with those commission chairs who confess to working for agreements that avoid complications with owners and officials.

NONCOMPLIANT PUBLIC PROJECTS

Do public projects in your district come under COA review? Even if they do, you may find the City bent on sidestepping the HPC.

We had a Public Works official who chafed at having to get projects approved by the City's "own" Commission. A new mayor refused to submit a major works project at a key historic site. Not that her plan was controversial: it was easily approvable. Though our ordinance prevailed on points, some City departments kept a different scorecard. Their attitude comforted process-dodgers and subverted public confidence.

In Lafayette, Indiana, an owner of two houses in the Perrin Historic District complained that the City had removed bricks along a historic street. Feeling "wronged and misled," she had "thought that the City was committed to historic preservation. Apparently, the City can do whatever it wants while expecting homeowners and property owners to follow the design guidelines."[6] The City's active sidewalk removal was political demolition by neglect of the district's tacit compact.

NEGLECT IN LEGISLATION

We secured district designation by weaving our interests in preservation with others of our neighbors. We expected elected officials would weigh the impact of new legislation on the community's well-being. Then we find to our chagrin that they are disquietingly oblivious to the big-picture promises we made.

New liquor licenses, bar closing times, rooftop dining, parking regulations, the proliferation of Airbnb's and VRBOs—name your own quality-of-life issues: city councils often approve or ignore them with little regard for residents.

So, what's up with city councils? Let's try to see it as they do.

NOTES

1. John Sharp, "Historic Preservation, Churches Struggling to Find Compromise," www.pjstar.com, October 11, 2010.

2. Richard Sharkey, "Alexandria Historic Preservation Commission to Downsize," www.thetowntalk.com, February 24, 2016.

3. Ken Byron, "Future Uncertain for Canton Center Historic District," www.courant.com, July 19, 2016.

4. Stephen Neal Dennis, "Problems Facing Local Preservation Commissions," National Park Service, www.nps.gov/tps/education/workingonthepast/problems. Italics added. Dennis lists six. Descriptions of the selected three are mine.

5. Tom Perkins, "Proposed Ordinance Would Give Ypsilanti Historic District Commission 'Teeth,'" www.mlive.com, September 8, 2016.

6. Elizabeth Mork, Letter to the Editor, "Why Did Lafayette Take 6th Street Brick?" www.jconline.com, August 29, 2016.

Chapter Forty-Eight

The View from City Council:
A Talk with a Council Member

Every man who says frankly what he thinks is doing a public service.

—Leslie Stephen

The average American credits the average City Council with too much insight into the communities they govern. If that sounds like a criticism, it is—*of us*, not the city councils. With them it's just a product of their nature.

Every municipality is different. But in all, historic districts have limited representation on city councils. In most every town and city, Council members have limited resources and time to attend to the many issues pressing them.

To help you appreciate the problem, I've invited Annapolis alderman Ross Arnett to talk with us about the view of our historic district from the Council chamber. He has served on the City Council for eleven of his fifteen years in town. Known for his commitment and his candor, Ross represents a ward outside of the historic district and so has distance and perspective. Before moving to Annapolis, he lived on Capitol Hill in Washington, D.C., where he was extensively active in historic preservation.

You would think that our historic district would be intimately known to the City Council in our small town by the Chesapeake that *National Geographic* has called "Camelot on the Bay." Is it so? Let's ask Ross, who has come to see me at our inn.

THE TALK

Me: Is the City Council as a whole well familiar with the historic district and its issues?

Ross: Not generally, unless there's a kerfuffle. The assumption is, "Well, that's the HPC, and they're going to take care of that." Or, "That's Joe's business," their own Council member's. There's a councilmanic courtesy, a matter of you don't mess in anybody else's ward. So there is a kind of benign neglect and no overall vision of what makes the City work. The Planning Department is siloed, and the preservation part of it is very much alone in its operations. The Council has no staff, just a clerical person working for us. So it's all on whatever you muster up the time to do.

Me: What am I missing? Isn't the success of the downtown historic district important to the City?

Ross: Yes, but Council members as a body aren't going to see themselves as its stewards. They're focused on getting results for their constituents and looking to the next election. It's hard to do the job as it is on ten hours a week. We have Council members who are very bright and very good who have full-time jobs and young families. Serving your community is really a full-time job that will consume you if you let it.

Me: Can anything be done to increase Council awareness? Is there any point in trying?

Ross: There's a point because you always have to try. The biggest problem we have throughout the country is ignorance and apathy. I'm not apathetic, but I do not know everything about the district and the HPC, its ordinance details and procedures. And that's just one set among very many that, in an ideal world, I would master. There's just so much to know and it's overwhelming. We have so many issues to consider. It's much easier to react than to act, and the pool for action on anything is very short-lived. Even so, there is a general understanding that development and redevelopment can profoundly change the character of Annapolis, though there's always a lot of pressure on the Council to look the other way.

Me: So it's wrong for HPCs to think their city councils are always looking over their shoulders with an interest in the districts they've created.

Ross: I think folks in general don't demand we take an interest because—and I mean nationally as well—they've already given up on government. As long as we don't do something that impinges on them *personally*—"Eh, who cares?" Every Council member will pay lip service to preserving the City's history. But who knows what that means to them? Jobs are more important to many of their constituents who have seen so many City resources going to the historic district.

Me: Is there open hostility there toward the historic district?

Ross: Some of my colleagues will talk about "urban removal" when people were marched out of the old homes because they did not have the money to preserve them and went into public housing. It's one of the less appealing sides of the historic district. And where that's happened, those who left the district aren't politically invested in it. That weighs on Council decisions. It's always going to be hard to make their Council representatives care about the district and its issues.

Me: But if there's councilmanic courtesy, shouldn't they support the interests of the member who represents the district?

Ross: If their interests coincide, then good. If they don't, then you may be in trouble. There is this schizophrenia. Annapolitans take pride in its history, association with the Naval Academy, its wonderful old buildings. But there's a feeling that the historic district gets everything that goes with that while they get very little.

Me: If the district ordinance were put up for reauthorization, could it win approval?

Ross: Yes, I'm sure it would. But the HPC can be its own worst enemy when it's a stickler for its guidelines. The City comes up with a proposal, or backs another, and the HPC will say, "Well, we've got this problem. . . ." That gets a *huge* reaction as a power grab that works against your interests."

Me: Understood. And thank you for your insights, Ross.

A thought occurred to me as Ross prepared to leave. If those we serve went before the City Council with their own complaints, *we* could have big problems like the ones we'll look at next.

Chapter Forty-Nine

Districts under Threat

Hell is truth seen too late.

—Thomas Hobbes, *Leviathan*

Showing administrative legalists and gatekeepers the pitfalls of their ways isn't all that hard. But getting them to change? Perhaps they need the fear of death in them.

If you're not focused on the public good, the Reaper for your district might be just around the corner. Even if you think you're doing well, you might be whistling past the graveyard. Every week brings new reports of attacks upon our districts. Sometimes we see the response coming. Other times we don't.

In Greece, New York, HPC chair Gina DiBella sent up a distress flare to the NAPC community in January 2017. Without so much as notifying the Commission, the Town Board had placed on its agenda a proposal to amend local legislation to dismantle the HPC and roll its responsibilities into the Planning Board.[1]

Whether we're to blame or others are, "There's always someone doing something stupid somewhere," as Jason Chaffetz says.[2]

IN MEMORIAM

City councils rarely go so far as killing off historic districts, but they do. Is it because they "don't get preservation," as we often say? Or are we the ones who don't get politics?

If we don't use politics, politicians will. They are creatures of interests for whom no position taken is ever final and no historic district, once established, is secure.

The following examples show that the threat of repeal is real if not pervasive.

- Residents of the Oliver Street Historic District in Owosso, Michigan, petitioned for and won repeal of their district.[3]
- Monterey, Virginia, disbanded its historic district.[4]
- The Estes Park, Colorado, historic district never had a chance. Three months after designation, the Town Board responded to a citizen petition and repealed designation.[5]
- In Palo Alto, California, the City Council voted unanimously to revoke its temporary preservation law following a public vote overturning a nearly identical law the previous month.[6]

THREATS

Other districts have come under attack from the sort of folks who originally opposed their designation and have not been mollified by their administration.

- In Albuquerque, 51 percent of business owners in the Huning Highland Historic District were seeking in 2004 to have the district abolished in favor of a less-regulated conservation zone. Bill Hoch of the Historic District Association said if the effort was successful, "then all the other districts are going to face the same dissolution."[7]
- Preservationists in Manitou Springs, Colorado, turned back a campaign by local property owners to create a "Swiss cheese option," allowing them to opt out of the district.[8]
- A member of the City Council of Saugatuck, Michigan, circulated a petition to abolish the local historic district. He was a party in a dispute who had lost a court appeal.[9]
- In Hartford, Connecticut, the 1974 historic district narrowly escaped repeal when a ballot fell just short of the 75 percent required for de-designation.[10]

Even when these efforts fail, one gets a feeling of districts living on the edge.

ROLLBACK

Elsewhere, we see city councils looking at paring down the size of districts or trimming their authority.

- In Irvington, Oregon, a fight developed over removing a twenty-seven square block section from the historic district in 2015.[11]
- Elkton, Georgia, also saw its Town Board consider shrinking its historic district to promote development.[12]
- In Park City, the City Council began considering a plan to streamline the approval process, eliminate the Historic District Commission, transfer some of its authority to the Planning Commission, and create a new HPC that would have no review authority. "I applaud this day," said local architect Peter Barnes.[13]
- Similarly, in Macon, Georgia, the Zoning Commission proposed eliminating the Design Review Board "to streamline the process" for district residents who wished to alter exteriors.[14]
- Houston has made it harder to designate districts, requiring support by owners of 67 percent of all tracts in a district for approval, while setting at 10 percent the number needed to initiate repeal—which requires only 51 percent support. Alternatively, district boundaries may be shrunk until 67 percent of remaining properties register support.[15]
- The Town Council in Strasburg, Virginia, suspended the administration and enforcement of its local preservation ordinance after being "thrashed" by residents who said that its guidelines were too intrusive.[16]

What happened in Monte Sereno, California, is especially chilling. The community "pulled the teeth of its own preservation ordinance by making preservation status on any home—regardless of its historic value—a homeowner option." This led to the mass resignation of the HPC's membership.[17]

OVERTURNING HPC DECISIONS

Vacating decisions on appeal is more common. When it happens, the effect on the HPC may be demoralizing.

- Rulings by the Fredericksburg, Virginia, City Council overturning two decisions of the Architectural Review Board led to resignations in 2005. "The City Council is not really interested in preserving the Historic District at this point in time," said ARB member John Sperlazza. "I've had enough."[18]
- In Hutchinson, Kansas, the Landmarks Commission was suspended between "their legal mandate to protect the integrity of the historic district" and the City Council's penchant for overturning their decisions: four in eighteen months. Faced with a COA for vinyl windows, a protracted silence ended in denial. The applicant already had a form in hand for an appeal.[19]

WARNING SIGNS

Repeal, rollback, and overturned decisions: each represents a different type of crisis. But all have deeper antecedents in rifts opening between communities and their HPCs.

- From Evansville, Indiana, we hear that "battle lines have been drawn between homeowners and the city's HPC."[20]
- Amy Skaggs in Oak Park, Illinois, spoke out with others to oppose the expansion of their historic district on the grounds that "whatever the process is right now, it is very difficult."[21]
- Properties for sale on the border of Ypsilanti, Michigan, are reported as listing "Not in the Historic District."[22]

Folks are wary of us anyway. I cannot overstress the fact that our district designation fight was over regulations, not historic preservation.

We won our neighbors' trust in our campaign, and after that our City Council's vote. Their hard-won trust in us gave legitimacy to our district process. So we need to keep in mind something Jeanne Kirkpatrick once observed: "Government is not legitimate merely because it exists."

EROSION OF LEGITIMACY

We lose legitimacy when folks perceive that the district process isn't working as it should or producing acceptable results. In Frederick, Maryland, "long-standing contention" between the HPC and some city residents "resulted in numerous attacks" that threw up a roadblock against the designation of a new district."[23]

That was in 2009. In 2015, Frederick city planners recommended demolition of a long-neglected log cabin as being too far gone to save. According to the local *News-Post*, HPC commissioner Carrie Albee told in a meeting, "Frankly, I would rather see it sit there and turn to dust than see it approved for premature demolition." The eyesore's neighbor, Carol Heatherly, called her statement "stupid" in a follow-up report in the *The Washington Post*.[24]

Is it "stupid" to take a hard stand against demolition by neglect? No, but how do we express it? As I wrote at the time in the *Post*, a "dismissive attitude toward competing interests on contentious issues, whatever the preservation merit, runs the risk of political demolition by neglect of public tolerance for governmental regulation, which is a community's most fragile preservation resource."[25]

Property owners may feel beholden to the law yet not rightfully bound by us to do as we require. Connie Phipps liked the bumper sticker she saw in Colorado: "What will you do when the government owns you?" "That's the way I feel," she said in supporting the repeal of the Estes Park historic district.[26]

"I'm really disappointed to say I'm even a member of this city," said a resident in Superior, Minnesota, in July 2011. Critical of the Historic Preservation Advisory Committee's stand against a developer's plans to revive the downtown Palace Theater, she was "ready to sell my house and move out tomorrow."[27]

Public contention over Dayton's preservation process led Pastor Dewayne Ramsey to comment, I think, directly on our compact there: "This is creating a rift in the moral fabric, or unity fabric, of our community that, left unchecked, is going to bring some divisive realities that we really don't want to see happen."[28]

A tragic commentary, isn't it, this separation from our neighbors? There is nothing more disheartening for former leaders of districting campaigns. They can't help but wonder what it is that today's district leaders have forgotten that they once understood about the nature of successful politics.

NOTES

1. Email to NAPC List-Serve, January 12, 2017.

2. Quoted in Scott Wong, "No Talk of Oversight between Trump, Chaffetz," www.thehill.com, February 7, 2017.

3. "Michigan County Libertarians Help Defeat Historic District Statute," www.lp.org, November 2001.

4. L. M. Schwartz, "Precedent-Setting Victory for Property Rights: Local Historic District Abolished," www.prfamerica.org, September 8, 2004.

5. Juley Harvey, "Repeal Granted: Town Board Votes to Repeal Historic District Ordinance; 3–3 Tie Broken by Mayor," www.eptrail.com, June 16, 2011.

6. Marcella Bernhard, "Community: Preservation Ordinance Gone for Good," www.paloaltoonline.com, April 26, 2000.

7. Rachel Alaimo-Monson, "Historic Districts May Lose Protection," www.dailylobo.com, April 8, 2004.

8. www.gazette.com, January 16, 2003; see also John Dicker, "Preservation or Coercion? Manitou's Historic District Polarizes Property Owners," www.csindy.com, October 3, 2002.

9. www.hollandsentinel.com, April 12, 2011.

10. Vanessa de la Torre, "Town's Historic District Survives Special Election," www.courant.com, September 27, 2007.

11. Mike Francis, "To Be or Not to Be in a Historic District: Irvington Residents Gear Up for a Debate about a Split," www.oregonlive.com, January 13, 2015.

12. Brianna Shea, "Elkton Discusses Narrowing Historic District," www.cecildaily.com, November 15, 2016.

13. Christopher Smart, "Historic District Panel Debated in Park City," www.sltrib.com, March 14, 2003.

14. Linda S. Morris, "Process for Making Changes to Design Review Board Stirs up Macon Historic Groups," www.macon.com/news, April 3, 2016.

15. "The Coming Historic District Repeal and Other Changes to Houston's Preservation Ordinance," www.Swamplot.com, October 13. 2010.

16. Preston Knight, "After Outcry, Strasburg Puts Historic District Rules on Hold," www.nvdaily.com, May 11, 2011.

17. Editorial, www.svcn.com, April 11, 2001; Susan Anawalt, "'Voluntary' Ordinance Threatens Preservation," www.svcn.com, April 27, 1997.

18. Historic Fredericksburg Foundation newsletter, November–December 2005.

19. Ken Stephens, "With No Good Option, Landmarks Commission Falls Silent," www.hutchnews.com, February 14, 2015.

20. Kristen Tucker and Sandra Hoy, "Price of Preservation," www.evansvilleliving.com, March–April 2002.

21. Jim Jaworski, "Residents Skeptical of New Historic District Boundaries," www.triblocal.com, March 22, 2011.

22. Comment by Flagshare following Tom Perkins, "'It's Absolutely Despicable,' Ypsilanti Council Member Says of Bill to Weaken Historic Districts," www.mlive.com, February 3, 2016.

23. Erica L. Green, "Historic Preservation Commission Criticism Not Supported by Numbers," www.gazette.net, January 22, 2009.

24. Michael S. Rosenfeld, "Plan to Level Historic Frederick Cabin Hits a Wall," *The Washington Post*, August 13, 2015, pp. B1–2.

25. William Schmickle, Letter to the Editor, "Preservation's Fragile Resource," *The Washington Post*, October 17, 2015.

26. Harvey, "Repeal Granted."

27. Richard Thomas, "Historic Restoration, Brick by Brick," www.businessnorth.com, July 3, 2011.

28. Dian Ver Valen, "Dayton Property Owners Call for Dissolution of Historic Homes Districts," www.union-bulletin.com, June 16, 2016.

Chapter Fifty

State-Level Interventions

Politics is the only art whose artists regularly disown their masterpieces.

—Raheel Farooq

So how's your district doing? Hard to say, isn't it? Then why not ask your neighbors and others with an interest? Afraid to poke the bear?

Better yet, how about a reset? Go and ask your City Council to put your district to a vote to prove you've kept your promises. Do it as a sunset clause. You know: by such and such a date you'll demonstrate broad community support for reauthorization.

Your gut reaction is indicative of how you're doing. Do you feel a new vote would reaffirm your community bonds, or blow things up? A commentator in Ypsilanti gives fair warning: "Most people I know . . . , including me, support THE IDEA of an HDC, but hate ours. If we had a vote on it today, I'd vote it out in a heartbeat."[1]

Well, his Michigan state legislature has considered making a re-vote an every-decade proof of popular support. Other states—we'll look at two—have considered bills that would make creating and sustaining districts much more difficult.

MICHIGAN

A failed 2014 districting campaign to stop a tear-down in East Grand Rapids led to an attack on all historic districts.[2] In January 2016, Rep. Chris Afendoulis introduced House Bill 5232 with twenty-three cosponsors amending Michigan's local district act of 1970. Before then, state law had required a simple-majority petition by property owners and a survey study before a City Council vote.

Under the new bill a municipal government would have to secure a written petition detailing boundaries from "at least 2/3 of the property owners" *before* initiating a study by a committee mandated to include an elected official and a builder. After a public meeting on the study, the City Council could draft a "conditionally effective ordinance" requiring majority approval by the entire municipality at the next general election.

HPC decisions would be based not only on preservation standards but any "different standard" deemed to be "in the best interest of the community." Appeals from a HPC would go straight to the City Council instead of, as before, the SHPO's Preservation Review Board.

A sunset clause stipulated that all existing and future districts would dissolve after ten years unless reapproved by a majority in a general election. A City Council could dissolve a district without petition or popular consent.[3]

Referring to the bill and "its evil twin Senate Bill 720," former Saginaw mayor Greg Branch said the bills would make it "virtually impossible to designate a new district."[4] Commentator Jack Lessenberry charged they "would put every historic district . . . out of business in a decade—and make it very hard and expensive to reestablish them."[5] Branch charged the sponsors with swatting "a fly with a sledgehammer" in the guise of "modernizing" the 1970 legislation.

WISCONSIN

Two senators in Wisconsin used a stiletto. As the State Reference Bureau summarized the provisions in its forward to Senate Bill 445 (December 2015), no local government could "require or prohibit any action by an owner of a property related to preservation of the historic or aesthetic value of the property without the consent of the owner."[6]

UTAH

Majority assistant whip, Rep. Brad Wilson's House Bill 223 in 2016 was triggered by discord over Salt Lake City's designating its Yalecrest neighborhood in 2011.[7] After the legislature slapped a state-wide moratorium on new districts the same year, Salt Lake shaped an ordinance under exceptions permitting small districts if 15 percent of property owners supported holding a vote and 51 percent approved designation. Wilson's bill raised those percentages for all local districts to 33 and 66 percent respectively, while also requiring approval by 50 percent of all parcels and condominiums in the district.

The bill stipulated that a municipality, after initiating the process, had to send out a "neutral" information packet to each owner and then distribute it again with the final mail-in ballot. This was, Wilson said, "to ensure that people know what they are signing and what the pros and cons of historic districts are."[8] A City Council could override an unfavorable outcome by a two-thirds vote. If that alternative also failed, no property owner could reintroduce a districting proposal covering more than 50 percent of the parcels/units before four years passed.[9]

WHAT HAPPENED NEXT?

Hey, I'm raising warning flags! As for the outcomes, just "be thankful," as Will Rogers said, that "we're not getting all the government we're paying for."

Except—I'll spill the beans—in Utah, where Governor Gary Herbert signed the legislation into law.

STATE VERSUS LOCAL CONTROL

The driving issue in all three of these legislative ventures wasn't *preservation* on its merits. From the Midwest to the Rockies, it was *property rights versus district regulations.*

In light of the 2016 election, Michigan and Wisconsin may be examples of conservative "red" state legislatures trying to make "blue" cities "toe the line," as *The Washington Post* reported. In Texas, an article on ending historic tree protections in Austin noted that a host of such proposed preemptive laws across the country were "designed to intimidate and bully local officials into doing the bidding of a smaller group of folks" whose interests centered on a different view of rights and freedom.[10]

In Michigan, Rep. Afendoulis put it bluntly: "I just want people to have a little bit more say over their property."[11] He and Rep. Jason Sheppard, co-sponsor of the bill, said that their "proposals strike the right balance between preserving *historic districts* while protecting *property rights.*"[12]

There's that "balance" thing again now employed as a red herring. We know that property rights and districts are already interwoven. When we fought this fight in designation, we persuaded our neighbors to *exercise* their property rights to support our district plan.

So this new battle at the state level was actually over *how* we did it under local law. As it played out in Michigan, the issue became one of *local versus state control* over the terms by which historic districts are both created and sustained.

Showing considerable chutzpah, Sheppard and Afendoulis actually claimed their bill would enhance local control in three specific ways: (1) by giving property owners more input in "establishing or eliminating a historic district," (2) taking appeals away from SHIPO, and (3) making HPCs more responsive and diverse, thus "allowing flexibility at the local level [with a] potential to spark—as opposed to discourage—reinvestment, improvements and upgrades to local properties." As they summed it up: "We will continue to focus on protecting property owners and preserving local control while allowing for historic preservation."[13]

City councils across the state rebelled. Ypsilanti council member Dan Vaught described the bill as "absolutely despicable" and as "extreme" property rights "ideology run amok." Member Pete Murdock spoke to the burdens the bill would impose on local governments while stripping them of power to decide things for themselves and politicizing appeals of HPC decisions.[14]

Preservation Detroit's Emily Bragg defended the status quo. "Private property owners," she said, "are part of the process every step of the way." As for increasing local control, she too said "this law does the opposite." The sunset clause in particular was "an unbearable level of [state] government overreach."[15]

While details differed state to state, the basic contest was the same in Utah, Wisconsin, and in the Texas case regarding trees. Austin's mayor, Steve Adler termed such legislative broadsides emblematic of a "war on cities."[16]

The League of Wisconsin Municipalities "voiced opposition" to the legislative bill "because it preempts local rule." State preservationists got the issue right. Even an aide to a Senate cosponsor of the bill observed that "they thought the legislation went a bit too far in knee-capping local government."[17]

Salt Lake City councilwoman, Lisa Adams, said she was "puzzled" by Rep. Wilson's bill in Utah. "The Legislature talks about local control and then acts as though they don't want us to have local control."[18] Attorney Katherine A. Fox charged that the state's proposed changes bucked the tide of public interest in "smaller government with more local control and less intrusion in our lives by big government." She argued: "Whether you agree with what local preservation seeks to accomplish is not the point here." What was: "government overreach and unnecessary control at its worst," making "a mockery of the democratic process."[19]

PERMANENT CAMPAIGNING

Across the board, cities had our back. Saginaw's Greg Branch observed: "Local historic districts are a key part of nearly every urban revitalization success story in Michigan." He affirmed that the existing act "is one of the things that we have in this state that works well," and then concluded: "It ain't broke; this attempt to fix it will render it useless."[20]

Such faith in us can be sustained, ironically perhaps, *by acting day to day as if we have a sunset clause.* So does a mental reset. Comport yourself in everything you do as though campaigning for your ordinance. It's not enough for mayors and city councils to defend us as FDR said of the dictator Anastasio Somoza, "He's an SOB, but he's *our* SOB."[21] We need to do much better.

At the very least, we need to carry out preventive political maintenance down at City Hall. As you become your Commission's chair, the task will fall to you. The key to your success will be navigating relations with your preservation planner and the mayor.

NOTES

1. Comment by "Balthasar" following Tom Perkins, "'It's Absolutely Despicable,' Ypsilanti Council Member Says of Bill to Weaken Historic Districts," www.mlive.com, February 3, 2016. Capitalizations original.

2. Nick Manes, "Controversial Historic Preservation Reform Bill 'Indefinitely Suspended,'" www.mibiz.com, April 26, 2016.

3. House Bill No. 5232, January 26, 2016, www.legislature.mi.gov/documents/2015-2016/billintroduced/House/pdf/2016-HIB-5232.

4. Mark Tower, "Saginaw Leaders Oppose Legislation Targeting Michigan Historic Districts," www.mlive.com, March 30, 2016.

5. Jack Lessenberry, "2 Bills Could Be a Disaster for Historic Districts in Michigan," www.toledoblade.com, February 26, 2016.

6. State of Wisconsin, 2015–2016 Legislature, 2015 Senate Bill 445, docs.legis.wisconsin.gov/2015/related/proposals/sb445.

7. Lisa Riley Roche, "Legislature OKs Yalecrest Historic District Moratorium," *Mojave Desert News*, March 8, 2011, at www.desertnews.com.

8. Christopher Smart, "Proposed Restrictions on Historic Districts Aimed at Salt Lake City," www.sltrib.com, February 23, 2016.

9. H.B. 223, Local Historic District Amendments, 2016 General Session, State of Utah, Chief Sponsor: Brad R. Wilson, le.utah.gov/~2016/bills/static/HB0223.

10. Sandhya Somashekhar, "Red States Try to Make Blue Cities Toe the Line," *The Washington Post*, July 2, 2017, pp. 1, 8.

11. Quoted in Mark Tower.

12. Chris Afendoulis and Jason Sheppard, "Michigan Must Modernize Historic Preservation Laws," *Detroit Free Press*, www.freep.com/story/opinion/contributors, February 13, 2016.

13. Chris Afendoulis and Jason Sheppard.

14. Quoted in Mark Tower.

15. Amy Elliott Bragg, "Leave Laws That Protect Historic Districts Alone," www. hometownlife.com, February 4, 2016.

16. Sandhya Somashekhar, p. 8.

17. Dean Mosiman, "State GOP Lawmakers Revise Bill on Historic Preservation, Tenant-Landlord Rights," *Wisconsin State Journal*, www.host.madison,com, January 15, 2016.

18. Quoted in Christopher Smart.

19. Katherine A. Fox, "Legislators Talk Local Control but They Want to Micromanage My Neighborhood," *Salt Lake Tribune*, www.sltrib.com, February 24, 2016.

20. Quoted in Mark Tower.

21. Whether Roosevelt said this is debated by historians.

Part VIII

NAVIGATING THE MUNICIPAL ADMINISTRATION

Chapter Fifty-One

The Preservation Planner's Role: A Discussion with Raleigh's Dan Becker

It's the most rewarding thing to be a civil servant.

—Sargent Shriver

You've joined your HPC and now, let's say, progressed to chair. Where do you fit into the City's administration? First and foremost I suggest you need to understand your preservation planner as the Planning Department's staffer attached to the HPC.

So now were on our way to Raleigh, North Carolina, to speak with one of the country's leading preservation planners. Dan Becker spent his career as executive director of the Raleigh Historic Properties and Districts Commission, and he later also served as the City's long-range planning manager. A former NAPC Board Chairman and co-founder of CAMP, he has trained commissioners and planners across the country.

As my wife and I drive up to his Craftsman-style bungalow in central Raleigh, I look forward to renewing our acquaintance. We begin our two-hour conversation by discussing the variety of employment situations planners find themselves in and how, in light of his experience, young professionals might prepare for them.

A CONVERSATION WITH DAN BECKER

Me: What is the proper term for the planner who works for the City and the HPC? Is it "staff?" "Preservation planner?"

Dan: Make it up. There's not a template. A lot is local custom. What if I'm a planner in a really small town and I have three areas of responsibility? What do

I call myself then? Maybe I'm "the planner" and I recognize among my duties I'm responsible for the preservation piece. But I've also got the zoning piece and I'm the inspector in the field. So understanding those hats you're wearing is really critical. Some people are lucky enough they only have to wear one hat.

Me: But many aren't so fortunate.

Dan: There are a lot of people out there who wear multiple hats. In fact, they may be trained and are really good in two areas, but actually they have seven. And so they're in this place where they have to work with the Commission— and it works on you: How am I supposed to learn to do this piece when I don't have any time with all the other things I have to do? It is a luxury to have had the career I had: a single focus in a large community as a dedicated public servant to one discretely identified area.

Me: Can you offer others comfort?

Dan: Well, on the other hand, it's rough to integrate if everything is segmented. Now if I wear all the hats I can make them all fit together, right? I can get them the right size; I can put them on at the same time and make sure all the plans and policies are supportive of one another across a broad range. I can interface with the HPC, with the Planning Board, and I can help them work collaboratively toward a broader vision for the community that really begins to integrate the multiple systems that make up life in that place: transportation, housing, com- merce—all those things that give communities their vitality.

Me: What would you say to someone starting out on a career path? How should they prepare?

Dan: I started out studying architecture. I thought I might be another Frank Lloyd Wright, then Buckminster Fuller—except he slept only one hour a day in twenty-minute naps. [Laughter.] Then I took a course, "Environmental Preser- vation Planning." That was in the mid-1970s and preservation was pretty new. Nobody really knew anything about it. I found my values matched up with that survey course and I figured out, "Oh, my gosh, I could be Dan Becker!"

Me: [Laughing with him.] And the rest is history.

Dan: Everything I did with my studios, I chose very carefully to support what I wanted to do. I just loved these old neighborhoods and that they felt good to people. They were the right scale, people enjoyed them, they had meaning to them—all the values we talk about in preservation. All of that was in play. But because of my design background—and this is what I think is really the key—what you fundamentally do is about real estate and real estate values and economic utility and vitality.

Me: I know some preservationists who would be aghast at that.

Dan: We talk about the tension between developers and preservationists? We're kin! We are the archivists of the development industry, because the stuff we are preserving now is what was put there by some developer some time way back. So understanding how real estate dynamics work, what the community role is in development in establishing regulations contributing to community growth—and then doing it in a responsible way: that's how preservation plays into the welfare piece of the government's charge to protect the health, safety, and welfare of citizens. A planner's job is helping people see that preservation is a welfare piece of a broad set of community values.

Me: So would you call yourself a preservation advocate?

Dan: I'm Dan Becker. I'm a preservationist. I'm mission-driven. But that's not my role in the governmental setting. I'm not the *driver*. I am the *deliverer* of the preservation program that the community tells me they want.

Me: And how do you know what it is they want?

Dan: I have to figure out where they are on the continuum of people who, on one end, just like the neighborhood and it's a nice place to come home to and walk the dog after a hard day at work, and they don't really know why they like it, they just do.

Me: And at the other end?

Dan: There are the people who are really gung-ho like in Salisbury, North Carolina, where preservation is the highest standard of the community and everything is done to museum standards. It's perfect Secretary-of-the-Interior-Standards work. Those are the two poles. So you figure out where your community is between them and show them over time how to ooch (sic) that value up. That's my public service.

Me: So it's following the community and leading at the same time?

Dan: I don't come at it by saying, "These are the Secretary's Standards that I'm going to impose on the community." That's when you have conflict. When I see a lot of newspaper articles about this fight and that difficulty that has taken over a community, I know that the application of the preservation program is not matched up to where their citizens are on the continuum. That's what needs figuring out: what regulations people will accept, that they find benefit their interests but don't impose on them too much?

Me: And yet many communities just adopt the Secretary's Standards.

Dan: Right. In developing their design guidelines, everybody just wants to use the Standards and that's miserable at the local governmental level. It's not what they were designed for, and they're obtuse to people. They don't represent the local community's values. They're a best practice to aspire toward.

Me: And still some preservationists will want to hold to the Secretary's Standards, right?

Dan: I have found that a lot of dyed-in-the-wool preservationists are black-and-white sorts of people. As a civil—public—servant, I must operate in the gray. I have to be able to always keep the community-wide perspective. I know my role. I'm here to enable and assist the preservation of our community's cultural resources however they manifest themselves. But this goes to who I work for. I work for the local government. I am there as support to the HPC to give it my professional knowledge and judgment related to preservation and lay out the potential. But commissioners are the ones who set the policy that then sets my work program in conjunction with what the Planning Department's program is. So it's a place you must navigate.

Me: How does the HPC make "policy" choices? In most places it just reviews applications.

Dan: That's the problem, isn't it? In my view, design review is maintenance. The real work is getting the district designated. Once I've got it designated, I'm just maintaining it.

Me: And your ties to the community?

Dan: We haven't talked about the distinction between advocacy and governmental roles. Again, I work for the city. I'm not there to advocate for preservation. It's the nonprofit advocate that convinces people this is a good thing and goes to the elected officials and says, "Give them a bigger piece of the pie." If I'm doing that as Commission staff I'm just the fox in the hen house. You're just providing the service the community wants. Giving advocacy to the nonprofit is what I call tossing the hot potato.

Me: But what if they're just into telling the stories?

Dan: I believe what I said about this being about real estate and design and affecting the physical environment. It is less about history. It is less about the stories of things. What we do in this part of the preservation world has everything to do with building design and economic and real estate dynamics. As a preservation planner, the best fundamental skill set to be helpful to your community is to understand those dynamics, how buildings go together, and to have good design sense.

Me: Isn't that a given in preparing for the job?

Dan: You'd be surprised how many people who come into this work don't know how to project two-dimensional plans into a vision of a three-dimensional reality. They can't figure out from what they're looking at how big a project is going to be, how it will relate to other things. It's not natural to most people. It's been a tremendous advantage in being a good public servant to my community. So when people came looking for a solution, I could work with them to find one using good preservation technology and practices.

Me: How did you work best with applicants?

Dan: You want to help people to success. That's the public service part of it. You develop relationships with architects who come to trust you. The more I can demonstrate to people that I'm there to help them and not torture them with these COAs—well, you create an atmosphere where they recognize that it is really in their best interest and it goes more smoothly.

Me: How did you deal with difficult applicants?

Dan: You just have to understand you can't take it personally. What was very important in my career was recognizing myself as an agent of the municipal government. It wasn't personal to me when owners got upset. I was playing a role.

Me: What are your views on enforcement?

Dan: Enforcement is not the commission's job. You are not the cop. You are the one determining whether or not what is proposed is in keeping with the design guidelines. Now the community's compact, their regulations say you may not make changes without a COA. So when it's not being enforced, that's the community's job to see to, the enforcement of its shared values.

Me: But how? What do you mean it's not our job? Don't we blow the whistle?

Dan: It has to be you, but not going to the preservation planner and saying it has to be enforced. You need to get everybody in the district to come back and say, "We want enforcement." We want the slice of the pie of governmental resources. We have laws. We believe that in fairness to all that we need to enforce them. But it's got to be the community saying how much enforcement they want. It's not up to the Commission. You have to look at overall enforcement in the community. Do we take this compact we made seriously? Or are we just putting it out there because it's supposed to be out there and then we turn a blind eye to it across a broad landscape of regulations? You can get wound up about it and rightfully so, but you can't enforce it without community support.

Me: Let's consider personnel. What did you look for in a commissioner? Did you have a hand in the Mayor's appointments?

Dan: Our Commission would write a letter every round naming at least one more candidate than there were vacancies. It gave the Mayor a choice and the Commission a sense that they were making the decision. Here in the state capital, we had access to people who knew how to do this stuff. That's not often the case in a small town where people want to help but don't know much about it. But I'll tell you that some of the best commissioners I ever worked with were people we didn't know, who came to us from left field and had an interest. They talked to their elected official and got themselves appointed. They didn't do it out of a sense of obligation or responsibility or because they needed some charitable work on their vita. They were there because they *just really wanted to do it*. The more you get commissioners who reflect the diversity of your community dynamics, the better off you will be. Period. What that does for you is it allows you to bring all the community-wide conversation so you don't get out of step with where the community is.

Me: And how it is changing?

Dan: Yeah. [Energetically.] There's *no* business for us in the Certificate of Appropriateness process if we haven't tacitly said that we are willing to accept change. The only time you have to get a COA is *when you are proposing change!* So it's built in: it's going to change.

Me: Some commissioners make hearings extremely contentious over change. How do you deal with those who give applicants a hard time? Do you counsel them?

Dan: No. I talk with my Chair who is the chief officer of the body who enforces the proper behavior of the HPC. You want the Commission behaving well so new members see a social standard there and adapt to it. But as the staff person, I never directly confronted a board member not appointed by me, over whom I had no authority about their behavior in public meetings. If it gets so bad that it's damaging your program, you have to face it as another difficult struggle then. You might have a Commission retreat and talk about it in generalities and try to include that person in the discussion. But that's up to the Commission and the Chair.

Me: Okay, now assume I'm the Chair. How do I work with you effectively?

Dan: What we see most often is that the person who knows the most becomes the Chair. That's almost always the architect. But the best person is the parliamentarian who helps the group to its decisions while maintaining harmony. And the relationship to staff is part of the package. So the Chair is the traffic cop, the manager of the dynamic. They set the tone of the public meetings. A strong working relationship with a staff member is critical. It's commonsense. But because people are individuals, it's not always the right type who takes on the job. As a public employee you don't exactly work for the commission. Sometimes you have to remind them, "Okay, I've got the Commission's work program and I've got the Planning Department's work program. I'm going to tell you what that program is and I'm going to carry your program back and we're going to try to make them work in support of one another. But you need to understand they're not the same. My work program is not necessarily your work program, but we each need an understanding of how they fit together."

Me: How do chairs differ?

Dan: I've had chairs who completely left policy and programmatic leadership to me. I've had others who saw me as their little worker bee, and they were in charge of everything.

Me: What do you do then?

Dan: You become that little worker bee. I was in the business long enough to know what I could do in that framework and that I'd outlast them all. [Chuckles.] So I'd park it for a little while and find something else to entertain myself that I enjoyed. It's just being accepting of my role as the public servant of the Commission. They set the policy. I work for the City. It's about human dynamics in the end, isn't it? You don't know who you're going to get, and people are funny.

Me: Do you talk about the relationship, or do you just let it evolve?

Dan: Sometimes you are direct. Other times . . . I think transparency is good and getting an eye-to-eye understanding with the Chair. That's when Commissions really functioned tremendously. We had shared goals, knew where we were going. Everybody was going in the same direction and had momentum. Other times you don't get much done.

Me: How do I deal with a less than ideal planner?

Dan: You don't have much control over that. You're the Chair and you've got who you've got. You can't predict personality, but you can find out what floats their boat and what chaps them. But what you've got and they don't is the leadership role and responsibility as Chair. Sometimes you have to be confrontational and run roughshod over them. Tell them what to do. Or find another way to get the job done. So you get your Commission together with your leadership skills and powers, set up a meeting with the City Manager or Mayor, with elected officials you know are sympathetic to what you're doing. You say, "We've looked at this and we need to do some work with our bylaws to set up a new operating structure in the Commission with some standing committees. We think it's going to make us much more efficient and make the planner's life easier."

Me: Does the preservation planner front for the HPC with elected officials on policy matters, like getting more resources to fund a preservation plan or expanding staff?

Dan: As a City employee, I have to be able to see the whole pie from the City's perspective, and in my experience ours is a pretty small piece of it. If I see a need, I might be told, "You can't do that." The only option then is for the Commission to demonstrate the public interest, the public will, the public desire to get that slice of the pie enlarged and express that to the elected officials who then, through their policies, tell the City administrator or manager who's saying "no" right now to tell me, "Yes, go ahead." So frankly, I always had the commissioners between me and the chief administrative officer of the City. They were the ones that made those policy choices. I was not the one.

Me: And they, of course, are beholden to the Mayor. And that's whose office I'll be visiting next.

I thanked Dan on your behalf, though we'll be hearing more from him later in chapters 70 and 71. When we break from our discussion, I find that Dan's wife, Laura Jean, has invited Charlotte and me to stay for dinner. After drinks on the spacious front porch, we sat down to a delicious meal of salmon and more sparkling conversation provided by our hosts.

Chapter Fifty-Two

Relations with Your Mayor: The Views of a Mayor's Adviser

Cities force growth, and make men talkative.

—Ralph Waldo Emerson

As a political appointee—nominated by the Mayor and confirmed by the City Council—do you have obligations to the Mayor now that you are Chair? What kind of relationship, if any, should you think about pursuing?

I've gone back to see Bob Agee. We first met Bob in chapter 36 as we prepared to testify before the City Council. He's now adviser to a first-term mayor in town. With no electoral interests of his own, I know I can count on Bob to speak his mind candidly.

DIALOGUE WITH BOB AGEE

Me: Assume I'm the newly elected Chair of our HPC. What is my position in the eyes of the Mayor as his or her appointee? Should I keep the Mayor apprised of likely contentious issues?

Bob: You have no legal obligation, but it would be good standard practice for you to have a session with the Mayor on a regular, not overly frequent, basis every three or four months for a conversation on what's going on, what you think is or isn't working. Have an initial discussion about your position first so you get a sense of areas of interest, what kind of engagement you should have, and take the measure of each other. That's not something you're going to be able to write down in a rulebook. It's going to be an informal understanding. But if you know there is something that could be controversial, you give a heads-up to the senior elected official as a courtesy.

299

Me: As a courtesy, but not in violation of *ex parte* ethical standards.

Bob: Well, you're not asking for permission. You're not asking him for his opinion. You're just saying, "You know, there's something coming up that from the public standpoint might be controversial," so he can be aware of it, maybe give it some thought.

Me: Would it be better to develop a relationship with you as the Mayor's adviser?

Bob: No. You do both, though you'll probably have more contact with the adviser who can filter what's important or not. At the same time you don't want it to interfere with the HPC's deliberations—or the other way around.

Me: Like intruding on his decisions?

Bob: You don't want somebody who's strong on the HPC coming in with a threat: "You support us or we're going to give you a hard time," drawing a line in the sand and saying, "We're going to go to war over this." You certainly have your formal protocols. But the real value is in sitting at the table with a cup of coffee when there's nothing particularly controversial. Because then, when there is, you'll understand each other's position a little better and maybe avoid an awkward situation.

Me: I can't be seen as the Mayor's lapdog.

Bob: [Laughing.] That will become self-evident over time, and it shouldn't be the case. In an ideal world—I stress "ideal"—you're appointed for your judgment. You're not appointed to make predetermined decisions or take instruction.

Me: What about the City's preservation planner?

Bob: In the staffer, you have a paid employee of the City. The professional staff is able to deal only with what's in their purview. A good elected official wants to hear from people out there on the HPC who are running into problems around town. Some will say they don't have to, because they have professional staff.

Me: Is that fairly common?

Bob: I call it the "Coke machine" approach to governance. If that's all we did, then you'd go to the soft drink machine and say, "Here's what I'm trying to do." I drop in a dollar and out pops the can. There's no deliberation, no concern. But when you're living in a dynamic city, with people living their lives, no, you want to hear how this affects them on a real-life daily basis.

Me: So the Chair should have a finger on the pulse of the community.

Bob: As Mayor, you want to bring in the more dynamic element of what the public may find of interest. Very few things are going to rise to a level of real difficulty. Ninety-five percent of everything is just normal everyday stuff and that's what staff are supposed to handle. But where you have a quasi-judicial authority like the HPC, I think it's important for the Chair to have some working relationship with the Mayor and the Mayor's staff to be able to get a quick read on emerging problems.

Me: Suppose I see that the City isn't paying attention to the impact other policies are having on the district. Do I have any policy-making standing with the Mayor on those issues outside the HPC's strict purview?

Bob: That's an easy one. Yes. What happens not just with the HPC but other commissions—they drift toward an insular point of view. They know *everything* going on in preservation and the historic district, and they assume therefore that *everybody* else does. They're the experts, and they become like snow globes. You shake them up and there's a whole lot of activity going on inside. [Laughter.] But no one else can get in it and they can't get out. It would be *extremely* helpful—and it seldom happens—to come in and say, "You know, we've been noticing some problems with this or that, we're seeing the effects on the neighborhood, and there are trends we're seeing as citizens on the HPC that need to be addressed. But they're not issues we normally deal with." That's something that the HPC, in its own little world, can do: observing, making comments that move on to those in policy-making positions who say, "You know, we *are* running into that. We're getting complaints." It would be helpful for such linked-up conversations to happen, but for the most part they don't. It helps to connect information from other sources, to see a pattern going on. Like trash collection at VRBOs and noise and nonresident owners ignoring their properties and a drop-off in community participation as other owners move away.

Me: If we're looking at altering our guidelines, is the Mayor interested in the niggling stuff we do?

Bob: No, he's not. But little stuff like that is not little and can go haywire. You might attempt to rewrite your ordinance and guidelines from an inside-the-snow-globe point of view that is perceived as now reaching out to grab traditionally unregulated practices. More information means better thought-out policies instead of folks saying, "Uh-oh, they're trying to sneak something through again!" You'll need to make sure you go out and talk with those I call the "push-button" people who'll want to know about it. Ask them to look at it and give their thoughts. Find out where potential problems are, and what they'd suggest. Even if you say, "No, we listened to you and this is something we still have to do," their opinions are out there so you don't get blindsided later on.

Me: And the Mayor . . .?

Bob: The Mayor doesn't know the push-button interest groups like you do. I think you have an obligation to apprise him on a hot-button topic that comes up. If everything is working as well, it should be *incredibly boring*! [Laughs.] If it's not boring, then you've got a problem.

Me: If the Mayor hears complaints about the HPC—"Terrible to work with!"—will he call in the Chair or is it hands-off?

Bob: It's both in this sense: You have to make new appointments and do it in the appropriate administrative way. The Mayor is going to address weaknesses and areas of concern. Suppose you had a HPC composed totally of experts in the field. Do you want average people, too? You can always hire experts. Maybe you don't want credentialed people out the kazoo. What about folks who are living here and have to go through the day-to-day activities and have a genuine constructive interest?

Me: What if I've got a problem with the performance of a commissioner the Mayor appointed?

Bob: We get a Chair coming in with members either taking rigid views—or doing little. You say, "I've got a problem, and here's why." The Mayor can take it as a constructive comment on a reappointment or he may actively encourage the person to do something else with their spare time.

Me: Many towns have just one district and its representative on the City Council. If I'm talking with the Mayor, do I also talk to the district's representative?

Bob: Why do you say "the district's representative?" Maybe they don't like historic districts, got elected saying, "I think the district is a pretty crummy thing, we really shouldn't have it." They're not representing the district. They just happen to have it in their district. They're not *representing* you; they want to get *rid* of you.

Me: But as Chair, should I talk to them?

Bob: Yeah, you have to. But talk to the City Council as a whole at one of its work sessions. Remember, the activity among a group of elected officials has each looking out for their particular interests—the personal and the public. What if they think the guy from your district's a complete jerk—and he is! [Laughs.] So they're going to vote against anything that character comes up with—even if he looks good from your point of view. "He's voted against five of my things and gave me a hard time. And *he* thinks *I'll* vote with him? You've got to be kidding me!"

Me: [Sighing.] So?

Bob: If you can separate the HPC from the personality element in a work session, you might attract others to what you see as good for the City, especially if their survival is not linked to a contentious issue in your district. They can be your best assets.

Me: If I go to them individually, am I crossing turf borders that I shouldn't?

Bob: [Smiling.] This isn't New York or Chicago! But in most places, don't underestimate the benefit of *informality*. Even in a work session, you're not establishing real rapport. It's better to take that walk to other districts, have a cup of coffee, and say, "I just want you to know what we're doing." It's the communication that is critical. You stop just being a name on a page to them.

Me: But what if they say they won't talk, as a matter of councilmanic courtesy?

Bob: That's only if there's some crisis, and it's why you want to go before that happens.

Me: Say there is a crisis. I'm thinking about talking to our Council member and the Mayor, and my view leans toward one. Do I say, "Oh, this stuff is too hot to touch?" What if I get squeezed between them?

Bob: Buy fundraiser tickets from both of them! [Laughs.] First ask why they're on different sides. Is it a legitimate policy disagreement or a clash of personalities? If it's policy, you can help. You are the management entity for the historic district. You have a certain knowledge base, the background to weigh in and comment. They don't have to accept it.

Me: Even then, won't it politicize the HPC?

Bob: Well, I don't like that term as it's used pejoratively. I like to say, "Politics is the exercise of public decision making." And you're in it because you have to be. Historic districts affect people's lives in an intimate way. So you have to be there. There's almost an *obligation* to come and make a reasoned commentary. That's ideal, again.

Me: And not ideal?

Bob: What if the policy being pushed by one side is deliberately designed to do harm to or destroy the whole pretext of good management in the historic district? Maybe not directly, but something in legislation that'll cause you to fall apart, be unable to do your job. Whatever they say publicly, we know the real reason is to undermine the HPC. Maybe you didn't support them in the last election, and they're going to rip out everything under you and let you float away.

Me: So I can't keep my head down.

Bob: Get it up! You've got an obligation!

Me: If it's the Mayor, he can always get rid of me.

Bob: No, you've got an appointment. The Mayor nominates. The Council confirms. The general rule is that you remain *until* your successor takes your place even *after* your term runs out. If the Mayor tries to get rid of you next time around and you've developed good relations with Council members, they might refuse to confirm your replacement. It's rare, and usually informally communicated to the Mayor, but it happens.

Me: What if the HPC has a problem with another City department like Public Works or Enforcement? As Chair, do I have the pull to iron it out?

Bob: First, why is there a problem? Is it a legal, regulatory, budgetary, or a priority problem? Is it just personalities—that what one gives the other to do goes to the bottom of the pile? If the problem's not resolvable or it's unreasonable, you have to go up. You're not going around. You're saying we've got an internal implementation problem here and it's preventing us from doing our job.

Me: I do it, not our preservation staff?

Bob: Often the staff can't do it. They have to go through their department head who may say your interest is too small a part of their heavy workload for them to go over and rock another department's boat for such a minor item. But you as Chair have been appointed for your judgment. You have to go up and say we've got this problem, because the City has to be thinking over time that there may be some potential lawsuits or grievances filed. We need to stop it at this stage.

Me: Do I anticipate success?

Bob: Don't be surprised if that department head comes back and says inspections staff are half of what he used to have, and there's a huge backlog of fire-safety inspections. "And you want me to look at painted masonry or awnings?"

Me: Neighbors in the district want City enforcers to police violations without turning each other in.

Bob: Big Brother isn't out there. A very significant portion of enforcement is complaint-driven. If they understand the importance of the district to them, then there shouldn't be a problem.

Me: Is there any way I can get a seat at the table for district interests when *ad hoc* study groups or commissions are being set up that affect them?

Bob: On the formal side, if you are silent, your interests will often be overlooked because nobody's been aware of them. Not as dramatic is to get the HPC to decide what other boards and commissions are impacting you and go to them and say, "Why don't we get together and have a little work session once in awhile?" Sometimes we get too caught up in the formalities of process when informality can get more done.

Me: Most commissioners come on board completely unaware of how the City operates.

Bob: And it's often overlooked, I know. We need to do some briefing. When you're appointed, it's with some expectation that you know how to perform in some fashion, especially when it has real consequences for people's lives. Otherwise you can stumble into unfortunate situations. A briefing can also help you decide if this is what you signed up for!

Me: What about getting the City to fund professional HPC training?

Bob: It'll differ among municipalities. There are always downward pressure on budgets, and lack of appreciation of the importance of training and professional relationships at conferences. Even if you can show value, what's important is the dollar on the table now, not the $10 you might be getting back later. If you can get outside help, like a matching grant, it helps. But if you just come in and say, "Give me some money," you've got ten more people behind you in line.

Me: When you get a quiet minute to think about commissions like the HPC, do you think "Oh, those people!" or "I'm glad they're there?"

Bob: It spans the board. From the view of elected officials, the best commissions make you say, "Thank heavens they're there!"—if they can provide a buffer, run interference, deal with an issue before it rises to the next level and you've got to deal with it.

Me: And the others?

Bob: They just come in and make demands, whine, and you say, "Dang, I've got to deal with these people. I'd rather go to the dentist." [Laughs.] When people are part of a subject-specific commission, they can take themselves too seriously. You hear that the entire universe revolves around this item and this is the only way to address it, and if you don't do it this way, right now, you're a terrible human being, you're a traitor, and we're going to hate you forever. As opposed to having a discussion about it and sometimes being able to laugh at yourself and not take it so seriously all the time. But they come in and [he pounds the table four times]—like that's going to get them someplace. I find it's funny, because they're going nowhere.

Me: Still, Bob, it's serious to them.

Bob: They have to understand other demands out there. Historic districts are important. They help culturally, economically—but people aren't dying in the street. We're not stepping over bodies. If we can keep things in perspective, it's wonderful to have the luxury to get into arguments over preservation in historic districts. And yet you get people who come in and say, "It has to be right now, or the whole place is going to fall apart!" Well, no, it's not.

Me: Any final thoughts?

Bob: I would like to stop using the term "preservation" in historic districts and move more to using the living aspect of a community in its day-to-day existence that happens to be in a historic district. Preservation is a component of it. But it's not about keeping Annapolis as it was in some idealized historical perspective, about the way it never really was. The City's always changing, and that's led to the contemporary town. I think the real challenge is how do you manage a living organism within the context of a historic district? It tends to be the life, the community structures functioning in the historic district that are most important. How do you deal with people living there?

Me: And new folks moving in. The problem, Bob, is also how we get new generations to buy into the ethos of our district.

And you and I will be looking at that next. So I thanked him for his help. As I leave his office in City Hall and cut back across the waterfront I am sobered by the thought that now fifty years along the appearance of the historic district has undergone considerable change—and its population even more.

Yours is changing, too. Over time none of us will escape the demographic crisis that comes to what I think of as "second-generation" districts.

Part IX

THE POLITICS OF AGING HISTORIC DISTRICTS

Chapter Fifty-Three

The Crisis of Second-Generation Districts

I used to have power, but old age is creeping up on me.

—Chief Dan George, *The Outlaw Josey Wales*

When Rep. Chris Afendoulis proposed his sunset law in Michigan he said, "If historic districts are so great and people really love them, then why would people get rid of them?"[1]

Yet "loving them" is not the case and never was. Then, too, the folks who lent us their support for district designation have been leaving ever since, and we can't count on their successors.

SECOND-GENERATION DISTRICTS

Sooner or later, our historic district enters its second generation. Our law remains in place. The HPC retains its statutory authority. Then the time comes when we pass a demographic halfway point. That's when a majority of owners have bought into the district without witnessing its birth. With the exception of a few, new owners:

- Have little understanding of its philosophy and purposes.
- Aren't up on its institutions, law, and procedures.
- Don't know its origins, unique local characteristics, defining community ethos, or their own social obligations and opportunities as newcomers to our compact.

"A lot of people move in and out of this town," a preservationist observes in Greenwich, Connecticut, "and they don't know the history, the historic neighborhoods, or the historic buildings we have."[2]

Without our noticing it, our political base has changed out from under us. We have a sense that "growing old is like being penalized for a crime you have not committed," as British novelist Anthony Powell observed.

TAKERS IN TRANSITION

If that doesn't make you sit up straight, it should. Remember how we divided up our neighborhood in our campaign among Makers, Breakers, and Takers? We won or lost those Takers one by one, and those who came our way made all the difference.

Though neither hot nor cold for districting, Takers were acculturated to the concept after designation. Now, by their proportion of the population, they make up most of those who've left. Most of those who have been coming in—by the same calculation—are politically like them. We can't suppose that they will be any less ambivalent about districting than were their predecessors when we first encountered them.

Do you recall how we missed the issue then, when we started our campaign? We *thought* "preservation" and *said* "historic district." Our neighbors *heard* "historic district" and *thought* "government regulation." *Preservation* didn't bother them half as much as *districting*.

Now it is reversed. Incomers *think* "Old Town spaces" and *talk* about the "historic district." We *hear* them say "historic district" and *assume* they include our HPC, our law, and our guidelines.

What we missed before we miss again. They may like the fruits of preservation, but districting is a different matter. They may be favorably disposed toward the convenient lifestyles of urban areas. Mostly they just have gauzy feelings for older places or want to profit from them. Many have only the vaguest notion of what's awaiting them in the COA process. Some not even that: it's simply where they land looking for a change. The district takes them in, but they're passively incurious about its operations.

Our political task remains the same as in the days of our campaign. One by one, we have to win these folks to districting for as long as our district lasts.

A VIGNETTE

To show you what I mean, I've asked Cathy Purple Cherry, a leading Annapolis architect, about why her clients move into our fifty-year-old historic district.

Cathy: It's for different reasons than thirty years ago. Today it's because of a general movement to urban areas, for walking, close proximity to restaurants and activities. They don't buy because of our limited parking, small lots, or historic structures. They may like the historic fabric, but not because of the historic district at all.

Me: And thirty years ago?

Cathy: I think because of the controls from development. The historic district overlay would give them some security in knowing they would not experience an overhaul of downtown by development. The town was on the rise and people understood and accepted the preservation part of it.

Me: But if they like the ambience today, why the lack of interest in district regulations?

Cathy: I apologize for that, but I think it's no different than trying to give your grandmother's dining room table to your children and they tell you it's a piece of junk. Our children of the Millennial generation don't want hand-me-downs. The significance of the historic component, the historic value, I think, is going away. What they do appreciate is the beauty in it, the character of it, but that doesn't mean they want the labor and expense to keep it up.

Me: So what are we looking at? How do they relate to our ordinance and guidelines?

Cathy: For example, in Annapolis where you have brand-new structures or additions you still have to build with traditional products and materials that rot, and that's not what the new generation wants. Concerns for the planet and energy efficiency also play a role when updating properties and doing repairs.

Me: Do they understand that district regulations represent a compact about what the community wanted at the time of designation?

Cathy: I don't think that thought even comes into their heads. All that does is, if they want to do anything to their structures they have to get approval. Still, they're likely surprised that there is control in their backyard.

Me: But they've bought into the district. Shouldn't they already know about the overlay? Is it up to you to tell them, then, when they come in?

Cathy: I'd say it's the real estate agents and the architects who are doing it. It doesn't mean they're doing it correctly, but yeah.

Me: And a lot of do-it-yourselfers and home repair professionals ignore requirements. Sometimes I think that less than one in ten district overlays will survive the century.

Cathy: That's not surprising, and I agree with you.

ENCOUNTERING THE DISTRICT

Many newcomers don't even know who we are or, as Cathy said, what we're about doesn't come "into their head." Although Anderson, South Carolina, has four historic districts as old as 1986, an article about the travail of new property owners in the *Independent Mail* refers to the Board of Architectural Review as a "little-known city panel."[3]

New owners will talk about the "historical society" instead of the HPC as an official government commission. An observer of the HPC in Edgartown, Massachusetts, says "historical societies do great work" when "they preserve the nature and character of an area."[4] This confusion is compounded when a high-profile preservation organization grabs all the local headlines or fronts for the HPC on education.

Even if these folks see government involvement—say, beneath a letterhead on our materials—they may take it as merely supportive, a kind of official imprimatur. Most folks haven't a clue about how municipalities work. They might be more or less aware that the Zoning Board has teeth. But a HPC speaking authoritatively to design or "taste"—come on, *really*?

So they'll also call the HPC a "committee," like an advisory group applying guidelines that aren't exactly rules.[5] As for COAs, newcomers hear complaints that "those preservationists"—not HPC *commissioners*, per se, but "style policemen"—are making owners do what the celebrity news website TMZ said Taylor Swift had to do after buying Samuel Goldwyn's Beverly Hills estate: "Hold the nail and hammer!!! She can't alter a thing without jumping through hoops."[6]

It gets worse. Even if they understand the HPC's official status, they convince themselves there must be a way *around* the process. This may be especially true of commercial investors who have been courted by the City and so expect special treatment. Or like the fellow in Annapolis when I chaired our HPC who took me aside after a difficult pre-application session and told me that he had many influential friends who would get his project through. When I told him the only appeal from us was to Circuit Court, his demeanor changed.

And when we think it can't get worse, it does. District arrangements get treated like a traffic light without a cop. "There's always going to be people who are trying to get away with it," says preservation planner Lisa Mroszczyk Murphy in Frederick, Maryland.[7] If property owners can slip projects by without approvals—projects which don't, as they see it, really injure anyone—then "no harm, no foul," they tell themselves. In Ann Arbor, an owner put up a fence without approval, and then had to tear it down or face a fine. "I didn't think it was going to be an issue," he said with honest candor.[8]

While the report bore no evidence of intentional evasion, it is the mindset that is telling.

Not everyone respects the law by ignoring or circumventing it. The first time many folks become aware of the district is when we hit them with a "cease and desist order," as City Councilor Dave Witham observes in Somersworth, New Hampshire. "It [says] to me that the property owners didn't know that living in the district came with some extra requirements."[9]

Whose fault is that? Sometimes political demolition by neglect begins with our laying no new foundations of support as our historic districts change.

EROSION OF HISTORIC RESOURCES

On the evidence, many folks who benefit the most from our arrangements—simply by owning properties—are rather casual about their responsibilities. Mistakes are made with disquieting frequency. Historic fabric is lost. Inappropriate alterations proliferate.

I don't think they actually set out to rob our community of heritage resources or pick their own pockets of value in the process. Commission chair Melissa Greene in Eureka Springs, Arkansas, says she detects "no malice" but, as reported, "an honest mistake" on the part of owners who replaced a stone wall without approval.[10] Still, some owners, like the purchaser of John Foster Dulles's former home in Georgetown, will still apologize for a "misunderstanding" when they undertake unapproved repairs and alterations even *after* entering the process.[11]

Others submit incomplete applications, miss deadlines, and then take umbrage at their treatment by the HPC. Some folks just can't help themselves. They'll procrastinate till time runs out. "When you start talking about the handy homeowner," says a Baltimore observer, "who has time to get permits?"[12] Then they'll do things on the sly, keep their fingers crossed they won't get caught. Then when they are, they apply for after-the-fact approvals when the damage has been done.

Some go through the formality of our HPC procedures, get a COA, and later violate its terms. Synthetic porch columns may show up where only wooden ones had been approved, as happened in Annapolis. A case might be made for their substitution. But that's a call the HPC should make.

Fortunately, these dodges rarely destroy large-scale historic resources. They are more on the order of a replaced window or a clumsy repair. Yet even if these depredations don't add up to death by a thousand cuts, their effect is scarring. They damage both our heritage and political support.

CAUGHT BETWEEN SUCCESS AND FAILURE

The hard truth is that HPCs get ground down between their successes and their failures in making their historic districts work. As Anton Chekhov said, "Any idiot can face a crisis—it is day to day living that wears you out."

Consider our successes first. Most districts begin in crisis. Then, as we avoid new crises, folks relax, become complacent. "Where's the fire?" they ask, and want us to ease up.

Planning Commissioner Dave Brauwer in Narberth, Pennsylvania, has warned against a "death by a thousand building permits," the "slow erosion" of support that Chair Jim Cornwell says is "almost imperceptible on a day-to-day basis."[13]

Similarly, early San Francisco activists are credited with "saving fantastic structures with true historic and aesthetic value." But "the process is so intrusive now," a critic says, that "such unnecessary interference would be amusing if not for the costs."[14]

Then there are our failures. Property owners expect fair and equitable enforcement. When we don't deliver, they grow cynical and disconnected. They start asking, "What's the use?"

Andrew Jones, a property owner in Manhattan's Greenwich Village, reflects on his difficult time with the Landmarks Commission over custom replacement windows. He is bitter that a neighboring building received an after-the-fact approval for aluminum windows after taking out originals dating to the 1830s. "The message that Landmarks sends is that if you try to comply, you get hassled, but if you do something illegal, you can get away with it."[15]

What Moliere once wrote we ought to take today as warning: "It is not only what we do, but also what we don't do for which we are accountable."

NONRESIDENT OWNERS

Even a record of uninterrupted success can wreak its own revenge. We all know examples of problems brought by large-scale projects, like new hotels and office buildings. We expect many of our small business buildings will be owned by outside interests.

But what about our homes? Successful and picturesque historic districts become magnets for second homes as well as short-term rentals. Year-round residents feel beset. They become strangers to their neighbors, watch property values grow less stable, and feel their sense of community evaporate in the resultant "best-of-times, worst-of-times" climate of the district.

There are exceptions, certainly. But most of us on HPCs are flummoxed by this outside erosion of our compact and our neighbors' culture of compliance. As we come ever more to rely upon enforcement in our dealings with nonresident owners, this problem of success threatens us with failure.

MISREPRESENTATIONS

How new district residents form their opinions of us adds to our distress. Many go a long time without setting foot near the HPC because they haven't undertaken projects. But here and there a neighbor does. Nine times out of ten, or ninety-nine out of a hundred, they get their COAs. Yet it's only human nature that they keep those stories to themselves. It's the small percent of those who've had real problems with our HPCs who tell their tales to others.

After awhile, everybody knows some woeful story second-hand. But most don't have an inkling about what we do time and again to reach accommodations.

- In Maryland, preservation planner Emily Paulus says, "There's a misconception that the HPC denies a lot of applications. . . . The one or two horror stories that have kind of permeated, often times from years ago and other commissions, don't die."[16]
- In Janesville, Wisconsin, the *Gazette* reported in 2010 that a recent count showed that out of 120 COA applications, only four had been denied, with just one appealed.[17] And yet a pervasive sense of difficulty led a member of the Planning Commission to suggest a procedure for mediating between applicants and the HPC.

The last year I chaired our HPC, the president of the local residents association invited me to speak. "A show of hands," I asked. "How many of you think we turn down 30 percent of applications?" A few hands went up. "Twenty percent?" Quite a lot. "Ten percent?" Almost everyone else. When I told them that over the previous three years it had been less than two percent, I could see the doubts.

And something else, less definable. Sensing it, I said, "Of course, maybe you think we should have turned some of those down." I said it smiling, but I knew I'd struck a nerve.

SERIAL MISUNDERSTANDINGS

Not everyone wants the HPC to find a way to get to "yes" on every project. They're not commissioners-in-waiting who have studied up on our ordinance, guidelines, and procedures or who stay abreast of how we reach decisions. What they think we do, or ought to do, is out of sync with us.

An example from Annapolis: Our guidelines direct the HPC to protect *public* views of the waterways that frame the district. Some residents overlooking a waterfront project testified that a new project blocked their *private* views. When we explained the difference in the law, they were *not happy.* A year or so later we had a similar situation a block or two away. Same testimony, same explanation, same result.

NIMBYism—"Not in my backyard!"—got them to the HPC. But another acronym now describes their serial disconnect from the COA application. Can you guess it? Turn the page.

NOTES

1. Anthony Pollreisz, "Republican Lawmaker Defends Historic District Reform Package, Says It Gives Homeowners and Cities Power Again," WKZO-AM, www.wtvbam.com, February 8, 2016.

2. Kai Sherwin, "Greenwich Preservation Network Hone [sic] the Gentle Art of Persuasion," www.greenwichfreepress.com, August 29, 2016.

3. Kirk Brown, "Preservation Poses Challenge for Anderson Residents," www.independentmail.com, September 24, 2016.

4. Comment by "Chris" following Steve Myrick, "Judge Rules against Edgartown Historic Commission," www.vineyardgazette.com, April 7, 2016.

5. Though the Annapolis historic district is fifty years old, a recent article referred to the HPC as "the city's Historic Preservation Committee." Chase Brown, "Annapolis Planning Commission Sends Historic District Code Changes Back to the Council for Amendments," www.capitalgazette.com, February 4, 2016.

6. See, www.tmz.com/2017/04/08/taylor-swift-beverly-hills-mansion-historic-landmark.

7. Nancy Lavin, "City Notes: City Employees Want to Set the Record Straight on Historic Preservation," www.fredericknewspost.com, December 20, 2015.

8. Tom Gantert, "Historic District Horror Stories," www.michigancapitolconfidential.com, February 15, 2016.

9. Judi Currie, "Somersworth Historic District May Discourage Repairs, Investment," www.fosters.com, March 23, 2015.

10. Nicky Boyette, "HDC Hits a Wall," www.lovelycitizen.com, September 14, 2011.

11. Elizabeth Wiener, "Historic Dumbarton Street Home Altered without Permit Review," www.thegeorgetowndish.com, January 21, 2015.

12. Comment by Fred Shoken following Ed Gunts, "Federal Hill Debates Whether to Become a City Historic District," www.baltimorebrew.com, February 15, 2016.

13. Cheryl Allison, "Narberth Considers Form Zoning to Preserve Town," www.mainlinemedianews.com, September 15, 2011.

14. Sherrie Matza, letter, www.nytimes.com, June 20, 2011.

15. Alexandra Bandon, "The Landmarks Commission Approves Most Requests, but Some Homeowners Complain about Arbitrary Decisions," www.nytimes.com, December 5, 2004.

16. Erica L. Green, "Historic Preservation Commission Criticism Not Supported by Numbers," www.gazette.net, January 22, 2009.

17. Marcia Nelesen, "Commission to Consider Historic Overlay Change," (MD) Gazette, April 7, 2010.

Chapter Fifty-Four

OIMBYism

To your health, gentlemen. I have doubts about your longevity.

—Sydney Greenstreet, *Malay*

Did you see it coming? Why, an acronym like this is worth a thousand ill-attended hearings, tossed information, and letters to the editor that are full of technical mistakes. It means that folks pay attention to the district when a project is *only* in their backyard.

The well-administered HPC may be consistent and predictable. The participation of our neighbors isn't. Unless a specific project affects them personally, we don't see them. Even then their engagement is undependable unless they're seeking COAs.

EMPTY ROOMS

As she resigned from her HPC in Lenox, Massachusetts, Chair Lucy Kennedy pointed to "the lack of widespread public involvement" in an important decision, adding, "there's not much backing" for "preserving the village as it is."[1]

Empty meeting rooms mean that folks aren't up on our practices. They don't show up in numbers even when their interests will be affected by proposed changes to our law and guidelines, or procedures for reviews.

In Cheshire, Connecticut, Chair Jeanne Chesanow of the Historic District Commission said she "was very disappointed in the turnout" for a hearing on changes to the review process. Only three of thirty-seven notified homeowners attended the meeting. If more didn't come to the next meeting, she said she'd just assume "they're satisfied with the changes."[2]

Good luck. More likely, owners in such situations have mentally checked out.

Without informed community consent, gatekeepers and administrative legalists will find it easier to tighten up oversight. Even if they don't, but HPCs just undertake to adjust some aspects of their laws and guidelines to reflect evolving practices, folks will assume the worst when they catch wind of such changes in the offing.

It's then that they turn up—in opposition. "What language bothers you?" a chair told me she asked. But not one testifying owner could cite a single passage in proposed amendments to the district's ordinance. Instead, their only interest was in attacking the HPC as a high-handed and unelected board bent on over-reaching.

On the other hand, better-informed supporters also aren't there when we need them. HPCs can't legitimately organize to bring them out to help with opposition. And private-sector preservation groups often offer little help.

It's like Yogi Berra said of absent fans: "If they don't want to come to the ballpark, ain't nobody gonna stop 'em."

MIRROR IMAGE DEMOLITION BY NEGLECT

When gatekeepers or administrative legalists make accommodation difficult, their unconcern with other interests gets repaid in kind by owners treating guidelines as afterthoughts instead of using them to shape compliant projects.

We can't expect them to work our goals into their plans when we ourselves have grown less creative about the role of preservation in their lives. It's then we find ourselves mired in monthly meetings processing noncompliant applications with jaded expectations reflecting mutual neglect.

RUNNING OUT OF TIME

What a pity! During our campaign, we inspired in folks a broader, optimistic interest. They raised their eyes beyond their own backyards to see the district as a whole. The arc of their involvement peaked at or in the period following designation, then waned.

We, too, dropped our eyes to the confines of our HPC and its administrative workload. With rare exceptions, we did little to acculturate newcomers to our district.

And so our compact's come and gone, unraveled. With its undoing, our signature community achievement looks like just another regulatory program imposed by local government.

The result is inescapable: OIMBYism is our district's greatest, though least acknowledged, problem in preservation circles. Wherever historic districts have been around awhile, OIMBYism gives them the appearance of running down like unwound clocks.

NOTES

1. Clarence Fanto, "Lennox Historic District Commissioner Resigns, Citing 'Growing Gap' in Preservation Mission," www.berkshireeagle.com, January 25, 2016.

2. Luther Turmelle, "Just Three Turn Out in Cheshire to Hear Proposed Historic District Rule Changes," www.nhregister.com, February 8, 2011.

Chapter Fifty-Five

Getting Helpful Local Coverage: The Perspectives of a Newspaper Executive Editor

Never pick a fight with a man who buys ink by the barrel.

—often attributed to Mark Twain

But why not pick his brain? Wouldn't it be great if your local newspaper could help you keep the value of your aging historic district in the public's eye?

We got a reporter's advice on working with him during our districting campaign. Now we want to ask an executive editor what we can do to get good coverage.

When I chaired our HPC, Tom Marquardt edited *The Capital* in Annapolis. He has since retired. He has accepted my request to talk with us. You'll find Tom mentions Rick Hutzell, the current editor, though he will be shifting back and forth into his former role.

As I prepare on your behalf, I wonder how to start. . . .

THE DIALOGUE

Me: Do I shoot off an email asking for a meeting? Do I state the topic only, or do I lay out an information-based request?

Tom: Email is most convenient. Yes, state the topic but in general terms, such as "how can we improve coverage." Rick will want to know if he needs to send a reporter, but it doesn't seem so at this point.

Me: I want to make a good impression. What do I do and what should I avoid?

Tom: Stop fretting over first impressions. Rick, like me, sees many people seeking something from the newspaper. I'd tell him your role in this and restate the importance of the newspaper's involvement. That's the right tone.

Me: I'm respectful of your time. Do I start off with an "elevator" pitch?[1]

Tom: Elevator speeches are best. He's busy. I'd concentrate on what and why: what do you want and why is it important? He'll ask questions if he wants more. To come in and say you want more coverage (a frequent request) without a suggestion on what to cover is doomed to fail.

Me: What sort of wrong assumptions do folks like me come in with?

Tom: There are lots! First, the results of newspaper coverage are vastly overestimated. Second, everyone wants extended coverage over a period of time when it just isn't there. In most cases, the request—at best—amounts to a single story. And then the paper's job is done. However, one story on one day will be forgotten in twenty-four hours. Maybe you'll get a couple of calls and your fellow volunteers will see the story, but often stories without controversy or substance fall with a thud.

Me: But, Tom, there's always some simmering conflict going on in a historic district.

Tom: With fewer reporters and fewer pages, Rick and his staff have to cherry pick stories. I'm sure he'll want to help, but the question will be time and availability for a story he may see as marginal.

Me: So where's the sweet spot in your interest?

Tom: Give me something I don't know. Surprise me. Tell me why readers will be interested, not why they *should* be interested. Make it compelling with facts, not opinion. Come with historical data, trends, and not generalizations and opinions. While you are talking, the editor is going to be looking for the hook—something that grabs his interest and something he feels is story-worthy. It could be totally different than what you wanted.

Me: Do I refer to the paper's unique position in the Internet age that trades in scandal and failure, making ever more vulnerable what is important to communities?

Tom: No. That doesn't sound relevant to me. With so little time, stay focused on the road ahead.

Me: Assume I've laid out the problem as I see it: that the place of the district in the public's eye has been on a slide for quite some time. Do I ask you if you see it, too, and agree that its decline ought to be reversed?

Tom: Sure. Engage him. An editor talks to a lot of people and has a pulse on the community. Here's what would pique my interest: "Perhaps you've seen this too, but doesn't it seem like historic preservation is no longer a priority here? And that residents no longer have the drive to protect the district? Here is what we have seen. . . ." And maybe you have some data here, such as more violations.

Me: Then do I ask you what role the paper might play to start up a discussion?

Tom: Yes, that'll work. But don't assume that the newspaper will just lead the way. It's a partner but not the leader. You need to give him a proposal. Don't go there with a problem and no solution, expecting him to go and find it.

Me: How do I talk about the coverage?

Tom: Ask me questions: is this of interest to you? How do you see it playing out in the paper? Do you visualize one story or more? Is there anything we can do to get more sustained coverage?

Me: Is it *unwise* to complain about past coverage?

Tom: Yes.

Me: Can I say that I'd like to see the paper change the frame? The HPC is often criticized for not seeing the "big picture." Is the same limited vision true for a newspaper?

Tom: Possibly, but it serves no purpose to accuse Rick of that. If you want him to see the big picture, give it to him. And that's the way I would frame it: "The HPC enjoyed a lot of public attention in the first decade because there were assaults on this town's history. But today the importance of the HPC doesn't seem to be understood or accepted. Rick, we're struggling to understand why and how to get our mojo back. Is it because the early high-octane leaders are no longer around or is it because the city takes historic preservation for granted or no longer cares about it?"

Me: Can I alter the paper's take on what the interesting conflict is? Instead of focusing on property owners versus the HPC, how about an obdurate owner's resistance to the HPC as reflecting dissent from the community's agreement to put the regulations in place?

Tom: You can't alter how a reporter reports conflict. Maybe you can help guide the editorial writer before he commits his thoughts to paper. Tell Rick how you feel. But he'll pass down the story and then it's the reporter who will identify the direction.

Me: Like Jeff Horseman.[2]

Tom: Then I'll tell you that you and Rick are basically out of it once Jeff looks for a lead. That's your real job: guiding Jeff to something that is very interesting.

Me: Then how does it play out?

Tom: After you leave Rick, Rick will say: "Hey, Jeff, Bill came in to talk to me this morning and I think there is a good story on the decline in interest for historic preservation. Here are a couple of things he told me. Set up an interview and work on a story that shows how perceptions have changed over the years."

Me: I want more than a story, Tom. I want to make sure it's substantively provocative enough to start a community-wide discussion.

Tom: That's a lot to ask. The paper is pumping out a dozen stories a day and always will gravitate to quick hits, like abuses in the district. That's what people read, sad to say. You're asking them to invest time and depth into something you haven't quite defined yet. To ask for "substantively provocative" reporting is far too general. He's going to ask, "Like what?"

Me: So what do you suggest?

Tom: You could frame your discussion along the lines of a semi-complaint. "Rick, you guys are doing a good job of covering the abuses and violations, but what we need is broader coverage that. . . ." You'll want to define it. "Here are some things you may not know. . . ."

Me: [Wryly smiling] Like we've got a real, historic community ethos that your paper has neglected?

Tom: Say that and he'll offer you space for an op-ed and then call it a day. I wouldn't put the blame on the paper, but instead you might just say that the HPC is too well known as a police force when their mission is much broader. Don't suggest that you want to erase this image. It's not the newspaper's job. Say that you want to expand it and see the newspaper as a vehicle.

Me: Would you assign a reporter the job of making it a regular piece of reporting?

Tom: It sounds like you're asking the newspaper to skew its coverage in an editorial direction. I like the subjects you are bringing up here, but you can't make governance interesting without an angle that it would help for you to define. Asking them to generally address issues isn't going anywhere. It is not uncommon for people to think that editors frame how the paper is going to cover something. Trust me, that doesn't happen. We're often oysters that wait for nutrients to swim by. We're reactive, occasionally proactive when it involves investigative reporting.

Me: What kind of angle might interest you if we're trying to reach newcomers to the district?

Tom: Here's what would interest me if I was still there: "Tom, very few people now were around when the city fought the early big battles over building heights and modern design in the historic district. I think it would be interesting to retell some of these stories for those who weren't here and use them as examples of why historic preservation is important." You can surprise and interest readers that way.

Me: Can we keep the coverage positive, to show the paper believes the juice is worth the squeeze?

Tom: You can't stop critical coverage, but you can help the reporter frame a story. We're not just going to sit around the table, say the paper has a new direction, and then frame its coverage for one small organization accordingly. It waits for the news to happen, then pounces.

Me: Even so, how would you think about a proposal for a quarterly special section just on the district? Who's Who? Who's New? Who's Making a Difference? A home tour, profiles of new residents or business owners, a skilled preservation builder, et cetera. Maybe a flashback story: "Whatever Happened to . . .?" And then "Coming Down the Pike" on rising issues? You could tie them in with seasonal appeal: holiday home tours, spring gardening, summer activities in the district, autumn.

Tom: I get it. Everyone wants a section. Forget it. The only way you could get one is with advertising support. Papers just don't have the money for newsprint that doesn't have a profit involved. Advertisers balk at buying an ad that does nothing to draw people or improve profits. Plus, I can't think of anyone in the historic district that advertises regularly. The "Whatever Happened to. . . " is worth a shot as an occasional column, but Rick will want to see an example.

Me: Finally, what issues have I missed? What parting words do you have for my readers?

Tom: Bill, your hope for greater coverage is common among struggling organizations but fraught with misunderstanding. I see in your questions and in the pleas of others a desire to seek help in arguing an opinion. It's wrong-headed to seek this broad endorsement of everything you do or want to do. When you turn to the newspaper, it should be for help on something specific. Otherwise, take advantage of guest opinion essays, letters to the editor, and help from the editorial writer.

Me: So that ball is in *my* court.

Tom: Also, don't underestimate your relationship with Jeff. It's probably more important in terms of coverage. Rick and the editorial writer are important in terms of editorials and assignments. But a reporter can take the story in a totally different and unpredictable direction. I'd cultivate a relationship with the beat reporter. He or she can be easily offended when a tip for a juicy story comes from an editor and not the source. I can't tell you how many times I've heard from a reporter, "I just saw him last week. Why didn't he tell me this?" Sometimes a story gets short shrift because of this.

Me: Point taken.

Tom: Finally, those like you should understand that historic preservation got more coverage in the old days of historic districts *because* of controversy. The first big tests elevated the profile of the HPC because it was being challenged. In all likelihood the magnitude of those controversies are no longer around because the precedents have been set. So, as much as you hate controversy, it can be your friend. Somehow you need to seize these moments to get the public on your side or at least more aware of your importance.

Me: [Laughing.] So I need to wreak some havoc. That's what we're trying to prevent!

Tom: [Smiling, too.] Then good luck.

Me: Thank you, Tom. This has really helped a lot.

After finishing with Tom, a thought occurred to me that maybe troubles you. If you are sitting on a HPC, what are the ethical dimensions of working with a paper? I went back for a follow-up.

ETHICAL CONCERNS

Me: Let's say I'm the chair or sitting member of our HPC, or the preservation planner. There are ethical concerns about *ex parte* communications on issues before a commission. Will you put a shot across my bow if I come through the back door to you or Jeff with "leaks" on a contentious issue? What if a COA applicant is challenging our authority, misstating fact, and bending Jeff's ear. Any advice?

Tom: The reporter won't have a problem because it's not his ethics at stake. Most likely, you'll have to deal with whether it's on the record, for background only, or off the record. "Leaks" work for reporters even if the leaker is violating the law, rule or ethical standard. If you are aware of a complainer bending an ear with error, absolutely I would advise you to pull aside the reporter. I can think of a number of times that has happened. But know first the conditions under which you are telling the reporter or editor: off the record, for background only? And do it yourself. Don't use a stand-in, a dreaded PR flak.

Me: Anything else?

Tom: Again, I highly advise your readers to be pre-emptive. If you know a controversy is about to air, give the paper a heads-up even if you have to ask them to embargo the release.

Me: Let's say we know a decision will be controversial.

Tom: Give the paper a candid background: how you reach the decision, the complications, the causes, et cetera. This puts in a reporter's mind what questions to ask your challengers and, if you talk to an editor or editorial writer, it gives them a perspective to think about before reaching a kneejerk decision.

You can't prevent a negative story if the news is negative, but you can at least balance it with fact and your position. Smart leaders I worked with followed this course and often benefitted from coverage, particularly in editorials.

Me: As before, thank you, Tom.

Tom has left the driving force to us. So, as we think about the newsworthy stories we might generate, we'll need a new strategic line suited to the political field of play in our second-generation district.

NOTES

1. A thirty-second to two-minute sales pitch, the length of an elevator ride.
2. See chapter 29.

Chapter Fifty-Six

Our New Strategic Line

King shall hold kingdom.

—Anglo-Saxon poem

The injunction comes from a review of a biography of Aethelred, the tenth-century English king known as "the Unready." The book's author concluded that he "held his kingdom with great toil and hardship for the length of his life."[1]

I think we should get ready to do better with our aging districts.

OUR ANALYTIC TOOL

First, we have to identify those (a) who stand behind our district, and (b) who harm it by intention or result. We'll need a tool to help us see them clearly, and not be like Casey Stengel: "All right, everyone, line up alphabetically according to your height."

What we'll use is sharp and simple. It stems from a later age than Aethelred's, when French was the language of diplomacy, when *raison d'état*—"reasons of state"—was everyone's preferred way of encapsulating the view that interests vital to the survival of a state were more compelling than all others. Now I'd like you to think of *raison du système*—"reasons of the system"—as summing up our overriding interest in the durability of our district institutions.

Those who stand with us will act from a basic understanding that the greater the support for the HPC and its authority, the better are the prospects for ensuring rooted growth and preservation in the process.

In practical terms, our perspective is:

* If we approve a controversial project—our authority must hold.
* If we hold to preservation—our authority must hold.
* In good times and in bad—our authority must hold.
* As our districts age—our authority should thrive.

We have already seen trouble brewing with changing attitudes and demographics. In administering our districts, we'll find our work is made difficult by the *willfulness* of some regarding their own interests and the *indifference* of many toward the compact that we won for district designation. Others, though, to varying degrees, have continued to practice good citizenship by abiding by district law and our institutional procedures.

We need a nuanced strategy for dealing with them all as we fight for our district in its troubled second generation.

A FLEXIBLE RESPONSE

The English philosopher Thomas Hobbes knew when and how to fight. "Be sociable with those who will be sociable," he wrote, "and formidable with those who won't."

By "sociable" he had in mind being faithful to one's promises, keeping social compacts, and seeking accommodations. In terms of those criteria we ourselves have not always been as sociable as we intended as public servants of our neighbors.

In our tendencies to narrow gatekeeping, underperforming on our preservation mandate, and administrative legalism, we've undermined our neighbors' trust. So we should pledge ourselves anew to administering our district in such sociable ways as to restore their belief that they are better off with us as than without the potent authority of our district institutions.

With those who will be sociable with us we will be solicitous, understanding, positive about accommodation, personable, considerate, compassionate, and encouraging. But we should be prepared to be formidable with anyone who is hostile to the district and our HPC.

As we pursue this flexible strategy we will be, as Ralph Waldo Emerson said of Walt Whitman, "half song-thrush, half alligator."

NOTE

1. Quotations from Tom Shippey, "King Shall Hold Kingdom," *London Review of Books*, March 30, 2017, p. 19.

Chapter Fifty-Seven

A New Political
Who's Who: An Overview

I believe you are your work.

—Rita Mae Brown

As we think about applying our new strategy we need to take an anticipatory survey of our community to see who by their sociable deeds may be labeled district *Rooters*—whose actions sustain our roots in the community—as opposed to *Rotters*, who are a source of rot.

OUR NEW READING OF THE LANDSCAPE

Neither group is homogeneous. I find it helpful to divide Rooters into three rough subgroups:

- **Actors**, who are actively engaged in sustaining the district process;
- **Backers**, who support but do not regularly engage the process; and
- **Slackers**, who accept but have loose ties to the process.

Similarly, Rotters are of three sorts:

- **Shirkers**, who by their casual property violations evade the district process;
- **Shredders**, who by their egregious behaviors pose more subversive threats; and
- **Should-Know-Betters**, who by their ideologies subvert community support.

LABELLING PRESERVATIONISTS

No one likes to be pigeonholed. Bear in mind that no individual except rarely is ever only one. Nor are the examples we'll consider exhaustive of each type. They are hortatory only, meant to spur reflection.

Preservationists are peppered through every category, except (I hope) the Shredders. Is it wise to point this out? Ronald Reagan once advised the party faithful not to criticize other Republicans in public. But what isn't "public" in this age of online living? If I don't call things as I see them, what good am I to you?

I prefer former Boston Celtics coach Red Auerbach to Ronald Reagan. "He was intensely loyal," John Feinstein had observed. "His motto seemed to be," when speaking to reporters, "I can criticize my players and my friends, but you can't."[1] He knew what we know, too: not everyone who wears the jersey is a team player.

We don't unfairly pigeonhole preservationists when we put them in their rightful places. They do so by their deeds. Where they cause us problems in relations with our neighbors and elected officials, we can whisper in their ear. But when all else fails, keeping the public's trust is a business better done in public. As former Labour Party leader Neil Kinnock observed, "Loyalty is a fine thing, but in excess it fills political graveyards."

NOTE

1. John Feinstein, "A Dynasty Maker, Like No Other," www.washingtonpost.com/archive/sports, October 30, 2006.

Chapter Fifty-Eight

Who's Who, Part One: District Rooters

As the twig is bent the tree inclines.

—Virgil

Rooters are favorably inclined toward the district after designation. As our district ages, their participation changes and shapes the future of its institutions.

1. ACTORS

Actors think and act as districtists. If they didn't do the district's work, it would not get done. They form the backbone of our community's investment in historic districting as they participate in HPC meetings or behind the scenes in the community.

Who they are: Not all Actors have the time or resources to take a leading role. Many would like to be able to do more. Others do more than their share. They may take a turn on the HPC or testify at hearings. They also tend to cycle through leadership positions in community associations with preservation interests.

Outside of HPC staff and commissioners we see such Actors as:

- The *politically engaged preservationist*, speaking out for the HPC and rooted growth;
- The *newspaper editor or reporter* and other opinion setters, accurately portraying district issues;

- The *president* and *other members* of a heritage organization, supporting the district process;
- *Business leaders* and *realtors*, who know and promote the value of a well-supported district;
- The *officers* and *other members* of a neighborhood association, maintaining community ties.

They may disagree with particular HPC decisions while consistently backing district institutions and the decision-making process as important to their interests. I chaired many meetings where the testifying representative of Historic Annapolis took positions on challenging COAs that differed from the outcome. After the vote we'd sometimes catch each other's eye, and in that glance we shared understanding. It was rather like the words of comfort spoken to a troubled war survivor in the 1948 film *Berlin Express*: "You did what you had to do, my friend."

A society of like-minded civic Actors who appreciate each other's views is more important than good laws in a historic district. But where one strong Actor dominates, others drift away. Samuel Johnson knew that "the most fatal disease of friendship is gradual decay, or dislike hourly increased by causes too slender for complaint, and too numerous for removal."

The alliance of disparate Actors peaks at designation and thins with time as the intensity of the moment passes, interests evolve, and activities compartmentalize. Supportive Actors circle further from the HPC in second-generation districts where its disengagement from the community has widened.

Some become *sunshine* Actors who duck contentious issues. They'll offer us boilerplate support in fights, though we have to do without them in the trenches. As this becomes habitual, they slip into the ranks of Backers.

Our response: We need to be invariably sociable in our affairs with other Actors. As our district ages, we should strive to keep all Actors in the loop, up-to-date on policies and practices, while tolerating one another's shortcomings and accepting criticism.

We also must guard against the narrowing of Actors to committed preservationists. The toughest task is socializing nonpreservationists to the work of preservation and making preservation work for the broad panoply of other interests in the community.

2. BACKERS

Backers are not as apt to think and act as districtists. If they helped to win the district, today they and others like them more passively support the district as a community institution. They can't imagine the community without it. But they are less imaginative than Actors about what it requires of them, politically, to keep it going.

Who they are: Among preservationists, the most engaged are often:

- *Keepers of the flame*, who work outside the HPC in preservation advocacy that sometimes crosses over to political support of the HPC;
- *Lodestar preservationists*, who seek to keep our compass pointing toward our stewardship for historic resources while not ignoring politics.

While these Backers value the district as a preservation tool, others support the district as a canvas for their work. Their professional or hobbyist interests are related to the district mainly by geography. Among them are:

- *Museum preservationists*, who care for iconic places;
- *History preservationists*, who work in studies of the local past;
- *Construction preservationists*, who work with special skills;
- *Philanthropic preservationists*, who underwrite the work of preservation.

All preservation Backers care about the district in different degrees, and all do useful things. Their various involvements reflect the healthy diversity of the preservation movement. Good thing, too, as none of us can do everything that needs doing. They free Actors up to focus on district operations, and the stronger preservation is because of their activities; the stronger is public appreciation for the importance of preservation in the life of the community.

Among nonpreservationists, *architects* and *builders* engage the HPC process as part of doing business in the district. While they might not be personally committed to the district, they support it by their deeds. The ones we see most often before our HPCs become adept at navigating the COA process and facilitating accommodations for their clients' projects. Backers in design and construction are likely to be, outside of commissioners and staff, the best informed students of our ordinance, guidelines, and procedures. As they impart their knowledge to their clients, they help us acculturate them to broader district goals and methods.

Above all else, let's remember the *good citizen*, whose law-abiding compliance with HPC procedures is the lifeblood of the district. In Carson City, Nevada, Alexander Kirsch says of his historic district neighbors: "They all live there and they have always followed the codes and rules of the district."[1]

Over time, Backers tend to subdivide. *Strong Backers* will still agree on the importance of sheltering historic resources while working for consensus with folks with other interests. *Weak Backers* may lean toward one side or the other:

- *Preservationists* may back the district as a heritage shelter without feeling especially obligated to support accommodations.
- *Nonpreservationists* may back the district as an engine of community development or business prosperity without caring as much about defending historic resources.

Our response: We'll strive to work sociably with all Backers to manage tensions that arise between them and HPC operations. We want to make sure that when they speak in the community they do so from informed perspectives on our ordinance and guidelines, up-to-date practices and procedures. Our being sociable helps to keep them from drifting further away from our common goals and support of HPC practices.

Otherwise, they slip into the third rank of district Rooters.

3. SLACKERS

These folks maintain only *loose ties* to our district, and that's what makes them Slackers. They support district institutions when and how it suits them. The looser their engagement, the more likely are they to have views formed outside the serious work of the HPC.

Who they are: Among Slackers we find unserious preservationists and those who take our district institutions lightly. Examples are:

- *Self-referential preservationists*, who hold their views to be as valid as the HPC's;
- *Cultured preservationists*, who value the refined patina of involvement;
- *Social preservationists*, who enjoy the society of volunteers;
- *Beautification preservationists*, who equate preservation with loveliness;
- *Good-taste preservationists*, who equate preservation with style;
- *Appearance preservationists*: "If I drive down the street and it looks okay," one said, "that's the standard."

They are preservation's dilettantes.

Nonpreservation Slackers may like districts for their atmosphere, lifestyle, economic boost, or protection of financial investments. They'll distrust us for overreaching and claim that we distrust them upon occasion. To them we are "hysterical" for not making "commonsense" decisions. Or they become hysterical when they think we've failed them.

Slackers are most egregious when they try to use the HPC process to settle scores with their neighbors or get at underlying use, such as a rescue mission's plans in Durham, North Carolina. They study up on technicalities, demand that we deliver, and sometimes sue us if we don't.

District Actors may encounter Slackers only in a crisis—"hearing today, gone tomorrow." Some come in with hair on fire. They speak out with only a cursory knowledge of the district. Many seem content with adopting emotionally satisfying positions in the moment.

Slackers are all over the board on regulation and enforcement. Some press for a strict approach, while others favor relaxed oversight, regardless of the law, depending on their interests and personal ideas of what preservation is.

Our response: Their ill-informed and episodic engagement wearies our sociability. We end up having to correct them pointedly—if civilly—in public forums when we shouldn't have to, and when doing so embarrasses everyone involved. Still, they might do better if their distant OIMBY orbit didn't make it so difficult for us to keep them in the loop and up to date on our policies, practices, and decision-making precedents.

Consequently, they don't embrace the tensions that we face in delivering good government. They want the advantages of the district without actually throwing in with us.

Slackers lend strength to the impression that there is no strong community consensus behind district institutions and the aims of rooted growth. To the extent that's true, it suggests slackness among Actors, too, for failing to retain their engagement support.

We'd like to like Slackers for our district's sake. Instead, we think of them as in the words of William Blake: "Thy friendship oft has made my heart to ache."

NOTE

1. Erin Breen, "Carson City Struggles with Development in Historic District," www.ktvn.com, January 6, 2015.

Chapter Fifty-Nine

Who's Who, Part Two: District Rotters

There's small choice in rotten apples.

—William Shakespeare, *The Taming of the Shrew*

Oh, Will, we wish t'were true! We've got three groups and choice of how to treat them to stop their rot from spreading.

1. SHIRKERS

Shirkers duck COAs and undercut the district:

• By harming the integrity of historic resources, and/or
• By harming the political integrity of the district process.

"Shirking" covers two different violations:

1. Doing *inappropriate* projects without approval.
2. Doing *appropriate* projects without approval.

Both are normally treated as a single violation with differing approaches to corrective measures, fines, and after-the-fact approvals.

Who they are: In truth, most folks shirk sometime, including Actors, Backers, Slackers. They earn the Shirker label by (a) willful neglect of the approval process, *plus* (b) repetition. A few, however, earn the name when the impact of their cheating on a single project gains widespread notoriety.

Explaining why folks shirk is like swimming through mashed potatoes.

They may be new owners oblivious to asking before embarking on their projects. Then there are the absentee owners for whom the district is a foreign country.

Others may be conscientious preservation stewards who act as if the law was made for everybody else. Take the former Midwest HPC chair who began an unapproved project out of sight behind his house. "What, *that*?" I bet he said when caught. "It's just in my backyard."

Yeah, JIMBYism sums him up, and a lot of other Shirkers too.

Most Shirkers' acts are small and mean. They install a vinyl window, use improper mortar for minor joint repairs, or fudge on business signage.

Some Shirkers can't be bothered, or are tired of going through the process. Perhaps they've had an unsatisfying experience with the HPC. Some believe their HPC lags behind the times in not approving longer-lasting new technologies that "look the same" for minor home repairs.

Others buck the process because they didn't have a hand in its creation. Some don't like those who run it now. Still others might not be especially law-conscious people in their daily lives, or just dislike property law in particular.

Some are merely cynical, having watched others get away with violations. Others grudge the fees and other costs involved in hiring architects and submitting applications. Few towns are as generous as Dayton, Ohio, where many COA permits are issued free of charge.[1]

A few will see the process judging *them*, and bristle at the prospect. Some are simple folks in fear of public forums, afraid they'll fail themselves.

All of these are speculative excuses—and you're welcome to add more— of which not one can justify the owner's bad behavior.

Our response: It's hard to label every Shirker antisocial. "The world is full of good people who do bad things," says Agatha Christie's wise and worldly sleuth, Hercule Poirot.

But shirking is the canary in the coal mine of our culture of compliance. The more we find folks dead to their district obligations, the more we find we've let our relations with the public be poisoned by neglect. Admitting this is difficult. Dealing with it is like staring down into the abyss of our own forgetfulness about our double legacies, double trusts, and double duties to care for *both* the historic and political resources of our second-generation districts.

Some of us get vertigo and look away. "The last administrator who went after them lost her job," I heard a planner plead.

We need to get to Shirkers early, and sociably, to return them to a culture of compliance. While instructing them in district law and processes, we must stress our compact with their neighbors. Meanwhile, we'll have to take on the distasteful business of processing after-the-fact COA applications. Because these folks are serial system gamers, we should treat both *appropriate* and *inappropriate* projects identically as violations of our process.

And if they're unrepentant? Fines are formidable weapons. Then, as Eli Wallach said in *The Good, the Bad and the Ugly*: "When you have to shoot, shoot, don't talk."

Most will stop at penalties. Others won't and will drop into the ranks of Shredders.

2. SHREDDERS

"Vulgarity begins at home," said Oscar Wilde—and shows up on some houses. Shredders are vulgarians who, as in Greensboro, North Carolina, "assert that they don't have to do what the rest of us have to do, which is abide by the historic district guidelines."[2]

As their public servants, we hold Shredders in our most minimal high regard. They do more than undercut the district. They swing axes at historic resources and shred our compact's understandings. They are aggressively antisocial and in our faces all the time.

"George Washington could've slept there," a Virginian says about his home. "I don't care. I sleep there now. History is just what it is, the past."[3]

Who they are: Shredders often include those Breakers and their allies who rode out our campaign and now remain a major reason for enforcement legislation. Among their number, we know them as:

- *Radical property-rightists*, who cloak their antisocial deeds in libertarian doctrine;
- *Egotists*, who are "my way" individualists, focused on their own self-regarding interests;
- *Contrarians*, who stand against community consensus;
- *Power-trippers*, who are out to prove us weak;
- *Deep pockets*, who threaten strapped public coffers with endless lawsuits;
- *Payback plotters*, who are out to get even for defeats; and
- *Too-big-to-fail investors*, who dare us to turn them down.

Shredders flaunt the law. The most egregious sorts are nonresident owners of investment properties and other bottom-line barbarians. Caring nothing for heritage or the good order of our district, they are themselves disorderly. They hold their interests sacrosanct,

- letting their properties deteriorate through neglect;
- bulldozing historic buildings on the slightest legal pretext;
- stripping their buildings of original architectural details;
- making major inappropriate repairs and alterations.

The worst throw junky work at properties like litter at a trash can. They hire the cheapest, least skilled workers. If they can't evade the HPC, they'll aim below our minimums, then afterward cut corners, change design, and substitute materials.

Confronted, they may raise the stakes and sue. A few will spend more money fighting us than it costs to do things right. Even when they're caught and fined, and fines hold up in court, they may drag their feet and never set things right.

These Shredders are like leeches. They suck value from the district, especially from neighbors. They are social cankers, and their properties often open sores.

As William Powell said in *The Last of Mrs. Cheney*, "Tragic. I blush for them."

Our response: Shredders bring out the best of the worst in us. We owe it to them, to ourselves, and to the rule of law to give them squeaky-clean due process. We should be civil in assigning fines. "When you have to kill a man," Winston Churchill said, "it costs nothing to be polite."

Still, they should know our limits. "Every normal man must be tempted, at times," H. L. Mencken wrote, "to spit upon his hands, hoist the black flag, and begin slitting throats." Is that us? Well, let them bring it on and see.

3. SHOULD-KNOW-BETTERS

Shirkers and Shredders take hammers to their buildings. These Rotters hammer at the HPC from opposite ends of the opinion spectrum. They are *hardcore anti-regulation* and *hard-line pro-preservation*.

Because they are excited, they attract attention. Because they know their minds, they have ready answers. Because the media like to sniff out conflict, newspapers and local TV stations will report their antipathies toward each other and the HPC. They threaten us with mischaracterization and the loss of public trust.

Who they are: Both sides reject the *politics of community* and the tradeoffs it entails. Because they are hostile toward all interests other than their own, they are insensitive to the new ethos of community that made our victory possible. Accordingly, the interiors of their images of the district are strangely depopulated:

- *Anti-regulationists* are individualists who live in a small world of their own, a world of one.
- *Pro-preservationists* see the district like the guest at our inn who said, when walking out at dawn with camera in hand, "It's so hard to get good pictures without people getting in the way."

Anti-regulationists deny that the exercise of rights carries community responsibilities. Pro-preservationists are oblivious to the truth that historic preservation can't exist without community support for regulations.
Both should know better, but they don't.
Now let's break them out by type.

1. Anti-Regulation Polarizers

These folks contend with us over paths to better futures. They come in two strong flavors:

1. *Extreme property rightists*, who seek to expand the scope of liberty; and
2. *Free-marketeers*, who place their trust in economic-driven change.

Other fellow travelers on this polarizing side assert that the future is so unknowable as to make impossible any such predictions as we make for rooted growth. They show themselves as:

- *Anti-expertise*, characterizing us as arrogant, dupes or liars;
- *Pro-commonsense*, trusting intuition;
- *Ahistorical*, holding that nothing ever really changes; or
- *Providentialist*, trusting in the beneficence of the existing order.

Still others may simply feel powerless in their own lives. The historic district is just one more oppressive force besetting them. Their opposition to the HPC extends no further than a hapless *cri de coeur*, "I know what's best—*for me!*"
Exponents seek to roll back district regulations, starve the HPC of administrative resources, block us where they can—and, where they can't, defame

us for their pleasure. On the latter, we may also find the fingerprints of the extremists we encountered in chapter 24.

2. Pro-Preservation Polarizers

These opposite Should-Know-Betters have joined the cloistered priesthood of preservation norms. They are loyal to an aesthetic so abstract as to reject the practical work of keeping intact community support for rooted growth.

Some may masquerade as Actors, or claim that they are Backers of district institutions. But by effect, they're Shredders of our compact with our neighbors.

Where Shredders make a principle of their own self-regarding interests, these pro-preservation polarizers make principles their interest and their guide to action. They believe our shared historic resources need protecting from everyone, including HPC commissioners who stray from any but the strictest lockbox reading of preservation norms.

Their views may strike us as intimidation. "Architecture is one of the great arts," we're told. "You wouldn't take a painting and rearrange it. Why do it with a building?"[4]

Preservation Should-Know Betters adore this sort of "case closed" flair. If we question their positions—"Do folks inhabit paintings?"—we're met with rolling eyes. If we pose it publicly, we're not being "helpful."

Resisting questioning is a hallmark of their hard-line take on things. During our campaign we embraced public Q&A to build community interest in the district, not divide our neighbors into camps. The one time that we did, to isolate our extremist opposition, they cheered us on. Now they endanger what we won. And *we're* not being helpful?

We encounter various subtypes of pro-preservation polarizers as:

- *White-glove preservationists*, who won't dirty their hands with politics;
- *Prophetic preservationists*, who project an ideal district beyond practicalities;
- *Phoenix preservationists*, who instigate or exacerbate crises to give rise to purer practices;
- *Vigilante preservationists*, who circumvent the HPC to scare off projects;
- *Scorched-earth preservationists*, who advocate enforcement minus justice;
- *Paranoid preservationists,* who see conspiracies against historic resources everywhere; or
- *Preservation martyrs*, who are proud to be attacked for the sake of preservation.

It's a sure bet that none of them has ever waged a districting campaign. If they have been a part of one, then others won it for them—or else they have been afflicted by political dementia in our aging districts. They give:

* *Anti-regulation types* ammunition for attacks;
* *Shirkers and Shredders* extra reasons to skirt the HPC process;
* *OIMBY Slackers* cause to keep their distance;
* *Backers* second thoughts; and
* *Actors* the added burden of having to defend the HPC on two fronts.

Our response: An old Central Asian proverb comes to mind: "The dog barks but the caravan continues on its way." If you can, ignore both polarizing types. But where you can't, confront them. And that deserves a chapter of its own.

NOTES

1. Cornelius Frolik, "Permits to Alter Historic Structures Are Up 36 Percent in 13 Years," www.mydaytondailynews.com, October 2, 2016.

2. Jim Schlosser, "Neighborhood Feud over Cleanup," *News and Record*, August 29, 1999.

3. Sally Voth, "Vinyl Siding, Windows among Concerns Expressed at Strasburg Joint Meeting," www.vdaily.com, May 10, 2011.

4. *Baltimore Sun*, October 26, 2005.

Chapter Sixty

Confronting Polarizers

Opposites attack.

—Rick Warren

Let's assume a worst-case scenario. Your second-generation district is in crisis. It's central ethos isn't holding. "Mere anarchy" isn't "loosed upon the world," as William Butler Yeats would have it. There's just simmering hostility, shirking, shredding, contentious HPC hearings, appeals and lawsuits in the offing, and warning signs of rollback.

As you labor over COAs, you are pummeled left and right by anti-regulation types and hard-line preservationists. The one attacks the HPC for being "overreaching" and "arbitrary and capricious," while the other charges it with "underperforming" on its preservation trust and being—well, "arbitrary and capricious."

Like owning two dogs, as Bob Newhart says, you don't know whom to blame.

WHERE TO CATCH THEM

You'll have to take them both on. If they show up at a hearing, you can't argue with their testimony. But any HPC commissioner can comment on its relevance.

- If *they* speak to what they like, *you* emphasize your guidelines.
- If *they* fall back on their principles, you underscore the law.

- If *they* say you're riding roughshod over testimony, *you* assure them of due process—and thank them for their interest.

You owe it to the applicant to put them in their place.

Outside the HPC, they're rather hit-and-run, especially online. So catch them as you can in other public forums. If any come from preservation groups or residents associations, go there. Meet them on their ground. Avoid speaking to specific issues that are before you now or in the pipeline.

HITTING BACK AT ANTI-REGULATIONISTS

We isolated and defeated *anti-regulatory types* in our campaign. We can do it all again, if need be, by holding to the compact that we won. They *say* they are opposed to regulations; we *know* that they reject the community of interests we stitched together that made the district possible.

Make that point, and then reach back to Plato's injunction that we're obliged to obey the law—either that, or change it. No one is above the law, nor are they outside it. If they want to change the law, we'll see. We might agree, or reach accommodations. If not, then we'll contend with them. But their ceaseless carping that undermines respect for law should be out of bounds by any measure of good citizenship, classical or modern.

CONFRONTING PRO-PRESERVATION POLARIZERS

We are linked to these folks by a singular bond of stewardship. But there is a limit to the criticism we'll take. It's not wrong to speak with them in private. In fact, we owe them better counsel.

But where they intrude upon the public sphere, we have no collegial obligation to remain silent about their political dysfunction when it challenges our authority and threatens to unsteady the community behind us. We're not looking for a fight. Still, Hillary Clinton has said it all: "You show people what you're willing to fight for when you fight your friends."

But you're not really fighting them on *preservation*. You are calling them to *citizenship*, to draw them to our vital center. If they're new to the district, you are also acculturating them to the ethos that underpins your district institutions.

Do I still need to stiffen your resolve? Then just imagine the travesty they'd make of administering the law if they sat on your commission.

Take the compulsive blogger who contended with our HPC in Annapolis over its reading of the law. Where our ordinance stipulates that the HPC "may" go after violators, his position was that commissioners "must" scour the historic district for even minor violations decades old. I was off the HPC by then. I countered as a private citizen that such an abuse of the HPC's authority could lead to the breakdown of community support for district regulations. He typed back in an email: "Preservation has standards that transcend politics, *n'est-ce pas?*"[1]

I rather like that "*n'est-ce pas,*" don't you? It's a French-fried version of "you dolt!" But the rest was overdone. So was a later reference to Lord Acton's observation that "power tends to corrupt" and its corollary that "absolute power corrupts absolutely."

You and I know something more important: such *absolutes* as his *corrupt power* on the HPC by undermining our authority with the neighbors whom we serve.

AN ENGAGING STRATEGY

I invited him to meet me at the HPC for a public airing of his views. He repeatedly refused, although it didn't stop his continuing attacks. He must have known his case was weak.

Imagine we encounter folks like him in a public meeting when we're drawing up our guidelines. The way that we'll respond is as we did in our campaign, reframing their positions.

But first some general observations. Pro-preservation polarizers drink deeply of preservation principles. Yet when it comes to *district* preservation they have only gargled. They demonstrate three weaknesses:

1. They don't think politically like districtists,
2. They treat preservation norms like moral verities, and
3. They disrespect the authority of the HPC's decision-making process.

Accordingly, if you meet them in public forums, you'll want to tackle them on issues of *stewardship* and *standards* and *authoritative preservation*.

A. Their argument against politics in stewardship.

They say: Our historic resources are too important to let politics interfere with HPC decisions.

Once they've plumped for this you are ready to reframe.

Reframe: *You mean there is no need for sustaining community support for regulations?*

You respond: *Surely you can't mean it. We can't do as you say* and *be good stewards of our preservation trust. Without community support for HPC decisions, we'll end up kissing what we care about goodbye. We* have to *tend to politics, now wouldn't you agree?*

If they concur, then good. Job done. If they don't, you'll be able to counter them on every point they make by talking like a districtist about our double legacies and trusts.

If they still resist, you'll want to push them into declaring that, compared to politics, preservation stewardship is uniquely virtuous. Say that when commissioners hear testimony, due process obliges them to hear private views on preservation and other interests all the same, including those of owners.

B. Their claim that HPC decisions that take cognizance of politics depart from the district's ordinance or guidelines.

Because they think that preservation norms are controlling, they prefer a narrow take on applying district guidelines. If your district uses only the Secretary's Standards, that's a problem. Anytime you work for accommodation, you are open to charges of straying from those norms.

They say: *HPC decisions are arbitrary and capricious.*

Variation: *What the HPC produces isn't preservation.*

That we work for rooted growth in which preservation plays its role is a different issue. Here your *decision-making authority* is under challenge. They assume they know better what preservation is and the decisions you should make.

You don't have to prove your preservation bona fides. Your response will be coldly assertive about what, objectively, preservation is in your historic district.

Reframe: *Who's to say what preservation is?*

You respond: *By its authority the HPC defines for the district what preservation is, decision by decision. In brief, it's how they call it.*

HPC commissioners are like those umpires in the story. Have you heard it? A sports reporter asked them how they called balls and strikes in baseball:

1. A brand new ump allowed, "I call them as they are."
2. An older ump said, and smiling, "I call 'em as I see 'em."
3. The oldest, wisest ump of all declared, "They ain't nothin' till I call 'em."

That's how it is with HPCs. In terms of preservation, they call the balls and strikes on project applications.

Outside of their decision there is—what? *Opinion.* That's true no matter who is testifying or morning-after grumbling about the ball that should've been a strike against a project—game over.

- Property-rights polarizers? Opinion.
- The OIMBY Slacker? Opinion.
- The well-informed Backer? Opinion.
- A legal-beagle commentator? Opinion.
- A SHPO representative? Opinion.
- A standard-bearing preservationist? Same thing.

And that's what you should tell them.

Say you respect them for their knowledge and their passion. But when it comes to testifying, they—just like you mom, whom you hold in high esteem—have to get in line according to due process. The HPC will take their testimony, weigh it, and decide. After that, *whatever else preservation might have been* was merely penciled in, erased.

This side of the appellate process, they should accept that your HPC is *the* authority on preservation for the district under law.

They are free to agree or not with HPC decisions. They may also work politically to change the ordinance and guidelines. Meanwhile they have to make up their minds. Withholding support for the conclusive authority of the process weakens the effective power of the HPC across the board. If they want the community to support HPC decisions they agree with, then they themselves must accept that HPC decisions are legitimate when they go against them.

Not just accept. "Say it," tell them. "Make your support public. Send out emails, write letters to the editor." Leave no doubt in their minds that siding with the HPC in good times and in bad is the best way they can corner anti-regulation polarizers who jeopardize their interests. They'll also gain deeper respect in the community and press—and with the HPC.

C. Their argument for the unique virtue of preservation stewardship.

They say: What owners want, they want. But we have an ethical obligation to protect our common heritage.

If they don't put it in these terms, then give it to them on a platter. Tell them you believe they're telling you that saving historic resources is uniquely good. When they say they do, continue.

Reframe: *Do* buildings and open spaces *deserve moral treatment the same way* people *do?*

You respond: *I agree that preservation is a social good. But the Secretary of the Interior's Standards aren't moral like the Ten Commandments. In fact, the real work of preservation* depends *upon the difference.*

This last essential point is so little understood in preservation circles that it needs elaboration. If you *particularize a moral principle*—saying when and where and how it's applicable—it *loses force and meaning.* Consider the difference between the Declaration of Independence and the Constitution, as an obvious example.

The one declares that "all men are created equal" with "right to life, liberty and the pursuit of happiness." As *self-evident truths*—that is, found and not created—they morally *compel our allegiance.* They can't be made time or place or group-specific without becoming hollowed out. We found that out in civil war and continuing fights over the particularized terms of our Constitution that treated free men and slaves differently and women were ignored.

Preservation standards are *created* as *norms of achievement* in areas of endeavor, *inviting our support.* They *gain force and meaning only* as they are made time and place specific to fit the needs of certain groups of citizens, the ones we call historic districts.

That's because the Secretary's Standards—shall we say our *standard* standards?—fly at 35,000 feet. The closer to the ground they get, the more they are particularized, admixed with other interests, and then given concrete *force and meaning* in our ordinances and guidelines. Those who would give such practical effect to abstract standards must concern themselves with other conditioning factors, such as concerns for justice and the consent of the governed.

In Oak Park, Illinois, the controversial plan to expand the boundaries of the Frank Lloyd Wright Historic District offers two distinctly different sorts of regulations for the four hundred homes to be included. Making the case for their distinctive aspirational goals, HPC chair Christina Morris assured residents that the Commission wanted their approval. "We don't want to plow it through," she said. "[This] is something we want to do, not something we have to do."[2]

See? In other words, there is no *there* there when it comes to moral imperative.

When you get them to this point, emphasize the split between private and public virtue as we struck it in chapter 40. They should know that when they testify before the HPC or comment in the press, they are doing so as *private* citizens. When they talk about the HPC, they need to be aware that commissioners must sublimate their *private* interests to their *public* obligation to make the system work for the happiness of citizens. The best way the folks you are addressing can demonstrate they do is by respecting HPC decisions.

Something else: When a moral ideal like justice is forgotten, "it is the vulnerable and powerless who suffer first and worst."[3] But when pro-preservation polarizers "remember" standards as ideals, they become insensitive to issues of legitimate property rights, economic justice, and the disfranchisement of the poorer and more helpless segments of our communities.

This, then, exacerbates the issue of gentrification as it affects our districts. It's time to look at it again.

NOTES

1. Name withheld, e-mail on file.
2. Jim Jaworski, "Residents Skeptical of New Historic District Boundaries," www.triblocal.com, March 22, 2011.
3. Michael Gerson, "What Lincoln Knew about America—and So Must We," *The Washington Post*, July 4, 2017, p. A17.

Chapter Sixty-One

Gentrification's Dissidents: On Displacement with Baltimore's Eric Holcomb

I agree with that you say. What do we do?

—Plato, *Crito*

If gentrification did not influence your campaign, it might impinge on district operations. Dissonant voices may come from residential and business owners, renters, and others aggrieved by change. You might not hear them in your HPC, but they can adversely affect your community compact and standing with elected officials.

Who they are: For analytical purposes relevant to us, I'll divide them into two types at either end of a continuum:

1. At one end are those whose *consciousness* of gentrification has been shaped by *life*. The harder their personal experience, the more they are inclined to think in terms of cash.
2. At the other end are those whose *conscience* regarding gentrification has been shaped by *observation*. The more distant their perspective, the more they are inclined to think in terms of class and culture clash.

As they move in toward one another, they gauge the situation differently. The one side gauges gentrification in terms of personal justice and opportunity, the other in terms of the defense of local culture and group solidarity.

This creates contests among competing interests that we can understand. We, too, have grappled with disruptive change and we're both concerned with justice. And yet we may find ourselves attacked for facilitating upscale change, while ignoring social justice.

Our response: You might find yourself *privately* moved by some or all of what such dissidents allege. But *publicly* as a HPC commissioner you have a duty under law to be just to all individuals as they come before you with their applications.

Even so, as we administer for happiness we have to factor in considerations involving social justice. We want to avoid policies and decisions that result in doing harm especially to the most vulnerable among us. How to think about gentrification as a practical challenge for our HPCs has put me on the road again to do an interview.

BALTIMORE

From the elevated freeway, "Charm City" opens up before me. The roadway drops me down by the home grounds of the Ravens and the Orioles. I'm on my way to meet Eric Holcomb, executive director of the City's Historical and Architectural Preservation Division to discuss his experience with justice in gentrifying change.

Eric sits behind a "partners" desk from an old police station. We begin by reviewing the arc of change in the City's north-central Mount Vernon local historic district, designated in 1964 and for which CHAP, the Commission for Historical and Architectural Preservation, was created to administer. In 1977, in the third of seven district expansions, Mount Vernon took in the great Victorian mansions of the Belvedere neighborhood.

THE DIALOGUE

Me: *Seven?* Were they easy?

Eric: Fairly easy. They were done at the behest of folks not in the district.

Me: So Mount Vernon was achieving its goals and people were pleased?

Eric: Not everybody, but yes. In fifty years Mount Vernon has really come into its own. The cumulative effects led in 2000 to the district's creation of a special tax benefits district to fund neighborhood maintenance—better lighting, trash collection. . . . You really see the synergy being created. It's about the community values that historic districting created.

Me: How did Mount Vernon get started?

Eric: The historic district was born out of the politics of urban renewal activity, actually, in concert with leaders working to pull a variety of resources together.

Me: How has gentrification figured in?

Eric: With the Great Recession, in 2010 you see the older generation of absentee landlords who were providing more affordable apartments selling out to folks doing more market-rate luxury, and you start to see this huge restoration effect in the neighborhood. So that's gentrifying.

Me: Is it a bad thing?

Eric: The term has become so toxic, I think, to the point where I don't know what people mean when they use it. So to sidestep it and drill-down on the issue I like to use "displacement." It's geographic—in a specific instance, a specific place, and always a unique situation, whatever the generalizations others talk about. The first question when you do revitalization using preservation tools is will there be displacement of folks who live there now, either owners or renters? And not just residential, like we think of first, but also local businesses serving the community.

Me: What's Mount Vernon's story?

Eric: The rich of the rich build the houses there in the 1830–1840s. Then, by the 1870–1880s, the rich kids who grew up there are jumping into other neighborhoods like Belvedere just north of the Square and along Eutaw Place. We start to see every generation going somewhere else. Mount Vernon Place was the exception where there were some tear downs and rebuilding in the latest architectural style.

Me: Are those demolitions gentrification?

Eric: In some ways, right? Or is it the new generation deciding to redo the neighborhood they grew up in? You start to see façade-ectomies as the affluent second generation starts taking them down and putting on the latest style, adding stories to their buildings, and building the adjacent Belvedere neighborhood.

Me: And then?

Eric: By the 1890s, the folks who grew up in the 1870s move out to Roland Park and Walbrook. By the early 1900s, you see a lot of those old homes in Mount Vernon, still owned by the families, being turned into multiple apartments or boarding houses. It kicks off the twentieth century residential development pattern. The great Baltimore fire of 1904 burned out 1,500 businesses, and many relocated along the Charles Street corridor in Mount Vernon.

Me: What would you call that?

Eric: Gentrification? Evolution. Change. In the 1920–1930s, you also have gays and lesbians showing up and starting to move into Mount Vernon, and the diversity remains today with the LGBTQ community being a notable and historic presence.

Me: Then after the war comes urban renewal?

Eric: With plans calling for the demolition of twenty-six square blocks in Mount Vernon. It begins with Robert Moses coming in 1945 with highway plans, and an off ramp is to be put directly south of Mount Vernon, adjacent to the Walters Art Museum. In a direct reaction to those renewal plans, Douglas Gordon and other affluent neighbors start fighting for historic preservation and by the 1960s there's a small contingent of preservation-minded folks in the community. There weren't many residential homes left but the mansions were still here. By 2017, only about 8 percent of properties were owner-occupied, with most renting out their upper floors.

Me: The others are still broken up into apartments?

Eric: A lot of them are, up to fifteen apartments in each. Twenty-nine properties were owned by one company who was not a good steward, and they put in as many units as they could. They went bankrupt around 2010. That was when deep pockets entered with an eye on the luxury market. They are a lot better stewards in terms of maintaining historic fabric. They are the ones who'll restore the brownstones, put on slate roofs, use preservation tax credits.

Me: And more affluent resident homeowners are coming back?

Eric: Not as many as you would like. In the mid-1990s, a row-house mansion of 3,000–5,000 square feet could go for $200,000. Today they're $600,000–700,000. We call that a success, right? And that's a question.

Me: How do you answer it?

Eric: If the neighborhood becomes revitalized using preservation tools and creates a really healthy real estate market, then you have to ask: how do we as government officials, politicians and advocates get in front of who gets displaced (and how to prevent it). That's the time to do it, when the market is coming back. You ask, what kind of neighborhood do we want, and the economic diversity? Then you work on creating the policies and strategies to implement what you're looking for.

Me: If you go into a neighborhood that's working on a district and then talk about displacement—you've got to have a hard hat on, don't you?

Eric: I'll put on my planner's hat here. You don't create a historic district in a vacuum. You do it within a larger planning and political perspective. And that brings in other experts. As a preservationist you don't need to know the answer to everything. But you need to know how to work with other experts, especially with regard to place making.

Me: Define place making for us.

Eric: Place making is when you start talking about making a physical neighborhood better. You need to work with your homeowners, your planners, architects, the advocacy groups on the ground, the neighborhood associations, and public health officials on issues like lead paint. In developing a master plan, you need to reach out to the community and have it guide the folks who have the tools (and training) to make the community better. The neighborhood residents are the ones who are coming together to create the vision, and it's the professionals—planners, preservationists, housing development folks—who have the expertise to lay out the plan and make it happen. Well that's the ideal anyway.

Me: But aren't there divisions in the community, and fears? Do historic districts do more to displace people, or keep them from being displaced?

Eric: Could be both. We have a couple of designations in the works. Displacement hasn't come up in terms of the designation process. Federal Hill is already a healthy real estate market and displacement is not a concern because it's already occurred. The Old Goucher neighborhood has diversity of owning residents and renters, but the community isn't asking CHAP to solve displacement. They're going to City offices and nonprofits to ask them to preserve their affordable housing units. The historic district is a tool in a bigger process. As preservationists we must learn to work better in the bigger process.

Me: So interest in affordable housing comes from residents who *also* want a district?

Eric: Affordable housing in Baltimore—and probably across the nation—is the result of a lack of a real estate market that can command rents that will kick people out. But in some of our neighborhoods, you're talking double-digit vacancy and abandonment rates. Owners have walked away, and the City assumes responsibility for the buildings. Getting those houses fixed up and back on the market isn't displacement, because nobody's living there. But hopefully it's creating a situation for a real estate market to come back. That's when you start to get displacement. When the market commands better rents and an owner says, "I can increase my rates."

Me: What can you do about it? Isn't displacement sort of like, with six you get eggroll? You might not want it, but you open up the bag and there it is.

Eric: I think we can and should learn to craft more equitable revitalization strategies. But the worst thing you can do to folks of little means is to leave them concentrated in one geographical area. Poor communities have less social capital and their social networks are so much weaker. So the idea would be to create mixed-income neighborhoods that are healthier than poor neighborhoods.

Me: And bring the rich into those downtown neighborhoods.

Eric: If a district becomes only affluent, it means folks are missing out on cultural richness and depth. On the other hand, a concentration of poverty is not good policy. It isn't good for the folks who live there, and not good for any communities around them.

Me: How do you create those mixed neighborhoods?

Eric: Look at the Barclay Greenmount neighborhood. You'd want to craft policies that allow folks living there to keep on living there by using low-income tax credits, preservation tax credits and other tools to build, and subsidize affordable housing. You'd work with nonprofit community developers. We have a good historic preservation property tax credit plan that offsets property taxes for ten years. It allows folks of up-means but not great means to buy rehabilitated houses and have a credit based on pre- and post-rehab appraisals that lowers your property tax for ten years.

Me: Has it worked anywhere?

Eric: Using post-2008 federal subsidies in East Baltimore, Habitat for Humanity built about 120 units that sold as lower-income and workforce housing. It helped stabilize the real estate market and values are rising. No apartment units. But it has allowed for a fireman or security guard to live in a diverse community and build equity with all the amenities they want. To date, since 1997 approximately 4,600 properties have applied, thousands of which have been in marginal neighborhoods.

Me: When you do this in a historic district, do you alter your design guidelines?

Eric: Right now, we have one set of guidelines that we apply consistently to our thirty-three districts. But we're working on a policy paper on what we call a "partial" versus "full control" historic district.

Me: What's the difference?

Eric: A partial historic district would be like a conservation district with a difference: the designation process would be the same as for a historic district, but we would apply our guidelines more leniently where there's less of a real estate market. We'd probably allow vinyl windows of acceptable color and style and alternative doors while keeping original façade openings. We'd review demolition and additions and new construction. *Any* window in many places in Baltimore would be a vast improvement over what's there now. And full control may be too expensive for developers. We've talked to our housing folks and community planners to see if this is another preservation tool.

Me: As historic districting shifts around the country toward less-affluent neighborhoods, judgment and flexibility on historic resources becomes important, doesn't it?

Eric: There's so much more to look at than just fabric. We have to address the market, economic hardship, community revitalization. But some preservationists won't even address lead paint. I've heard, "I grew up in a lead-painted house, and I'm fine." But CHAP spent two years with health officials on how to preserve and be safe. It's an incredibly serious problem.

Me: Beyond displacement, what are your observations regarding social justice?

Eric: I want to get it on the record that in the last three years the Baltimore City Planning Department, of which CHAP staff is a part, has been looking at equity and justice. We're starting to create policy papers. Equity and gentrification aren't new issues. But we're looking to make sure that what we do on a *day-to-day* basis—"we" meaning all of planning, CHAP staff, the comprehensive planners, the land-use/urban-development folks—that we're all looking through the equity lens.

Me: Like what, specifically?

Eric: How do we prepare residents to come into CHAP and the Planning Commission and testify? What's the best way to get their testimony together to have the biggest impact? Some CHAP applications for exterior work in local districts are handwritten, scrawled, almost in crayon, with just basic sketches. How do we help them through the review process? When we go out with a district revitalization plan—are we listening to all the folks in the community, talking with everybody? It's a concerted effort to listen better, so we can create plans to serve all the community.

Me: And that's apart from gentrification.

Eric: It's a more nuanced view of how to address gentrification. It's exciting, and especially after the 2014 Baltimore riots. We're looking at what people really need to make sure we're not always greasing the same squeaky wheels. Looking through the equity lens, we want to celebrate the history of overlooked communities.

Me: Any last comments?

Eric: In terms of gentrification, we can look at South Baltimore in the 1980s. Many old-time residents did not want to live there. Property values were awful, and lots of folks owned their houses. Then the real estate market took off. The first thing that a lot of those folks who owned houses did was sell. They had their golden tickets to go out into the county and live their dreams, which is what they wanted.

Me: And that was a kind of social justice.

Eric: A kind of social justice. They finally got enough money to go do what they wanted to do. That's displacement, right? But it's a positive outcome.

Me: And willing. The issue is complex, and we thank you for your insights.

After leaving Eric's office I grab a donut and a cup of coffee. I find a place to sit outside—in the middle of the street, looking northwards toward Mount Vernon. Traffic bends around me: I'm in a monumental plaza to the War of 1812 and the victory at Ft. McHenry.

I see the City with new eyes. Not the buildings that preservation dotes on but the ghosts of generations past. Today, I wonder who is leaving and who is coming next.

As you envisage your community, you might not have all of Eric's tools to deflect the adverse costs of gentrifying as displacement. Yet his flexible response instructs us to set aside abstract ruminations and focus on our concrete situations as we find them on the ground. Bottom line: If you'd be just, be just today to people as they are.

Part X

DISTRICT DECLINE
AND ITS REVERSAL

Chapter Sixty-Two

Political Personalities: Who Leads?

The measure of a man is what he does with power.

—Plato

We have parsed who's who in our historic district and put us in the forefront. Are we up to the job? Now we need to be as objective with ourselves as we have been with others.

POLITICAL PERSONALITY

Leadership reveals itself in many forms. Not all of them are equal or equal to the task of mastering the tension at the heart of district service. Change in our aging district puts stress on historic resources and the standing of our HPC. It also stresses *us*. Some of us are energized. Others batten down the hatches and just soldier on. Some facilitate accommodation, and others throw up roadblocks.

The innate traits inclining each of us one way or another are *intellect and temperament*—or, in other words, our comprehension and compulsions. The combination of the two defines our *political personality*.

FOUR TYPES OF PERSONALITIES

Of course, we're all unique. And yet those who handle tension best do so in pretty much the same way as a group. And those who don't? They respond in several different ways.

We will be using what we've learned from Hobbes to break out four distinctive personality types, though no one person is one type all the time.

In their relationships with others, leaders may be by intellect and temperament:

1. Sociable and formidable;
2. Sociable, not formidable;
3. Formidable, not sociable;
4. Neither formidable nor sociable.

This typology can help us better see ourselves, understand our differences, and compensate each other as we can. Leadership starts at the top. I mainly have in mind commission chairs and planners assigned to HPCs. Even so, a single strong personality among rank and file commissioners can make a telling difference in a HPC's success.

TYPE 1: SOCIABLE AND FORMIDABLE

These Actors are self-confident and flexible in their roles. They take pleasure from positions of authority. As sociable optimists, they anticipate change as affirming the vitality of the community even as it brings them problems.

They are assertively positive about the role of government, enthusiastic about working with others, and comfortable with exercising power. Their priority lies in making the district work, and they look for better ways to do it.

They are proactive in conflicts. They seek out the toughest issues, cultivate support, and expect to win. They assume the district is only as strong as the HPC's last success and its next decision.

They are not unnerved by loss. Whether they succeed or fail—and they expect to lose sometimes—they don't take it personally or demonize their critics. They know that politics isn't about them. So they readily adapt to fluid situations and change their minds as conditions warrant.

They are team leaders, power sharers, consensus builders, facilitators. When singled out for credit, they deflect it off on others to empower them to do new things tomorrow. They inspire confidence and loyalty to the district by their example.

Relaxed in their own political skins, they're not laid-back but energetic. Never ones to flinch from exercising power, they prefer jawboning and brokering to relying on the law or their procedural prerogatives. They will put their foot down when things get out of hand and enforce the district vigorously when they have to.

They take their cues from observing what's going on around them rather than from abstract notions about what's right and proper. Being solution oriented, they are ideologically neutral. They think like Deng Xiaoping who said that it doesn't matter if a cat is black or white as long as it catches mice. They are pragmatic decision makers.

In HPC meetings they are fast off the mark and quick to get to the heart of things. They use the process to accommodate conflicting interests, which they see in positive-sum terms. They know how to run smooth meetings, and they handle political tension well.

Being both sociable and formidable, they are happy prosecutors of the district's interests vis-à-vis its Rotters. They leave highly charged sessions energized.

Though obviously enjoying commission service, they may be rather less attentive to administrative details. Used to thinking politically, they prefer to be where the action is. If they cycle through the HPC, they look for other things to do to make a contribution. They take on public education to draw others into their arc of service and accomplishment.

Privately, they like to think that, with them, the historic district is in capable hands.

TYPE 2: SOCIABLE NOT FORMIDABLE

These Actors are compliant, politically passive, and easygoing folks with ingratiating attitudes. Their impulses are social rather than political.

They lead from the center, optimistically encouraging others to get along to go along. They want to be a friend to everyone, and have everyone be a friend. They desire all the drama of a Doris Day movie.

This preference for sociability reflects their discomfort with exercising power over neighbors. They enjoy authority for the chance to help, though they also like to be admired for their contributions.

Because politics puts them ill at ease, their priority lies in being well-received as the key to job performance. They substitute likability for political success in sustaining community support. They figure if folks warm to them, they will like the district, too.

They are receptive to change, while counting on an outwardly sunny disposition to see them through its challenges. Risk averse, they have a "sure, why not?" kind of optimism.

This makes them reactive problem solvers. They like to be thought of as Mr. or Ms. "Fix-it," typically telling others, "I'm here for you," "Bring me your problems," and "Let me know what I can do." They say it with a smile that often masks an underlying personal uncertainty about their ability to handle conflict. Confronted by a difficult project, they'll say "We'll see what we can do," while meaning, however, that they'll let the district process run its course.

While they look to good outcomes, they prefer to stay above the fray. They favor accommodation to disarm conflict rather than for working through it. They are sympathetic, scene-setting shapers more than doers. With them, as Mark Twain once said, "Action speaks louder than words, but not nearly as often."

In the HPC, they like to get things off on a friendly footing, sit back, see what develops, join the popular side if need be, or pour oil on troubled waters in the role of peacemaker. If they take an active role in deliberations, it is often as the go-to master of technical requirements, detail, and precedent, which they use to press for happy outcomes.

They see themselves as team players more than leaders, preferring to sit in circles and defer to others. Not quite sure of themselves, they readily adapt their views in a changing climate of opinion.

In confrontations, they verge on being genial nonentities, not foxhole sorts of folk. They sense they can't be formidable without jeopardizing their own and the district's reputation for being helpful. They dread saying no.

This opens them up to being manipulated and marginalized when the chips are down. So they aren't eager enforcers. If they have to do it, they'll passively let others take the lead in bringing Shirkers and Shredders to heel.

They convey a friendly competence and efficiency, which inspires a kind of trust. They may be able, open-door administrators. As long as things are going well in a stable district, they can do a splendid job, friendly at the helm.

Privately, they like to think they put the right face on the district.

TYPE 3: FORMIDABLE NOT SOCIABLE

Al Capone would tell Type 2 folks, "You can get much farther with a kind word and a gun than you can with a kind word alone." Type 3 Actors like the gun part best.

Formidable and rarely sociable, they see themselves as hard-duty district sheriffs, shooting down noncompliant projects and enforcing process. They expect little but problems to come from change—although they know it is inevitable—and for them everything is zero-sum.

They are anxious about staying ahead of the curve or falling behind. For them, "losing feels worse than winning feels good," as Vin Scully said about baseball. They value wins mostly for what others lose. When they lose, they think of getting even. They like to tote up wins and losses on their private scorecard.

Being offensively inclined, they head in the direction of gunfire. They watch for emerging problems and then ride out to head them off, brandishing their authority.

They like to exercise power, but don't take much pleasure from it. They come across as highly driven to deliver good government to a less than deserving community, often feeling they give better than they get in recognition.

They are, as a type, pessimistic about others. As loners who distrust team playing unless they're in control, they are disinclined toward power sharing. Just the opposite: they jealously protect their roles and HPC prerogatives. To the extent they're politically astute, they'll put on a sociable performance if it will get them what they want.

Yet they tend to be confrontational in and outside of HPC meetings. Conflicts over interests and policy quickly become personal, creating situations that end up confirming their negative preconceptions.

Often perfectionists themselves, they are drawn to the exactness of the law. They take a rather hard line on guidelines and equate accommodation with compromise and weakness.

This makes them rigidly incapable of adapting to any other point of view. They feel betrayed by colleagues on the HPC who don't support them, and they rarely hesitate to cast dissenting votes when it suits them, often as a point of honor.

As administrators, they're feared more than valued for their my-way-or-the-highway thoroughness and tenacity. In outreach education they are aggressively assertive about the HPC's authority. They think of it as putting the community and public officials on notice.

Type 3 Actors seem to have tough hides, but they're thin-skinned underneath. Challenges to heritage and the HPC are taken personally as threats to their authority and what they care about. They sense that the district is only as strong as they are.

Privately, these embattled Actors believe the district can't survive without them.

TYPE 4: NEITHER FORMIDABLE NOR SOCIABLE

These folks are leaders only in the sense of holding a leadership position. They often find themselves with authority they neither want nor enjoy. They may serve as commissioners because they've been dragooned or as staff because it is a delegated job.

It's hard to know how they see themselves, but low self-esteem seems to fit. Certainly they tend to be thin-skinned and withdrawn. Like tortoises, they're slow to act, and quick to retreat into the protective shells they build around themselves. They don't go the extra mile—or, indeed, an extra step—to make the district work. They might wonder why the tortoise ran at all in Aesop's fable.

Theirs is a self-protective fortress mentality. They prefer to work "behind the scenes," as they might call it, where they labor miserably at what they see as thankless tasks for the sake of duty or employment. They mean well, but do only what they have to do in clearly defined tasks that they perform unimaginatively and sometimes not at all. They are often good folks who, battered and disheartened, have just burned out.

Feeling isolated and underappreciated, they're quick to defend their inaction in terms of their role descriptions or the limits of their authority. "My hands are tied" is a common comment, or "I'm just the planner." One told me she was "really a historian" more interested in recording district resources than dealing with the public. Rather than increasing their own or sharing power, Type 4 folks are relieved to cede initiative and authority to others.

As HPC commissioners, they let others lead, while they may come unprepared and then sit back. They offer applicants neither help nor useful criticism, except pro forma. They prefer to agree with other commissioners in meetings that end early.

These unsociable and passive pessimists have a stop-the-world-I-want-to-get-off attitude toward change. Insensitive to its opportunities, they react slowly to its threats while waiting for our HPC procedures to kick in for them. They seem to think that the district, having been wound up at designation, will keep on ticking with or without concerted effort to sustain it.

Uncomfortable with politics, they insist on law and principle, even though their aptitude for self-protection makes them malleable. They cringe at enforcement and fear reprisals. They'll bend or ignore regulations and procedures to extricate themselves from trouble. When forced into accommodating change, they'll do it to be rid of problems.

They tend to be both principled in their own minds and inconsistent in practice. If they get caught with their necks out, they'll turn turtle quickly.

As administrators, they see themselves as functionaries, processing project applications. As in-box, out-box types, they believe folks ought to know the rules and shouldn't need a nursemaid. "The form is self-explanatory" may be a favorite phrase.

They're averse to outreach education. Unless they're tasked to do it, they don't. They dread public forums and are quick to turn defensive under questioning.

If working with others is unavoidable they'll comply, while expecting they'll get little out of it and viewing everything a bother. They know if they do more, more will be expected. They seek refuge in chains of command and run from turf battles. They think like Martin Cruz Smith in his thriller *Wolves Eat Dogs*: "Figure out the food chain, and you figure out the world."

Privately, they want to be somewhere else. But we may find them, as Texan Hickey Freeman says, "hangin' in there like a hair in a biscuit."

SUMMARY

So how does each type respond to the challenges of change? We can sum them up in four brief phrases:

1. Sociable and formidable: Good government.
2. Sociable, not formidable: Good me.
3. Formidable, not sociable: Good offense.
4. Neither formidable nor sociable: Good grief!

Most of us have to work with some version of every type in district operations. What's more, our constituents have to deal with all of us.

As we make COA decisions, we reveal the temperaments that shape our public image. So how do people see us? Can we see ourselves objectively?

"Many a man's reputation," essayist Elbert Hubbard wrote, "would not know his character if they met on the street."

I once turned the corner and saw a vaguely familiar face studying a building. "I know you, don't I?" he greeted me. I told him I chaired the HPC. "That's right," he said. "You're the rat bastard who approved my roof."

Who, *me*? Why, I thought, he must mean someone else! Or did he mean us as a group?

Well, now, that's an interesting notion, isn't it? Let's see what we can do with it.

Chapter Sixty-Three

The Stages of Declining Districts

If I had my life to live again, I'd make the same mistakes, only sooner.

—Tallulah Bankhead

What kinds of HPCs would we get if each one were populated or even just dominated by one personality type, descending from the best to worst?

In the *Republic*, Plato develops a typology of societies based on the intellects and temperaments of those who shape their politics. He ranks them top to bottom. Then he traces how a society declines step-by-step as it descends the list.

You're ahead of me already, aren't you? Yep, we'll do that with our districts. What I'll be unspooling is an allegory of the collapse of public service like bumping down a flight of steps. Think of it as some other district's history of mistakes that no one, even Ms. Bankhead, should look back on with nostalgia.

THE DECLENSION OF OUR HPCs

But that doesn't mean we can't have a little fun. I'm going to give each successive type of HPC a music group or pub name to lighten up the story. Here goes:

Type 1. Sociable and formidable: The Up & Doing
Type 2. Sociable, not formidable: The Open Arms
Type 3. Formidable, not sociable: The Regulatory Spanking Machine
Type 4. Neither formidable nor sociable: The Muddle On

We'll assume that the best HPC is found right after designation. Its members still act from the political lessons they learned from winning the compact with their neighbors. From that point on, our district starts to come apart politically as it ages.

So here we go again, aware that if Plato wrote today it would be for cable television and likely with a soundtrack. Let's make it R&B. Did Plato ever get his groove on? I would like to think so.

STAGE 1: THE UP AND DOING

As we start, our HPC is filled by those who handle tension well, aware of our twin legacies and trusts.[1] They are aiding applicants, making good decisions, and enforcing the district process. We hear Marvin Gaye and Tammi Terrell singing "Ain't No Mountain High Enough," you know, "to keep me from you," whether sociably or formidably.

But our Type 1 commissioners don't get much positive feedback from their neighbors. The press won't cover the good work they do, nor will local gossip chains. Both, however, trade in failures and distortions.

Those outside the process—Slackers most of all—begin to feel there's something wrong going on inside the HPC, even if there really isn't. Commissioners are flummoxed by whispering campaigns. We catch snatches of Marvin Gaye singing all alone, "I Heard It through the Grapevine," as OIMBYism turns its cold shoulder to district operations.

STAGE 2: THE OPEN ARMS

Old campaign pros cycle off the HPC, and those who take their places want to put a better face on district operations. They are determined to get along with everyone and have a good reputation.

They try to smooth things over easing up, overlooking slights, and smiling as they cozy up to owners' interests. Al Green's version of "What a Wonderful World" sets the scene as they see only "skies of blue and fields of green."

But soon the HPC is accused of rubber-stamping COAs. Then these sociable Type 2 commissioners are taken advantage of one too many times by those who aren't sociable with them. Now the pendulum starts swinging the other way with strains of the Tams' "What Kind of Fool Do You Think I Am?" rising in the background.

STAGE 3: THE REGULATORY SPANKING MACHINE

Type 2's formidable successors enter to the tune of the "Tighten Up," by Archie Bell and the Drells. Sociability takes a powder on all sides. The process shifts from amicable to adversarial. Predictably, the Drells play on in an endless loop to Stage 3 fadeout.

STAGE 4: THE MUDDLE ON

At rock bottom finally, everyone is dispirited about the prospects for preservation and making preservation work. Isolated from public opinion and crabbed in its operations, the HPC slogs along under uninspired leadership. Now it's all B.B. King singing "The Thrill Is Gone" from somewhere in the shadows.

In this final stage, because the HPC is neither sociable nor formidable, the historic district is disoriented and disordered. The ranks of Actors thin, Backers lose conviction, and Slackers spin still farther from the HPC. Shirkers damage historic resources with near impunity. Shredders get away with murder. Should-Know-Betters rail on behalf of their ideologies, while those owners grow cynical who once were model citizens.

A culture of complaint prevails. Then, as Plato writes of his last stage before collapse, we find impeachments everywhere. Commissioners and staff are set upon in the press and public forums. The political landscape is dotted with lawsuits and appeals.

Something's got to give, something to bring order.

Those who have authority—the courts and/or city council—start to overturn HPC decisions, tinker with the district, and then begin considering wholesale changes or repeal. The mayor is drumming fingers and humming Sam Cook's classic, "A Change Is Gonna Come."

THE ANTIDOTE

Can nothing save the day, to protect us from decline? There are two parts to the antidote:

- **Defen-*si*-ble** decision making, that tracks along with law, and
- **Defen-*da*-ble** decision making, that keeps its eye upon our political support in the community and at City Hall.

So let's turn the page and as we do we'll hum "What a Difference a *da* Makes," with apologies to Dinah Washington.

NOTE

1. See chapter 43.

Chapter Sixty-Four

The Politics of Decision Making: Defensible and Defendable

To do something right does not mean that doing it is right.

—William Safire

Let's take stock of what we've done since our designation victory. We have:

- Learned to cope with the problems of transition to administration.
- Identified the nature of good government.
- Analyzed our practices.
- Tracked the arc of political change in aging districts.
- Opted to deal with others, sociably and formidably, as they engage the district process.
- Taken our own measure as fit or less than able leaders.

Now we want to make sure what we do next in decision making won't pull the roof down on us.

MADISON'S CHARGE TO US

James Madison summed up our central problem. "In framing a government," he wrote, "the great difficulty lies in this: you must first enable the government to control the governed; and in the next place oblige it to control itself."

Administrative legalism's singular strength lies in focusing on the rule of law in district operations. But all well-run HPCs work very hard at self-regulation by following procedures, ensuring due process, and basing our decisions on their ordinance and guidelines. Taken together, these are hallmarks of *defensible* decision making.

DEFENSIBLE DECISION MAKING

How often have you heard it said you should "think outside the box?" Have you ever wondered, *what* box? Let's make our commission room our mental box, to set an image. It is filled with us, our law, our guidelines, and our procedures.

Now we districtists, acting on our twin duties to historic resources and the people, think inside the box and out, beyond it, to the *ripple effects* of our decisions on political support for districting, the HPC, and rooted growth.

Administrative legalists avoid chasing after these unpredictable and politically elusive criteria. They say to us, stay in the box and master it professionally. The best that we can do, they believe, hearing after hearing for the aggregate of applicants, is ensure an efficiently administered district according to the law.

We do that, too. All of us, regardless of our attitude toward politics, are *formidable with ourselves*: we turn the law on ourselves and hold ourselves accountable for due process and defensible decisions. We are, in a way, like COA applicants. The law squeezes them, and the law squeezes us. And while the squeeze itself can't ensure that the juice is sweet, the squeeze is still essential.

PROPER PROCESS

Here's how decision making ought to look in broad-brush:

- Administrative staff or some other authority oversees the submission of the application, making sure that it satisfies requirements.
- An HPC session is convened in accordance with the law, including provisions for public notification.
- The meeting is conducted to assure due process.
- The project is presented.
- Testimony is taken.
- Commissioners deliberate.

Picture the scene as though you were making a model educational video. Commissioners come to the meeting prepared. As they arrange the application in front of them, you show footage of prior site visits, members' quiet study of the project's documentation, and their review of the ordinance and guidelines. Then a gavel raps. The meeting is opened. Commissioners listen to testimony, ask pertinent and well-framed questions, look judicious, nod their heads or frown thoughtfully—all the while consulting the variety of materials in front of them. A decision begins to take shape. Next:

- A motion is put forward citing chapter and verse reasons for the project's compliance or noncompliance with local law and guidelines.
- After further discussion, the motion takes final form and the vote is held.

Done properly, the HPC's process is efficient and its decision is defensible.

COMMISSION TRAINING

Reality is almost always different. One example should suffice. A commissioner in California announced that a project would never be approved because as a seagull in a former life he had flown over the site and hadn't seen it.

Oh. My. Gosh. Do you think if you stood close to his head, you could hear the ocean?

Most failings aren't so spectacular—*to us*. But to applicants, even some minor procedural confusion can seem significant. So will unprepared commissioners who take part in deliberations, or any talk about what we do or don't "like" about a project instead of whether it complies. The list of such mistakes is almost endless, as you must know from your own experience.

Regular training sessions in proper decision making are invaluable any time, anywhere, to guard against such errors. And no matter how many training programs you attend, it's like in sports: repetition develops muscle memory. Repeated training helps to make professionalism second nature.

DEFENSIVENESS IN DECISION MAKING

Defensible decision making has to do with quality control, as if Madison himself were holding us to exacting public-service standards. Yet much of our sub-rosa interest in defensible decisions is *defensive*, too.

- *Defensible* decision making means doing things properly, above reproach, within the scope of law.
- *Defensive* decision making means taking care to get what we want against those who do not share our interests.

A common example of defensive intent is the temptation to use our guidelines to redesign projects to please our own aesthetic sense. "Meeting preservation standards doesn't necessarily equate with good design," says a Baltimore observer.[1]

So the question frequently arises, how does a guideline differ from a rule? I once heard preservationist Pratt Cassity cite the following pop culture reference that has worked rather well for me since then in public presentations.

Did you see *Ghostbusters*? On report of a disturbance, Bill Murray goes up to Sigourney Weaver's apartment. He knocks, she answers. She has a wildly supernatural look as she invites him in. He says he makes it a "rule" not to become involved with women who are possessed by demons. She plants a big one on his lips. "Actually," he says, "it's more of a guideline."

We are tempted, too, to use guidelines to get us what we want when we know we really shouldn't go there.

Charleston's Eddie Bello said pretty much the same thing when I visited him in his busy office when he helped oversee the City's role in preservation. While we briefly chatted, he said the biggest problem they had was in attracting quality design in new construction. In fact, during his last year in office, Mayor Riley made a push in that direction.[2] As things stood then, however, Bello said the BAR would press applicants for better than they offered. He wasn't unsympathetic. But he had to make a special effort to impress upon commissioners that if an application met minimum requirements it had to be approved.

His care was rare enough that the opposite is not uncommon.

If applicants can be strong-armed or "plum" worn down, most any outcome wrenched out of them can be justified within the latitude of guidelines. And as long as we've ensured due process, our decision is defensible.

QUACKERY

But applicants aren't dumb. They know that "defensible" is not the same as "just."

"This ain't some lowlife dirt bag you're dealing with here," Baltimore mystery writer Tami Hoag writes in *A Thin Dark Line*. "He's an architect, for Christ's sake!"

You can bet an architect knows when he's being pecked to death by a duck. It doesn't matter how the duck does it. A professionally competent and efficient duck, a law-abiding duck, a duck that follows all the rules of duckdom, is still a pecking duck.

DEFENDABLE DECISION MAKING

This makes defensible decision making very much like advocacy at the start of our campaign: absolutely necessary for us to master, but not enough to win the day or last for long.

Simply put, what is legally *defensible* if it gets before a circuit judge is not the same as politically *defendable* in the court of public opinion. Close attention to law and administration can guard against missteps. But it can't insulate us from the politics that judge us. Bottom line:

- *Defensible* decision making is about protecting our findings by hewing to the law within the boundaries of discretion.
- *Defendable* decision making aims at securing the political standing of our decisions in the district and beyond, including down at City Hall when they're brought up on appeal.

We can get everything legally and administratively right *defensibly* and still get bad results.

PROCESS PROUD

In fact, it seems perversely likely.

A lot of us find the field of preservation law and administration to be compelling. It can dominate our attention and eat up all our time. And then as we apply it, it can make us process proud.

We can get so wrapped up in our administrative practices that we let ourselves get boxed inside our heads—and out of politics, as though it doesn't exist. We are lucky then if we don't find ourselves entangled in enforcement as our neighbors drift away.

NOTES

1. Comment by Fred Shoken following Ed Gunts, "Federal Hill Debates Whether to Become a City Historic District," www.baltimorebrew.com, February 15, 2016.
2. Bruce Smith, "80 Years On, Charleston Worries about New Building Design," www.thestate.com, March 15, 2015.

Chapter Sixty-Five

Enforcement: The Third Rail of Historic District Politics

The first law of law enforcement is, when your shift is over, go home alive.

—Sean Connery, *The Untouchables*

We want an *enforceable*, yet not so much an *enforced* district. Even Thomas Jefferson—no political slouch himself—admitted that "an honest man can feel no pleasure in the exercise of power over his fellow citizens." And *they* don't like it either. This is why districting, not preservation, was our designation problem.

It also makes enforcement like the third rail on a subway line. We need its power to make our district run, but it is deadly if not approached with care.

LEVERAGE

I'll own up. There were times on our HPC when I wanted to use enforcement to mete out punishment to Shredders, pure and simple. A few of them really frosted my socks. But then, as Dwight Eisenhower said: "You don't lead by hitting people over the head—that's assault, not leadership."

Yet a formidable ability to punish violators and enforce our process gives us leverage. We should use our potential to inflict hurt to get everyone to pull up a chair to our table to talk through problems.

A BROKEN CONVERSATION

Looked at this way, the necessity of actually having to enforce the district may be, in columnist David Brooks's useful phrase, "a symbol of the broken

377

conversation" between owners and the HPC. The rule of thumb should be that the greater the need for enforcement, the less attention we've paid proactively to politics.

This makes some commissioners and staff wary of enforcement as an admission of failure. Apart from that, any number of reasons may be adduced for inaction, up to and including care for preservation.

Consider this actual example. Three property owners are within a stone's throw of each other. Each needs roofing work.

- The first, who has an average income, gets approval to replace an asphalt shingle roof, not with in-kind materials, which were permissible, but with an expensive, hand-crafted standing-seam metal roof, which would take the property back toward its original condition. The nearly flat pitched roof is barely visible from the ground.
- The second owner, with a more modest income than the first, asks the HPC for permission to replace a much-deteriorated, seriously leaky, structure-damaging, and by expert testimony irreparable original metal roof with an affordable substitute material. Though this roof, too, is hardly visible, the application is denied.
- The third, a wealthy owner with a poor preservation record on numerous properties, avoids the HPC, has a crew hammer down the standing seams of an original metal roof, and clads it in bitumen. The well-pitched roof is visible.

In the third case no enforcement action is brought against the violator, even after he has been advised to stop mid-action. Why? The argument is that he owns so many properties in such poor condition, and has been such a serial problem for preservation, that some other, more positive incentives must be found to reset the conversation.

We can sympathize . . . and wait . . . and see what happens. The argument has *preservation* merit. But as Julius Caesar said, "All bad precedents began as justifiable measures."

A BROKEN TRUST

But is our *district* based on the tractability of Shredders? Of course it isn't.

We argued just the opposite in our designation campaign. We spoke to our neighbors' concerns about districting because we couldn't win them with our views on preservation. We connected with them differently. We proceeded partly on the sly understanding that while they weren't themselves eager for regulation, they wanted their neighbors under the thumb. So we undertook to shield their interests from the minority of willful owners who made the district necessary. We assured them that their neighbors, too, would be made to comply with district rules or suffer consequences. As preservation economist Donovan Rypkema has said, "Homeowners have a level of assurance that their neighbors will comply with the rules."[1]

Putting preservation first again will look like bait and switch. We need to enforce our procedures to uphold our end of the district bargain. Not following through on violations constitutes a broken trust, a reneging on our compact.

THE CHUMP FACTOR

Neglecting owners' interests in enforcement will make them feel like chumps. Can you blame them? What's more, they will have lost a crucial measure of self-interest in the district and be less inclined themselves toward working for compliance. There comes a point in their cynicism when "What's the use?" becomes "Get off my back!"

Our well-intentioned neighbors have only so much tolerance and goodwill. On the other hand, Shirkers and Shredders will take advantage of our weakness. As soon as we lose the threat of credible enforcement, they will be on us like rats.

JUDICIOUS ENFORCEMENT

Thomas Hobbes has instructed us to be formidable with those who will not be sociable. Yet there is a caveat. Petty, overzealous enforcement is unattractive to those who would be sociable with us. Enforcement with a human face—and an eye to justice—is appealing.

So we need to take Hobbes's dictum as a guideline, not a rule. In fact, a restrained use of the cudgel can enhance our power to enforce. The opposite can cream us.

Our HPC is a quasi-judicial body, but justice can't be blind. We must always act judiciously in our exercise of authority on behalf of law. It is madness to enforce the law without a decent respect for justice and the feelings of our neighbors.

THE CITY AND ENFORCEMENT

Higher ups in city governments and especially on city councils don't like enforcement. There are exceptions: In Easton, Pennsylvania, Mayor Sal Panto,

Jr. wanted to streamline the bureaucracy but not "water down the historic district" while he also aimed "to look at more effectively enforcing the law."[2]

When I chaired our HPC, the Mayor told me she never got complaints about nonenforcement, but only the opposite. Well, *we* heard about it regularly on the HPC. Even so, one of OIMBYism's costs is that a large segment of the community may expect enforcement but won't press the issue consistently with one voice. A local heritage society may be loath to get involved. Homeowners are reluctant, too. When Strasburg, Virginia, town manager Judson Rex suggested complaining neighbors should report violations, "one woman yelled, 'I'm not a tattletale.'"[3] When the HPC asks for help from the heads of other City departments, we often find to our consternation that authority comes down the line, not up.

There's no easy solution. The best that we can do is conduct ourselves in such a way that those others on whom enforcement depends find it in their interest to work with us. They have to see us as part of their power base, perceive the community as being behind us, and understand that enforcement works for them.

THREADING THE NEEDLE

We have to thread the needle. If we gain a community reputation either for neglecting or for overzealous enforcement, two things will happen:

1. Folks will impeach our judgment and withhold support.
2. Some will appeal our findings, while making *us* the issue.

If appeal is to the courts, we may be shielded by *defensible* decision making. But where appeal is to politically complected bodies, ultimately the City Council, *defendable* decision making can make the difference.

If we've already lost in the court of public opinion—or retain only lukewarm support—then we can't like our chances. Then, too, no matter what, going to the City Council on appeal will always be a crapshoot.

NOTES

1. "Preservation Haul," www.chicagotribune.com, December 28, 2003.

2. Daryl Nerl, "Easton Mayor Sal Panto Jr. 'Wants Review of Historic District Law,'" www.mcall.com, February 25, 2016.

3. Sally Voth, "Vinyl Siding, Windows among Concerns Expressed at Strasburg Joint Meeting," www.vdaily.com, May 10, 2011.

Chapter Sixty-Six

The Politics of Appeals

Compromise is the best and cheapest lawyer.

—Robert Louis Stevenson

The appellate process is a meat grinder, whether it is to a City Board, City Council, or the Circuit Court. Do whatever it takes to stay out of it while getting acceptable results.

A CASE IN POINT

There is no gambling in district politics like inviting an appeal. Let's see what happened in Madison, Wisconsin, with the hotel issue we encountered earlier. The Historic Landmarks Commission (HLC) denied the application for rehabilitating and expanding the Edgewater Hotel. Then the Common Council overturned the Commission on appeal.

Adding "insult" to "injury," according to the Madison Trust's Jason Tish, the Council then "suggested some debilitating changes to the ordinance and Commission." "No matter how you interpret" it, he says, "the integrity of the Landmarks Commission and the Mansion Hill Historic District took a serious hit."

"There were strong arguments on both sides of the debate," he goes on to tell us in his most admirable review.[1] "At its core, this project pitted job creation and economic development against the value of preserving the character of a historically significant neighborhood."

But the issue wasn't all that stark, and some features of the project tracked along with rooted growth. Tish acknowledges there were "positive aspects to the proposal: the rehabilitation of the [hotel] and the improvement of the failed public space of the 1970s addition." He also says that both preservation and economics "are important pursuits, essential to any healthy city with a sense of identity, but in a depressed economy, job creation is a tough opponent."

The Commission's decision was agonizing. One commissioner said it was the hardest decision he ever made.

In the end, the vote to protect the integrity of the ordinance turned out to be, in novelist Dorothy L. Sayers's fine phrase, "about as protective as a can opener." It further threatened the integrity of historic resources by laying bare the ordinance to "major changes by," as Tish claims, "people less qualified to make them, whose motives would likely be to remove guidelines perceived as obstacles to development."

A QUESTION OF LAW AND ETHICS

What lessons can we learn? Well, none to second-guess the HLC. As political commentator Jeff Greenfield has said, "Victory has a thousand fathers; failure a thousand kibitzers." Still, trying to learn from their experience honors their travail.

We may find ourselves in our own districts confronted by a situation in which the law prevents us in good conscience from approving a worthwhile project that's noncompliant. If that's the case, then as the *Code of Ethics* suggests, perhaps it's time to change the law.

But this case also warns us against proving the advisability of revision to our City Council in such a way that inclines them (a) to take the law out of our hands and (b) to take it out on us, our district and our HPC, and the community we serve.

If our law and guidelines still serve our district well, and what's before us is an important one-off issue likely not to be repeated, then we ought to find the strength to approve it. But if we can't find a way to say "yes," then we're better off working toward an exception on appeal that leaves our district law and guidelines still intact.

And don't forget our campaign promise to the City Council. That was when we pushed for the district with our politically inspired claim that we could keep such issues off their plate. It was good strategy. We believed, as does Tish, that we are better suited for dealing with these problems than they are. We owe it to our basic trusts to prove it.

THE IRON LAW OF SETTLEMENT

I have an iron law for any HPC staring at a volatile issue:

Let it end with you.

Don't just find for your ordinance and guidelines. Find a way to make them work, or change them. You have a district to defend.

This imperative does not make the dilemma of politics any less disturbing than it actually is. Don't engage in plea deals just to avoid punishing appeals.

Take the example of another hot hotel issue, in Milwaukee, which followed closely on the Madison affair. Here, after project backers conducted a withering campaign, the HPC gave them "everything they wanted," said James Draeger, the deputy officer for the Wisconsin Historical Society. "They folded like a house of cards," agreed Alderman Robert Bauman, who also sits on the HPC.

The outcome? Mayor Tom Barrett decided, as reported, that it was "time to look at the 30-year-old law and see if it still reflects what the community wants."[2]

The lesson? Work aggressively for mutual accommodation and think politically. Remember, folks are judging you as strong or weak. If you can make the process work to find a way to crack the hardest case without giving in, you will be seen as formidable.

Getting to "yes" has a caveat. If the other side is simply bloody-minded, then let them know you'll take them to the mat and fight them on appeal. It may give them a religious moment and convert them to tractability.

Alderman Bauman said of the HPC: "The only way you could blunt a campaign like that is if everyone stood together." He himself was considering resigning from the HPC. "There's no sense in staying if the commission ceases to perform its core function."

Sometimes, as Vince Lombardi said, you don't lose the game so much as time runs out. Yet every coach knows that if the game was played with the same determination all along as it was when the clock ran down, the outcome could be different. With a solid reputation for pragmatic accommodation and clean due process, you will be in a stronger position if you have to play in overtime on appeal.

DEALING WITH A LOSS

When you win appeals, it's great. "Nothing in life is so exhilarating," Churchill said from his experience in the Boer War, "as to be shot at without result."

Losing wounds, but don't complain.

The best advice comes from Phoenix attorney Rory Hays, who told a NAPC training session that if the decision goes against you, "accept it and move on."

THINKING THE UNTHINKABLE

The time may come when folding is nonetheless the wiser choice. "No man has ever yet been hanged for breaking the spirit of the law," Grover Cleveland said. If you find that unthinkable, then keep this analogy in mind. It stunned me when I heard it.

It came from no appeaser, but the author of the hard-nosed doctrine of "containment" that won the Cold War. George F. Kennan was a career diplomat, adviser to presidents, and Pulitzer Prize–winning historian. As the dean of political realism in American foreign policy, he argued that had every country that declared victory at the end of the First World War simply surrendered at the opening shot in August, 1914, every one of them would have been better off, stronger, safer, and more prosperous in the long run.[3]

What he knew is this: some good fights aren't worth the fighting. We need to be careful in choosing which hills to climb and die on.

NOTES

1. Jason Tish, "Edgewater: Losing the Preservation Argument," Executive Director's Blog, www.madisonpreservation.org, June 10, 2010.
2. Marie Rohde, "Milwaukee's Historic Preservation Commission Alderman Robert Bauman Considers Leaving Commission over Marriott Debate," *Daily Reporter*, January 24, 2011.
3. I heard him speak when I was a student. You can find the basic analysis in George F. Kennan, *American Diplomacy, 1900–1950* (Chicago: University of Chicago Press, 1950).

Chapter Sixty-Seven

Choosing Our Battles

When you go up the mountain too often, you will eventually encounter the tiger.

—Chinese Proverb

We districtists are human. We can't help but think in terms of preservation wins and losses in our HPC and on appeal, even though we are the people's servants. But then they think the same way, too.

Wins invite confidence. Losses pile on doubt. Yet some wins cost us future battles, while a loss may conserve our power for another day. "The side that knows when to fight and when not to," Sun-Tzu wrote in *The Art of Warfare*, "will take the victory."

ADVENTURISM

There is a term we can take from the East—well, Moscow anyway. The Kremlin used it to describe ill-advised foreign forays: "adventurism."

"There are roadways not to be traveled," Sun-Tzu said, "armies not to be attacked, walled cities not to be assaulted"—and rose trellises not to be assailed.

Yep, you heard me right. It lives in lore as "the case of the plastic trellis" from before my time in Annapolis. Resident Bianca Lavies put one up in her garden and was forced to take it down. The case became a cause célèbre as it progressed through the courts on appeal. Local folks still refer to the HPC's "hysteria." That's all that they remember, though in the end the commission reversed itself before the final courtroom hearing.

A few around here still contend that the drag-'em-to-account action on the trellis should have become our standard practice. But the blowback from that case helped for years to chill the City's will to take all sorts of far more egregious miscreants to task.

PYRRHUS AND FAUBUS

We find it far too easy to let our ordinances choose our battles for us. But ordinances are written in the language of empowerment, not command.

They invest us with authority, but their authors surely knew that power of accomplishment is something different. The link between the two is judgment, about when and how to apply the law and to what effect. Judgment lets us choose most battles. "What it lies in our power to do," wrote Aristotle, "it lies in our power not to do." This has all the tension in it that we expect from politics.

All sorts of folks—for example, gatekeepers, polarizers, administrative legalists—would take power from us by limiting our room for judgment. They would have us choose fights for purity of ideals or jots and tittles in our laws and guidelines. We know them by their heavy breathing over minor affairs. The unwise paths they lead us down may end in the following:

- *Pyrrhic victories*, named for Pyrrhus, king of Epirus, whose costly victory over the Romans at Asculum was his undoing;
- *Faubian defeats*, which I adapt from the talent former Arkansas governor Orville Faubus had for losing in such a way as to take everybody down with him.

Such wins and losses are neither sociable nor formidable. They are plagues on our communities. They weaken our body politic and diminish our effectiveness. We simply cannot afford to let these folks make a sacrifice of good government the litmus test of our devotion to our duty to protect historic resources.

The benefits of fighting the wrong battles are small and cramped compared to the large and dispersed damage done to our commission's standing in the community and before elected officials. That's the way it's always been, and even more so now in the age of Twitter and the blogosphere.

OUR ELEVENTH STANDARD

The Secretary of the Interior has given us ten standards for historic preservation. Politically, as districtists, we need only one:

Community support for the historic district shall be sustained.

Phrased as a guide to action, it can serve as a law of power conservation:

**Do nothing that may reasonably be avoided that diminishes
the political standing of the district and the HPC.**

Richard Moe editorialized in *Preservation*: "Obviously, we must always be prepared to fight—and fight hard—to protect . . . historic places. . . . But on the other hand, we must avoid the kind of unwarranted rigidity that can cripple our efforts by destroying our credibility and robbing us of public support." He concluded that "we must choose our battles carefully, saving our energy and resources for the fights that really matter."[1]

As William Bennett said of a politician, "He picks fights with the right people. As an old Irishman," he added, "I think that's a good sign." It's prudent, too. And no, you cynics out there, prudence isn't cowardice. It is more on the order of what Rhett said to Scarlett in *Gone with the Wind*. As he handed her a pistol, he told her to shoot anybody who tried to take their horse. "But don't misaim," he said, "and shoot the horse."

Allow me to pose a rhetorical question: If something isn't good politically, can it ever be good for preservation? Picking proper fights is about more than husbanding resources for future battles, as Dick Moe said. The wrong fight weakens us for even routine daily tasks.

Remember Frank Whitaker? He was the one who defended our campaign for district designation in Oak Ridge, North Carolina, with "The juice is worth the squeeze." In Annapolis, my successor as HPC chair, Sharon Kennedy, has put a twist on it. When confronted with a difficult issue, she says she asks herself, "Is the squeeze worth the juice?"

Gee, I wish I'd thought of that. Now I'm glad to pass it on.

WINNING WITHOUT FIGHTING

There are mountains we must climb and fights which must be fought. The trick is figuring out which ones. So let's narrow down the field.

Prussian general Karl von Clausewitz helps. In his treatise *On War* he famously stated that war is a continuation of politics by other means—that is, by means other than diplomacy. Diplomacy is sociable and preferable, while war is formidable and uncertain. As Sun-Tzu said, "In war the highest excellence is never having to fight." That's why we practice politics as diplomacy, which is the search for proximate solutions—that is, accommodations. The need to fight evaporates if we can find a political solution to a conflict.

We should work at all times on shaping a political environment conducive to agreement. I think Sun-Tzu would agree. Before our historic ages out, we should renew our community compact. We'll be starting with what I call "transformative education."

NOTE

1. "President's Note," *Preservation*, March–April 2007.

Part XI

REPAIRING OUR
COMMUNITY COMPACT

Chapter Sixty-Eight

Transformative Education

It takes a long time to become young.

—Pablo Picasso

To get at what I mean by "transformative education," let's go back to the beginning of our districting campaign. We started out as preservation advocates, believing in persuasive education. We became political when we ran up against advocacy's inherent limitations. But others missed that lesson.

New folks may now act on the misbegotten story line that merit won the district, though with one important difference. Their faith in advocacy as *persuasion* has been replaced by *outreach education* centered on informing folks on district law and operations.

INFORMATIVE, NOT TRANSFORMATIVE

Now, I'm a strong believer in outreach education. It is absolutely necessary. Folks have to be informed in a timely fashion about their responsibilities under district law and the penalties for evasion. Dennis Au, city preservation officer in Evansville, Indiana, says that "in almost every complaint from a homeowner against the Preservation Commission, it is because the homeowner did not come to us first."[1] If that's because they didn't think to, then outreach education can help prevent casual violations. But even the best outreach education can't work miracles. Folks won't let it.

I'll bet you've seen it, too. Someone from the HPC attends a community forum and makes a presentation. The latest thing is to have online information. So they direct their listeners to the official website. A few folks write it down, maybe on hard-copy handouts. As the meeting adjourns you sense what happens next. Even if the materials are taken home, they won't be read. If we're lucky they'll get filed away for a later day—*if* they are remembered. As for the website? Most folks just forget it.

And whose fault is this? Not ours, we say. We showed up, talked, and downloaded information to attendees. Been there, done that, and checked the box on our to-do list. And, like as not, no single attitude has changed.

Why? Because we never even tried. We engaged the community in *informative* rather than *transformative* education. We've restructured no one's thinking about their role in rooted growth.

You can lead people to a watered-down presentation, but you can't make them think. "The Labour Party," British politician William Whitelaw said, "is going about the country stirring up apathy." Are we, too?

TRANSFORMING THINKING

To win newly incoming folks over and those we missed before, we want to transform their interests and win support for our historic district practices. We'll get the best effect when folks share our objectives. We can't just tell them what they are. They'll think we don't respect them.

We learned this in our campaign, after stalling out with advocacy. Our reset put their interests first and wove them in with ours. Still, we didn't stop at that. We couldn't leave them to themselves to work out their response. Left alone, folks will tend to put themselves before community. We had to involve them publicly in meetings, sociably let's say, to forge community consensus.

That put them among their neighbors where they had to take a public stand. We built community by leading them to a *civic*, not merely a personal, response, adjusting their own interests to harmonize with others.

This we have to do again, especially with newcomers as our district ages. For many of them it will be their first real involvement in community. So we want to give them a shared experience beyond their interests that turns their thoughts toward our common future.

Our problem now is that we lack the campaign setting and the advantages of calling district meetings. Yet we have other options, as we'll see.

NOTE

1. Kristen Tucker and Sandra Hoy, "Price of Preservation," www.evansvilleliving.com, March–April 2002.

Chapter Sixty-Nine

Reconstructive Programs

Pull up a chair. Take a taste. Come join us.

—Ruth Reichl

There are many ways to oil the engine and tune-up community support for the district and its process. They involve in-reach and outreach programs, "tell us" sessions with professionals, keeping bridges open, and one-on-one transformations.

IN-REACH EDUCATION

The easiest way is through the HPC. Why not bring folks in and familiarize them with our purposes and processes *before* they come to us as applicants? Invite new owners to a meeting. Welcome them with a "here's what you will see" introduction, say, fifteen minutes before the meeting. Acknowledge them publicly by name so they know they're in the public eye. Then send them on their way after a brief post-meeting Q&A session.

More ambitiously, give them a few applications with annotations pointing to relevant guidelines. Let them follow along—as silent partners, to protect due process—while grappling with the issues, making their own determinations, and getting a feel for how we work with applicants to reach accommodations and serve the greater good. After the session is adjourned, have at least one commissioner conduct a roundtable discussion with them about their experience.

But—and here's a caution—you had better be delivering good government. As essayist and journalist Walter Bagehot once observed in Britain, "The cure for admiring the House of Lords is to go and look at it."

OUTREACH PROGRAMS

Use outreach programs for transformative education. Don't just tell—*show* others in civic forums what we do on the HPC, and involve them.

When James Gibb served as our archaeological consultant in Annapolis, he observed that "most people do not realize the scope of the commissioners' responsibility, the hours of donated service, and the emotional conflicts of critiquing their neighbors' plans. Wearing their shoes might engender a little respect."[1]

Yes, but how? Well, we commissioners use in-house mock training sessions to improve our own understanding and performance. Why not do it for them, too? Organizations are always looking for program ideas. Go to your local residents association, historical society, Main Street business association or newcomers group, for example, and offer to do a mock COA review using their own members. The locus needn't be geographically centered in the district. Folks all over town may take an interest, too, and you will always need broader support if you go again before your City Council.

Make it engaging. Devise a couple of credible applications on an easy and a sticky topic. Instruct them briefly in the relevant law and guidelines. Get them into playing realistic roles as applicants and commissioners. Others can offer comments from the floor.

Select participants by asking who's for strict preservation or accommodation, for district regulations or against them. The public's gaze is civilizing even in these sessions. Folks will round their edges, pull their punches. Tell them to get real.

Let them deal with the possibilities and limitations of our law and guidelines, the dilemmas of decision making, and the political importance of working to good effect.

Back in our campaign we told our neighbors how the process would work. It helped build confidence. Now you're showing them. Our goal is the same today: to shore up and broaden our political base.

Now, as then, we'll do our best educational work as we answer questions that arise from a *need to know*, driven by their reflection on their obligations and own real interests. This is a far better way of changing thinking than telling them what they *ought to know*.

Reach out to difficult property owners and polarizing types. If they reject our sociable intention, let the others know you tried. It will incline them more sympathetically toward the HPC for its willingness to listen.

"TELL US" SESSIONS

In Charleston, Joe Riley advises us as public servants to "always *listen* to people—especially the people who are saying things you don't want to hear."[2]

But first you've got to get them talking. Invite various constituencies to HPC administrative meetings for "tell us" consultations. Among these are architects, contractors, landscapers, home-improvement specialists, realtors, and anyone involved in community-development programs.

These folks have a direct interest in our work. We want to ask them two things:

1. How do you think we're doing?
2. What can we do to help you do what you do better?

My experience is that they will appreciate our interest and be frank. This will improve our relationship with them and, indirectly, with those they serve.

Such sessions support our HPC training on best practices. They instruct us on effectiveness—and they're free. They speak to *actual* in contrast to *hypothetical* performance, keep us abreast of change, and give us insights into the kinds of adjustments we should be making to our law, guidelines, and practices. Then we need to follow through, as we will do in the next chapter.

This also suggests calling in representative samplings of other groups from time to time, such as recent applicants and even work-project violators. We'll want to know how they found our process: was it accessible and understandable, open, fair, and transparent? Don't just echo Samuel Goldwyn's attributed instruction, "Tell me how much you loved my picture." We want to hear their gripes, questions, and their suggestions, too.

At the same time, be aware that they may feel gambits like "tell-us" sessions are like poking a beehive. They may also fear the sessions like citizen reviews of job performance. Remember, too, that you don't pay their salaries and, unlike them, you have nothing personally at stake.

These sessions can be transformative for both sides. On ours, they hold a mirror up to dispositional gatekeepers, underperformers, and administrative legalists. They help all of us reflect on public service and the place of justice in decision making.

KEEPING BRIDGES IN REPAIR

Those we've labeled district Actors are our hardpan allies. We need to keep them close and tighten our connections with other Rooters, too. Personal relationships are transformative. When we befriend new folks whose support we need, we come to share more common views and interests.

It's always a good idea to establish open lines of communication with Backers, especially the leaders of other preservation groups as well as resident and business associations, including the local board of realtors. Asking elected officials for input keeps their interested support, as does periodically attending their meetings.

While the HPC chair should be careful about stepping in between staff and their local governmental colleagues, it helps to have at least a nodding acquaintance with folks in municipal departments who are involved in public projects in the district.

MEDIA CONTACTS

We are the face of the district in our community. But apart from picturing us through gossip, the public mostly sees us through the press.

The HPC chair should establish a relationship with a key reporter on a basis of mutual trust along the lines discussed with Jeff Horseman in chapter 29. As we learned then in campaigning, getting good press takes tact. Our interest lies in two places:

1. Getting accurate coverage
2. Influencing the questions reporters ask that shape their stories

Reporters want to do good work. We can help by furnishing deep background information, providing open and timely responses, and explaining the law, process, and technicalities. Helping them be successful works a special kind of magic. Consider, too, Tom Marquardt's observations in chapter 55 on how to interest an editor in the issues of your aging district.

USING REGULAR HPC HEARINGS

"Always remember," Dean Acheson said, "that the future comes one day at a time." Our monthly meetings are like the movie "Groundhog Day." Each meeting is the same; but each time around we get a chance to do better.

Tweak your meeting's message. When we run our sessions by the book, the book is like the one the boy got in Dylan Thomas's *A Child's Christmas in Wales*. It told him "everything about the wasp, except why." So tell attendees why you have the district.

Applicants come in thinking we're just about the past. Start with that. But do it as political context. Have the chair or vice-chair start each meeting with a very brief "canned" sketch of when and why the community originally decided to shoulder the personal responsibilities of districting. Tell applicants that you look forward to working with them to uphold your tacit compact to work for preservation while making preservation work for the community. Then introduce the commissioners and their qualifications to review their applications.

THE SMILE FACTOR

Remember James Madison on the nature of good government: it conduces to "the happiness of the people." The smile factor is all important.

The only time some HPCs put on a pleasant face is when a meeting's called to order. It's rather as though the chair has taken W. C. Fields seriously: "Smile first thing in the morning and get it over with." One of the nicest comments I ever got was from an applicant who, after a difficult project review, said he appreciated my good humor.

A friendly disposition says you value people and their interests. It might sound corny, but when you're sheltering historic resources from the storm, a smile may be your best umbrella. When folks leave smiling when the hard work's done, you know you've reached them at a deeper level than just an appreciation of the law.

ONE-ON-ONE TRANSFORMATIONS

We've suffered a couple of devastating Main Street fires in Annapolis. After the second one, the mayor called a next-day meeting. The owner had his people there, and so was I as chair.

When it was my turn to speak, I didn't talk about what he had to do to rebuild. I affirmed the HPC's interest in getting good design. This was, I said, the owner's unparalleled chance to put his stamp upon the district with a structure that would bear his name. I promised we would do all we could within the discretion of the law to expedite rebuilding—even calling special meetings at his behest—while working to accommodate his interests.

He sat back and said no one had ever explained it to him like that. Goodwill prevailed. Afterwards, we worked with him on a first-class project.

The larger point is that transformative education can be most effective—and is immediately easier—as we handle COAs, especially in preapplication sessions. Then it's in our district's interests for us to stress opportunities over obligations and our cooperation. When folks want to do something positive, their attitudes toward regulations are transformed. They stop seeing review regulations as "restrictions" and instead elevate them to the status of a "helpful process."

REACHING OTHER INDIVIDUALS

Many district owners never come before us. They also aren't members—or regular attendees—of organizations where we conduct outreach programs. They may not read the press. In effect, they play hard to get.

Send them regular newsletters, or emails if you can. Public relations maven Rick Tyler, a contributor to MSNBC's "MTP Daily," has said "the human heart is conditioned to hear stories." Update them on what has been going on in the district to deepen their awareness of the HPC.

A major problem is that most local governments do not have the interest or resources to send a mailing to each property owner of record—and only one mailing to owners of multiple properties. Instead, it's easier to use water-bill or street addresses in the historic district. Where business premises are leased or there are renters, the mailing can end up in the trash. Work on getting City Council support for the database you need.

The fallback is your website. Make sure it is user-engaging, not passive. I once was a member of a group that advised the National Trust on a new website. My take was that folks had to work too hard to find what they wanted. When you create or update yours, think through what site visitors are looking for and need to know rather than what you want to tell them.

How about this? Title a dropdown click-through "New Owners." In the menu that pops up, list:

- "Welcome to the District"—relating the community ethos they've bought into;
- "Your Opportunities"—explaining the benefits of districting;
- "Why Regulations?" affirming community support;
- "The HPC Serving You"—laying out district intuitions and the HPC's mission;
- "Bringing in Your Project"—focusing on process;
- "Working with Design Guidelines"—relating their scope and functions.
- "Getting Help"—stressing the practical dimension of your opening welcome: and
- "Email Updates"—offering them a chance to register.

If you want them to learn independently how the process works, that's the way to do it.

EXPANDING YOUR DISTRICT

That is, unless you have a plan to expand your district's boundaries. In that case, you have an excellent opportunity of involving everyone vicariously, by extension, in your original districting campaign. And a chance to get across your record.

TRANSFORMATIVE LEADERSHIP

Good educators don't just know their stuff. They also know what makes people tick. To succeed they must be leaders with the right kind of political personality for the job.

Getting the right person in the right place with the right sort of program is all-important. Just make sure you don't dump any of the gambits I've outlined in your preservation planner's lap. They can help, but recapturing the youthful district ethos we created at the time of designation is not in their job description.

Many of these ideas require a lot of extra work and not every districting arrangement makes them practical. Perhaps you can find a way to make good use of former commissioners. They are an underutilized resource practically everywhere. But where we can we'll delegate responsibility among our members, even to the point of restructuring district operations.

NOTES

1. Email on file.
2. Jay Walljasper, "5 Questions for Joe Riley" (undated 2016 interview), www.aarp.org/livable-communities/livable-in-action/info-2016/interview-mayor-joe-riley.

Chapter Seventy

Institutionalizing Community Relations

Our age will be known as the age of the committee.

—Ernest Benn

Do you imagine Ernest Been as not being a fan? Why's that? Are you yourself a committee-phobe? Have you had *ad hoc* committees that haven't been as effective as you hoped, like messages in bottles that then are set afloat? And yet as you read through the last chapter you might have foreseen more.

Well, there is no *ad hoc* fix for reviving and sustaining community support. It will take more permanent campaigning by involvement, inspiration, information, and example.

Most of our HPCs are institutionally ill-prepared to carry out the task when "design review fills their windshield," as Dan Becker put it when I visited him in Raleigh. Then, too, like most of those we serve today in our second-generation districts, our own commissioners are new and unfamiliar with community relations.

Dan saw the basic problem early on in his tenure with the City. So let's go back to Raleigh and look at how he handled it through institutional innovation that—yes—centered on committees.

CONTINUING OUR CONVERSATION WITH DAN BECKER

After Raleigh's first district was created in 1975, the City Council packed the Commission with thirty-two people doing design review. Because of a gap in legislation, they were "putting anybody they wanted on it," Dan observed.

Over time, he got it cut to twelve, with five to do design review. What happened with the other seven? They created four committees: one for Design Review, one for Research, one for Public Awareness, and an Executive Committee for coordination and agenda setting. Each Commission member then had two meetings per month, or three if they were on the Executive Committee formed up by committee chairs and Commission officers. The Commission as a whole met monthly to consider policy.

I asked him how the system works.

Dan: The Executive Committee members meet to set the agenda for the main Commission meeting. We bring the reports from the committees up. We hear what's hot, what needs a decision: here's what we're working on, we need a strategic plan, and when are we going to schedule that? The members are the planning and management of the Commission. We spend all our time on the Executive Committee figuring out preservation and how to run the design review in its specially tasked committee.

Me: What are the advantages?

Dan: How much time do HPCs spend on the machinery of running their commissions?

Me: Not much in my experience.

Dan: Right—and it's super critical! It means we can be effective in everything we do. Design review typically gets all the attention. But in visualizing our committee structure, it is the equal of the Research and Public Awareness committees. We can force whatever is current into a standing committee and resist too many ad hoc committees. I recommend the book, *Essentialism: The Disciplined Pursuit of Less.*[1] It's fabulous. Learning how to say no, like with priority lists. That's an oxymoron. There's only one priority. Work on it, get it done, move on. Keep a very short list. The Executive Committee defines what we're working on now, what we're moving toward. With our three primary committees we can cover everything we have to cover in our mission.

Me: How did it work in practice?

Dan: So we would have the business meeting for policy, the three committee meetings for doing the work, then the Executive Committee that kept the good ship of state running where it needed to go.

Me: Do you find this done in many other communities?

Dan: It's rare. I have a sense when I talk about this at workshops that light bulbs are going off. They didn't realize they could be different than they are. They struggle with these other things but they don't know how to deal with them in the context of the design review committee which the whole HPC is acting as.

CONSIDERING YOUR OPTIONS

So, do you think you could do this? Your City Attorney should be able to clarify your authority to emulate or create a variant of Dan's structure or what special legislation might be needed. Double-check with your SHPO for advice.

If your HPC already meets twice monthly for design review and administrative matters, you might consider rotating months between committee and administrative meetings, with an Executive Committee preparing the agenda and making policy recommendations for decisive action. Too often, our administrative meetings are taken up by COA review matters, like pre-application sessions, with other matters considered on an ad hoc basis. Without a standing committee to carry out decisions, they tend to fall into the crack between commissioners and staff—or burdening the latter.

The point is to create the equivalent of a standing Public Relations Committee tasked with community programming on a dedicated basis.

THE WORK OF THE PUBLIC RELATIONS COMMITTEE

I asked Dan to speak some more about the work of the Public Relations Committee.

Dan: There's the preservation planning piece, working with the town on the comprehensive plan, making sure that our preservation values are represented in that. Their job was to make people aware of the value of the historic resources the City had. Not to sell people on why they should be preserved: that's the advocacy part that government doesn't do. It is educational programs about the district, newsletters, community conversations through events we'd tape and put on the cable TV public access channel.

Me: So you had folks going out into the community and holding meetings?

Dan: We ask people to come to our turf all the time, every time they need something. They have to come to us. So what's the flipside? Our going out to their neighborhood association meetings and talking about what's going on in the City to get them involved. Helping them to understand that being part of the public process is in their own best interest. Yes—it takes a lot of work.

Me: What else can the Public Relations Committee do?

Dan: You make sure when you're doing your design guideline revisions that the Committee is very much a part of it, because they're the ones getting all the people in the room.

Me: How often did you do guidelines revisions?

Dan: Every ten years. Time goes on—

Me: Wait a second—what was that? Every *ten*?

Click! Now I saw a light bulb too. Do you?

NOTE

1. Greg McKeown, Crown Business, 2014.

Chapter Seventy-One

Renewal through Revising Design Guidelines

The quarrels of lovers are the renewal of love.

—Jean Racine

What's love got to do with it? Recall that when Rep. Chris Afendoulis proposed his sunset law in Michigan he said, "If historic districts are so great and people really love them, then why would people get rid of them?"[1] He wanted them reviewed every ten years. And now Dan Becker has told us that Raleigh revises its guidelines every decade.

Hmmm. . . . Maybe that's the way to out-do Afendoulis and make us more secure.

RENEWING VOWS

In our designation campaign, we pledged to work for preservation and make preservation work for the community. The locus of our compact with our neighbors was our ordinance, with the terms of its application specified by our design guidelines.

By analogy, our compact was a marriage, our guidelines were our vows mutually agreed upon. Decades later, couples may renew their vows. Then back before the altar they may recite the same words as before, as proof of mutual constancy or out of grim determination. But like as not they change the terms to reflect their maturation and, perhaps, the problems they've encountered as they've drifted separate ways.

Again by this analogy, a revision of our guidelines reaffirms our compact and makes our district stronger. It reflects our mutual respect, our record of accomplishment, a determination to address problems that have arisen—and, unlike with Afendoulis, divorce isn't on the table.

At the very least, it doesn't hurt to think this way. So how are we to do it?

THE POLITICS OF REVISION

When I chaired our HPC, I went through one revision exercise that became an object lesson. The goal was to harmonize our guidelines with the evolution of our practices and address problems that had dogged us and new ones we foresaw. With the draft in hand, we announced a public workshop to generate responses.

To this day, I remember how relieved many on our side were when few showed up and none expressed concern. I left the evening's meeting with a sense of a missed opportunity to reengage our second-generation district's population. I figured out too late that we had worked for preservation without gaining important insights into how we were doing in making preservation work in the life of our community.

Now as I think politically about revising guidelines, I see it as a pretext for renewing bonds. The work itself is serious: to produce a better set to work from. That *end* is our immediate, *technical goal*. Our *political goal* actually becomes the *process* itself that engages the community to bring citizens to a revivified understanding of the district and our HPC. So we will use the process to put a new face on our compact in our ever-changing district.

Because I like the way he phrases it, I'm going to let you hear Dan Becker express his views on generating guidelines. Though we'll be talking about guidelines in general, the process he describes can be made to fit revisions.

THE PROCESS TUSSLE

Me: Dan, you said earlier that the Secretary of the Interior's Standards don't represent the local community's values. Then how do you come up with design guidelines that do?

Dan: You talk to your community. I'd much rather have a wrestling match putting each other in headlocks. [He chuckles.] I want to bring them all together and have a knock-down, drag-out tussle while we're putting the guidelines together so we can get them to fit where we are as a community right now and get it over with. Why would I want to have that fight each and every application month after month when I can get it all worked out at the front end? Now people know what the deal is and it seems fair.

Me: How do you know when you've got what you need?

Dan: My touchstone was, if I could get about an equal number saying "Oh, these are to strict, nobody can do anything!" and the other side, a bunch of people saying "They're not firm enough, they don't give people any guidance at all and they'll run over them"—if I can get equal numbers of people on either side, then I've found the *sweet spot*. [Laughter.] So you have to have a robust feedback as you go through your draft: What do you like? What do you not? You keep track of it and you're trying to navigate yourself to find the sweet spot of your community's *present preservation personality*. That's what I call it.

And I'd call that a bravura encapsulation of how you should proceed.

A WORKING DRAFT

Dan mentioned working through your draft. He was talking about drawing up a basic set of guidelines, and what he said fits neatly into the process we considered in chapter 42, especially regarding community meetings.

But for a *revision*, you already have a draft: your established guidelines. Yet just like for your kickoff community meeting during your campaign, you don't want to call people in and ask them what they think without giving them something in particular to think about. You can discharge that by having an *ad hoc* taskforce work on a preliminary markup that the HPC should approve as *talking points*.

The point is not to press for them. Rather say, "These could work for us. What do you think? We're your HPC, and we just want to make sure that the guidelines we are using work for you."

WHO PARTICIPATES?

Your Public Relations Committee will bring everybody in. You'll want to see:

- Residents, investment property owners, and businesses.
- Architects, builders, developers and realtors who have professional interests and specific knowledge.
- Representatives from residents associations and heritage societies.
- The district's City Council member.

But that's not all. Your long-term goal is a revived core consensus on the terms of your community compact. To that end, you'll want to include those who affect the tenor of the district, such as anti-regulation and pro-preservation polarizers, gentrification dissenters and those concerned with social justice. You never can tell what positive synergies may result, like Jean Racine's "quarrels" that result in "renewal."

Offer observation to your media contacts. If you can get a story, work to see that it's not just about the revision but also your open links to the community.

Make sure all HPC commissioners are in attendance. Listening to the community will hold a mirror up to difficult members, especially dispositional gatekeepers and administrative legalists. You can't afford to have them engage the process at a later stage and cause problems. Besides, they're partners in the compact, too.

VICARIOUS CAMPAIGNING

You are a leader. Don't approach the process with a technical frame of mind. You may leave that to your preservation planner.

Remember you have two legacies and two duties to discharge. The details of your guidelines are for your preservation trust. Think also of your place in the long arc of how the HPC has ensured or neglected its political trust for sustaining the community trust it inherited from the time of your district's designation. You are campaigning in all ways but in name for the renewal of that compact.

If you yourself have never done campaigning and are unfamiliar with community relations, then study up on our lessons in the first five sections of this book. Focus on the strategy of creating new consensus in the midst of continuing disagreements. Learn how to respond to discord. Think about giving folks a vision based on the practical and civic understandings that the district designated.

A professional guidelines writer can make the mechanics easier. Just be sure they understand the political purposes as well that you've carried into the process.

TEACHABLE MOMENTS

All community sessions are transformationally educational for conveners and participants alike. Those moments are both large and small. They work upon groups as well as individuals.

Make sure that everyone appreciates that, unless mandated by ordinance, our undertaking of these revisions is not something that *we have to do* but *want to do* with them to keep the district close. They should know that we are *their* HPC, and that we want their support and confidence for a culture of compliance that will enhance the district's benefits for everyone.

Portray our compact as the community's signature achievement. Leave no doubt that nothing would be as good or better for the community without the district. Make sure to deflate the impression that the district is a dictate by the City rather than the community's empowerment of itself.

Community participants will newly see us as their public servants. They will also raise their eyes to see the whole community again. Even more important for our day-to-day operations, they will get a bracing sense of the difficult milieu their HPC is working in to facilitate rooted growth. Newcomers will find themselves imbibing the community ethos that underpins the district even as we revive it.

HPC commissioners will reacquaint themselves with the "big picture" of the role of preservation in the lives of the participants. They will also reconnect with the elemental nature of their service to the community.

A well-done revision makes COA reviews go more smoothly. It puts us on a firmer political footing and reverses demolition by neglect.

When presenting the final document, you might employ Dan Becker's phrase. Tell your audience that it represents the "present preservation personality" of the community. Say it is the new face of your compact for rooted growth.

LOOKING FORWARD

Record your sessions. Keep notes of your impressions. Listen for observations on HPC performance and decision making that you can work on later. This holds true as well for ways you may want to amend your enabling ordinance.

One of the more difficult things you'll face throughout the process is suppressing your inclination to contain conversations and keep them focused on the guidelines. And why shouldn't you do that?

As long as you can get the work done, there is an advantage to tolerating discussions of extraneous concerns. What other areas of concern are highlighted? Is it the City's own adherence to our guidelines in public projects? Not enough resources being detailed to the district, like enforcement? These are matters you can carry forward.

And they can generate interest in a larger preservation plan.

NOTE

1. Anthony Pollreisz, "Republican Lawmaker Defends Historic District Reform Package, Says It Gives Homeowners and Cities Power Again," WKZO-AM, www. wtvbam.com, February 8, 2016.

Chapter Seventy-Two

A Preservation Plan? Looking Ahead with Consultant Elizabeth Watson

Think ahead. Don't let day-to-day operations drive out planning.

—Donald Rumsfeld

As we transitioned from designation to administering our district we saw how we could lose the "big picture" of the community compact we inherited from campaigning. We've put a great deal of effort into seeing and repairing it since then.

We have rethought district education, looked at institutionalizing community relations, and treated guidelines revision as campaigning to draw our neighbors close. Now we might think about a preservation plan to invigorate widespread public interest and do a reset with the City: the Mayor, the City Council, and administrative departments.

Elizabeth Watson, who teams with Peter Benton[1] in Heritage Strategies, is the preservation planner in their national practice. When I read praise for their work in Joplin, Missouri, I asked Elizabeth to speak with us to explain the planning process. Before I turn to our dialogue, she has a basic perspective that's instructive.

Like Bob Agee in chapter 51, she uses the term "silo" to refer to our "phenomenal" district institutions and processes. "It's well understood in most places," she says, "but the story is so much more than that. Preservation is the one issue that touches on every issue in a city. What we've done in focusing on the silo—we've forgotten all those other aspects, the issues and decisions that affect the place of preservation in our communities. Without that, people aren't ready to hear about regulations because they don't understand the *why*."

410

Bear that in mind. As we begin, I've filled her in on our concepts of twin legacies and trusts and second-generation districts. "Great framework," she allows.

A DIALOGUE ON PRESERVATION PLANNING

Me: Thank you for driving over from the Eastern Shore today. I was delighted to hear you live nearby. Now, I'll be that person who comes to you from an aging district and says we're thinking about a preservation plan. What is it that you do?

Elizabeth: I focus on historic preservation, storytelling, heritage tourism—all the things that contribute to quality of life and community character. I help communities figure out where they are and where they want to go, using every possible asset.

Me: To avoid or reverse demolition by neglect in terms of policy and action?

Elizabeth: You've hit upon an interesting concept. Historic preservation is the most radical idea of the twentieth century, and historic districts are an overlay approach for a reason. They haven't been integral to planning. Most planners are not trained in preservation, and it's startling to encounter them in my practice. They can be downright hostile when they're new to it. Why? Because they're already full of the regulatory burdens of the other jobs they've had and want no part of this one. They may have a problem with how preservation is practiced at the local level.

Me: Why aren't they trained in preservation, given its ubiquity across the country?

Elizabeth: Programs are slow to catch up. Remember: as late as the 1960–1970s, preservation was mostly done by volunteers doing inventory surveys. Then as historic districts took off, they were hardly ever hardwired into underlying zoning, which can be at odds. In Erie, Colorado, a town I fell in love with through my practice, underlying zoning has allowed demolition-on-demand and three-times larger replacements in the historic heart of town. You can add guidelines all day long and get nowhere if people believe it's better to buy and tear those buildings down. Which is happening.

Me: But not everywhere.

Elizabeth: Cities like D.C. and Charleston have figured out urban design with preservation. Historic district overlays since the 1970s have generally become very high practice. Even so, we want to go into planning in a community at just the right moment.

Me: Like when?

Elizabeth: Asheville voted down demolition of half the city as it boomed, but had no preservation plan. The Historic Resources Commission was completely focused on the regulatory piece in their numerous historic districts. The Preservation Society was outside of the silo telling the stories and doing the archival work, and there was constant confusion among the public. That happens, too, in other places where there are maybe other outside advocacy groups. In Connecticut and Massachusetts you have Historic Commissions besides the HPCs that look more broadly at the picture. In their silos, those who are reviewing projects are not doing community cultivation.

Me: And the role of planning?

Elizabeth: Two things. One is general programming and the other is getting a lot more deliberate about your interpretation of how the resources tell the story.

Me: So it isn't just the HPC.

Elizabeth: You need an alliance among all of those involved. They're all out there being passionate, and you've got to tap into that.

Me: Can they work together?

Elizabeth: Sometimes, though not always. Very often you'll see they don't even think of one another. The Historical Society loves telling stories, but they don't pay attention to—even like—the regulatory aspect. And the regulatory people have their silo and they're not worried about telling the story because the Society does.

Me: And what I see falling in the crack between them in older districts where it's quite forgotten is the all-important *historic district story* to keep community support for regulations going.

Elizabeth: Because they're not strategic thinkers, and that's what we offer in preservation plans. That's why your sense that renewal is important. Planning is a giant strategy for having a great community conversation on all the things a community should be doing.

Me: Do you think of the plan's end-users, the citizens and property owners?

Elizabeth: Sure, sure.

Me: How does it work? Do you involve them bottom-up, or are you doing plans top-down?

Elizabeth: You are aiming at the public-participation piece.

Me: But the private-sector people are already interested in preservation, and city planners are responsible to others upwards. How do you get the rest involved? Do you hold community meetings?

Elizabeth: It's standard practice—and I'll tell you it's expensive.

Me: *Financially?*

Elizabeth: In *meetings*. How many can you put a community through? Planning is divided into three stages. We'll get to all of them, but first there's what I call "scoping." You go in and figure out the issues. That's the time to go to the community in a general meeting to engage the leaders among stakeholders: private-sector owners, businesses, the Historical Society, a residents association. . . .

Me: Do you select them, or simply call the meeting?

Elizabeth: The mechanism we use first puts together a steering committee. The idea is that those who initiate the plan will call in a representative group of people who have some kind of connection to help with long-range planning.

Me: Do they ever invite hostile elements?

Elizabeth: I would recommend it for the initial assessment, not for your steering committee. The steering committee helps you reach out to the wider body of people who might be interested, including hostile elements. Everybody ought to be at the first community meeting you hold. You want to get a really good conversation going then, both pro and con.

Me: What are you looking for?

Elizabeth: We look at what's happening with historic resources and the administration of the preservation ordinance. Are there tweaks that could be done, processes that could be fixed? A sense of all of that. I'm looking for who's engaged and why. Is it economics; is it storytelling, heritage tourism, or just because they like the beauty of the place? You look at each of those and you come up with chapters for the plan, historical, topical, and at the heart—the silo.

Me: I read you planned for eight in Joplin.

Elizabeth: We're being orderly because the average person doesn't do planning, except in their own lives. The key to planning is creating lists and categories of the things you need to know. So that's the second stage.

Me: Suppose we know we need to work on our design guidelines for the district. Are you more concerned with what makes sense for preservation, or to the end-users?

Elizabeth: Both. But I think it would be a very big job to do the plan and guidelines at the same time instead of in a sequence. Plans are tailored to discovering the needs of each community first.

Me: After your community meeting and analyzing needs, to whom do you present your findings?

Elizabeth: To the steering committee for an internal discussion *and* you should go back to the community for another facilitated general conversation. Probably do them back-to-back, factoring for travel. The larger community doesn't know there is a list. We're using what we've found to energize the conversation, and new questions may come through.

Me: So you're listing still and not persuading.

Elizabeth: Definitely. I think the really interesting conversation is the second one with the stakeholders. The real payoff is you come back and say, "Here are the issues, a framework. Do we have it right?"

Me: Who's with you up in front?

Elizabeth: Generally the client representative, the preservation planner who helps to administer the ordinance.

Me: Can you profile the type who works the best?

Elizabeth: Generally, they've gotten up to a certain point and want to water ski—they're up, but not yet skiing. They need a plan to help them figure out what's best to do—and they're energetic.

Me: Do you ever hear from people who say they need a plan because City Hall isn't doing anything? Someone from the private sector?

Elizabeth: Not the private sector. We do it for officials. But it can be from another official group outside of planning—an advisory board, for instance.

Me: I've read about one case where a planning department withheld support in another planning project. They had a hard time coming to the table. The odd thing was that they were good at planning other areas, just not preservation. I guess that if you run into that, it must be discouraging.

Elizabeth: We've been fortunate. But in small towns and cities they may be just overwhelmed with over-meeting and a too-packed schedule. Folks sometimes just don't have enough energy to add on preservation.

Me: I assume drawing up the final plan is stage three. What happens to it once you leave? Who carries the ball, public officials or the private sector?

Elizabeth: Usually the planner. But if you have luck, somewhere in the process other voices will emerge. They will be on the steering committee, come to the community meetings, take an active part. And you'll see that people respect their opinions and suggestions. It's a big help where you can get it. It might be a long-term, well-connected resident or a member of the City Council. They might emerge in your third public meeting when the plan is revealed, confirming what they expected.

Me: What about press coverage? Is the local paper interested?

Elizabeth: Sometimes there's no coverage at all. Many communities no longer have a local paper. But if they do, they'll usually come, seem to enjoy the meetings, and cover them pretty well.

Me: Let's switch to some general observations. Can you reflect on what you see out there?

Elizabeth: [Pausing and considering.] In an ideal world, preservation would take place without historic districts. We as preservationists still don't know how to add new layers to the old. We cherish the old, but we don't trust ourselves and owners in designing the "new" safely enough that we don't need regulations. Where you get people uncomfortable with change and others unhappy with rules, it's a real ugly combination.

Me: Can planning overcome it?

Elizabeth: I see entropy in preservation, where there's not in environmentalism. Everywhere you look there are cities seeking the "green," creating new walkable communities, et cetera. Why is this happening successfully while preservation is getting a little bit creaky? I believe the reason lies in education, in our schools. Environmentalism has been hardwired into schools by very clever, strategic environmentalists through state curricular requirements. Kids get something of it in all twelve years of school. But they aren't being taught well enough how our communities work and that preservation is integral.

Me: My concern is that we haven't been inculcating the community ethos of districts into newcomers. But you think the problem is even deeper?

Elizabeth: As a nation, we lack basic civics education linked up with preservation. There was a chance for it years ago that we missed at the national level of advocacy in the Reagan administration when environmentalists began their push. There are a few pockets around the country that do better.

Me: How do you encounter the problem?

Elizabeth: You see its effects on cub reporters who don't really understand how governments work for the public good. They'll sit and watch the head-butting at a commission meeting and don't know what to make of it because they have no education either. I hear complaints from people that each time they get a local historic district up and running well, new people walk in the door and they don't know a thing about how their town is supposed to work. Then it hit me. I thought it was a problem for preservation. But it was a much larger problem. It's the societal blind spot bar none.

Me: How can we open eyes?

Elizabeth: [An exasperated shrug.] How great it would be to do a five-day charette with an eighth-grade class with a planner or your mayor working on a problem as a team. You're giving them a civics education using a preservation issue for problem solving through design. It would teach kids how to look at up-options, how to identify issues, come up with solutions, decide which ones are optimal, and consider how to introduce them in the public sphere and make decisions on their implementation. That's a whole world you and I have experienced, but it isn't taught.

Me: And those who know politics don't do it, while those who know preservation don't know civics. They just want to download regulatory information.

Elizabeth: You have to promote community culture first and foremost. You have to find the pressure points, ways of nudging, shaping willing Actors. There's a limit that perhaps preservationists don't recognize to what people will do because it's so close to their skin. Our historic resources are like endangered species. Once they're gone, you can't have Jurassic Park. You can't bring back what's lost. And I'm worried we're losing ground in new urban design also.

Me: Leadership is key.

Elizabeth: Back in the 1970s it was all grassroots preservation. The passion and interest at the ground level was phenomenal. I worry that we have over-professionalized. We have absolutely marvelous people in many places. But there is a view at the state and local level that once you put these systems in place—the silos—that they're supposed to keep on going by themselves. There's politics and strategy and community education for a culture of preservation—and I'm not sure it's in the lexicon or that we're pulling in leaders who can give us what we need to keep preservation vital and alive.

Me: That's what you meant by "entropy" a bit ago.

Elizabeth: If you don't keep up. You have real opportunities to talk to your neighbors and commenting to folks on the street with all kinds on interests that tie into preservation. The threshold of what you need to do is very steep. It should be a series of steps.

Me: Such as?

Elizabeth: Is it the buildings, is it the people, is it the history, is it the future that interests them? Those are the four quadrants.

Me: How do you manage them together?

Elizabeth: As elements of strategy. But I think you're right: it's politics. But how can you build communities through a sense of place in the digital world today? It's a profoundly human task. You have to have face-to-face conversations to find common values in community.

Me: If cities were once reluctant to take on new districts, how do you persuade them that community re-building is important to them now?

Elizabeth: The crystal ball is pretty cloudy. Municipal coffers are declining and employees are expected to take on more and more. We're running out of the ability to do what we have to do to sustain ourselves and make sure historic districts can do all they can do for communities.

Me: And the plan we ended up with earlier? How do we sustain its momentum?

Elizabeth: The plan itself should ask that question in addressing what programs will work for the city. Do we come back together every year to talk about it, to show excitement and renew our energy? You need to shape every program around the plan from here on out. In the HPC it's not just application reviews but also, "What are we doing about neighborhoods, our downtown, tax credits. . . ."

Me: The big picture.

Elizabeth: The silo is just one piece of it. At least quarterly you need to check in with the plan in an administrative meeting, prioritizing what your contribution should be, and when. You can't afford to lose the juice of your plan. And it's a great way to have that continuing conversation on building community together with an open heart.

Me: That's a nice way to put it. Thank you for demystifying the process for us.

If your community is in a position to pursue a preservation plan, remember what we learned in chapter 5: a plan is just a plan until it runs into opposition. For that you need a strategy and a sustaining vision.

NOTE

1. See chapter 42.

Chapter Seventy-Three

Our Sustaining Vision

The older I get the better I used to be.

—Lee Trevino

What golfer Lee Trevino said is often true of districts, too, when it comes to politics. We played the game early on and won our district's designation. Over the years, some of us seemed to turn our backs upon the game entirely.

In the last sections we took strides to repair our original community compact with our neighbors. To keep the momentum going we will need a vision to sustain us, one derived from the political lessons of our successes and misfortunes.

Long before Michigan's state-level foray into local meddling, a report came out of Traverse City about a state senator who wanted to give local city councils authority to settle disputes between HPCs and property owners. "I'm a strong supporter of historic preservation," he affirmed, "but there are times that . . . other community needs . . . also must be considered." A critic claimed that this would "dangerously invite politics into a process designed to save a community's most treasured neighborhoods."[1]

But on this evidence alone, politics was there already.

OUR PECULIAR AGE

For all his foresight, I don't remember James Madison, or any of the Founders, ever imagining we'd do such a thing as repudiate politics in a vain attempt to save our districts. Such would have been unthinkable. They mastered politics to better serve the people.

So, to go back to where we started, why is it that folks don't love us more? I think we know the answer. As we've traveled down the road, we've lost our story line: the one about public service.

OUR STORY LINE

The story of our district—the one that we've been working on—is the epic of our compact: the building of community, creating our historic district, and then administering the law to fit the ever-changing needs and interests of our neighbors, as we work with them for rooted growth.

The essence of our tale has been the politics of change. Once we changed the law to get our district designated. It turns out we often haven't been as good at working at the intersection of our district law and change.

Why is that? We have mistaken our authority. Instead of serving people, we've been tempted to bend our power to the service of our preservation interests.

POWER AND PUBLIC SERVICE

When power is uncoupled from the politics of public service, it tempts us to gatekeep historic resources, hew to the details of our law, or take guidance from our principles. These misbegotten approaches show, to borrow Michael Gerson's line, "all the creativity and strategic positioning of a stop sign."

If we let them define the basic ways we think, then indeed our districts are in danger. Folks with crossing interests in their properties, businesses, and lives won't forever tolerate delays and disappointments on our say-so. If we don't succeed with them, we run the risk of district failure.

POLITICS AND VISION

In order to succeed we need a steady tone with a historic vision. The vision that we need to sustain us isn't some projected future of our liking, or one inherent in our law and guidelines. It is right insight into politics. "Genuine politics," Vaclav Havel said, "is simply a matter of serving those around us, serving the community, and serving those who will come after us."

As well as caring for our heritage, we must focus on the three basic political imperatives of success that have been with us from the start:

Get power. Keep it. Govern well.

Those who think this way are districtists. The signs that guide them on their way are the perspectives of fusion preservation. As capable public servants, they

- Are versed in the precepts and practices of preservation;
- Are familiar with the district's ordinance and guidelines and how the HPC works;
- See the entire community as a set of legitimate competing interests;
- Honor our community compact;
- Define the district's role in terms of contributing to rooted growth;
- Consistently strive to deliver good government;
- Orient their efforts toward mutual accommodation; and
- Sustain political support for districting in the community and with public officials.

One characteristic above all else marks them out as leaders. They don't flee from, but instead eagerly embrace, the ambiguity, uncertainty, and inherent tensions that suffuse the politics of decision making.

Edmund Burke, who was Madison's British equal, had high praise for them—for *us*, because by now I trust we all are districtists. "A disposition to preserve and an ability to improve, taken together," he said, "would be my standard of a statesman."

USING POWER WELL

Successful leaders acting as public servants know the uses and abuses of power. In our historic districts, enforcement may *compel* compliance by violators, and it may *deter* others from behaving badly. These things we have to tend to.

But we also shouldn't underestimate the *allure* of power for drawing our neighbors into a culture of compliance. Secretary of State Henry Kissinger once was asked about his legendary attractiveness to women. "Power," he deadpanned, "is the ultimate aphrodisiac." The appeal of power isn't force, as well he knew. It's the magnetic pull of those who know how to move the world along.

Our neighbors will never love us, but then we didn't ask them to. We campaigned to work through change with them to ensure a living role for heritage in our community. The vision that sustains us now is service through good government that keeps the public's trust.

NOTE

1. Marjory Raymer, "Decisions in Historic Districts May Shift," www.record-eagle.com, October 10, 1999.

Epilogue

Now my consolidation is in the stardust of a song.

—Hoagy Carmichael, "Stardust"

I've enjoyed the time I've spent with you, the preservation star I said you were in the preface. That was where we met Taylor Wilson gazing heavenwards, identifying fusion as the power of the stars.

She has dreamed of bringing "cold" fusion down to earth to power towns and cities. So has Stephen Hawking's brilliant mind. But even IBM's supercomputer, "Watson," hasn't solved the problem that has eluded such bright mortals.

But you and I have powered up our communities by fusing politics with preservation in historic districts. The result has been transforming.

Before they fused, preservation had limited appeal and politics no goal. When we collapsed them into one another, a chain reaction started. It energized our campaign that grew in power as others joined our cause. We reached critical mass by bonding diverse interests. The light and heat it generated won the vote for designation in our community and then at City Hall.

The City Council bound our power over to administering the district. In the HPC, we set our faces toward sustaining and controlling the energy we created. We learned to think as districtists, and then encountered problems that threatened us with meltdown. As our power plant showed signs of age, we undertook to repair our district operations and reconnect with the community. Then we shaped a final vision to sustain us.

421

THE STARS IN US

Leadership is an art, not science. Maybe that's why you and I have been able to master the cold fusion of my metaphor to empower our historic districts.

Where we neglected politics, we found the fault lay "in ourselves" not "in our stars," as Cassius tells Brutus in Shakespeare's *Julius Caesar*. As for our success in making districts work: well, physicists will tell you we are made of stardust, atoms from above. So, if IBM's human-voiced computer ever asks you how you pulled it off, just say—sorry, Sherlock—"It's *elemental*, my dear Watson."

The elements of success have been in you all along. If I have helped you see and hone them for the future, that's the consolation of my song.

Index

About the Author

William E. Schmickle, PhD, is past chair of the Annapolis Historic Preservation Commission and cofounder of the Oak Ridge, North Carolina, Historic District. His services are available through his website, www.preservation-politics.com. A former college professor, he lives with his wife Charlotte in Annapolis.